A Text Book of

APPLIED MECHANICS

FOR

SEMESTER – I & II

FIRST YEAR DEGREE COURSES IN ENGINEERING

COMMON FOR ALL BRANCHES

AS PER NEW REVISED SYLLABUS OF SHIVAJI UNIVERSITY, KOLHAPUR

Effective From Academic Year 2012-2013

Prof. S. B. HIVAREKAR
M. Tech.
Head, Deptt. of Civil Engg.
Annasaheb Dange College of Engineering
ASHTA (DIST. SANGLI)

Dr. SURESH R. PAREKAR
B.E. (Civil), M. E. (Structure)
Professor of Civil Engg.
Sinhgad Academy of Engineering,
Kondhawa (BK), PUNE.

Prof. UTTAM R. AWARI
B.E. (Structure), M.E. (Structure)
Asstt. Professor, Deptt. of Civil Engg.
AISSMS's College of Engineering
PUNE.

Mrs. SEEMA V. JOSHI
B.E. (Civil), M.E. (Const. & Mgt.)
Asstt Professor, Deptt. of Civil Engg.,
P.V.G's College of Engineering & Tech.
PUNE.

N2403

APPLIED MECHANICS (S.U.)   ISBN 978-93-83971-57-2

Second Edition : July 2015
©   : Authors

The text of this publication, or any part thereof, should not be reproduced or transmitted in any form or stored in any computer storage system or device for distribution including photocopy, recording, taping or information retrieval system or reproduced on any disc, tape, perforated media or other information storage device etc., without the written permission of Authors with whom the rights are reserved. Breach of this condition is liable for legal action.

Every effort has been made to avoid errors or omissions in this publication. In spite of this, errors may have crept in. Any mistake, error or discrepancy so noted and shall be brought to our notice shall be taken care of in the next edition. It is notified that neither the publisher nor the authors or seller shall be responsible for any damage or loss of action to any one, of any kind, in any manner, therefrom.

Published By :	Printed By :
NIRALI PRAKASHAN	**REPRO INDIA LTD.**
Abhyudaya Pragati, 1312, Shivaji Nagar,	50/2 TTC MIDC Industrial Area
Off J.M. Road, PUNE – 411005	Mahape
Tel - (020) 25512336/37/39, Fax - (020) 25511379	NAVI MUMBAI
Email – niralipune@pragationline.com	

☞ DISTRIBUTION CENTRES

PUNE
Nirali Prakashan : 119, Budhwar Peth, Jogeshwari Mandir Lane, Pune 411002, Maharashtra
Tel : (020) 2445 2044, 66022708, Fax : (020) 2445 1538
Email : bookorder@pragationline.com, niralilocal@pragationline.com

Nirali Prakashan : S. No. 28/27, Dhyari, Near Pari Company, Pune 411041
Tel : (020) 24690204 Fax : (020) 24690316
Email : dhyari@pragationline.com, bookorder@pragationline.com

MUMBAI
Nirali Prakashan : 385, S.V.P. Road, Rasdhara Co-op. Hsg. Society Ltd.,
Girgaum, Mumbai 400004, Maharashtra
Tel : (022) 2385 6339 / 2386 9976, Fax : (022) 2386 9976
Email : niralimumbai@pragationline.com

☞ DISTRIBUTION BRANCHES

JALGAON
Nirali Prakashan : 34, V. V. Golani Market, Navi Peth, Jalgaon 425001,
Maharashtra, Tel : (0257) 222 0395, Mob : 94234 91860

KOLHAPUR
Nirali Prakashan : New Mahadvar Road, Kedar Plaza, 1st Floor Opp. IDBI Bank
Kolhapur 416 012, Maharashtra. Mob : 9850046155

NAGPUR
Pratibha Book Distributor
: Above Maratha Mandir, Shop No. 3, First Floor,
Rani Jhanshi Square, Sitabuldi, Nagpur 440012, Maharashtra
Tel : (0712) 254 7129

DELHI
Nirali Prakashan : 4593/21, Basement, Aggarwal Lane 15, Ansari Road, Daryaganj
Near Times of India Building, New Delhi 110002
Mob : 08505972553

BENGALURU
Pragati Book House : House No. 1, Sanjeevappa Lane, Avenue Road Cross,
Opp. Rice Church, Bengaluru – 560002.
Tel : (080) 64513344, 64513355,Mob : 9880582331, 9845021552
Email:bharatsavla@yahoo.com

CHENNAI
Pragati Books : 9/1, Montieth Road, Behind Taas Mahal, Egmore,
Chennai 600008 Tamil Nadu, Tel : (044) 6518 3535,
Mob : 94440 01782 / 98450 21552 / 98805 82331,
Email : bharatsavla@yahoo.com

niralipune@pragationline.com | www.pragationline.com

Also find us on www.facebook.com/niralibooks

Dedicated to ....

Dynamic F.E. Students

...... Authors

PREFACE TO SECOND EDITION

We have great pleasure in presenting Second edition of "**APPLIED MECHANICS**" as per the New Revised Syllabus of Shivaji University for the students of First Year (F.E.) Degree Course in Engineering. We are happy to receive very good response to the previous book of old syllabus by the students and faculty members.

The **Applied Mechanics** is one of the core subjects for engineering students irrespective of branch as it develops the thinking and imagination power of the students at the initial stage of engineering, which may be utilised in future study. The engineering mechanics is one of the most difficult subjects to pass in first year engineering for the student, hence it is necessary to come down to the lowest level of the student's understanding to explain the concepts in easiest way with simple language so that the fear in mind of student should be wiped out.

The present edition is presented in twelve chapters as per the new syllabus of Pune University.

The theory of each chapter is written in **simple language** and **number of solved numerical examples** considering practical aspect of each and every chapter are given. **Every solved example is presented in the form of free body diagram** and **kinetic diagram**, which will help the reader to imagine and understand the practical application of the theoretical concept.

Attempts have been made to minimize the errors in the text as well as in the figures to the maximum extent. We are thankful to the readers for their suggestions which have been incorporated to rearrange it more systematically. Precautions are taken to minimize the errors. Constructive suggestions, criticisms and comments are highly appreciated and will be incorporated in the next edition.

We take this opportunity to express our sincere thanks to Shri Dineshbhai Furia and Shri Jigneshbhai Furia, pioneer in publication field. We are also grateful to Shri M. P. Munde for constant follow up and encouraging to write the book.

We appreciate this efforts taken by Mr. Santosh Bare, Mrs. Anupama Pingle and Miss Chaitali Takale of Nirali Prakashan, which has made the timely publication of this book possible.

We hope that this edition will also be useful to the students as well as the Teachers and Readers.

AUTHORS

SYLLABUS

SECTION - I

UNIT - 1 : FUNDAMENTALS OF STATICS (7 Hours)

Basic concepts and Fundamental laws, Force, Moment and Couple, System of forces, Resultant, Resolution and Composition of forces, Varignon's theorem, Law of moments.

UNIT - 2 : EQUILIBRIUM (7 Hours)

Lamis' theorem, Free body diagram, Equilibrium of forces, Equilibrium conditions, Surface friction for bodies on horizontal and inclined planes.

Beams : Types of loads, Types of supports, Analysis o simple beams, Virtual work method for support reactions.

UNIT - 3 : ANALYSIS OF TRUSS (7 Hours)

Types of trusses, Assumptions, Methods of analysis : Method of joints, Method of section, Analysis of simple truss with maximum seven members.

SECTION - II

UNIT - 4 : CENTROID AND MOMENT OF INERTIA (7 Hours)

Centroid and Center of gravity, Moment of inertia of standard shapes from first principle, Parallel and perpendicular axis theorem, Moment of inertia of plain and composite figures, Radius of gyration.

UNIT - 5 : KINETICS OF LINEAR AND CIRCULAR MOTION (9 Hours)

Introduction to kinematics of linear and circular motion (no numerical on kinematics), Kinetics of linear motion, Newton's laws, D'Alembert's principle, Work-energy principle, Impulse momentum principle, Kinetics of circular motion.

UNIT - 6 : IMPACT AND COLLISION (5 Hours)

Impact, Types of impact, Law of conservation of momentum, Coefficient of restitution, Numerical on direct central impact.

•••

CONTENTS

SECTION - I

1. Fundamentals of Statics — 1.1 – 1.48

2. Equilibrium — 2.1 – 2.70

3. Analysis of Truss — 3.1 – 3.22

SECTION - II

4. Centroid and Moment of Inertia — 4.1 – 4.48

5. Kinetics of Linear and Circular Motion — 5.1 – 5.66

6. Impact and Collision — 6.1 – 6.16

   University Question papers (Dec. 2014 & May 2015) — P-1 – P-6

• • •

SECTION-I

CHAPTER ONE

FUNDAMENTALS OF STATICS

1.1 INTRODUCTION

Mechanics can be defined as the branch of science which deals with the state of rest or motion of bodies under the action of forces.

Mechanics is classified as follows :

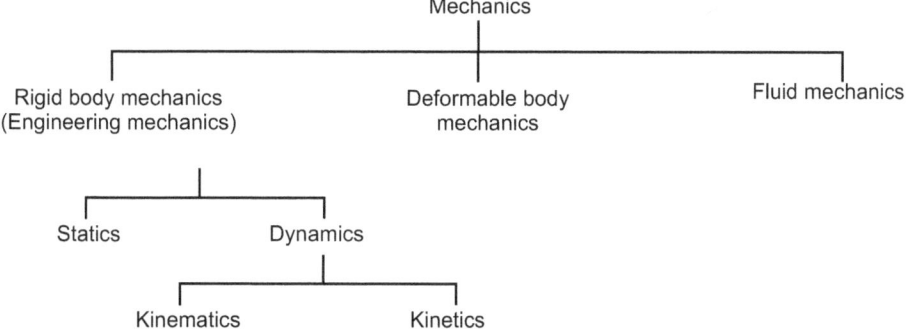

Engineering Mechanics treats only rigid body mechanics. It is divided into two sub-branches.

Statics : It deals with the study of bodies at rest or at uniform motion under the action of forces.

Dynamics : It deals with study of bodies in motion under the action of forces.

1.2 FUNDAMENTAL CONCEPTS

Particle : A particle is a point mass.

Rigid body : A rigid body can be defined as 'a combination of a large number of particles in which all the particles remain at a fixed distance from one another before and after applying the forces'.

Force : Force can be defined as 'any action that tends to change the state of rest or motion of the body upon which it acts'. A force is a vector quantity. The characteristics of a force are :

1. Magnitude.
2. Direction.
3. Point of application.
4. Sense i.e. pull or push.

Scalar quantities : Physical quantities having only magnitude are called scalar quantities. For example, time, speed, density etc.

Vector quantities : Physical quantities having both magnitude as well as direction are called vector quantities. For example, force, velocity, displacement etc.

1.3 FORCE SYSTEMS

A force system can be classified into 2-D force system or coplanar force system, and 3-D force system or space forces.

The characteristics of force system are as follows :

Table 1.1

Force system	Diagram	Description
1. Coplanar forces		Lines of action of all forces lie in the same plane.
2. Collinear forces	$F_1 \leftarrow\ F_2 \rightarrow\ F_3 \rightarrow\ F_4 \leftarrow$	Lines of action of all forces lie in the same line.
3. Concurrent forces	(forces F_1, F_2, F_3, F_4 intersecting at a point)	Lines of action of all forces intersect at a single point.
4. Parallel forces	(parallel arrows F_1, F_2, F_3, F_4)	Lines of action of all forces are parallel to each other.
5. Non-concurrent and non-parallel forces	(3-D box with forces F_1, F_2, F_3, F_4 along x, y, z axes)	Lines of action of all forces do not intersect at a single point and are not parallel to each other.

1.4 PRINCIPLES OF STATICS

Law of Parallelogram :

Two coplanar concurrent forces can be replaced by a single resultant force by law of parallelogram.

If two concurrent forces are represented by the adjacent sides of the parallelogram, then the diagonal of the parallelogram passing from a common point of two forces represents resultant in magnitude and direction.

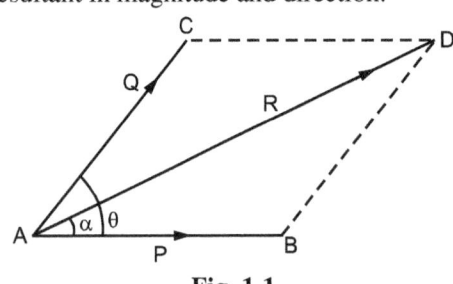

Fig. 1.1

Forces $\bar{P}$ and $\bar{Q}$ are acting at point A making an angle θ with each other. Refer Fig. 1.1.

$$\text{Magnitude of resultant, } R = \sqrt{P^2 + Q^2 + 2PQ \cos \theta}$$

Direction of resultant w.r.t. force $\bar{P}$,

$$\tan \alpha = \frac{Q \sin \theta}{P + Q \cos \theta}$$

Principle of Transmissibility of Forces :

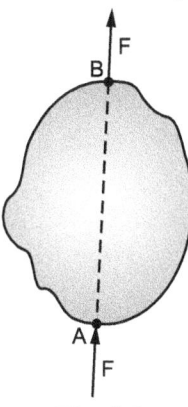

Fig. 1.2

The state of rest or motion of a rigid body will remain unchanged if a force acting at a given point of the rigid body is replaced by a force of same magnitude and same direction acting at any point on the same line of action. Refer Fig. 1.2.

Sense of force has changed from push at A to pull at B.

Newton's First Law :

Every body continues to be in its state of rest or of uniform motion along a straight line unless it is acted upon by an external unbalanced force to change that state.

Newton's Second Law :

If the resultant force acting on a particle is not zero, a particle will have an acceleration proportional to the magnitude of the resultant force and in the direction of this resultant force along a straight line. 'The rate of change of momentum of a body is directly proportional to the force acting on it and is in the direction of force'.

Newton's Third Law :

The forces of action and reaction between bodies in contact have the same magnitude, same line of action, but opposite in direction.

Newton's Law of Gravitation :

It states that two bodies of mass 'm' and 'M' are mutually attracted with equal and opposite forces of same magnitude. Refer Fig. 1.3.

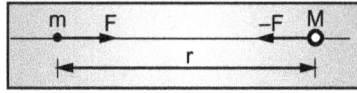

Fig. 1.3

$$F = G \frac{Mm}{r^2}$$

where,   G = Constant of gravitation

1.5 RESOLUTION OF A FORCE

Resolution of a force is the process of replacing a force by several component forces having the same effect as that of a single force.

A force is resolved into two component forces acting at a point along any direction by using law of parallelogram (Analytically).

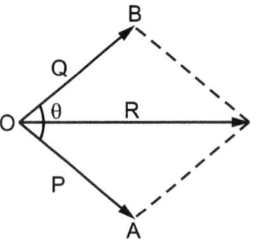

Fig. 1.4

Force $\bar{R}$ can be resolved along directions OA and OB into component forces $\bar{P}$ and $\bar{Q}$ by law of parallelogram. Refer Fig. 1.4.

A force is resolved into two component forces making an angle of 90° with each other. Component forces are called rectangular components of a force.

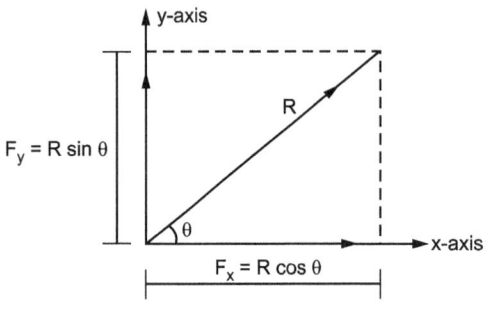

Fig. 1.5

Magnitudes of rectangular components of force $\bar{R}$ along x-axis and y-axis are $F_x = R \cos \theta$ and $F_y = R \sin \theta$ respectively. Refer Fig. 1.5.

A force is resolved into two component forces along any direction by using law of triangle. (Graphically).

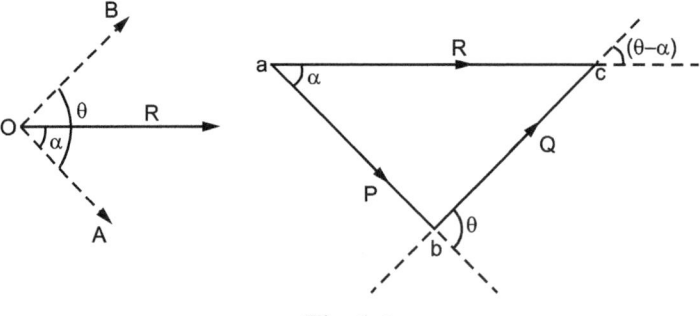

Fig. 1.6

Force $\bar{R}$ can be resolved along directions OA and OB as shown in Fig. 1.6. Side 'ab' represents component force $\bar{P}$ along direction OA. Side 'bc' represents component force $\bar{Q}$ along direction OB. Side 'ac' represents a force $\bar{R}$. Refer Fig. 1.6.

1.6 COMPOSITION OF FORCES

Composition of forces is the process of adding two or more forces to obtain a single force having same effect as that of number of its component forces. This single force is called resultant of number of forces.

Resultant of two forces acting at a point is obtained by law of parallelogram.

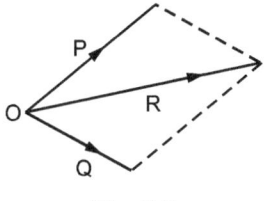

Fig. 1.7

$\bar{R}$ is the resultant force of two forces $\bar{P}$ and $\bar{Q}$ acting at point 'O'. Refer Fig. 1.7.

Resultant of two forces can be obtained by law of triangle. (Graphical method).

Law of Triangle : If two forces are represented in clockwise or anticlockwise order as the adjacent sides of a triangle, the resultant force is represented by the third closing side of the triangle directed from starting point of first force to end point of second force.

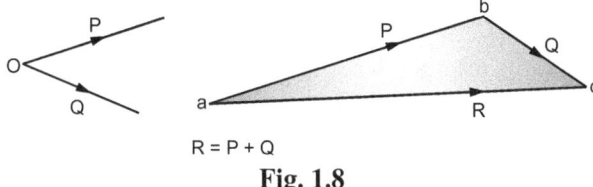

R = P + Q

Fig. 1.8

Side 'ab' represents force $\bar{P}$. Side 'bc' represents force $\bar{Q}$. Side 'ac' represents force $\bar{R}$. Refer Fig. 1.8.

1.6.1 Composition of Concurrent Force System

Analytical Method :

1. Resolve each force along x and y axes. Refer Fig. 1.9.
2. Sum up components of forces along x-axis. (ΣF_x) i.e. R_x.
3. Sum up components of forces along y-axis. (ΣF_y) i.e. R_y.
4. Magnitude of resultant, $R = \sqrt{(\Sigma F_x)^2 + (\Sigma F_y)^2}$.
5. Direction of resultant w.r.t. x-axis = $\alpha = \tan^{-1}\left(\dfrac{\Sigma F_y}{\Sigma F_x}\right)$. Refer Fig. 1.10.

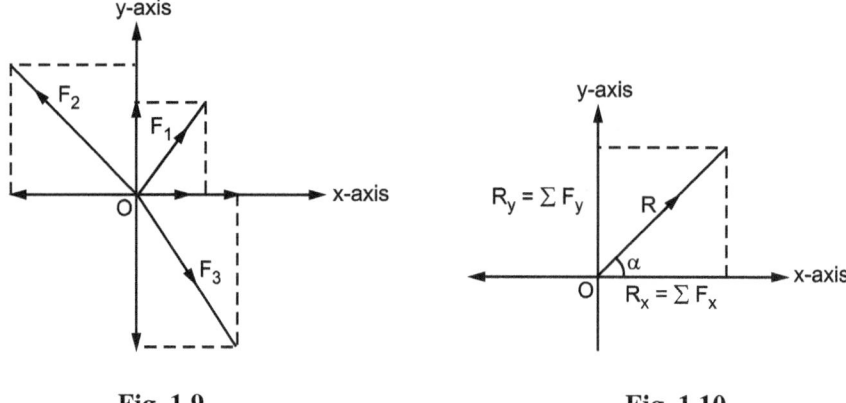

Fig. 1.9 Fig. 1.10

$\Sigma F_x = F_{1x} + F_{2x} + F_{3x} = R_x$ = Component of resultant along x-axis

$\Sigma F_y = F_{1y} + F_{2y} + F_{3y} = R_y$ = Component of resultant along y-axis

Let R be magnitude of resultant.

$$R = \sqrt{R_x^2 + R_y^2} = \sqrt{(\Sigma F_x)^2 + (\Sigma F_y)^2}, \quad \theta = \tan^{-1}\left(\frac{R_y}{R_x}\right) = \tan^{-1}\left(\frac{\Sigma F_y}{\Sigma F_x}\right)$$

Graphical Method :

Resultant of several concurrent forces can be obtained by law of polygon.

Law of polygon : If number of forces are represented sequentially by the sides of polygon in clockwise or anticlockwise order, the resultant force is represented by the closing side of the polygon directed from starting point of first force to end point of last force.

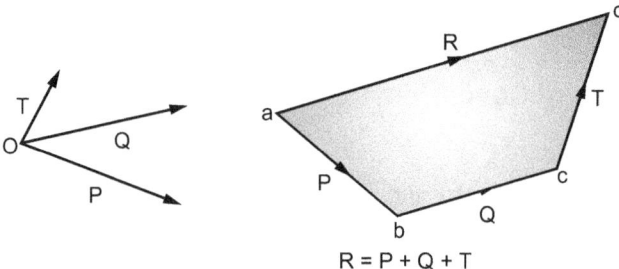

R = P + Q + T

Fig. 1.11

Side 'ab' represents force $\bar{P}$. Side 'bc' represents force $\bar{Q}$. Side 'cd' represents force $\bar{T}$. Side 'ad' represents resultant force $\bar{R}$. Refer Fig. 1.11.

NUMERICAL EXAMPLES ON COMPOSITION AND RESOLUTION OF CONCURRENT FORCES

Example 1.1 :

Determine the x and y components of each of the forces shown.

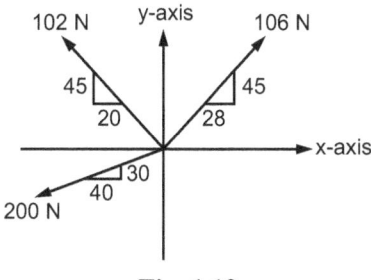

Fig. 1.12

Solution :

Give data : $F_1 = 106$ N, $F_2 = 102$ N, $F_3 = 200$ N. Dimensions are as shown in Fig. 1.12.

To find : x and y components of each force.

(a) Force $F_1 = 106$ N

$$\text{Direction of } F_1 \text{ w.r.t. x-axis} = \tan^{-1}\left(\frac{45}{28}\right) = 58.11°$$

Component of force 106 N along x-axis = 106 cos 58.11° = **56 N** ... Ans.

Component of force 106 N along y-axis = 106 sin 58.11° = **90 N** ... Ans.

(b) Force $F_2 = 102$ N

$$\text{Direction of } F_2 \text{ w.r.t. negative x-axis} = \tan^{-1}\left(\frac{45}{24}\right) = 61.93°$$

Component of force 102 N along negative x-axis = 102 cos 61.93° = **48 N** ... Ans.

Component of force 102 N along y-axis = 102 sin 61.93° = **90 N** ... Ans.

(c) Force $F_3 = 200$ N

$$\text{Direction of } F_3 \text{ w.r.t. negative x-axis} = \tan^{-1}\left(\frac{30}{40}\right) = 36.87°$$

Component of force 200 N along negative x-axis = 200 cos 36.87° = **160 N** ... Ans.

Component of force 200 N along negative y-axis = 200 sin 36.87° = **120 N** ... Ans.

Example 1.2 :

For a particular position, connecting rod BA of engine exerts a force $P = 25$ kN on the crank-pin at A. Resolve force into two rectangular components :

(a) P_h and P_v acting horizontally and vertically.

(b) P_r and P_t along radius AO and perpendicular to AO respectively.

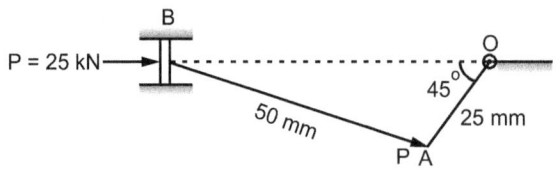

Fig. 1.13

Solution :

Given data : P = 25 kN acting at point A.

l (AB) = 50 mm, l (AO) = 25 mm, ∠ BOA = 45°

To find : (a) Components of force P along horizontal (P_h) and vertical (P_v) direction.

(b) Components of force P along AO and perpendicular to AO (P_r and P_t).

(a) From geometry of Δ BAO. [Refer Fig. 1.13 (a)]

Let ∠ OBA = α

By sine rule,

$$\frac{25}{\sin \alpha} = \frac{50}{\sin 45°}$$

∴ $\sin \alpha = \dfrac{25 \times \sin 45°}{50}$

∴ α = 20.7°

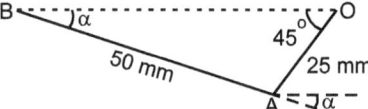

Fig. 1.13 (a)

(b) Component of force P along horizontal direction, [Refer Fig. 1.13 (b)]

P_h = P cos α = 25 cos 20.7°

= **23.39 kN** ... Ans.

Component of force P along vertical direction,

P_v = P sin α = 25 sin 20.7°

= **8.84 kN** ... Ans.

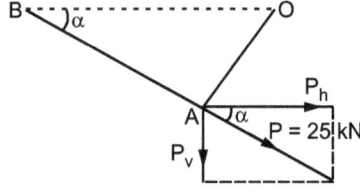

Fig. 1.13 (b)

(c) Component of force P along AO,
[Refer Fig. 1.13 (c)]

P_r = P cos (45° + 20.7°)

= 25 cos 65.7° = **10.3 kN** ...Ans.

Component of force normal to AO,

P_t = P sin (65.7°) = 25 sin 65.7°

= **22.8 kN** ... Ans.

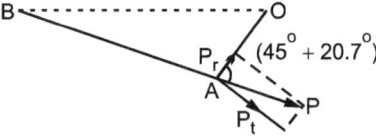

Fig. 1.13 (c)

Example 1.3 :

Find value of α if resultant of given three forces is parallel to the inclined plane. Also find corresponding magnitude of the resultant.

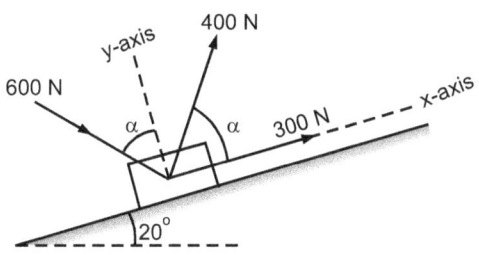
Fig. 1.14

Solution :

Let axis parallel to inclined plane be X-axis.

(a) Since resultant of three forces along X-axis is
$$\Sigma F_y = 0$$
∴ $400 \sin \alpha - 600 \cos \alpha = 0$

∴ $400 \dfrac{\sin \alpha}{\cos \alpha} - 600 = 0$

∴ $400 \tan \alpha - 600 = 0$

∴ $\tan \alpha = \dfrac{600}{400}$

∴ $\alpha = \mathbf{56.31°}$ ... **Ans.**

(b) Magnitude of resultant $= \Sigma F_x$

∴ $\Sigma F_x = 300 + 400 \cos 56.31° + 600 \sin 56.31°$
$= \mathbf{1021.11 \ N}$ ... **Ans.**

Example 1.4 :

Determine components of 2 kN force along oblique axes a and b. Determine projections of F on a and b axes.

Solution :

(a) By triangle law : Refer Fig. 1.15 (a)

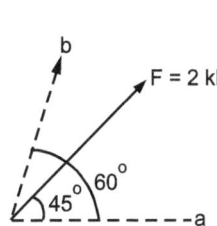
Fig. 1.15

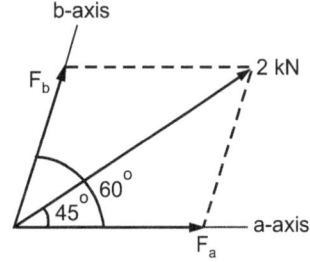
Fig. 1.15 (a)

By Law of Parallelogram :

(a) Direction of force 2 kN w.r.t. axis a :
$$\tan 45° = \dfrac{F_b \sin 60°}{F_a + F_b \cos 60°}$$

$\therefore \quad F_a + 0.5 F_b = 0.866 F_b$

$\therefore \quad F_a = 0.366 F_b$ ... (i)

(b) $\quad (2)^2 = F_a^2 + F_b^2 + 2F_a \cdot F_b \cos 60°$ ... (ii)

Using equations (i) and (ii), we get

$F_a = \mathbf{1.633\ kN}$ ... Ans.

$F_b = \mathbf{0.597\ kN}$ ... Ans.

Example 1.5 :

Determine components of the 1000 N force shown along aa' and bb' axes shown in Fig. 1.16.

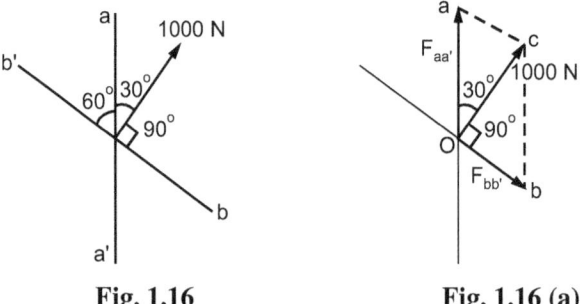

Fig. 1.16   Fig. 1.16 (a)

Solution :

By law of parallelogram (Refer Fig. 1.16 (a)).

Side of parallelogram opposite to force $F_{bb'}$ is equal to $F_{bb'}$ in magnitude and direction.

Redrawing half portion of parallelogram as shown in Fig. 1.16 (b).

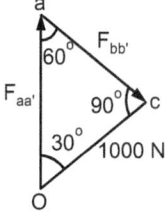

Fig. 1.16 (b)

Applying sine rule to triangle oac,

$$\frac{1000}{\sin 60°} = \frac{F_{aa'}}{\sin 90°} = \frac{F_{bb'}}{\sin 30°}$$

$\therefore \quad F_{aa'} = \mathbf{1154.7\ N}$ ... Ans.

$F_{bb'} = \mathbf{577.35\ N}$ ... Ans.

Example 1.6 :

Resultant force R = 400 N has two component forces P = 240 N and Q = 200 N as shown. Determine direction of component forces i.e. α and β w.r.t. resultant force.

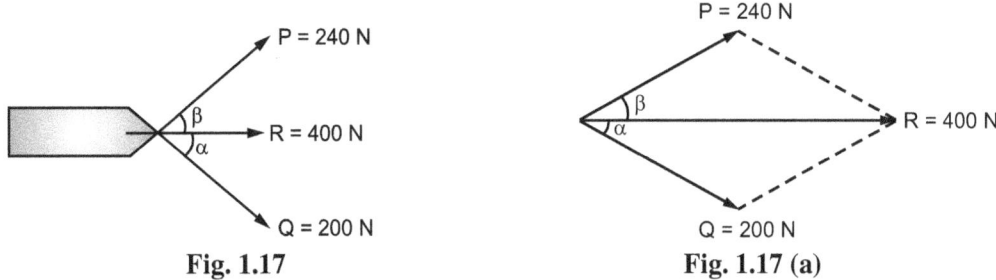

Fig. 1.17   Fig. 1.17 (a)

Solution :
Given data : Resultant force R = 400 N
Components of force R are P = 240 N and Q = 200 N.
To find : Direction of component forces w.r.t. force R i.e. β and α as shown in Fig. 1.17 (a).

Let $\theta = (\alpha + \beta)$

(a) By law of parallelogram, [Refer Fig. 1.17 (a)]

$$R = \sqrt{P^2 + Q^2 + 2\,PQ\cos\theta}$$

∴ $(400)^2 = (240)^2 + (200)^2 + 2 \times 240 \times 200 \times \cos\theta$
∴ $\cos\theta = 0.65$
∴ $\theta = 49.46°$
∴ $\alpha + \beta = 49.46°$

(b) Direction of resultant force 400 N w.r.t. force 240 N :

$$\tan\beta = \frac{200 \sin(\alpha + \beta)}{240 + 200 \cos(\alpha + \beta)}$$

But $(\alpha + \beta) = 49.46°$
∴ $\beta = 22.33°$ and $\alpha = 27.12°$ ... Ans.

Example 1.7 :

The vertical force F = 60 N acts downward at A as shown in Fig. 1.18. Determine the angle $\theta\,(0° \leq \theta \leq 90°)$ of member AB so that the component of F acting along the axis of AB is 80 N. What is the magnitude of the force component acting along the axis of member AC ?

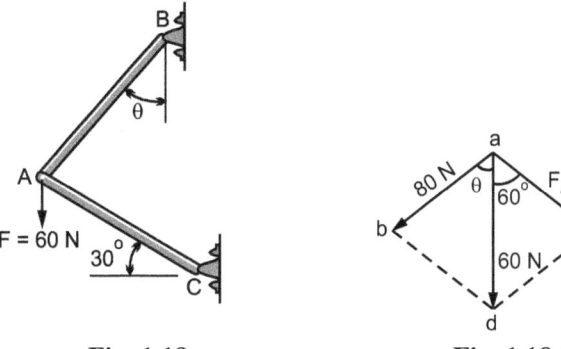

Fig. 1.18   Fig. 1.18 (a)

Solution :

Given data : Resultant force F = 60 N acting vertically downward. F_{AB} = 80 N and F_{AC} are components of force F.

To find : Direction of F_{AB} w.r.t. vertical = θ = ?

Component force, F_{AC} = ?

Triangle abd as shown in Fig. 1.18 (b) represents half of parallelogram shown in Fig. 1.18 (a).

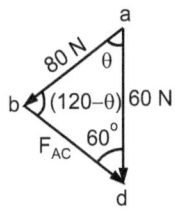

Fig. 1.18 (b)

Angle θ can be determined by law of sine :

$$\frac{80}{\sin 60°} = \frac{60}{\sin (120 - \theta)°}$$

$\therefore \quad \theta = 79.49°$ ... Ans.

$$\frac{80}{\sin 60°} = \frac{F_{AC}}{\sin \theta}$$

$\therefore \quad F_{AC} = 90.83 \text{ N}$ ... Ans.

Example 1.8 :

The log is being towed by two tractors A and B. If the resultant F_R of the two forces acting on the log is to be directed along positive x-axis and have a magnitude of 10 kN, determine the angle θ of the cable attached to B such that the force F_B in this cable is a minimum. What is the magnitude of force in each cable for this situation ?

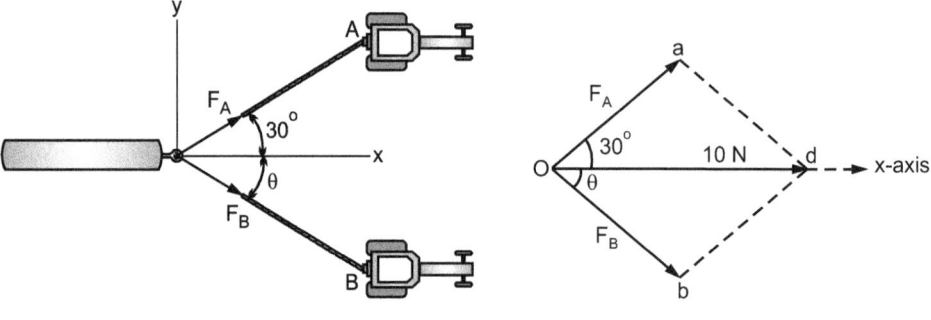

Fig. 1.19   **Fig. 1.19 (a)**

Solution :

Given data : F_R = 10 N is the resultant of component forces F_A and F_B.

Direction of component force F_A w.r.t. resultant F_R = 30°.

To find : Direction of force F_B w.r.t. resultant F_R = θ = ? when F_B in this cable is minimum.

Redrawing half portion of the parallelogram as triangle oad.

(a) Side of parallelogram opposite to F_B is equal to F_B in magnitude and direction. (Refer Fig. 1.19 (a).

Hence, Refer Fig. 1.19 (b)

Force F_B is minimum, if forces F_A and F_B are perpendicular to each other.

i.e. from Fig. 1.19 (b).

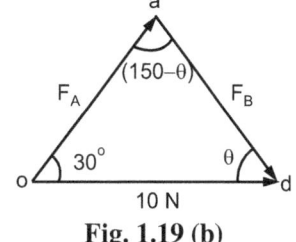

Fig. 1.19 (b)

$$150 - \theta = 90°$$
$$\therefore \quad \theta = 60° \quad \text{... Ans.}$$

(b) By sine rule to triangle oad,

$$\frac{10}{\sin 90°} = \frac{F_A}{\sin 60°}$$

$$\therefore \quad F_A = 8.66 \text{ N} \quad \text{... Ans.}$$

$$\frac{10}{\sin 90°} = \frac{F_B}{\sin 30°}$$

$$\therefore \quad F_B = 5 \text{ N} \quad \text{... Ans.}$$

Example 1.9 :

The post is to be pulled out of the ground using two ropes A and B. Rope A is subjected to a force of 600 N and is directed at 60° from the horizontal. If the resultant force acting on the post is 1200 N vertically upward, determine force T in rope B and corresponding angle θ.

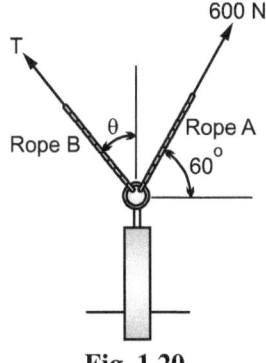

Fig. 1.20

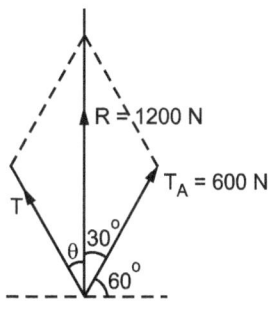

Fig. 1.20 (a)

Solution :

Given data : Tension in the rope A = T_A = 600 N

Resultant is vertically upward.

Angle made by force T_A with resultant R = α = 30°.

Magnitude of resultant of force T_A and T = 1200 N.

To find : Tension in rope = T = ?

Direction of T = θ w.r.t. resultant R.

(a) By law of parallelogram, [Refer Fig. 1.20 (a)]
Let θ_1 be the included angle between forces T_A and T.

$$R = \sqrt{T_A^2 + T^2 + 2\,T_A \cdot T \cos\theta_1}$$

$\therefore \quad (1200)^2 = (600)^2 + T^2 + 2 \times 600 \times T \cos\theta_1$

$\therefore \quad T^2 + 1200\,T \times \cos\theta_1 = 1080000 \qquad \ldots (i)$

$$\tan\alpha = \frac{T \sin\theta_1}{T_A + T \cos\theta_1}$$

$\therefore \quad \tan 30° = \dfrac{T \sin\theta_1}{600 + T_B \cos\theta_1}$

$\therefore \quad 0.577\,(600 + T_B \cos\theta_1) = T \sin\theta_1$

$\therefore \quad 346.2 + 0.577\,T \cos\theta_1 = T \sin\theta_1 \qquad \ldots (ii)$

By solving equations (i) and (ii) simultaneously,

$T = 743.6\text{ N}$ and $\theta_1 = 54.79°$

$\theta = \theta_1 - 30 = 53.79 - 30 = 23.79°$

$\therefore \quad T = \mathbf{743.7\ N}$ and $\theta = \mathbf{23.79°}$ ... Ans.

Example 1.10 :

Determine resultant R of two forces 400 N and 600 N.

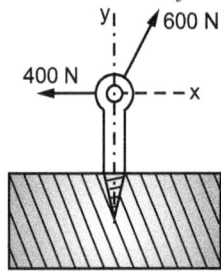

Fig. 1.21

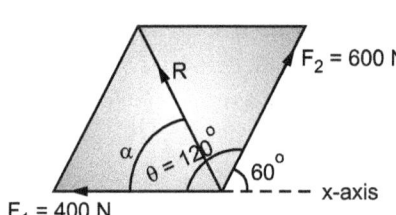

Fig. 1.21 (a)

Solution :

Given data : Let $F_1 = 400$ N, $F_2 = 600$ N, Included angle between two forces F_1 and $F_2 = \theta = 120°$.

To find : Magnitude of resultant = R
Direction of resultant = α (with force F_1)
By law of parallelogram, [Refer Fig. 1.21 (a)]

(a) $\quad R = \sqrt{F_1^2 + F_2^2 + 2\,F_1 F_2 \cos\theta}$

$\therefore \quad R = \sqrt{(400)^2 + (600)^2 + (2 \times 400 \times 600 \times \cos 120°)}$

$\therefore \quad R = \mathbf{529.15\ N}$ ... Ans.

(b) $\quad \tan\alpha = \dfrac{F_2 \sin\theta}{F_1 + F_2 \cos\theta} = \dfrac{600 \sin 120°}{400 + 600 \cos 120°} = 5.196$

$\therefore \quad \alpha = \tan^{-1}(5.196) = \mathbf{79.10°}$ ... Ans.

Example 1.11 :

Determine magnitude of the resultant force of F_1 and F_2. Determine its direction from positive x-axis.

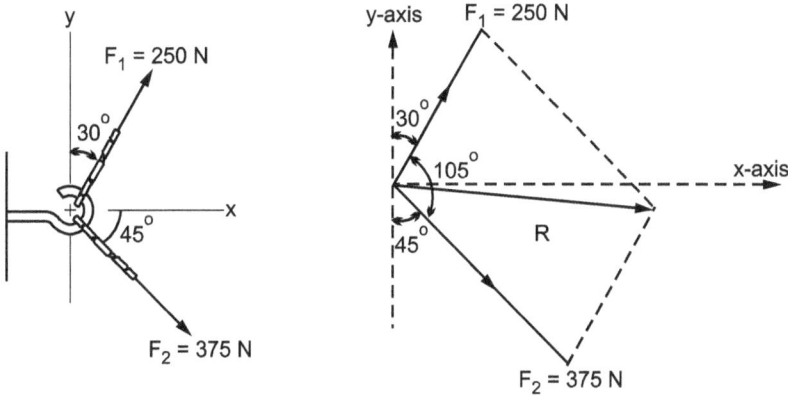

Fig. 1.22   Fig. 1.22 (a)

Solution :

Given data : $F_1 = 250$ N, $F_2 = 375$ N, Included angle θ between F_1 and $F_2 = 105°$.

To find : Magnitude of resultant force R.

Direction of resultant force w.r.t. x-axis.

(a) Let R be the resultant force of F_1 and F_2. By law of parallelogram,

[Refer Fig. 1.22 (a)]

$$R = \sqrt{F_1^2 + F_2^2 + 2\,F_1 F_2 \cos\theta}$$
$$= \sqrt{(250)^2 + (375)^2 + (2 \times 250 \times 375 \times \cos 105°)}$$
$$= \mathbf{393.18\ N} \qquad \text{... Ans.}$$

(b) Let θ be the direction of resultant force w.r.t. force F_1.

$\therefore \qquad \tan\theta = \dfrac{375 \sin 105°}{250 + 375 \cos 105°} = 2.368$

$\therefore \qquad \theta = 67.1°$

Since direction of force F_1 w.r.t. x-axis is 60°.

Direction of resultant force w.r.t. x-axis measured in clockwise direction is $(67.1° - 60°)$ i.e. $7.1°$. ... Ans.

Example 1.12 :

Two forces, one 400 N and the other P, are applied as shown in Fig. 1.23 to remove the spike from timber. Compute the magnitude of P necessary to ensure a resultant T directed along the spike. Also find T.

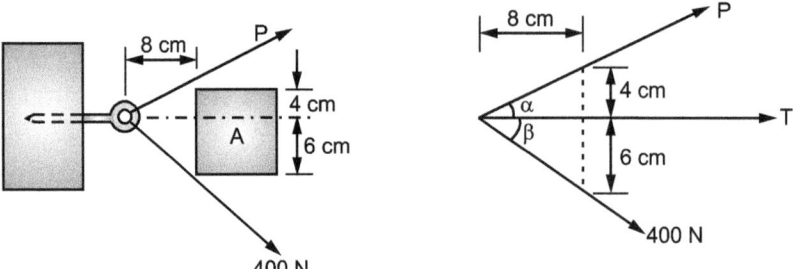

Fig. 1.23   Fig. 1.23 (a)

Solution :

Given data : Resultant of force P and force 400 N is force T acting along x-axis as shown.

From geometry,

$$\text{Direction of force P w.r.t. resultant} = \tan^{-1}\left(\frac{4}{8}\right) = 26.56°$$

$$\text{Direction of force 400 N w.r.t. resultant} = \tan^{-1}\left(\frac{6}{8}\right) = 36.87°$$

Included angle between component forces = $\alpha + \beta = 63.43°$

To find : Magnitude of component force P.
Magnitude of resultant force T.

(a) By law of parallelogram, [Refer Fig. 1.23 (a)]

$$T = \sqrt{P^2 + (400)^2 + 2 \times P \times 400 \times \cos 63.43°}$$

∴ $T^2 = P^2 + 160000 + 357.83\, P$ ... (i)

$$\tan 36.87° = \frac{P \sin 63.43°}{400 + P \cos 63.43°} = \frac{0.894\, P}{400 + 0.447\, P}$$

∴   **P = 536.67 N**   ... Ans.

Substituting P = 536.67 N in equation (i),

                 T = 800 N   ... Ans.

Example 1.13 :

Determine the angle θ ($0° \leq \theta \leq 90°$) between the two forces so that the magnitude of the resultant force acting on the ring is a minimum. What is the magnitude of the resultant force ?

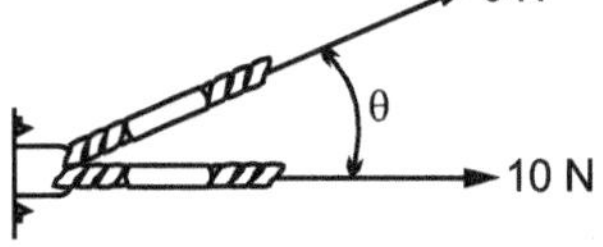

Fig. 1.24

Solution :

Given data : Let P = 10 N and Q = 6 N

To find : Included angle between two forces = θ = ? When resultant force acting on the ring is minimum, magnitude of resultant force R = ?

(a) By law of parallelogram,
$$R = \sqrt{P^2 + Q^2 + 2PQ\cos\theta}$$
∴ $\quad R^2 = P^2 + Q^2 + 2PQ\cos\theta$ ... (i)

R is minimum when last term of equation (i) equals to zero.

i.e. $\quad 2PQ\cos\theta = 0$

⇒ $\quad \cos\theta = 0$

⇒ $\quad \theta = 90°\ (0° \le \theta \le 90°)$

∴ **R is minimum when θ = 90°** ... Ans.

(b) Substituting θ = 90° in equation (i), we get,
$$R^2 = P^2 + Q^2$$
⇒ $\quad R = \sqrt{P^2 + Q^2}$

⇒ $\quad R = \sqrt{(10)^2 + (6)^2}$

∴ $\quad \mathbf{R = 11.67\ N}$ ... Ans.

Example 1.14 :

Resolve 60 N force into components acting along u and v axes.

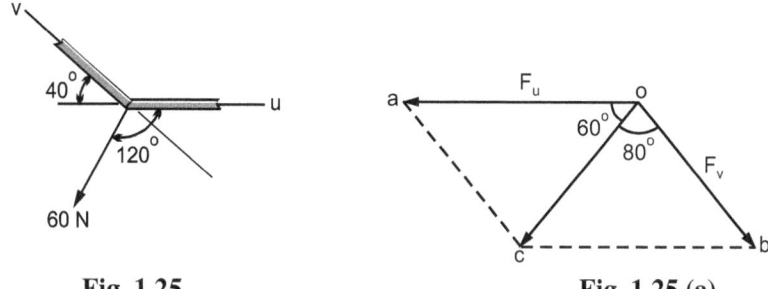

Fig. 1.25   **Fig. 1.25 (a)**

Solution :

Given data : Force F = 60 N

Direction of force F w.r.t. negative u-axis = 60°

Direction of force F w.r.t. negative v-axis = 80°

To find : Components of force F along u and v directions : F_u and F_v.

By law of parallelogram (Refer Fig. 1.25 (a)), side of parallelogram opposite to force F_v is equal to F_v in magnitude and direction.

Redrawing half portion of parallelogram, as shown in Fig. 1.25 (b).

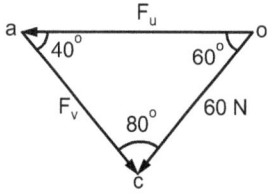

Fig. 1.25 (b)

Applying sine rule to triangle oac

$$\frac{60}{\sin 40°} = \frac{F_u}{\sin 80°}$$

∴ $F_u = $ **91.92 N** ... Ans.

$$\frac{60}{\sin 40°} = \frac{F_v}{\sin 60°}$$

∴ $F_v = $ **80.83 N** ... Ans.

Example 1.15 :

Two forces are shown in Fig. 1.26. Knowing that magnitude of P is 600 N. Determine :
(a) The required angle θ if the resultant R of the two forces is to be vertical.
(b) The corresponding value of R.

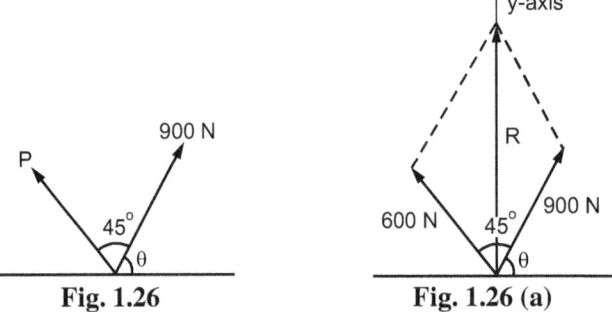

Fig. 1.26   Fig. 1.26 (a)

Solution :

By law of parallelogram (Refer Fig. 1.26 (a)).

(a) $R^2 = 900^2 + 600^2 + (2)(900)(600)\cos 45°$

∴ $R = $ **1390.57 N** ... Ans.

(b) Direction of resultant R w.r.t. force 900 N is $(90 - \theta)$.

$$\tan(90 - \theta) = \frac{600 \sin 45°}{900 + 600 \cos 45°}$$

∴ $\theta = $ **72.23°** ... Ans.

Example 1.16 :

The resultant of two forces P and Q is 1200 N vertical. Determine force Q and the corresponding angle θ for the system of forces as shown in Fig. 1.27.   **(May 2013/4 Marks)**

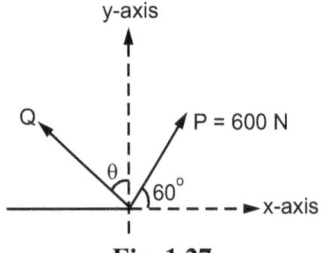

Fig. 1.27

Solution :

Resultant is vertical.

So, Component of resultant along X-axis = 0

and Component of resultant along Y-axis = 1200 N.

$\therefore \quad \Sigma F_x = 600 \cos 60° - Q \cos (90 - \theta) = 0$

$\therefore \quad 300 - Q \sin \theta = 0$ ... (i)

$\quad \Sigma F_y = 600 \sin 60° + Q \cos \theta = 1200$

$\therefore \quad 519.61 + Q \cos \theta = 1200$

$\therefore \quad Q \cos \theta = 680.38$ ... (ii)

Solving equation (i) and (ii),

$\quad \theta = \mathbf{23.75°}$ ... Ans.

$\quad Q = \mathbf{743.33\ N}$ ... Ans.

Example 1.17 :

Determine the magnitude and direction of the resultant force.

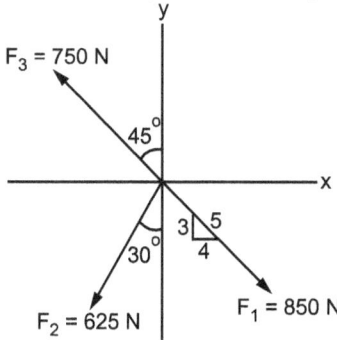

Fig. 1.28

Solution :

Given data : $F_1 = 850$ N, $F_2 = 625$ N and $F_3 = 750$ N are acting at a point.

Directions of forces are as shown in Fig. 1.28.

$\theta_3 = 45°$, $\theta_2 = 30°$ and $\theta_1 = 53.13°$ w.r.t. y-axis in respective quadrants.

To find : Magnitude and direction of resultant.

(a) Resolving forces along x-axis,

$\quad \Sigma F_x = 850 \sin 53.13° - 625 \sin 30° - 750 \sin 45°$

$\quad\quad\quad = -162.83$ N

Resolving forces along y-axis,

$\quad \Sigma F_y = -850 \cos 53.13° - 625 \cos 30° + 750 \cos 45°$

$\quad\quad\quad = -520.93$ N

Magnitude of resultant $= \sqrt{(\Sigma F_x)^2 + (\Sigma F_y)^2}$

$\quad\quad\quad\quad\quad\quad\quad\quad = \sqrt{(-162.83)^2 + (-520.93)^2}$

$\quad\quad\quad\quad\quad\quad\quad\quad = \mathbf{545.78\ N}$ ... Ans.

Direction of resultant, [Refer Fig. 1.28 (a)]

$$\tan \alpha = \frac{\Sigma F_y}{\Sigma F_x} = \frac{520.93}{162.83}$$

∴ $\alpha = 72.64°$ **w.r.t. negative x-axis** ... Ans.

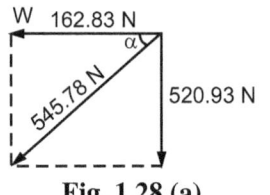

Fig. 1.28 (a)

Example 1.18 :

Determine the range of values for the magnitude of P so that the magnitude of the resultant force does not exceed 2500 N. Force P is always directed to the right.

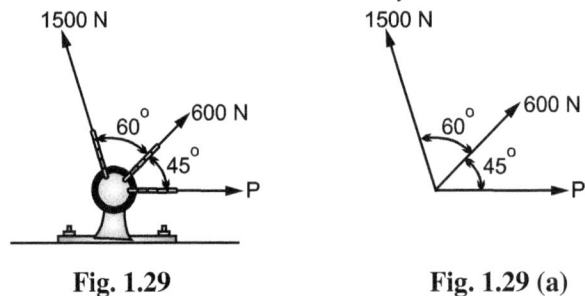

Fig. 1.29   Fig. 1.29 (a)

Solution :

Given data : Magnitudes of two forces are 1500 N and 600 N.

Direction of three forces are as shown in Fig. 1.29.

Resultant R ≤ 2500 N.

To find : Force P.

(a) By law of parallelogram, [Refer Fig. 1.29 (a)]

Magnitude of resultant of forces 600 N and 1500 N

$$= \sqrt{(600)^2 + (1500)^2 + (2 \times 600 \times 1500 \cos 60°)}$$
$$= 1873.5 \text{ N}$$

Direction of resultant w.r.t. force 600 N

$$= \tan^{-1}\left(\frac{1500 \sin 60°}{600 + 1500 \cos 60°}\right)$$
$$= 43.9°$$

∴ Resultant of forces 1500 N and 600 N is 1873.5 N.

Direction of this resultant is 88.9° w.r.t. force P.

(b) Resultant of 1873.5 N and force P [Refer Fig. 1.29 (a)] does not exceed 2500 N.

∴   P = 0   OR

By law of parallelogram,

$$2500 = \sqrt{(1873.5)^2 + P^2 + (2 \times P \times 1873.5) \cos 88.9°}$$

∴ $(2500)^2 = (1873.5)^2 + P^2 + 72\,P$

∴ $P^2 + 72\,P - 2739997.75 = 0$

∴ $P = 1619.72$ N

Range of P is between 0 N and 1619.72 N ... Ans.

Example 1.19 :

Determine magnitude and direction of force F so that the resultant of three forces is zero.

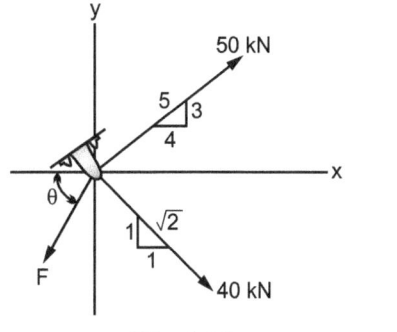
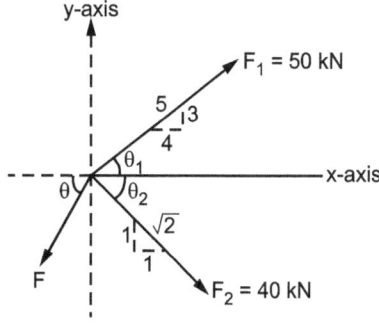

Fig. 1.30   Fig. 1.30 (a)

Solution :

Given data : Magnitude of forces $F_1 = 50$ kN, $F_2 = 40$ kN

Direction of forces : $\theta_1 = 36.87°$, $\theta_2 = 45°$ w.r.t. positive x-axis. Resultant R = 0

To find : Magnitude and direction of force.

(a) Since resultant is zero, $\Sigma F_x = 0$ and $\Sigma F_y = 0$

Resolving forces along x-axis,

$$\Sigma F_x = 50 \cos 36.87° + 40 \cos 45° - F \cos \theta = 0$$

⇒ $68.28 - F \cos \theta = 0$

⇒ $F \cos \theta = 68.28$ ... (i)

Resolving forces along y-axis,

$$\Sigma F_y = 50 \sin 36.87° - 40 \sin 45° - F \sin \theta = 0$$

⇒ $1.71 - F \sin \theta = 0$

⇒ $F \sin \theta = 1.71$ ... (ii)

From equations (i) and (ii),

$\theta = \mathbf{1.43°}$ and $F = \mathbf{68.30}$ **kN** ... Ans.

Example 1.20 :

Knowing that tension in cable BC is 145 N, determine resultant of three forces exerted at point B of beam AB.

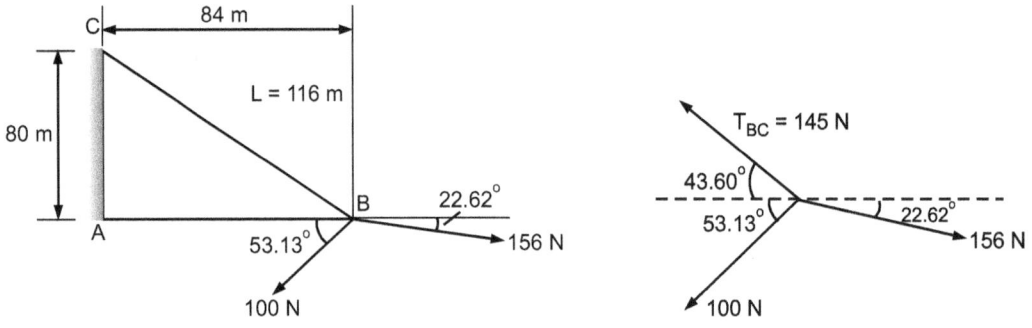

Fig. 1.31   Fig. 1.31 (a)

Solution :

(a) From Fig. 1.31 (a),

$$\angle ABC = \tan^{-1}\left(\frac{80}{84}\right) = 43.60°$$

(b) Resultant of forces at B,

$$\Sigma F_x = -145 \cos 43.60° - 100 \cos 53.13° + 156 \cos 22.62°$$
$$= -21 \text{ N}$$
$$= 21 \text{ N } (\leftarrow)$$

$$\Sigma F_y = 145 \sin 43.60° - 100 \sin 53.13° - 156 \sin 22.62°$$
$$\Sigma F_y = -40 \text{ (N)} = 40 \text{ N } (\downarrow)$$

∴ Magnitude of resultant :

$$R = \sqrt{(\Sigma F_x)^2 + (\Sigma F_y)^2} = \sqrt{(21)^2 + (40)^2}$$
$$= \mathbf{45.18 \text{ N}} \qquad \text{... Ans.}$$

Direction of resultant

$$\alpha = \tan^{-1}\left(\frac{\Sigma F_y}{\Sigma F_x}\right)$$

$$= \tan^{-1}\left(\frac{40}{21}\right) = \mathbf{62.30°} \qquad \text{... Ans.}$$

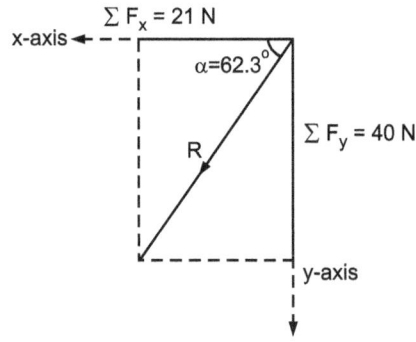

Fig. 1.31 (b)

Example 1.21 :

The resultant of two forces P and Q is 1200 N horizontally leftward. Determine the force Q and the corresponding angle θ for the system of forces as shown in Fig. 1.32.

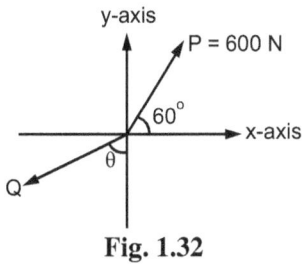

Fig. 1.32

Solution :

Resultant is horizontally leftward :

Component of resultant along X-axis = – 1200 N

So, Component of resultant along Y-axis = 0.

$$\Sigma F_x = -1200$$
$$\Sigma F_y = 0$$

∴ $\Sigma F_x = 600 \cos 60° - Q \sin \theta = -1200$ ... (i)

$Q \sin \theta = 1500$

$\Sigma F_y = 600 \sin 60° - Q \cos \theta = 0$ ... (ii)

$Q \cos \theta = 519.61$

Solving equations (i) and (ii), **Q = 1587.45 N** ... Ans.

θ = 70.89° ... Ans.

1.7 MOMENT OF A FORCE

The moment of a force is the cause of rotation. The magnitude of rotation or turning depends on the extent of moment.

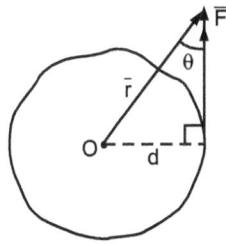

Fig. 1.33

Moment of a force about a point O

$$\overline{M}_o = \overline{r} \times \overline{F}$$ $\overline{r}$ is the position vector.

∴ $$M_o = F r \sin \theta$$

$$M_o = Fd$$

M_o = Force × Perpendicular distance between moment centre and line of action of force.

For example :

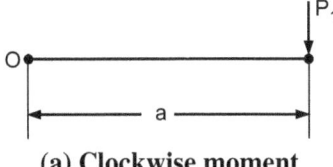

(a) Clockwise moment

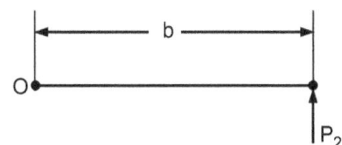

(b) Anticlockwise moment

Fig. 1.34

Here the moment of force P_1 about point O is given by
$M_O = (P_1 \times a)$ (clockwise)

Here the moment of force P_2 about point O is given by
$M_O = (P_2 \times b)$ (anticlockwise)

The moment is zero when either the force is zero or when the perpendicular distance is zero.

Sign convention : Clockwise moment is taken positive.
Anticlockwise moment is taken negative.

1.8 GRAPHICAL REPRESENTATION OF MOMENT OF FORCE

Refer Fig. 1.35.

Force $\bar{F}$ is represented by a vector AB.
'O' is the moment centre and d is the perpendicular distance.
(Moment of force F about point O = Fd)

$$\text{Area of } \triangle AOB = \frac{1}{2} Fd$$

∴ Moment of force at point O = Fd = 2 × Area of △ AOB.

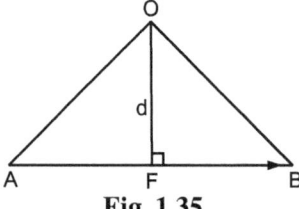

Fig. 1.35

1.9 VARIGNON'S THEOREM OF MOMENTS

The theorem states that the algebraic sum of the moments of all forces about any point is equal to the moment of their resultant about the same point. Moment of forces about point 'O' is

$$\boxed{-(P_1 \times d_1) + (P_2 \times d_2) - (P_3 \times d_3) = -(R \times d)}$$

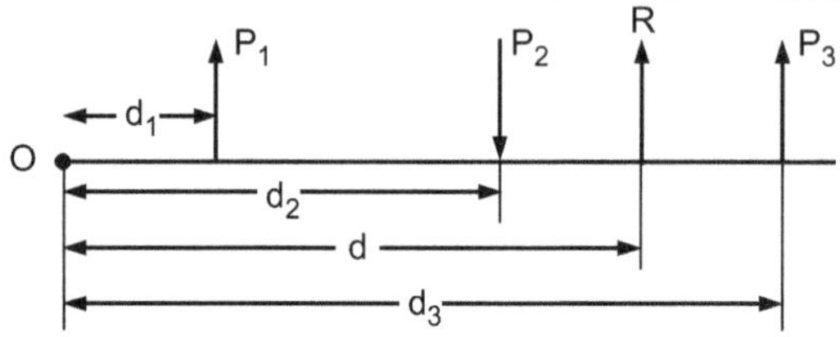

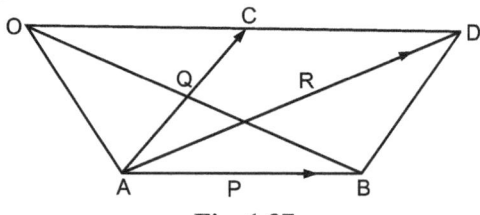

Fig. 1.36

Proof : Two concurrent forces P and Q acting at A are shown in Fig. 1.37. The resultant of P and Q is R, given by the diagonal AD of the parallelogram ABDC. Extend DC to O, which is considered as the moment centre for all forces.

Fig. 1.37

Moment of P about O = $M_{PO} = 2 \Delta ABO$

Moment of Q about O = $M_{QO} = 2 \Delta ACO$

Adding, $M_{PO} + M_{QO} = \Sigma M_o = 2 [\Delta ABO + \Delta ACO]$

But, $\Delta ABO = \Delta ABD = \Delta ACD$

∴ $\Sigma M_o = 2 [\Delta ACD + \Delta ACO] = 2 \Delta ADO$

$= M_{RO}$ = moment of R about O.

Thus, $(M_{PO} + M_{QO}) = \Sigma M_o = M_{RO}$

Now we conclude that, the sum of the moments of two concurrent forces about a point O in their plane is equal to the moment of their resultant about the same point O. This is known as Varignon's theorem of moments.

Only for simplicity we had taken the moment centre on the line DC extended, but this is not a required condition. By successive application, the theorem can be extended to any number of concurrent forces.

1.10 COUPLE

Two equal, opposite and parallel forces having different lines of action are said to form a couple.

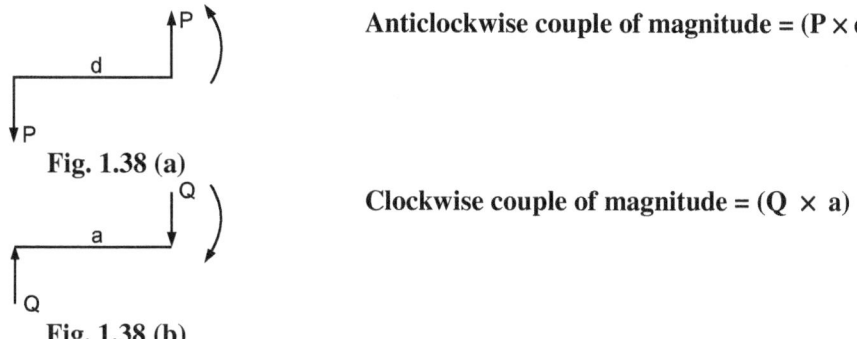

Anticlockwise couple of magnitude = (P × d)

Fig. 1.38 (a)

Clockwise couple of magnitude = (Q × a)

Fig. 1.38 (b)

Characteristics of a Couple :
1. The sum of two forces along any direction is zero. But the sum of moments about any given point is not zero.
2. The couple does not translate a body but tends to rotate it.
3. Moment of couple about any point is equal to the product of the force and perpendicular distance between the two forces.
   i.e. M = (P × d)
   where, 'd' is the distance between two forces and is known as *lever arm*.
4. Moment of couple is independent of the distance of the point "O" about which moment is taken i.e. couple is always constant.

1.11 COPLANAR GENERAL FORCE SYSTEMS

Coplanar general force system consists of several non-concurrent and non-parallel forces acting at different points in a plane.

The general force system can be reduced to a resultant force and a resultant couple.

The general force system is in equilibrium if a resultant force is zero and moment of couple is also zero.

1.12 COMPOSITION OF GENERAL FORCE SYSTEM

Resultant of general force system can be obtained both analytically and graphically.

Analytical Method :

(i) **Magnitude of resultant :** Resolve each force in general force system along x-axis and y-axis.

Sum up the components of forces along x-axis and y-axis. This summation gives component of resultant along x-axis and along y-axis i.e. $R_x = \sum F_x$ and $R_y = \sum F_y$.

Magnitude of resultant = $R = \sqrt{(\sum F_x)^2 + (\sum F_y)^2}$

(ii) **Direction of resultant :** Let $'\alpha'$ be the inclination of the resultant with x-axis.

$$\tan \alpha = \left(\frac{\sum F_y}{\sum F_x}\right)$$

Direction of resultant = $\alpha = \tan^{-1}\left(\frac{\sum F_y}{\sum F_x}\right)$.

(iii) **Location of resultant w.r.t. any point :** Let 'd' be the perpendicular distance of resultant from point 'O'.

By Varignon's theorem,

Moment of resultant about point 'O' = $\sum$ Moment of component forces about point 'O'.

i.e. $\quad R \times d = F_1 d_1 + F_2 d_2 + F_3 d_3 + \ldots\ldots$

where $F_1, F_2, F_3 \ldots$ are component forces and $d_1, d_2, d_3, \ldots$ are perpendicular distances of component forces from point 'O'.

NUMERICAL EXAMPLES ON MOMENT, COUPLE AND EQUIVALENT FORCE COUPLE SYSTEM

Example 1.22 :

Determine the magnitude and directional sense of the resultant moment of the forces about point P.

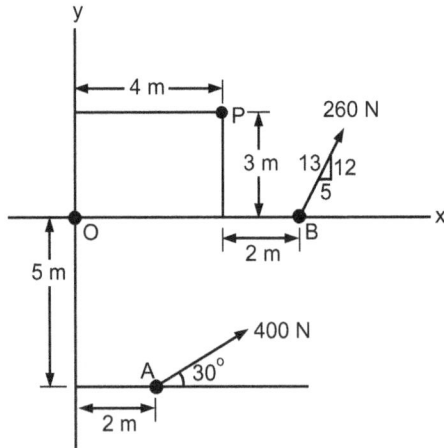

Fig. 1.39

Solution :

Given data : $F_1 = 260$ N, $\theta_1 = \tan^{-1}\left(\dfrac{12}{5}\right) = 67.38°$

$F_2 = 400$ N, $\theta_2 = 30°$

To find : Magnitude and direction of resultant moment at point P.

(a) Moment of 260 N about point P,

$= -260 \cos 67.38° \times 3 - 260 \sin 67.38° \times 2$

$= -780$ Nm   i.e.   780 Nm (↻)

(b) Moment of 400 N about point P

$= -400 \cos 30° \times 8 + 400 \sin 30° \times 2$

$= -2371.28$ Nm   i.e.   2371.28 Nm (↻)

∴ Resultant moment of forces about point P = **3151.28 Nm (↻)**   ... **Ans.**

Example 1.23 :

Replace the couple and force shown by a single force F applied at a point D. Locate D by determining the distance b.

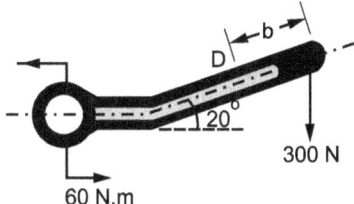

Fig. 1.40

Solution :

Given data : Force = 300 N at angle 20° with horizontal.

Moment of couple = 60 Nm.

To find : Distance b.

(a) To find distance 'b' :

Resultant force = 300 N acts at D

By Varignon's theorem,

Moment of resultant at point D = $\sum$ Moment of forces at point D.

∴ $\quad 300 \times 0 = 300 \times b \cos 20° - 60$

$281.9\, b - 60 = 0$

∴ $\quad b = \mathbf{0.213\ m}$ ... **Ans.**

Example 1.24 :

A force $F = 60$ N is applied to the gear. Determine moment of F about point O, $r = 100$ mm.

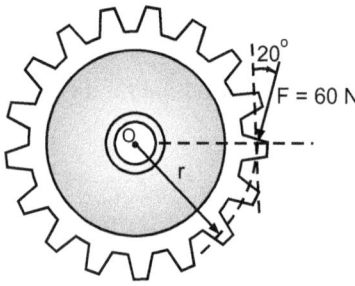

Fig. 1.41

Solution :

Force $F = 60$ N is resolved along x-axis and y-axis.

∴ Component of force 60 N along x-axis

$$F_x = 60 \sin 20°$$

Component of force 60 N along y-axis

$$F_y = 60 \cos 20° = 56.38 \text{ N}$$

Moment of F_x about centre O = 0 N-m

Moment of F_y about centre O = $56.38 \times 0.1 = 5.638$ N-m (↺)

By Varignon's theorem,

Moment of force F about point O = $0 + 5.638 = 5.638$ N-m (↺)

Example 1.25 :

Calculate the moment of 250 N force on the handle about centre of the bolt.

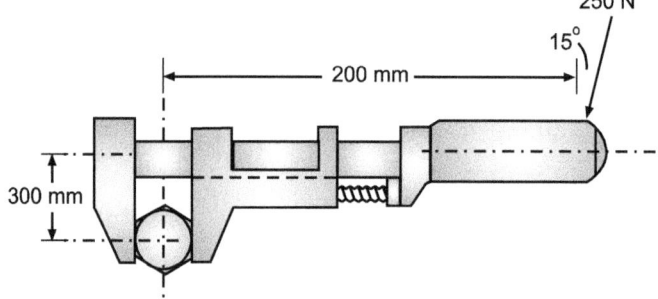

Fig. 1.42

Solution :

Force 250 N is resolved along x-axis and y-axis.
Component of force 250 N along x-axis.

$$F_x = 250 \sin 15° = 64.7 \text{ N}$$

Component of force 250 N along y-axis

$$F_y = 250 \cos 15° = 241.48 \text{ N}$$

Moment of F_x about centre of bolt = $F_x \times 0.03$ = 1.94 N-m (↻)

Moment of F_y about centre of bolt = $F_y \times 0.2$ = 48.3 N-m (↺)

By Varignon's theorem,

Total moment of force 250 N about centre of bolt

$$= -1.94 + 48.3 = -46.36 \text{ N-m} = \textbf{46.36 N-m (↻)} \qquad \text{... Ans.}$$

Example 1.26 :

If the resultant moment about point A is 4800 Nm clockwise, determine the magnitude of F_3 if $F_1 = 300$ N and $F_2 = 400$ N.

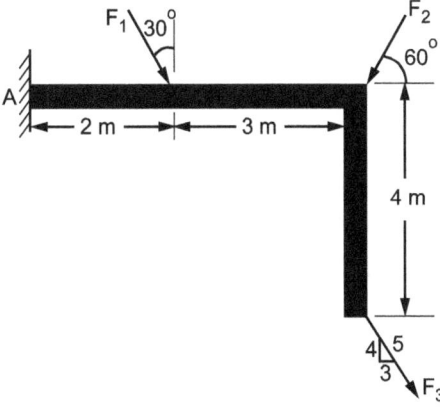

Fig. 1.43

Solution :

Given data : Moment of forces about point A = 4800 Nm (↺)

$F_1 = 300$ N, $F_2 = 400$ N.

Direction of force $F_3 = \tan^{-1}\left(\dfrac{4}{3}\right) = 53.13°$ with horizontal.

Dimensions are as shown in the Fig. 1.43.

To find : Magnitude of force F_3.

(a) Resultant moment about point A = 4800 Nm.

i.e. $\sum$ Moment of forces about point A = 4800 Nm.

∴ $300 \cos 30° \times 2 + 400 \sin 60° \times 5 + F_3 \sin 53.13° \times 5 - F_3 \cos 53.13° \times 4 = 4800$ Nm

∴ $\qquad\qquad\qquad 1.6 F_3 = 2548$

∴ $\qquad\qquad\qquad F_3 = \textbf{1592.5 N} \qquad \text{... Ans.}$

Example 1.27 :

If F = 180 kN, determine the magnitude and sense of the resultant couple moment. Also find where on the beam of the resultant couple act ?

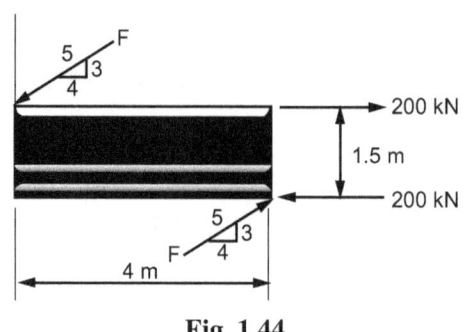

Fig. 1.44

Solution :

Given data : Forces of magnitude 200 kN and 180 kN are acting as shown in Fig. 1.44.

To find : Magnitude and sense of the resultant couple moment.

(a) To find magnitude and sense of resultant couple moment.
(i) Moment of couple due to force 200 kN = 200 × 1.5 = 300 kNm (↻).
(ii) Moment of couple due to force 180 kN :

Resolving force 180 kN along x and y axes

∴ Moment of couple due to force 180 kN
$$= -180 \sin 36.87° \times 4 - 180 \cos 36.87° \times 1.5$$
$$= 648 \text{ kNm } (↺)$$

(iii) Magnitude of resultant couple moment = 348 kNm (↺).
(iv) Couple can act anywhere.

Example 1.28 :

Compute combined moment of two 180 N forces about (a) point O, (b) point A.

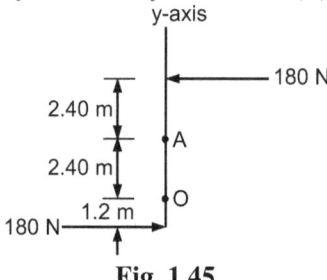

Fig. 1.45

Solution :

Since given two forces of magnitude 180 N each are parallel and opposite in direction, so they form a couple.

The characteristic of couple is :

Moment of a couple about any point is independent of distance about which moment is to be found out.

∴ Moment of a couple about point A
= Moment of a couple about point O
= Force × Perpendicular distance between the two forces
= 180 × 6
= **1080 N-m (↻)** ... Ans.

Example 1.29 :
Find resultant moment of two couples for the loading as shown in Fig. 1.46.

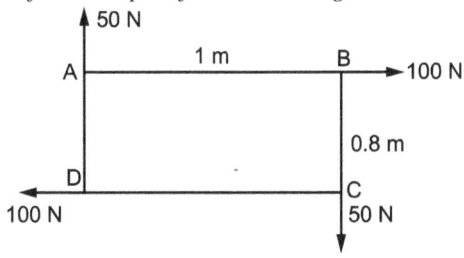

Fig. 1.46

Solution :
Moment of couple of forces of magnitude 50 N = 50 × 1 = **50 N-m (↻)** ... Ans.
Moment of couple of forces of magnitude 100 N = 100 × 0.8 = **80 N-m (↻)** ... Ans.
∴ Resultant moment of two couples = 50 + 80 = **130 N-m (↻)** ... Ans.

NUMERICAL EXAMPLES ON RESULTANT OF PARALLEL FORCE SYSTEM AND GENERAL FORCE SYSTEM

Example 1.30 :
Four parallel forces of magnitude 100 N, 200 N, 50 N and 400 N are as shown in Fig. 1.47. Determine the magnitude of the resultant and also the distance of the resultant from point A.

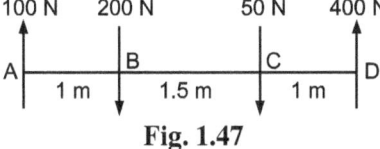

Fig. 1.47

Solution :
Magnitude of resultant of four parallel forces = – 100 – 200 – 50 + 400 = **250 N (↑)**
... Ans.

Position of resultant from point A :
Assume resultant R = 250 N is at a perpendicular distance x from point A.

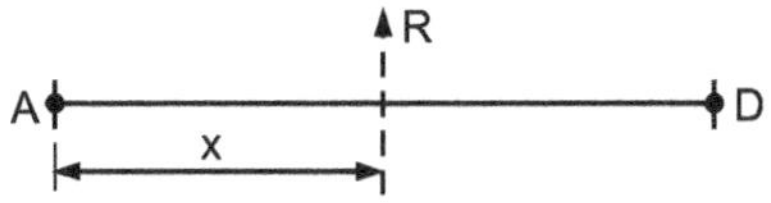

Fig. 1.48

By Varignon's theorem

Taking moments about point A,

$$-R \times x = 100 \times 0 + 200 \times 1 + 50 \times 2.5 - 400 \times 3.5$$

$$\therefore \quad -250 \times x = -1075$$

$$\therefore \quad x = \mathbf{4.3\ m}$$

Distance of resultant is 4.3 m from point A to the right. ... **Ans.**

Example 1.31 :

If resultant R = 600 N of three forces 100 N, F and 300 N is acting as shown in Fig. 1.49, find magnitude of force F and its distance 'x' from point A.

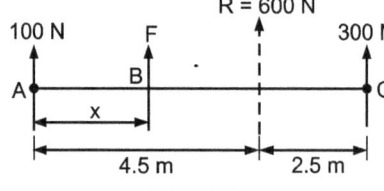

Fig. 1.49

Solution :

Magnitude of resultant of three parallel forces = $100 + F + 300 = 600$ N

$\therefore$ Magnitude of force F = **200 N** ... **Ans.**

Position of force F i.e. distance x :

By Varignon's theorem,

Taking moments about point A,

$$-600 \times 4.5 = 100 \times 0 - F \times x - 300 \times 7$$

$$\therefore \quad -2700 = -200x - 2100$$

$$\therefore \quad x = \mathbf{3\ m}$$ ... **Ans.**

Example 1.32 :

Determine the resultant of four forces tangent to the circle of radius 1.5 m as shown. Determine its location w.r.t. 'O'.

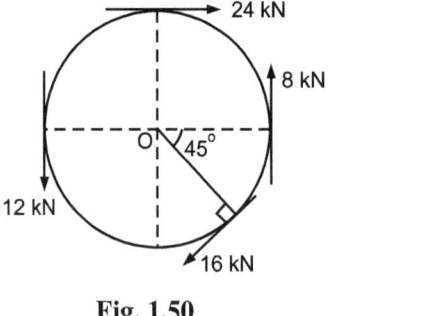 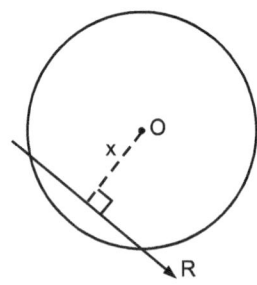

Fig. 1.50   Fig. 1.50 (a)

Solution :

Given data : Forces $F_1 = 24$ kN, $F_2 = 12$ kN, $F_3 = 8$ kN, $F_4 = 16$ kN are acting as shown in Fig. 1.50 (a).

To find : Magnitude and direction of resultant. Location of resultant w.r.t. point O.

(a) Magnitude and direction of resultant :

$$\Sigma F_x = 24 - 16 \cos 45° = 12.68 \text{ kN}$$
$$\Sigma F_y = -12 - 16 \sin 45° + 8 = -15.31 \text{ kN}$$

$$\text{Magnitude of resultant} = \sqrt{(\Sigma F_x)^2 + (\Sigma F_y)^2}$$
$$= \sqrt{(12.68)^2 + (-15.31)^2}$$
$$R = \mathbf{19.88 \text{ kN}} \quad \text{... Ans.}$$

$$\text{Direction of resultant} = \theta = \tan^{-1}\left(\frac{\Sigma F_y}{\Sigma F_x}\right) = \tan^{-1}\left(\frac{15.31}{12.68}\right) = 50.37°$$

Refer Fig. 1.50 (b).

(b) Position of resultant R : Let resultant R act at a perpendicular distance of x from centre 'O'. Refer Fig. 1.50 (a).

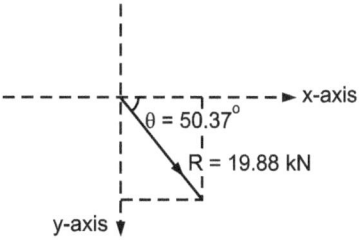

Fig. 1.50 (b) : Resultant

By Varignon's theorem,

Moment of resultant at point O = Σ Moment of forces at point O

∴ $-R \times x = 16 \times 1.5 - 8 \times 1.5 + 24 \times 1.5 - 12 \times 1.5$

∴ $-19.88 \times x = 30$

∴ $x = \mathbf{-1.51 \text{ m}}$ ... Ans.

Since, value of x is –ve, assumed position of resultant is wrong, resultant acts on the right hand side of centre at perpendicular distance 1.51 m.

Example 1.33 :

Find the resultant and its point of application on y-axis for the force system acting on triangular plate as shown in Fig. 1.51.

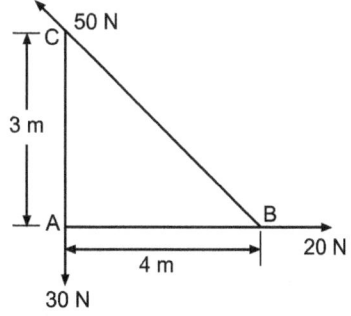

Fig. 1.51

Solution :

$$\tan \theta = \frac{3}{4} \qquad \therefore \theta = 36.87°$$

Magnitude of resultant of 20 N, 30 N and 50 N forces.

$$\therefore \quad \Sigma F_x = 20 - 50 \cos 36.87° = -20 \text{ N}$$

$$\Sigma F_y = -30 + 50 \sin 36.87° = 0 \text{ N}$$

$\therefore$ Magnitude and direction of resultant $= \sqrt{(\Sigma F_x)^2 + (\Sigma F_y)^2} = \textbf{20 N} (\leftarrow)$ ... **Ans.**

Position of resultant :

By Varignon's theorem,

Let position of resultant be as shown in Fig. 1.51 (a). Taking moments at point B,

$$-R \times x = 50 \times 0 - 30 \times 4$$

$$\therefore \quad x = \frac{30 \times 4}{20} = 6 \text{ m} \qquad \text{... Ans.}$$

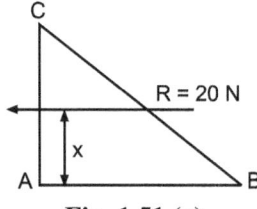

Fig. 1.51 (a)

Example 1.34 :

Reduce system of forces to an equivalent force. Determine its magnitude, x and y intercepts.

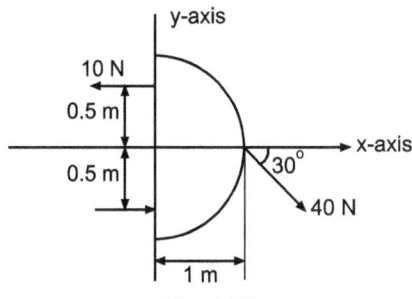

Fig. 1.52

Solution :

$$\Sigma F_x = -10 + 10 + 40 \cos 30° = 34.64 \text{ N} (\rightarrow)$$

$$\Sigma F_y = -40 \sin 30° = 20 \text{ N} (\downarrow)$$

Magnitude of resultant $= \sqrt{(34.64)^2 + (20)^2} = \textbf{40 N}$ ... **Ans.**

Direction of resultant $= \alpha = \tan^{-1}\left(\frac{20}{34.64}\right) = \textbf{30°}$ ... **Ans.**

Example 1.35 :

The three forces shown in Fig. 1.53 create a vertical resultant acting through point B. If P = 361 N, compute the values of T and F.

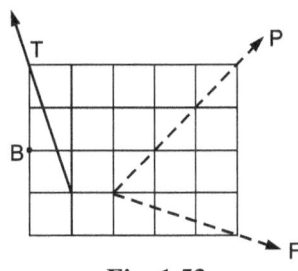

Fig. 1.53

Solution :

Inclination of forces :

Inclination of force T $= \alpha = \tan^{-1}\left(\dfrac{3}{1}\right) = 71.56°$

Inclination of force P $= \beta = \tan^{-1}\left(\dfrac{3}{2}\right) = 56.31°$

Inclination of force F $= \gamma = \tan^{-1}\left(\dfrac{1}{2}\right) = 25.56°$

Magnitude of resultant of forces T, P and F i.e. $\Sigma F_x = 0$ and let $\Sigma F_y = R$.

∴ $\Sigma F_x = -T \cos 71.56° + P \cos 56.31° + F \cos 26.56°$
$= -0.316\,T + 200.24 + 0.894\,F = 0$ ... (i)

$\Sigma F_y = T \sin 71.56° + P \sin 56.31° - F \sin 26.56°$
$= 0.948\,T + 300.37 - 0.447\,F$ ... (ii)

Position of resultant : Resultant passes through point F.

By Varignon's theorem,

Taking moments of forces about point B,

$R \times 0 = (T \cos \alpha) \times 1 - (T \sin \alpha) \times 1 - (P \cos \beta) \times 1 - (P \sin \beta) \times 2$
$- (F \cos \gamma) \times 1 + (F \sin \gamma) \times 2$ ... (iii)

∴ $0.316\,T - 0.948\,T - 200.24 - 600.74 - 0.894\,F + 0.894\,F = 0$

∴ From equation (iii), T $= -1267.37$ N ... **Ans.**

From equation (i), F $= -671.95$ N ... **Ans.**

Example 1.36 :

A beam AB of 6 m span is subjected to a concentrated load and a distributed load as shown. Replace system of forces by an equivalent force-couple system at supports A and B.

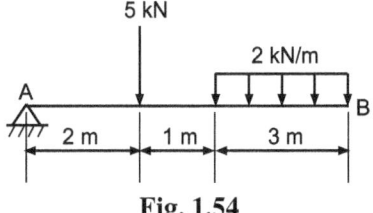

Fig. 1.54

Solution :

Magnitude of resultant :

$\Sigma F_y = -5 - (2 \times 3) = -11$ kN $= 11$ kN ($\downarrow$)

Position of resultant : By Varignon's theorem,

Let resultant 'R' act at distance 'd' from A.

Taking moments about point A,

$$R \times d = 5 \times 2 + (2 \times 3) \times (3 + 1.5)$$

$\therefore \qquad 11 \times d = 10 + 27$

$\therefore \qquad d = 3.36$ m

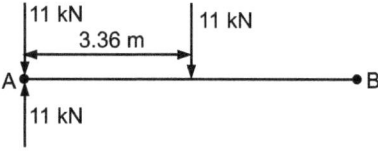

Fig. 1.54 (a)

(a) Equivalent force-couple system at 'A' :

(i) Adding two forces of 11 kN with opposite direction at point A, so that effect of these two forces is zero.

(ii) It forms a force = 11 kN ($\downarrow$) acting at point A and a couple of moment = $11 \times 3.36 = $ **36.96 kN-m** ($\circlearrowleft$) ... Ans.

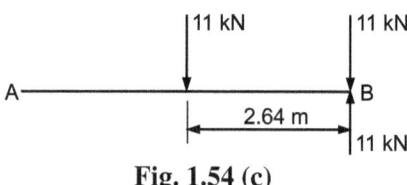

Fig. 1.54 (b)

(b) Equivalent force-couple system at 'B' :

(i) Adding two forces of 11 kN with opposite direction at point B, so that effect of these two forces is zero.

(ii) It forms a force = 11 kN ($\downarrow$) at point B and a couple of moment = $11 \times 2.64 = $ **29 kN-m** ($\circlearrowleft$) ... Ans.

Fig. 1.54 (c)

Example 1.37 :

System of forces acting on a frame is as shown in Fig. 1.55. Calculate the magnitude and direction of the resultant. Also find the position of the resultant w.r.t. point A.

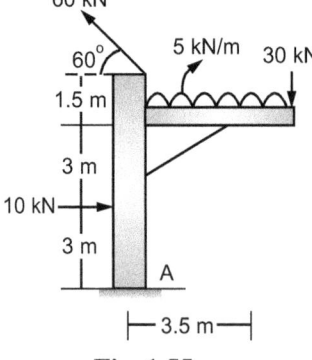

Fig. 1.55

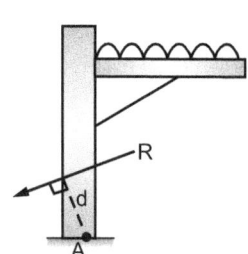

Fig. 1.55 (a)

Solution :

(a) Magnitude of resultant :

$$\Sigma F_x = -60 \cos 60° + 10 = -20 \text{ kN}$$
$$\Sigma F_y = 60 \sin 60° - (5 \times 3.5) - 30 = 4.46 \text{ kN}$$

∴ Magnitude of resultant $= \sqrt{(-20)^2 + (4.46)^2} = 20.5$ kN ... **Ans.**

(b) Direction of resultant $= \alpha = \tan^{-1}\left(\dfrac{4.46}{20}\right) = 12.57°$ ... **Ans.**

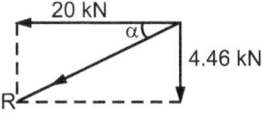

Fig. 1.56

(c) Position of resultant w.r.t. point A : Refer Fig. 1.55 (a).

Let resultant acts at a perpendicular distance 'd' from point A.

By Varignon's theorem, (↻ + and ↺ −).

$$-R \times d = -60 \cos 60° \times 7.5 + 30 \times 3.5 + (5 \times 3.5 \times \dfrac{3.5}{2}) + 10 \times 3$$

∴ $d = \textbf{2.89 m from A}$ ... **Ans.**

PROBLEMS FOR PRACTICE

Problem No. 1 : R = 18 kN is the resultant of four concurrent forces out of which only three are known. Find the fourth force in magnitude and direction.

Answer : (1) P = 31.44 kN

(2) θ = 24.5° (fourth quadrant)

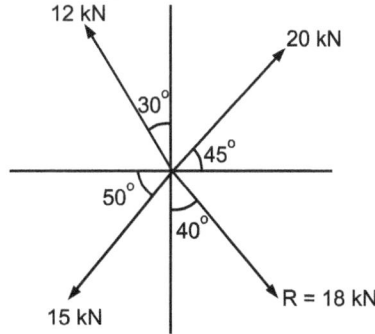

Fig. 1.57

Problem No. 2 : A force P of magnitude 800 N is to be resolved into two components along the lines aa and bb. If the component of force P along the line bb is 300 N, determine the angle α and component of the force along line aa.

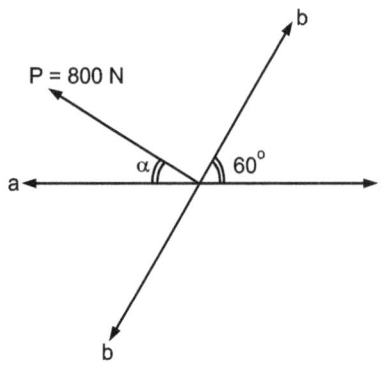

Fig. 1.58

Answer : (1) $\alpha = 18.95°$

(2) Force along line aa = – 906.64

Problem No. 3 : A motor boat is crossing a river. The flow of water pushes the boat East-wards with a force of 500 N. The wind tends to push the boat with a force of 200 N towards North-west, while the engine of the boat drives it towards the North with a force of 1000 N. Find the resultant force on the boat and the direction in which it will finally move.

Answer : (1) R = 1196.11 N

(2) $\theta = 72.56°$ North to East.

Problem No. 4 : A vertical pole 60 m high has a socket connection at the base and is pulled by two wire forces of 4 kN and 8 kN making an angle of 5° and 25° with the horizontal. Another wire which is attached to the top of the pole is anchored at the ground at a point 80 m from the base of the pole. If the resultant of all the wire forces at the top of the pole is known to act vertically downwards, towards the centre of the base, calculate the tension (force) in the wire and the magnitude of the resultant.

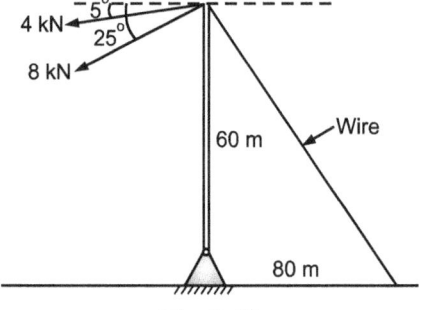

Fig. 1.59

Hint : It is given that the resultant of all the forces is acting vertically downwards i.e. the resultant has only one component which is in negative y-direction i.e. component of resultant in x-direction is zero i.e. $\sum F_x = 0$.

Answer : (1) T = 14.04 kN

(2) R = 12.15 kN (downwards)

Problem No. 5 : A car is to be lifted in the vertical direction with a force of 20 kN. This is done by applying two forces P and Q as shown in Fig. 1.60.
(a) Determine the value of force P if force Q is to be minimum.
(b) In the above case, what is the distance between the two pulleys ?

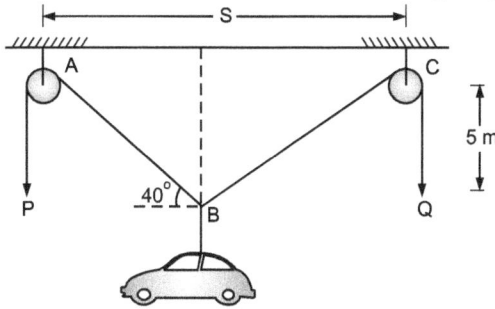

Fig. 1.60

Answer : (a) For the force Q to be minimum, the angle ABC should be 90°.

$$Q_{min} = 15.33 \text{ kN}$$
$$P = 12.86 \text{ kN}$$

(b) S = (5.959 + 4.195) = (10.154) m

Problem No. 6 : Resolve the force of 500 kN into its components along the directions OA and OB as shown in Fig. 1.61.

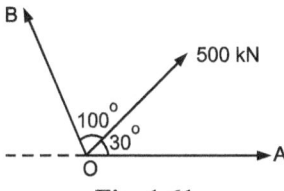

Fig. 1.61

Problem No. 7 : Fig. 1.62 shows free body diagram of joints 'A' and 'B' of truss which is in equilibrium. Draw representative force polygon for both the joints.

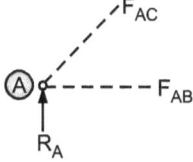

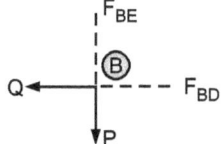

Fig. 1.62

Problem No. 8 : A 200 N force is to be resolved into components along lines a-a' and b-b' as shown in Fig. 1.63.

(i) Determine the angle 'α' knowing that the component along a-a' is to be 150 N.
(ii) What is the corresponding value of the component along b-b' ?

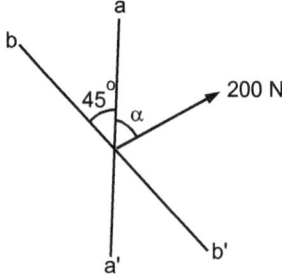

Fig. 1.63

Problem No. 9 : Determine x and y components of the 800 N force.

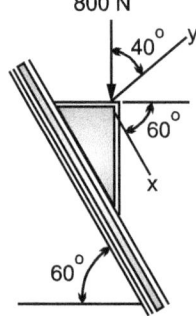

Fig. 1.64

Answer : (a) Component of force 800 N along x-axis = 514.23 N
(b) Component of force 800 N along negative y-axis = 612.83 N

Problem No. 10 : Resolve a force of 20 N into components acting (a) along the n and t axes, (b) along the x and y axes.

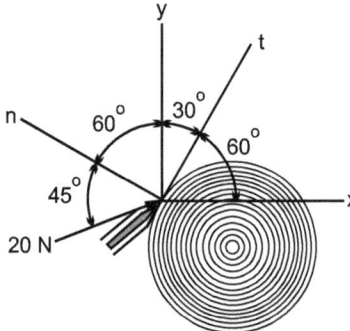

Fig. 1.65

Answer : (a) Component of force 20 N along negative n-axis = 14.14 N
  Component of force 20 N along t-axis = 14.14 N
(b) Component of force 20 N along x-axis = 19.32 N
  Component of force 20 N along y-axis = 51.76 N

Problem No. 11 : Resolve resultant force of force L = 1500 N and force D = 200 N along x and y axes. α = 5°.

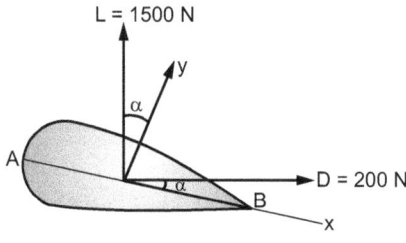

Fig. 1.66

Answer : Component of force 1513.27 N along x-axis = 68.65 N

Component of force 1513.27 N along y-axis = 1511.71 N

Problem No. 12 : Determine angle θ so that magnitude of resultant of two forces 1400 N and 800 N is 2000 N. For this condition, determine angle α between resultant and vertical force of magnitude 1400 N.

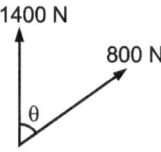

Fig. 1.67

Answer : θ = 51.32°, α = 18.2°

Problem No. 13 : Express resultant force R exerted on pulley by two tensions in vector notation. Determine magnitude of R. Pulley is of negligible radius.

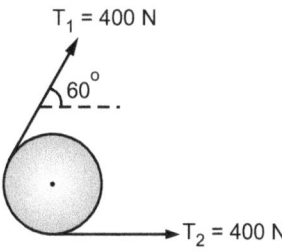

Fig. 1.68

Answer : R = 692.66 N.

Problem No. 14 : Replace two forces 800 N and 900 N by two equivalent forces along x-axis and a-axis.

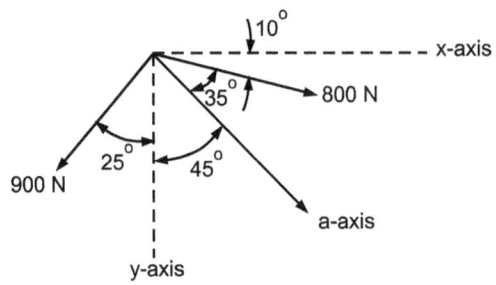

Fig. 1.69

Answer : $F_x = 547.53$ N, $F_a = 1350.2$ N

Problem No. 15 : Show that the resultant force is zero for the given force system.

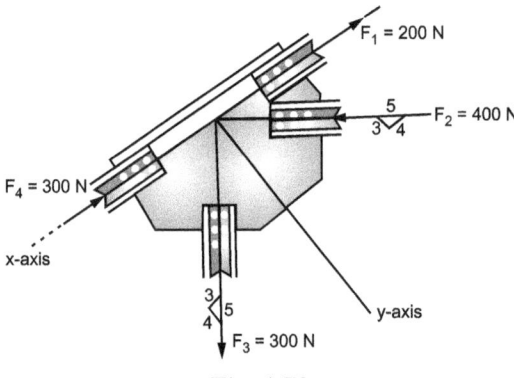

Fig. 1.70

Answer : Resultant force is zero for the given force system.

Problem No. 16 : Determine resultant of given force system.

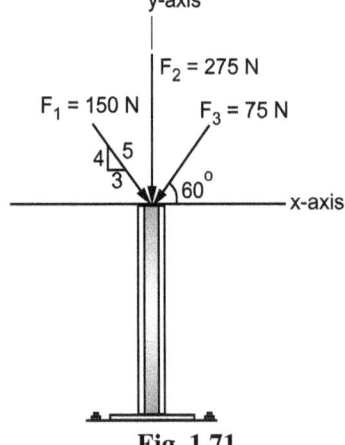

Fig. 1.71

Answer : Magnitude of resultant = 463 N, Direction of resultant = 83.49° w.r.t. positive x-axis in clockwise direction.

Problem No. 17 : Determine the magnitude of force F so that magnitude of the resultant of the three forces is as small as possible. What is the minimum magnitude of the resultant ?

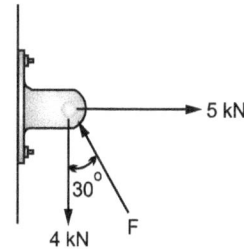

Fig. 1.72

Answer : R = 2.36 kN, F = 5.96 kN

Problem No. 18 : If resultant of three concurrent forces is zero, determine θ and required magnitude of F_3.

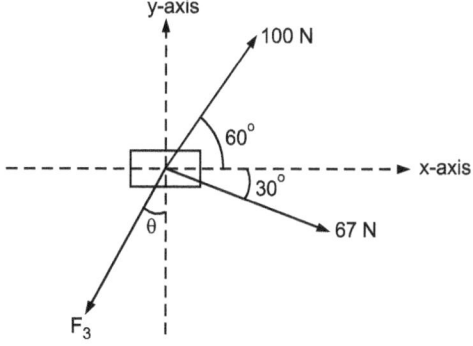

Fig. 1.73

Answer : θ = 63.82°, F_3 = 120.36 N

Problem No. 19 : Determine magnitude F and direction θ of force F, so that resultant of three forces acting on the hook is zero.

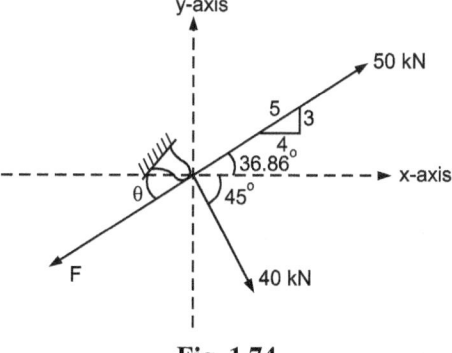

Fig. 1.74

Answer : θ = 1.43°, F = 68.32 kN

Problem No. 20 : A cantilever ABC 1.8 m long is fixed at end A and carries loads P, Q, R as shown. Due to these loads, there is a pull of 4 kN at end A and an anticlockwise moment of 3.5 kN-m at end A. Determine the values of forces P, Q, R.

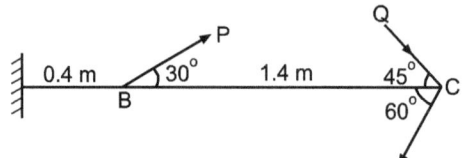

Fig. 1.75

Answer :

(1) P = 5 kN, (2) Q = 1 kN, (3) R = 2 kN

Problem No. 21 : Find the magnitude, direction and position of the resultant of the system of forces shown.

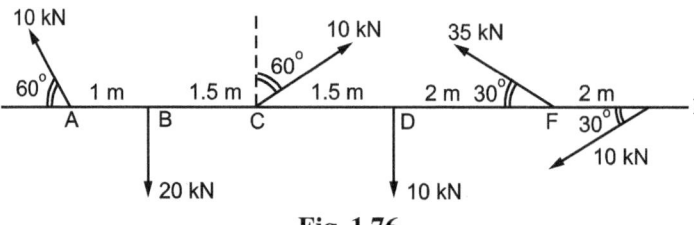

Fig. 1.76

Answer : (1) R = 35.5 kN

(2) θ = 6.2° (third quadrant)

(3) x = − 4.55 m (on LHS of point A)

Problem No. 22 : (a) Compute the simplest resultant force for the loads shown acting on the cantilever beam.

(b) What moment is transmitted by this force on the supporting wall at A ?

(c) Find the position on the beam where the resultant force acts.

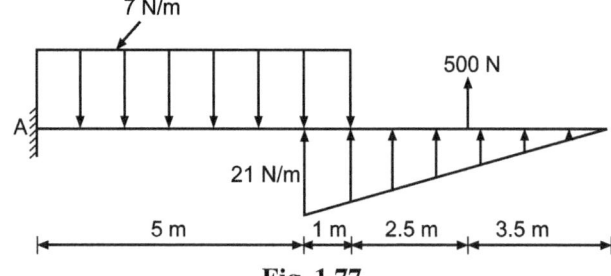

Fig. 1.77

Answer : (a) R = 531.5 N (↑)

(b) M_A = 4662.75 Nm

(c) x = 8.77 m (from A)

Problem No. 23 : A slender homogeneous wire is bent into shape as shown. Determine the dimension 'a' so that the centre of gravity of the wire will coincide with the centre C of the semicircular portion.

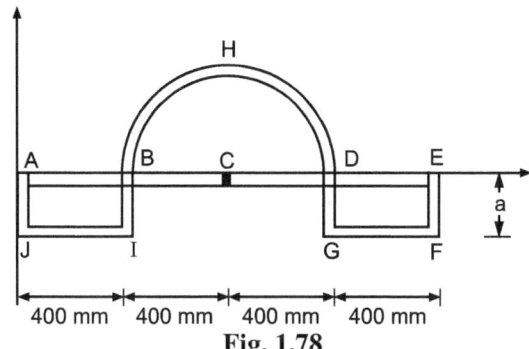

Fig. 1.78

Answer : a = 247.17 mm

Problem No. 24 : A Z-shaped lamina of uniform width of 20 mm is subjected to four forces as shown in Fig. 1.79. Find equilibrant in magnitude and direction.

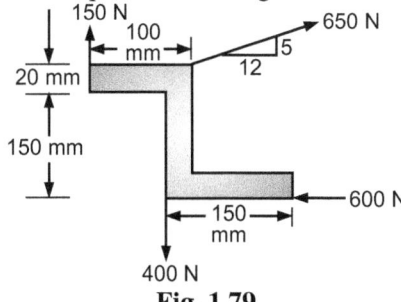

Fig. 1.79

Problem No. 25 : Compute moment of force F = 450 N about points A and B.

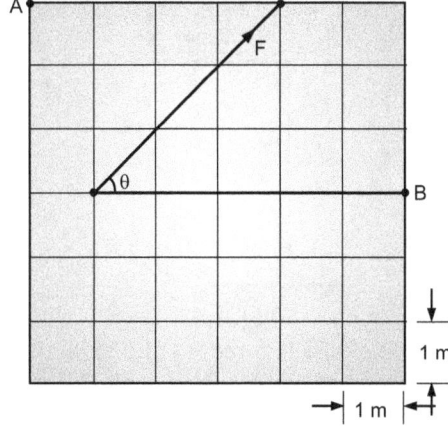

Fig. 1.80

Answer : (a) Moment of force F about point A = 1350.14 N-m (↻)
(b) Moment of force F about point B = 1350 N-m (↻)

Problem No. 26 : Two couples act on the frame. If d = 4 m, determine the resultant couple moment. Compute the resultant by resolving each force into x and y components (a) finding the moment of each couple, (b) summing the moments of all the force components about point B.

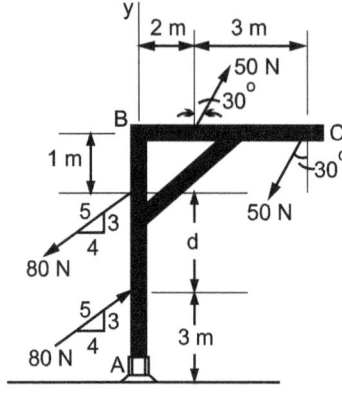

Fig. 1.81

Answer : (a) Moment of couple of 50 N force = 130 Nm (↻)

Moment of couple of 80 N force = 256 Nm (↺)

Resultant moment of couple = 126 Nm (↺)

(b) Resultant moment of forces about point B = 126 Nm (↺)

Problem No. 27 : A 400 N force is applied at an angle $\theta = 20°$. Determine the equivalent force-couple system acting at (a) point A and (b) point O.

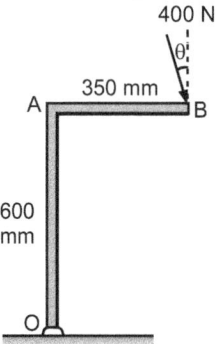

Fig. 1.82

Answer : Moment of couple of 400 N force = 131.55 Nm (↻)
Resultant force acting at A = 400 N at angle 20° with vertical
Moment of couple = 213.64 Nm
Resultant force acting at O = 400 N at an angle 20° with vertical

Problem No. 28 : Replace the forces and couple system by an equivalent force and couple moment at point P.

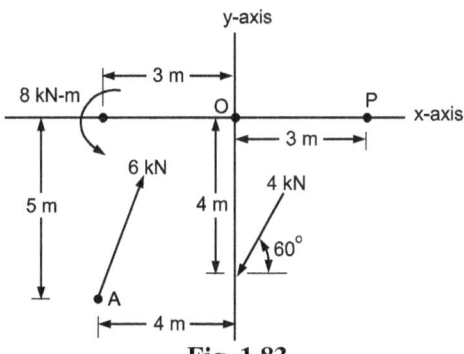

Fig. 1.83

Answer : Force acting at point P = 2.09 kN

Problem No. 29 : Replace the loading on the frame by a single resultant force. Specify where its line of action intersects member CD measured from end C.

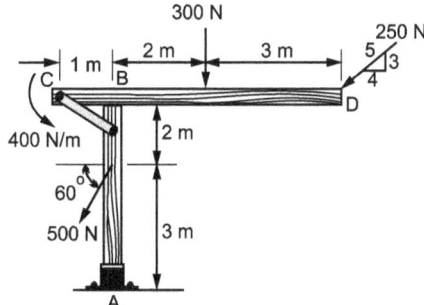

Fig. 1.84

Answer : R = 990.16 N, θ = 63°, x = 2.64 m from point C on the member CD.

Problem No. 30 : Find magnitude of two like parallel forces acting at a distance 2.4 m whose resultant is 200 N and its line of action is at a distance of 0.6 m from one of the forces.

Answer : $F_2 = 50$ N (↓), $F_1 = 150$ N (↓)

Problem No. 31 : For the semi-annular area, determine the ratio of "a" to "b" for which the centroid of the area is located at the point of intersection of the inner circle and the y-axis.

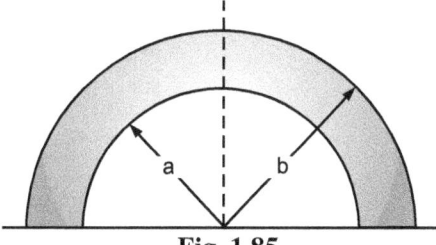

Fig. 1.85

Answer : $\dfrac{a}{b} = 0.495$

Problem No. 32 : Find the value of distance 'a' so that the centroid of the uniform lamina shown in Fig. 1.86 remains at the centre of rectangle ABCD.

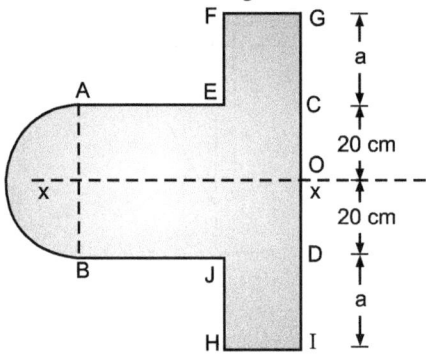

Fig. 1.86

Answer : Value of a = 21.58 cm

CHAPTER TWO

EQUILIBRIUM

2.1 INTRODUCTION

When a particle acted upon by a system of forces is in equilibrium,
(i) it remains at state of rest if originally at state of rest.
(ii) it moves with constant velocity if originally in state of motion.
This illustrates Newton's first law of motion.
In statics, when a rigid body acted upon by a system of forces is in equilibrium,
(i) it remains at state of rest as resultant force is zero, and
(ii) there is no rotation of rigid body as resultant moment of forces about any point is zero.

2.2 FREE BODY DIAGRAM (F.B.D.)

Free Body Diagram is a sketch of the particle or rigid body representing it as being isolated or free from its surroundings (like supports, bodies in contact or attached cables etc.). All the known and unknown forces that act on the particle or rigid body are shown on F.B.D.

These forces are active (which tend to set the motion due to weight or attached cords etc.) and reactive (which tend to prevent the motion due to constraints or supports etc.).

F.B.D. helps to apply conditions of equilibrium correctly.

Steps to draw F.B.D. :
1. Isolate the particle or rigid body from its surroundings and sketch the shape of the same.

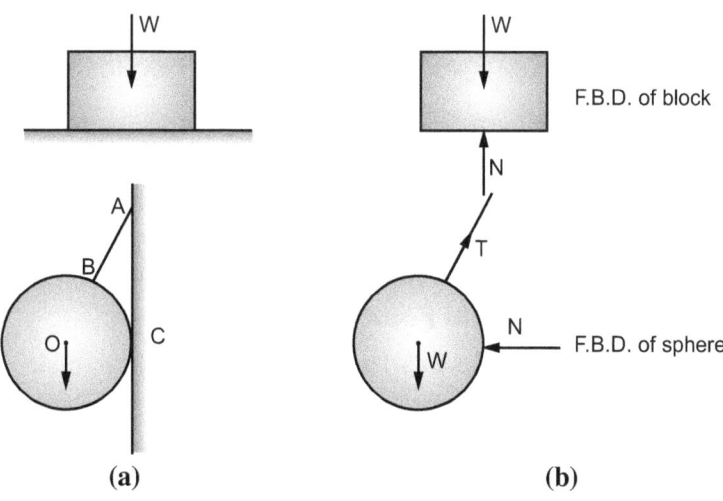

(a) (b)

Fig. 2.1

2. Show all the active and reactive forces on the sketch. Note carefully each force by tracing around the boundary of particle/rigid body.
3. Show all the known forces with proper magnitude and direction.
4. Show all the unknown forces with letters for magnitude and arrow head for direction as assumed force i.e. push/pull. The correct direction becomes apparent after solving for conditions of equilibrium. If magnitude of unknown force is positive, assumed direction is correct and if negative, force is opposite to originally assumed direction.

2.3 EQUILIBRIUM OF COPLANAR FORCES

When a body is in equilibrium, the resultant of all the forces acting on it is zero. Also, the resultant moment of forces acting on it about any point is zero.

Mathematically, it may be stated as :

(i) $\bar{R} = \sum \bar{F} = 0$

(ii) $\sum$ Moment of force about any point on or off the body = 0.

Analytical conditions of equilibrium of number of forces may be stated as :

$\sum F_x = 0$, $\sum F_y = 0$, $\sum M_{\text{at any point}} = 0$.

These are necessary and sufficient conditions of equilibrium.

In this topic, equilibrium of different coplanar force systems is studied.

2.3.1 Equilibrium of Two Forces Only

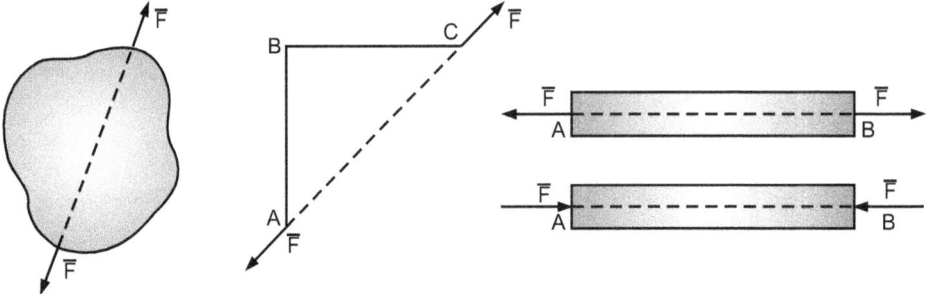

Fig. 2.2

For equilibrium, two forces must be equal, opposite and collinear as shown in Fig. 2.2.

2.3.2 Equilibrium of Concurrent Force System

1. Equilibrium of Three Forces (Lami's Theorem) :

Three forces are said to be in equilibrium only when they are coplanar concurrent forces. (Refer Fig. 2.3 (a)).

Such a force system forms a closed force triangle. Sine rule is used to find the unknown forces of force triangle. (Refer Fig. 2.3 (b))

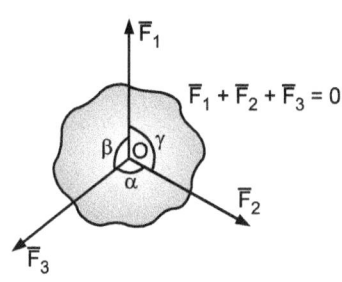
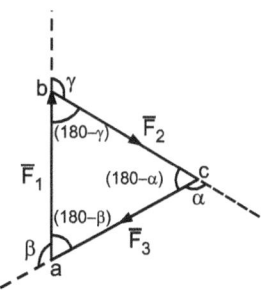

(a) Forces $\bar{F}_1, \bar{F}_2$ and $\bar{F}_3$ are in equilibrium (b) Force triangle

Fig. 2.3

Applying sine rule to the force triangle abc,

$$\frac{F_1}{\sin(180-\alpha)} = \frac{F_2}{\sin(180-\beta)} = \frac{F_3}{\sin(180-\gamma)}$$

$$\therefore \quad \boxed{\frac{F_1}{\sin\alpha} = \frac{F_2}{\sin\beta} = \frac{F_3}{\sin\gamma}} \qquad \text{... Lami's theorem}$$

2. Equilibrium of More than Three Forces :

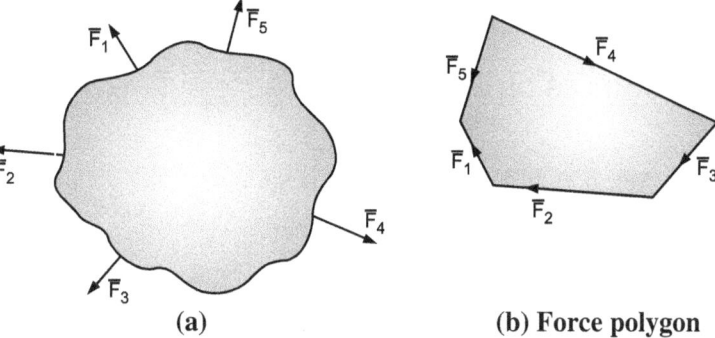

(a) (b) Force polygon

Fig. 2.4

When a number of concurrent forces are in equilibrium, they must satisfy conditions of equilibrium as follows : $\sum F_x = 0$ and $\sum F_y = 0$

Graphically, polygon of forces must be a closed polygon. Refer Fig. 2.4 (b).

2.3.3 Equilibrium of Parallel Force System

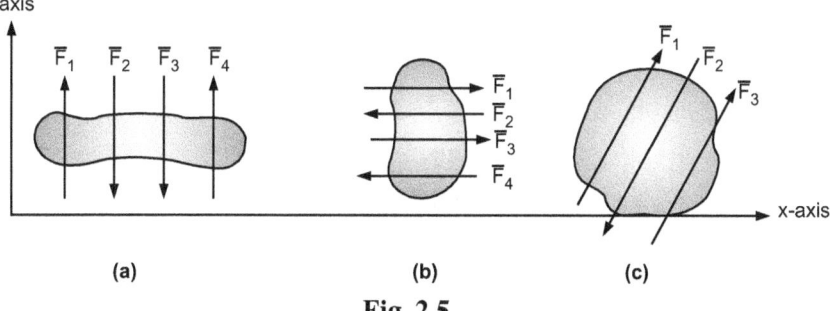

(a) (b) (c)

Fig. 2.5

Applied Mechanics — Equilibrium

When a number of parallel forces are in equilibrium, they must satisfy conditions of equilibrium as follows :

$\sum F_y = 0$ and $\sum$ Moment of forces at y-axis = 0.   ... Refer Fig. 2.5 (a)

$\sum F_x = 0$ and $\sum$ Moment of forces at x-axis = 0.   ... Refer Fig. 2.5 (b)

$\sum \overline{F} = 0$ and $\sum$ Moment of forces at any point = 0.   ... Refer Fig. 2.5 (c)

2.3.4 Equilibrium of General Force System

When a number of non-concurrent, non-parallel forces are in equilibrium, they must satisfy the following conditions of equilibrium :

$\sum F_x = 0, \quad \sum F_y = 0$ and

$\sum$ Moment of forces about any point = 0.

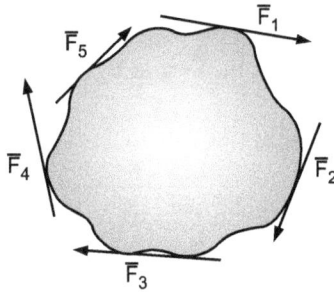

Fig. 2.6

Graphically, polygon of forces must be a closed polygon and funicular diagram must be a closed polygon.

NUMERICAL EXAMPLES ON EQUILIBRIUM OF CONCURRENT FORCE SYSTEM

Example 2.1 :

Determine the mass that must be supported at A and the angle θ of the cord in order to hold the system in equilibrium.

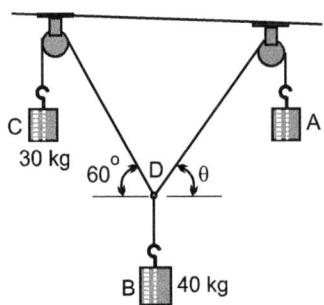

Fig. 2.7

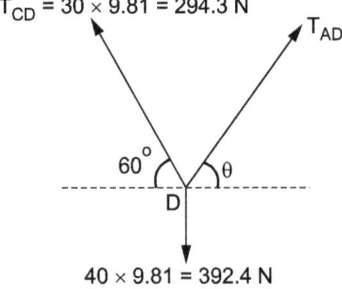

Fig. 2.7 (a) : F.B.D. of joint D

Solution :

Given data : Load = $40 \times 9.81 = 392.4$ N

Assume that pulleys are smooth and of negligible size.

Tension in the rope CD = $T_{CD} = 30 \times 9.81 = 294.3$ N

To find : Tension in rope AD = T_{AD}

Inclination of rope AD = θ

(a) Consider F.B.D. of joint D. Refer Fig. 2.7 (a).

Forces acting at joint D are T_{AD}, T_{CD} and load joint D is in equilibrium.

By Lami's theorem,

$$\frac{T_{CD}}{\sin(90° + \theta)} = \frac{T_{AD}}{\sin(90° + 60°)} = \frac{392.4}{\sin(180° - 60° - \theta)}$$

$\therefore \quad \dfrac{294.3}{\cos \theta} = \dfrac{T_{AD}}{\cos 60°} = \dfrac{392.4}{\sin(60° + \theta)}$

$\therefore \quad \dfrac{294.3}{\cos \theta} = \dfrac{T_{AD}}{\cos 60°}$

$\therefore \quad T_{AD} = \dfrac{147.15}{\cos \theta}$ ... (i)

$\dfrac{T_{AD}}{\cos 60°} = \dfrac{392.4}{\sin(60° + \theta)}$

$\therefore \quad T_{AD} = \dfrac{196.2}{\sin(60° + \theta)}$ ... (ii)

From equations (i) and (ii),

$\dfrac{147.15}{\cos \theta} = \dfrac{196.2}{\sin(60° + \theta)}$

$\therefore \quad \dfrac{\sin(60° + \theta)}{\cos \theta} = \dfrac{196.2}{147.15} = 1.33$

$\therefore \quad \dfrac{\sin 60° \cos \theta}{\cos \theta} + \dfrac{\cos 60° \sin \theta}{\cos \theta} = 1.33$

$\therefore \quad 0.866 + 0.5 \tan \theta = 1.33$

$\therefore \quad \theta = \mathbf{42.86°}$ ... Ans.

$T_{AD} = 200.74$ N

$\therefore \quad$ Mass supported at A $= \dfrac{200.74}{9.81} = \mathbf{20.96\ kg}$ ... Ans.

Example 2.2 :

The 30 kg pipe is supported at A by a system of five cords. Determine the force in each cord for equilibrium.

Solution :

Given data : Load attached at A = 294 N

Direction of tension in cord is as shown in Fig. 2.8.

To find : T_{AB}, T_{AE}, T_{BC}, T_{BD}.

(a) Consider F.B.D. of joint A. Refer Fig. 2.8 (a).

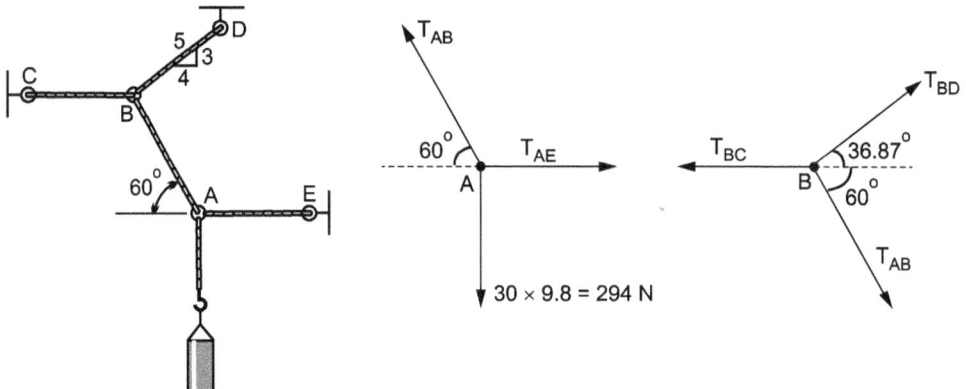

Fig. 2.8 **Fig. 2.8 (a) : F.B.D. of joint A** **Fig. 2.8 (b) : F.B.D. of joint B**

Forces acting at joint A are T_{AB}, T_{AE} and 294 N. Joint A is in equilibrium.

By Lami's theorem,

$$\frac{294}{\sin 120°} = \frac{T_{AB}}{\sin 90°} = \frac{T_{AE}}{\sin (90° + 60°)}$$

∴ $$\frac{294}{\sin 120°} = \frac{T_{AB}}{\sin 90°}$$

∴ $T_{AB} = \mathbf{339.48 \ N}$ ... Ans.

$$\frac{294}{\sin 120°} = \frac{T_{AE}}{\cos 60°}$$

∴ $T_{AE} = \mathbf{169.74 \ N}$ ... Ans.

(b) Consider F.B.D. of joint B. Refer Fig. 2.8 (b).

Forces acting at joint B are T_{AB}, T_{BC} and T_{BD}.

Joint B is in equilibrium.

By Lami's theorem,

$$\frac{T_{AB}}{\sin 143.13°} = \frac{T_{BC}}{\sin 96.87°} = \frac{T_{BD}}{\sin 120°}$$

∴ $$\frac{339.48}{\sin 143.13°} = \frac{T_{BC}}{\sin 96.87°}$$

∴ $T_{BC} = \mathbf{561.74 \ N}$ ... Ans.

$$\frac{339.48}{\sin 143.13°} = \frac{T_{BD}}{\sin 120°}$$

∴ $T_{BD} = \mathbf{490 \ N}$ ... Ans.

Example 2.3 :

Determine smallest angle θ to hold the given system in equilibrium if each rope can withstand a maximum tension of 2500 N before it breaks.

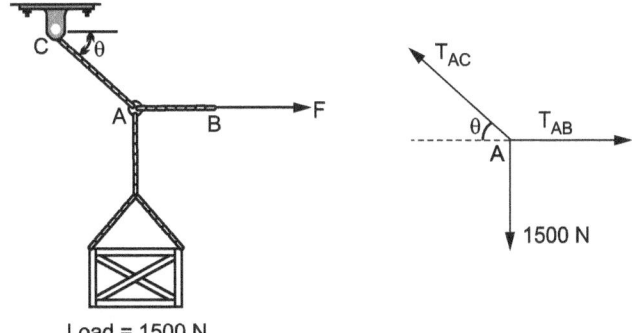

Fig. 2.9   Fig. 2.9 (a) : F.B.D. of joint A

Solution :

Given data : Load = 1500 N.

Maximum tension in each rope is 2500 N.

To find : Smallest angle θ to keep the system in equilibrium.

(a) Consider F.B.D. of joint A. [Refer Fig. 2.9 (a)].

Joint A is in equilibrium.

By Lami's theorem,

$$\frac{1500}{\sin(180°-\theta)} = \frac{T_{AC}}{\sin 90°} = \frac{T_{AB}}{\sin(90°+\theta)}$$

$\therefore \quad \dfrac{1500}{\sin\theta} = \dfrac{T_{AC}}{\sin 90°}$

$\therefore \quad T_{AC} = \dfrac{500}{\sin\theta}$ ... (i)

and $\quad \dfrac{1500}{\sin\theta} = \dfrac{T_{AB}}{\cos\theta}$

$\therefore \quad T_{AB} = 1500 \times \cot\theta$ ... (ii)

(b) Since maximum tension in each rope is 2500 N.

From equation (i),

$\sin\theta = 0.20$

$\therefore \quad \theta = 11.54°$

From equation (ii), $\cot\theta = \dfrac{2500}{500} = 5$

$\therefore \quad \theta = 11.31°$

Smallest angle θ to keep the system in equilibrium is 11.31°. ... Ans.

Example 2.4 :

The motor at B winds up the cord attached to the 65 N crate at A with a constant speed. Determine the force in cord CD supporting pulley and the angle θ for equilibrium. Neglect size of the pulley at C.

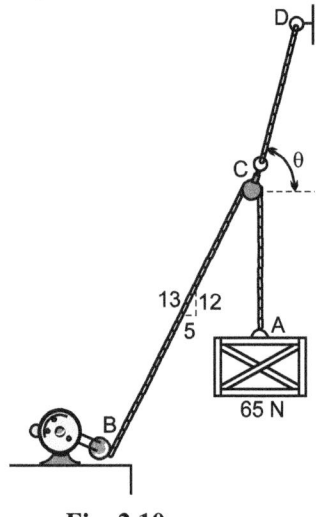

Fig. 2.10   **Fig. 2.10 (a) : F.B.D. of joint C**

Solution :

Given data : Weight of the crate = 65 N

Tension in the cable CB = 65 N

Direction of tension with horizontal = $\tan^{-1}\left(\dfrac{12}{5}\right) = 67.38°$

To find : Tension in the cable CD = T_{CD} = ?

Direction of T_{CD} for equilibrium = θ

(a) Forces acting at point C are : [Refer Fig. 2.10 (a)]

$$\text{Weight of the crate} = 65 \text{ N}$$
$$\text{Tension in the cable CB} = T_{CB} = 65 \text{ N}$$
$$\text{Tension in the cable CD} = T_{CD}$$

(b) Since forces are in equilibrium,

$$\Sigma F_x = 0 \text{ and } \Sigma F_y = 0$$

Resolving the forces along x-axis,

$$\Sigma F_x = T_{CD} \cos\theta - 65 \cos 67.38° = 0$$

$\therefore \quad T_{CD} \cos\theta = 25$ ... (i)

Resolving the forces along y-axis,

$$\Sigma F_y = T_{CD} \sin\theta - 65 \sin 67.38° - 65 = 0$$

$\therefore \quad T_{CD} \sin\theta = 125$ ... (ii)

From equations (i) and (ii),

$$\frac{T_{CD} \sin \theta}{T_{CD} \cos \theta} = \frac{125}{25}$$

∴ $\tan \theta = 5$
∴ $\theta = 78.7°$ ... Ans.

Substituting $\theta = 78.7°$ in equation (i),
$$T_{CD} = 127.5 \text{ N}$$ ... Ans.

Example 2.5 :

A horizontal prismatic bar AB of length l is hinged to a vertical wall at A and supported at B by a tie rod BC that makes an angle α with the horizontal. A weight P can have any position along the bar as defined by the distance x from the wall. Determine tensile force T in the bar.

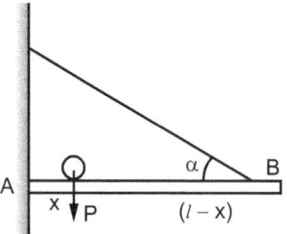

Fig. 2.11

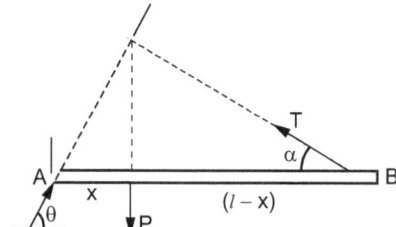

Fig. 2.11 (a)

Solution :

Given data : Weight P acting at distance x from A.

Angle of the tie bar with horizontal = α

Length of the tie bar = l

To find : Tension T in the tie bar = ?

(a) Let R_A be reaction at hinge A at an angle θ with horizontal.

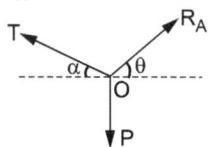

Fig. 2.11 (b)

Since forces T, P and R_A are keeping the bar in equilibrium, lines of action of three forces are intersecting at point 'O'.

Refer Fig. 2.11 (a).

By Lami's theorem, [Refer Fig. 2.11 (b)]

$$\frac{R_A}{\sin(90 + \alpha)} = \frac{T}{\sin(90 + \theta)} = \frac{P}{\sin(180 - \alpha - \theta)}$$

Since bar is in equilibrium,

Σ Moments of forces about point A = 0

∴ $P \times x - T \sin \alpha \times l = 0$

∴ $$T = \frac{Px}{l \sin \alpha}$$ ... Ans.

Example 2.6 :

Determine the axial forces produced in the bars of the system due to horizontal force P applied at hinge B.

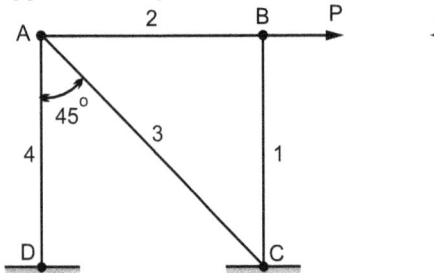 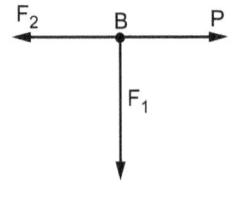 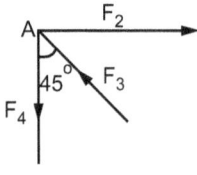

Fig. 2.12   Fig. 2.12 (a) : F.B.D. of joint B   Fig. 2.12 (b) : F.B.D. of joint A

Solution :

Given data : Force P is acting at B.
Forces in bars are axial forces, tensile or compressive.
To find : Axial forces in bars 1, 2, 3 and 4.
(a) Consider F.B.D. of joint B. [Refer Fig. 2.12 (a)]
Joint B is in equilibrium.
By conditions of equilibrium,

$\Sigma F_x = 0$ $\therefore$ $F_2 = P$ ... Ans.
$\Sigma F_y = 0$ $\therefore$ $F_1 = 0$ ... Ans.

(b) Consider F.B.D. of joint A. [Refer Fig. 2.14 (b)] Joint A is in equilibrium.
By conditions of equilibrium,

$\Sigma F_x = 0$ $\therefore$ $F_3 \sin 45° = P$ $\therefore$ $F_3 = 1.414\ P$ ... Ans.
$\Sigma F_y = 0$ $\therefore$ $-F_4 + F_3 \cos 45° = 0$ $\therefore$ $F_4 = P$ ... Ans.

Example 2.7 :

Weight of the cylinder is 800 N. Cords are passed over two frictionless pulleys. Loads 600 N and 200 N are attached to the end of cords. Determine angle θ and normal reaction between cylinder and smooth horizontal surface.

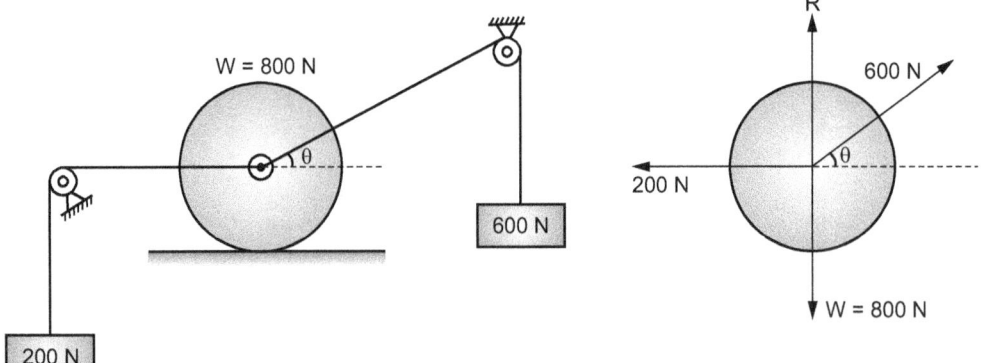

Fig. 2.13   Fig. 2.13 (a) : F.B.D. of cylinder

Solution :

Given data : Weight of cylinder = 800 N

Loads attached to the cords = 600 N and 200 N.

To find : Angle θ, Normal reaction between cylinder and smooth horizontal surface.

(a) Since pulleys are smooth, tension in the cord is same as load attached to the cord.

Consider F.B.D. of the cylinder. Cylinder is in equilibrium under four forces i.e. tension in two cords, weight of the cylinder, normal reaction R. [Refer Fig. 2.13 (a)]

By conditions of equilibrium,

$\Sigma F_x = 0$ ∴ $-200 + 600 \cos \theta = 0$

∴ $\cos \theta = \dfrac{1}{3}$ ∴   **θ = 70.52°**   ... Ans.

$\Sigma F_y = 0$ ∴ $-800 + R + 600 \sin 70.52° = 0$

∴   **R = 234.38 N**   ... Ans.

Example 2.8 :

A roller of weight 500 N is to be pulled over a step of height h = 0.06 m by a horizontal force P applied to the end of a string wound around the circumference of the roller. Find the magnitude of P required to start the roller over the step. Radius of the roller is 0.12 m.

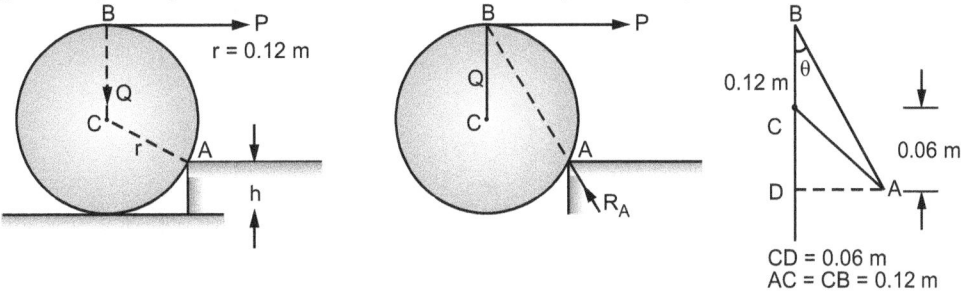

Fig. 2.14   Fig. 2.14 (a)   Fig. 2.14 (b)

Solution :

Given data : Radius of the roller = 0.12 m

Height of the step = 0.06 m

Weight of the roller = 500 N

To find : Horizontal force P required to start the roller.

(a) When the roller is about to roll over the point A, it loses its contact with the ground.

(b) Consider F.B.D. of the roller. Roller is in equilibrium under three forces : Q, P and reaction at A. Since, three forces are in equilibrium, they must be concurrent at point B. [Refer Fig. 2.14 (a)]

(c) By Lami's theorem, [Refer Fig. 2.14 (c)]

$$\dfrac{500}{\sin (90° + \theta)} = \dfrac{P}{\sin (180° - \theta)} = \dfrac{R_A}{\sin 90°} \quad \ldots \text{(i)}$$

To find θ, consider the triangle ADC.
[Refer Fig. 2.14 (b)]

$$\cos(\angle DCA) = \frac{0.06}{0.12}$$

∴ $\angle DCA = 60°$

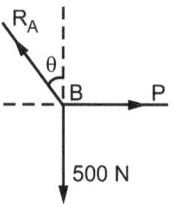

Fig. 2.14 (c)

Since AC = BC = r, and ∠ DCA = ∠ CBA + ∠ BAC = 2θ = 60°, ∴ θ = 30°

Substituting θ = 30° in equation (i),

$$\frac{500}{\cos 30°} = \frac{P}{\sin 30°} = \frac{R_A}{\sin 90°}$$

∴ $\frac{500}{0.866} = \frac{P}{0.5}$ ∴ **P = 288.68 N** ... Ans.

and $\frac{500}{\cos 30°} = \frac{R_A}{\sin 90°}$ ∴ **R_A = 577.35 N** ... Ans.

Example 2.9 :

If three cylinders, each of weight 20 N and diameter 380 mm, rest in a box of 790 mm wide as shown in Fig. 2.15, find the reactions at each contact point.

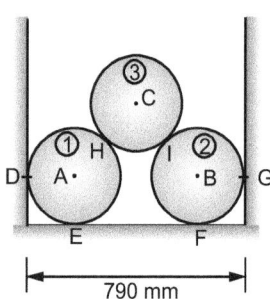

Fig. 2.15

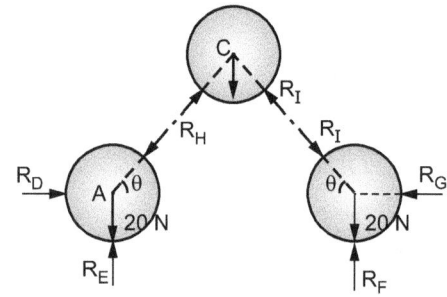

Fig. 2.15 (a) : F.B.D. of cylinders

Solution :

Given data : Weight of each cylinder = 20 N

Diameter of each cylinder = 380 mm

To find : Reactions R_E, R_D, R_H, R_I, R_G, R_F of cylinders (1) and (2).

Since position is symmetrical, as well as weight and diameter are same,

$R_D = R_G$, $R_E = R_F$ and $R_H = R_I$

(a) Consider F.B.D. of the cylinder (3). [Refer Fig. 2.15 (a)]. Cylinder (3) is in equilibrium under reactions R_H, R_I and weight W.

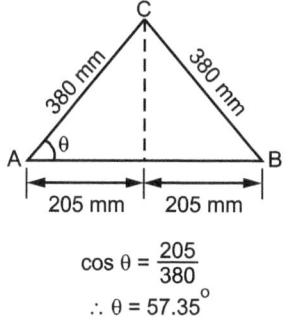

$\cos\theta = \dfrac{205}{380}$

$\therefore \theta = 57.35°$

Fig. 2.15 (b)

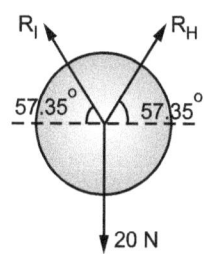

Fig. 2.15 (c) : F.B.D. of cylinder (3)

By Lami's theorem, [Refer Fig. 2.15 (c)]

$$\dfrac{20}{\sin[180° - (2 \times 57.35°)]} = \dfrac{R_H}{\sin(90° + 57.35°)}$$

$\therefore \quad R_H = \dfrac{20 \cos 57.35°}{\sin 114.70°} = 11.88$ N

$R_H = R_I = \mathbf{11.88\ N}$ ... **Ans.**

(b) Consider F.B.D. of cylinder (1). Cylinder (1) is in equilibrium under reactions R_H, R_E, R_D and weight 20 N. [Refer Fig. 2.15 (d)]

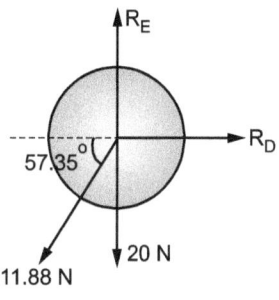

Fig. 2.15 (d) : F.B.D. of cylinder (1)

By conditions of equilibrium,

$\Sigma F_x = 0$

$\therefore R_D - 11.88 \cos 57.35° = 0$

$\therefore R_D = 6.41$ N

$R_D = R_G = \mathbf{6.41\ N}$ ... **Ans.**

$\Sigma F_y = 0$

$\therefore R_E - 20 - 11.88 \sin 57.35° = 0$

$\therefore R_E = 30$ N

$\therefore R_E = R_F = \mathbf{30\ N}$ ... **Ans.**

NUMERICAL EXAMPLES ON EQUILIBRIUM OF PARALLEL FORCE SYSTEM

Example 2.10 :

Two identical prismatic bars AB and CD are welded together in the form of 'T' as shown. Calculate angle α that bar CD will make with vertical when vertical load P = 10 N is applied at B. Weight of each bar Q = 5 N.

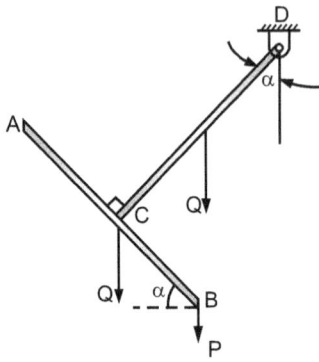

Fig. 2.16 (a)

Solution :

Given data : As shown in Fig. 2.16 (a).

To find : Angle 'α'.

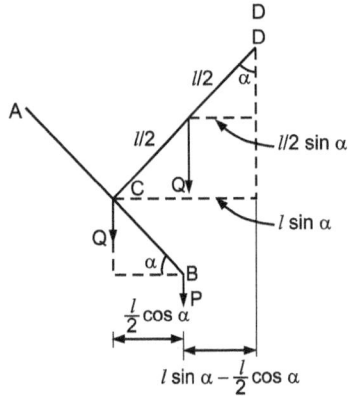

Fig. 2.16 (b)

Since bars are in equilibrium,

$$\Sigma M = 0$$

$\therefore$ Moment of force P at D

$$= -P \times \left(l \sin \alpha - \frac{l}{2} \cos \alpha \right)$$

$\therefore \quad \Sigma M_D = 0$

$\therefore -Q \cdot \frac{l}{2} \sin \alpha - Q \, l \sin \alpha - P \left(l \sin \alpha - \frac{l}{2} \cos \alpha \right) = 0$

$\therefore -Q \sin \alpha - 2Q \sin \alpha - 2P \sin \alpha + P \cos \alpha = 0$

$\therefore -3Q \sin \alpha + P (\cos \alpha - 2 \sin \alpha) = 0$

$\therefore -15 \sin \alpha + 10 (\cos \alpha - 2 \sin \alpha) = 0$

$\therefore \sin \alpha - \frac{2}{3} (\cos \alpha - 2 \sin \alpha) = 0$

Dividing by $\sin \alpha$,

$\therefore \quad 1 - \frac{2}{3} (\cot \alpha - 2) = 0$

$\quad \frac{2}{3} (\cot \alpha - 2) = 1$

$\quad \cot \alpha - 2 = \frac{3}{2}$

$\quad \cot \alpha = \frac{3}{2} + 2 = \frac{7}{2}$

$\therefore \quad \tan \alpha = \frac{2}{7}$

$\therefore \quad \alpha = 15.94°$ ... **Ans.**

NUMERICAL EXAMPLES ON EQUILIBRIUM OF GENERAL FORCE SYSTEM

Example 2.11 :

Three lines of power pole exert a vertical force on pole as shown in Fig. 2.17. Determine reactions at fixed support D. Determine which line when removed creates a condition for the greatest moment reaction at D.

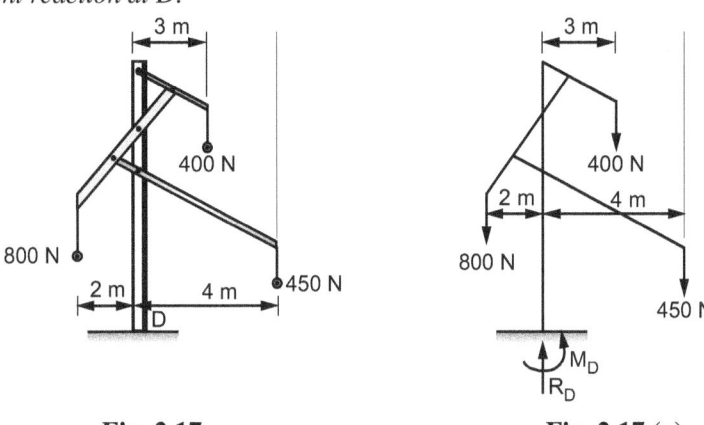

Fig. 2.17   Fig. 2.17 (a)

Solution :

Given data : Forces 800 N, 400 N and 450 N are acting as shown in Fig. 2.17 (a).

To find : Vertical reaction at D.

Moment at D.

(a) Let R_D be the vertical reaction at D and M_D be the moment at D as shown in Fig. 2.17 (a). Pole is in equilibrium.

Applying conditions of equilibrium,

$\therefore \quad \Sigma F_y = 0 \quad \therefore \quad -400 - 800 - 450 + R_D = 0 \quad \therefore \quad R_D = \mathbf{1650\ N}$ ... **Ans.**

$\therefore \quad \Sigma M_D = 0 \quad \therefore \quad 400 \times 3 + 450 \times 4 - 800 \times 2 - M_D = 0$

$\therefore \quad M_D = \mathbf{1400\ Nm\ (\circlearrowleft)}$ ... **Ans.**

(Since value of M_D is positive, assumed direction of moment at D i.e. anticlockwise is correct.)

(b) **A condition of greatest moment reaction is produced when a line carrying weight of 800 N is removed.** ... **Ans.**

Example 2.12 :

Force of 200 N is acting on the middle of the rod as shown. Floor and wall are perfectly smooth and slipping is prevented by string DE. Find (a) tension S in the string DE, (b) reactions at A and B.

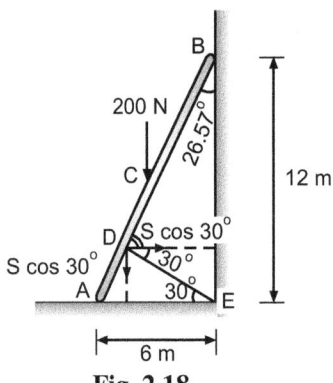
Fig. 2.18

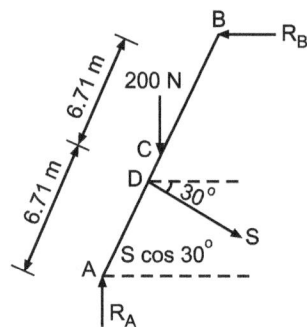
Fig. 2.18 (a) : F.B.D. of rod

Solution :

Given data : Force = 200 N is acting at the centre of the rod.

Dimensions are as shown in Fig. 2.18 (a).

To find : Tension in the string DE = S. Reactions at floor and wall i.e. R_A and R_B.

(a) Rod is in equilibrium under forces : Refer Fig. 2.18 (a).

$$\text{Force} = 200 \text{ N}$$
$$\text{Reaction at wall} = R_A$$
$$\text{Reaction at floor} = R_B$$
$$\text{Tension in string DE} = S.$$

(b) From geometry, Refer Fig. 2.18 (b)

$$l(AB) = \sqrt{6^2 + 12^2} = 13.42 \text{ m}$$
$$l(BC) = l(AC) = 6.71 \text{ m}$$

Consider △ BGA,

$$\angle BAG = \tan^{-1}\left(\frac{12}{6}\right)$$
$$= 63.43°$$

Consider △ BCE,

$$\cos 63.43° = \frac{CE}{CB} = \frac{CE}{6.71}$$

∴ $$CE = 6.71 \cos 63.43°$$
$$= 3 \text{ m}$$

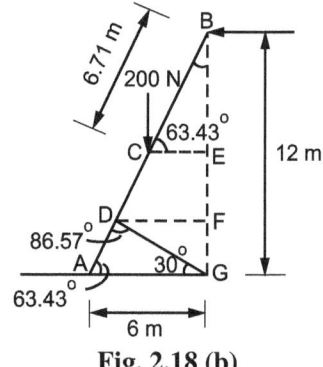
Fig. 2.18 (b)

Consider △ ADG,

By sine rule,

$$\frac{6}{\sin 86.57°} = \frac{DG}{\sin 63.43°}$$

∴ $$DG = 5.37 \text{ m}$$

Consider Δ DFG,

$$\cos 60° = \frac{FG}{DG} \quad \therefore FG = DG \cos 60° = 5.37 \cos 60° = 2.685 \text{ m}$$

$$\sin 60° = \frac{DF}{DG} \quad \therefore DF = DG \sin 60° = 5.37 \sin 60° = 4.65 \text{ m}$$

(c) By conditions of equilibrium,

$\Sigma M_B = 0 \quad \therefore -200 \times CE + S \cos 30° \times BF + S \sin 30° \times DF + R_A \times 6 = 0$

$\therefore -200 \times 3 + S \cos 30° \times (12 - FG) + S \sin 30° \times 4.65 + R_A \times 6 = 0$

$\therefore -600 - 8.067 S - 2.325 S + 6 R_A = 0$

$\therefore -10.392 S + 6 R_A = 600$ ... (i)

$\Sigma F_y = 0 \quad \therefore R_A - 200 - S \sin 30° = 0$

$\therefore -0.5 S + R_A = 200$ ... (ii)

$\Sigma F_x = 0 \quad \therefore -R_B + S \cos 30° = 0$

$\therefore R_B = 0.866 S$ ... (iii)

Solving equations (i) and (ii),

$S = 81.17$ N and $R_A = \mathbf{240.58}$ **N** ... Ans.

Substituting $S = 81.17$ N in equation (iii),

$R_B = \mathbf{70.29}$ **N** ... Ans.

Example 2.13 :

Determine tension in the cable ABD and the reaction at C when θ = 60°, a = 1 m, P = 100 N. Neglect friction in the pulley.

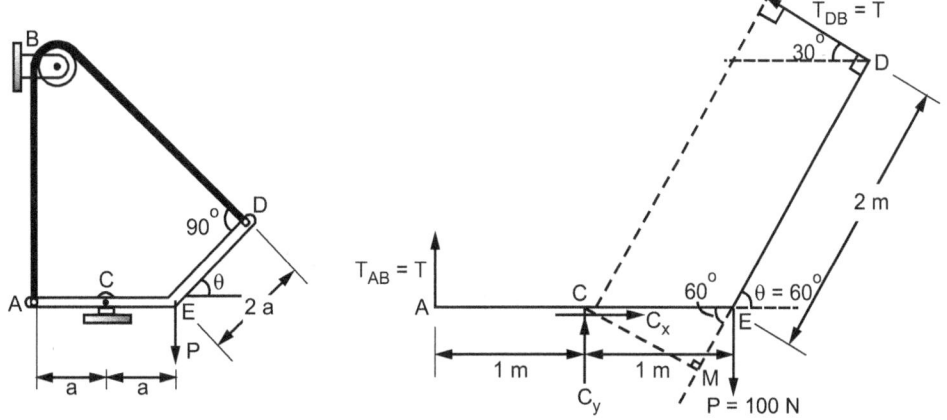

Fig. 2.19   Fig. 2.19 (a) : F.B.D. of ACD

Solution :

Given data : Force P = 100 N is acting at E

Dimensions are as shown in Fig. 2.19 (a).

To find : Tension in the cable ABD i.e. $T_{AB} = T_{DB}$

Reaction at C i.e. R_C

(a) Lever ACD is in equilibrium under forces :

Reaction at C = R_C

Tension in the cable i.e. $T_{AB} = T_{DB} = T$

Force P = 100 N

(b) From geometry, Refer Fig. 2.19 (a)

Consider $\triangle$ CME, $\cos 60° = \dfrac{ME}{CE} = \dfrac{ME}{1}$

∴ ME = 0.5 m

∴ MD = 2.5 m

(c) Applying conditions of equilibrium to the lever,

$\Sigma M_C = 0$ ∴ $T \times 1 + 100 \times 1 - T(MD) = 0$

∴ $T \times 1 + 100 - T(2.5) = 0$

∴ **T = 66.67 N** ... Ans.

$\Sigma F_x = 0$ ∴ $C_x - T \cos 30° = 0$

∴ $C_x = 66.67 \cos 30° = 57.73$ N ($\rightarrow$)

$\Sigma F_y = 0$ ∴ $T + T \sin 30° + C_y - P = 0$

∴ $66.67 + 66.67 \sin 30° + C_y - 100 = 0$

∴ $C_y = 0$ N

∴ **Reaction at C = R_C = 57.73 N ($\rightarrow$)** .. Ans.

Example 2.14 :

Determine the tension in each cable and the reaction at D.

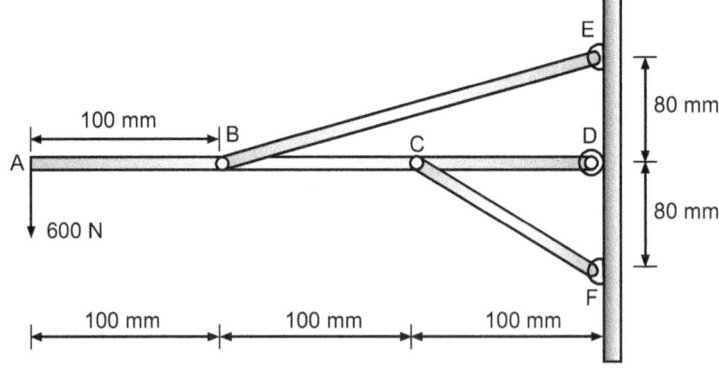

Fig. 2.20

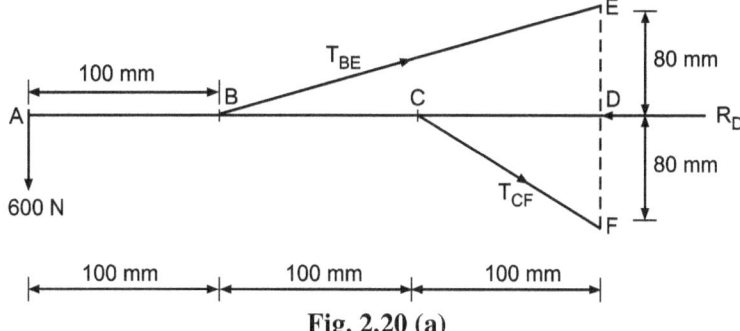

Fig. 2.20 (a)

Solution :

Given data : Force 600 N is acting at A.
Dimensions are as shown in Fig. 2.20 (a).
To find : Tension in the cables T_{BE} and T_{CF}.
Reaction at D i.e. R_D.

(a) Bar AD is in equilibrium under forces : [Refer Fig. 2.20 (a)]
Force of 600 N at A.
Tension in the cables T_{BE} and T_{CF}.
Reaction at roller at D i.e. R_D.

(b) From geometry, [Refer Fig. 2.20 (a)]
Consider Δ EDB,

$$\tan(\angle EBD) = \frac{ED}{BD} = \frac{80}{200}$$

$\therefore \quad \angle EBD = 21.8°$

Consider Δ CDF,

$$\tan(\angle DCF) = \frac{DF}{CD} = \frac{80}{100}$$

$\therefore \quad \angle DCF = 38.66°$

(c) Applying conditions of equilibrium,

$\Sigma M_C = 0 \quad \therefore \quad -600 \times 200 + T_{BE} \sin(\angle EBD) \times 100 = 0$

$\therefore \quad T_{BE} \times 100 \times \sin 21.8° = 120000$

$\therefore \quad T_{BE} = \mathbf{3231.3 \ N}$ ... **Ans.**

$\Sigma F_y = 0 \quad \therefore \quad -600 + T_{BE} \sin 21.8° - T_{CF} \sin 38.66° = 0$

$\therefore \quad T_{CF} \sin 38.66° = -600 + 3231.3 \sin 21.8°$

$\therefore \quad T_{CF} = \mathbf{960.47 \ N}$ ... **Ans.**

$\Sigma F_x = 0 \quad \therefore \quad T_{BE} \cos 21.8° + T_{CF} \cos 38.66° - R_D = 0$

$\therefore \quad R_D = \mathbf{3750.22 \ N}$ ... **Ans.**

Example 2.15 :

A lever AB is hinged at C and attached to a control cable at A. If the lever is subjected to a 75 N vertical force at B, determine (a) the tension in the cable, (b) the reaction at C.

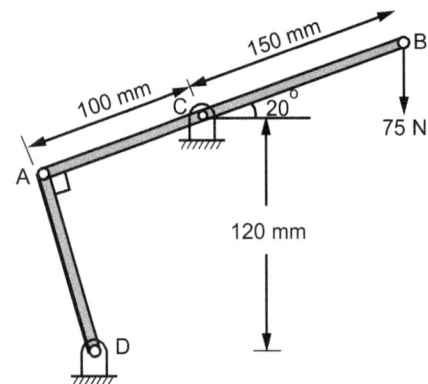

Fig. 2.21   Fig. 2.21 (a)

Solution :

Given data : Force 75 N is acting at B.
Dimensions are as shown in Fig. 2.21 (a).

To find : Tension in the cable AD : T_{AD}
Reaction at C : R_C

(a) Lever AB is in equilibrium under forces : [Refer Fig. 2.21 (a)]
Force 75 N.
Tension in the cable AD i.e. T_{AD}
Reaction at hinge C i.e. R_C

(b) Applying conditions of equilibrium,

$\Sigma M_C = 0$ ∴ $-T_{AD} \times 100$

∴ $T_{AD} = \mathbf{105.71\ N}$ ... Ans.

$\Sigma F_x = 0$ ∴ $+C_x + T_{AD} \cos 70° = 0$

∴ $C_x = -36.15\ N$

(Since value of C_x is negative, assumed direction of C_x is wrong.)

∴ $C_x = 36.15\ N\ (\circlearrowleft)$

$\Sigma F_y = 0$ ∴ $-T_{AD} \sin 70° - 75 + C_y = 0$

∴ $C_y = \mathbf{174.33\ N\ (\circlearrowleft)}$ ... Ans.

Reaction at C $= \sqrt{C_x^2 + C_y^2} = \sqrt{(88.10)^2 + (155.44)^2}$

∴ $R_C = \mathbf{178.04\ N}$ ... Ans.

Direction of $R_C = \tan\alpha = \dfrac{C_y}{C_x}$

$\therefore \quad \alpha = \tan^{-1}\left(\dfrac{C_y}{C_x}\right)$

$= \tan^{-1}\left(\dfrac{174.33}{36.15}\right)$

$= 78.28°$ ... **Ans.**

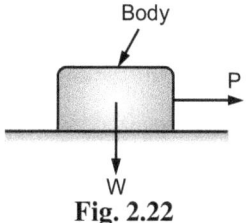

Fig. 2.21 (b)

2.4 FRICTION

Introduction : When a body is intended to move over the surface, due to the application of a tractive force P, a force which automatically appears on the application of the force P that prevent or oppose any possible sliding motion of body over the surface is known as **frictional force**. Frictional force always acts in a direction opposite to that in which motion is sought. It is denoted by the letter F.

Fig. 2.22

The property of the surfaces by virtue of which the frictional force exists is called **friction**.

2.5 CHARACTERISTICS OF THE FRICTIONAL FORCE

The following are the basic characteristics of frictional force :

(a) It is a passive and self-adjusting force. This force exists only if the tractive force P is there, so it is called passive force. As we go on increasing the force P, the frictional force F also goes on increasing till the maximum frictional force.

(b) It always acts in a direction opposite to that in which motion occurs.

2.6 LAWS OF COULOMB FRICTION

We exert a continuously increasing force (a tractive force P), which is completely resisted by friction until the body begins to move. At this stage, maximum frictional force exists.

This maximum frictional force (F_{max}) is called the **limiting force of friction** or **limiting friction**, and the frictional force less than F_{max}, is called the statical friction because the body remains static over the surface. When we again increase tractive force, body will move with unbalanced force ($P - F_{max}$).

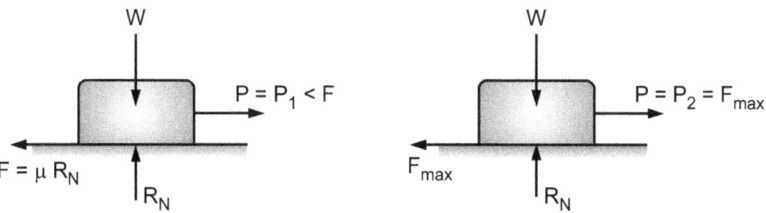

(a) Body at rest (statical friction)   (b) Limiting friction (about to move)

At this instant, the friction existing between body and surface is less than the static friction and is called **dynamic friction**. At the condition of impending motion, it is possible to relate the frictional and normal components of force F, as given by Coulomb in 1781.

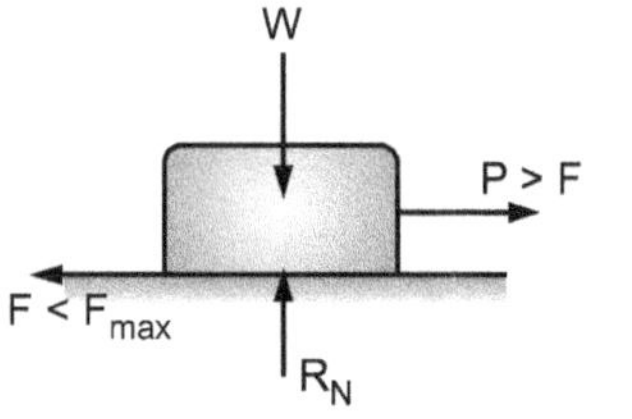

(c) Dynamic friction
Fig. 2.23

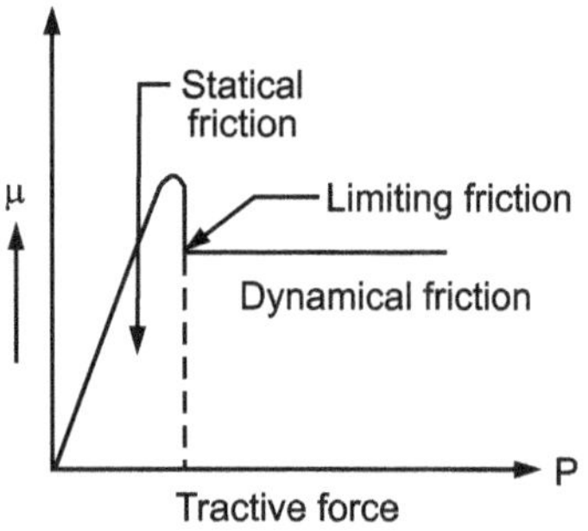

The laws are :
(i) The total amount of friction that can be developed is independent of the magnitude of the area of contact but it depends upon the nature of the surface in contact with each other.
(ii) The maximum frictional force that can be developed is proportional to the normal force transmitted at the surface of contact.

$$F_{max} \propto R_N$$
or $$F_{max} = \mu \cdot R_N$$

where $\mu \rightarrow$ Coefficient of friction

$R_N \rightarrow$ Normal force or reaction at the surface of contact.

2.7 DEFINITIONS
2.7.1 Coefficient of Friction

It is the ratio of limiting friction or maximum frictional force to normal reaction.

$$\mu = \frac{F_{max}}{R_N}$$

Theoretically, for ideally smooth surface, $\mu = 0$, but there exist hardly any such surface in practice. The coefficient of friction μ increases as the tractive force is gradually increased. The coefficient of limiting friction is slightly more than the coefficient of dynamic friction.

2.7.2 Total Reaction

At the stage of limiting friction, equilibrium of body, under the action of the following forces.
(i) The tractive force, P
(ii) Frictional force, F_{max}
(iii) Normal reaction, R_N
(iv) Weight of the body, W.

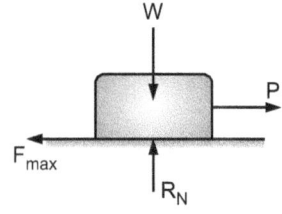

Fig. 2.25

The frictional force F_{max} and normal reaction R_N, which acts at right angles to each other, may be combined into a single force.

$$R_T = \sqrt{F_{max}^2 + R_N^2}$$

This single force is called the total reaction.

2.7.3 Angle of Friction (ϕ)

It is the inclination of the total reaction R, with the normal reaction R_N.

$$\tan \phi = \frac{F_{max}}{R_N}$$

But, $\dfrac{F_{max}}{R_N} = \mu$, the coefficient of friction

$\therefore \quad \tan \phi = \mu = \dfrac{F_{max}}{R_N}$ or $\dfrac{F}{R}$

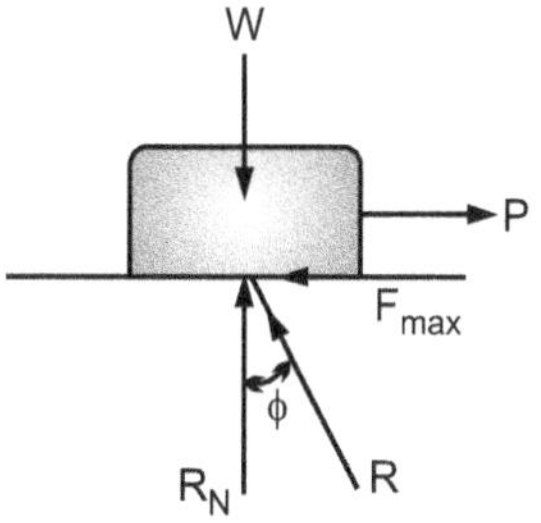

Fig. 2.26

This angle ϕ which is the maximum inclination of total reaction makes with normal reaction is called the angle of friction. From above relation,

$$\phi = \tan^{-1} \mu$$

2.7.4 Angle of Repose

The angle of repose is defined as 'the maximum inclination of a plane at which a body remains in equilibrium over the inclined plane by the assistance of friction only'.

Let us consider a body of weight W rest on rough inclined plane, which makes an angle α with horizontal.

Resolving force along and perpendicular to plane at the stage of just sliding,

$W \sin \alpha = F$ ... (i)
$W \cos \alpha = R$ ... (ii)

Dividing equation (i) by equation (ii),

$$\tan \alpha = \frac{F}{R}$$

$$\tan \phi = \mu = \frac{F}{R}$$

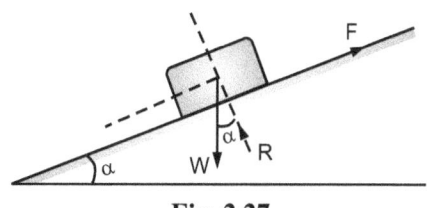

Fig. 2.27

Hence from the above equation,

$\tan \alpha = \tan \phi \quad \therefore \quad \alpha = \phi$

Thus, **Angle of repose = Angle of friction.**

2.7.5 Cone of Friction

It is defined as 'the right circular cone with vertex at the point of contact of the two bodies, axis in the direction of normal reaction (R) and semi-vertical angle equal to angle of friction (ϕ)'.

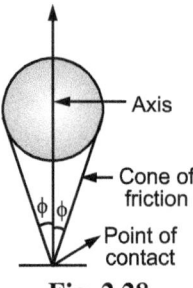

Fig. 2.28

2.8 ROUGH INCLINED PLANE

We know that an inclined plane is a plane lying at a certain angle to the horizontal. Such planes are quite common, a steep hill road or a ramp in a building. The analysis of problem related with inclined plane is similar to other problem of friction. In this case, the frictional resistance F is acting in the opposite direction of impending motion tangentially to the plane. (If block moves up the plane, F is acting down the plane and vice-versa and reaction is acting normal to the plane).

Consider F.B.D. of block of impending motion down and up the plane and applying condition of equilibrium in any two mutually perpendicular directions. (It is convenient to resolve force along and normal to the plane.)

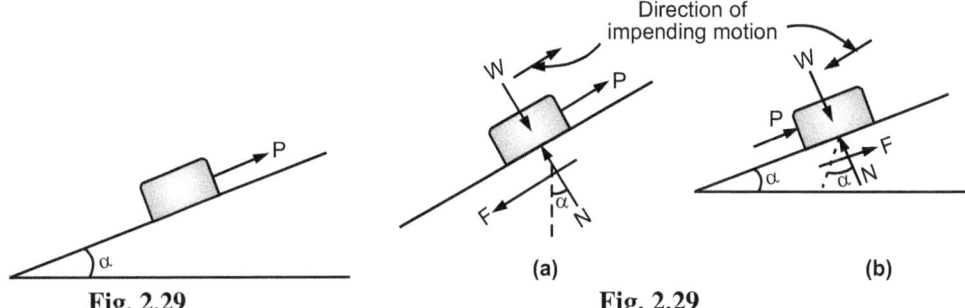

Fig. 2.29   Fig. 2.29

Case - I : Impending motion down the plane.

$$N - W \cos \alpha = 0 \quad \ldots (i)$$
and
$$P + F - W \sin \alpha = 0 \quad \ldots (ii)$$

Solving these equations for required unknown force P,
$$P = W \sin \alpha - \mu W \cos \alpha$$
$$P = W (\sin \alpha - \mu \cos \alpha)$$

Case - II : Impending motion up the plane.

$$N = W \cos \alpha \quad \ldots (iii)$$
$$P = F + W \sin \alpha \quad \ldots (iv)$$

Solving equations (iii) and (iv), we get,
$$P = W (\sin \alpha + \mu \cos \alpha)$$

We shall solve all problems related to inclined plane by above approach.

NUMERICAL EXAMPLES

Example 2.16 :

Determine whether the block shown is in equilibrium and find the magnitude and direction of the friction force when $\theta = 35°$ and $P = 100$ N.

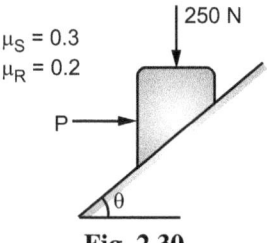

Fig. 2.30

Solution :

Given data : $P = 100$ N, $\theta = 35°$, $\mu_s = 0.3$,

To find : Friction force.

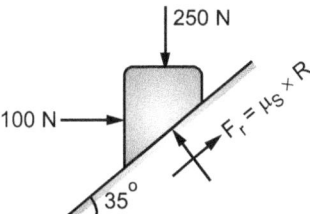

Fig. 2.31 : F.B.D. of block

(Incline plane as x-x axis and perpendicular to incline plane as y-y axis).

Let F_r be the frictional force required to maintain equilibrium.

$$\therefore \quad \Sigma f_y = 0$$
$$-250 \cos 35 - 100 \sin 35 + R = 0$$
$$\therefore \quad R = 262.15 \text{ N}$$

Let $\Sigma f_x = 0$.

$$\therefore \quad \Sigma f_x = F_r - 250 \sin 35 + 100 \cos 35 = 0$$
$$F_r - 250 \sin 35 + 100 \cos 35 = 0$$
$$\therefore \quad F_r = \textbf{61.48 N} \qquad \ldots \text{Ans.}$$

Maximum friction force which may be developed is,

$$F_m = \mu_s \times R = 0.3 \times 262.15 = \textbf{78.65 N} \qquad \ldots \text{Ans.}$$

Since the value of force required to maintain equilibrium (61.48 N) is lesser than the maximum value which may be obtained (78.65 N), equilibrium will be maintained.

Example 2.17 :

Determine whether the block shown is in equilibrium and find the magnitude and direction of the friction force when $\theta = 40°$ and $P = 400$ N.

Applied Mechanics 2.26 Equilibrium

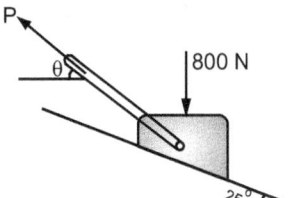

Fig. 2.32 : F.B.D. of block

Solution :
Given data : P = 400 N, θ = 40°.
To find : Is block in equilibrium and frictional force.

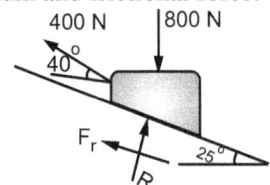

Fig. 2.33 : F.B.D. of block

(Incline plane as x-x axis and perpendicular to plane as y-y axis).
$$\Sigma f_y = 0$$
R + 400 sin 15 − 800 cos 25 = 0
For equilibrium $\Sigma f_x = 0$
F_r + 400 cos 15 − 800 − 800 sin 25 = 0
∴ F_r = − 48.27 N
∴ F_r = **48.27 N**   … Ans.

Maximum frictional force which may be developed.
$F_m = \mu_s R = 0.2 \times 621.51 =$ **124.30 N**   … Ans.

Since value of force required to maintain equilibrium (48.27 N) is less than the maximum frictional force (124.3 N), so equilibrium will be maintained.

Example 2.18 :

Knowing that the coefficient of friction between the 25 kg block and the incline is $\mu_s = 0.25$, determine (a) the smallest value P required to start the block moving up the incline, (b) the corresponding value of β.

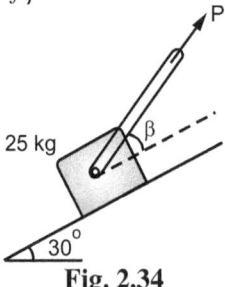

Fig. 2.34

Solution :
Given data : m = 25 kg, μ_s = 0.25, θ = 30°.

To find : P and β.

(Incline plane as x-x axis and perpendicular to incline plane as y-y axis).

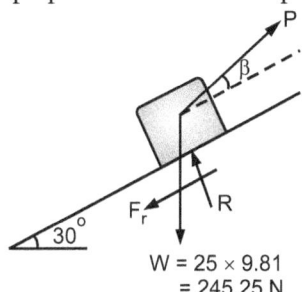

Fig. 2.35 : F.B.D. of block

$$\Sigma f_x = 0$$

$$P \cos \beta - F_r - 245.25 \sin 30 = 0$$

$$P \cos \beta - 0.25 R - 122.63 = 0$$

∴ $$R = 4P \cos \beta - 490.52$$

$$\Sigma f_y = 0$$

$$R + P \sin \beta - 245.25 \cos 30 = 0$$

$$4P \cos \beta - 490.52 + P \sin \beta - 212.39 = 0$$

$$4P \cos \beta + P \sin \beta = 702.91$$

∴ $$P (4 \cos \beta + \sin \beta) = 702.91$$

∴ $$P = 702.91/(4 \cos \beta + \sin \beta)$$

The value of P will be minimum when the denominator $(4 \cos \beta + \sin \beta)$ is maximum. Take the derivative of the denominator with respect to β and set it equal to zero to determine the value of β which will make P a minimum.

$$\frac{d}{d\beta} (4 \cos \beta + \sin \beta) = 0$$

$$- 4 \sin \beta + \cos \beta = 0$$

∴ $$\tan \beta = 0.25$$

∴ $$\beta = 14.03°$$ ... Ans.

Hence, the maximum value of P is,

$$P = \frac{702.91}{(4 \cos 14.03 + \sin 14.03)} = 170.48 \text{ N}$$ ... Ans.

Example 2.19 :

The force required to pull a body of weight 80 N on a rough horizontal plane is 22.5 N. Determine the coefficient of friction if the force is applied at an angle of 17° with the horizontal.

Solution :

Consider the F.B.D. of a body at the time of motion due to force of 22.5 N acting at an angle of 17°, hence a force of friction equal to μR will be acting in the opposite direction of motion. Thus, body is in equilibrium under the action of forces shown in Fig. 2.36. Resolving force along and perpendicular to the plane,

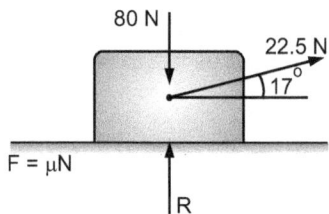

Fig. 2.36 : F.B.D. of body

$$22.5 \cos 17° - F = 0 \qquad \ldots (i)$$
$$R + 22.5 \sin 17° - 80° = 0 \qquad \ldots (ii)$$

Solving equations, we get, $\quad R = 73.422 \text{ N} \quad \text{and} \quad F = 21.517 \text{ N}$

$$\text{Coefficient of friction, } \mu = \frac{F}{R} = \textbf{0.293} \qquad \ldots \textbf{Ans.}$$

Example 2.20 :

A force of 40 N is required to pull a body of weight W and which is inclined at 25° with a rough horizontal plane. But the force required to push a body is 50 N. If the push is inclined 20° to the horizontal, find the weight of the body and coefficient of friction.

Solution :

Consider the equilibrium of a body under the action of pull force as shown in Fig. 2.37 (a). Resolving the forces along and normal to the plane,

$$-F + 40 \cos 25° = 0 \qquad \ldots (i)$$
$$-N + W - 40 \sin 25° = 0 \qquad \ldots (ii)$$

Solving equations (i) and (ii), we get,

$$N = W - 16.905 \qquad \ldots (iii)$$
$$\mu (W - 16.905) = 36.25 \qquad \ldots (iv)$$

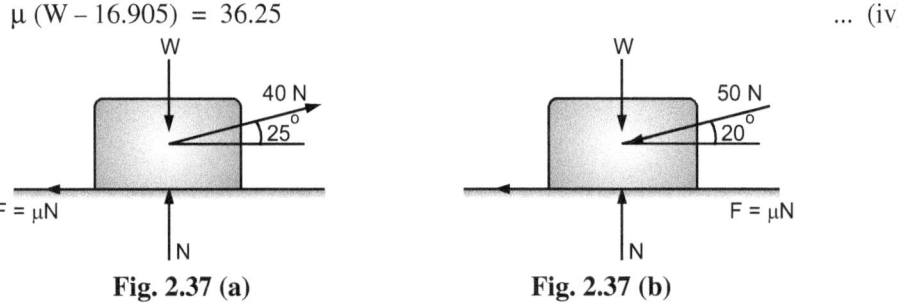

Fig. 2.37 (a)   **Fig. 2.37 (b)**

Now, consider the equilibrium of a body under the action of pull force [Fig. 2.37 (b)]

Resolving the forces along and normal to the plane,

$$F - 50 \cos 20° = 0 \qquad \ldots (v)$$
$$N - W - 50 \sin 20° = 0 \qquad \ldots (vi)$$

Solving equations (v) and (vi), we get,

$$N = W + 17.1 \quad \text{...(vii)}$$
$$\mu(W + 17.1) = 46.985 \quad \text{...(viii)}$$

Dividing equation (iv) by equation (viii),

$$\frac{\mu(W - 16.905)}{\mu(W + 17.1)} = \frac{36.25}{46.98}$$

∴ $46.98\,W - 794.19 = 36.25\,W + 619.875$

∴ $10.73\,W = 1414.06$

∴ $W = \mathbf{131.79\ N}$ and $\mu = \mathbf{0.316}$ ...Ans.

Example 2.21 :

In Fig. 2.38, a block B of weight 8 kN rests on another block A of weight 16 kN. A string passing round a frictionless pulley connects both these blocks as shown. What would be the value of the horizontal force P to drag the block A towards left ? Coefficient of friction for all sliding surfaces is 0.25.

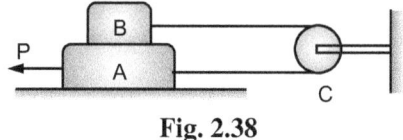

Fig. 2.38

Solution :

As block A moves towards left due to force P, block B will move towards right, due to tension in the string connect both blocks. Draw F.B.D. of both blocks, frictional forces are acting opposite to the direction of motion.

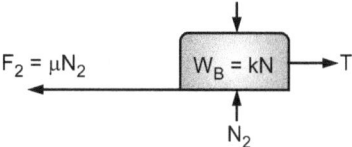

(a) F.B.D. of block B

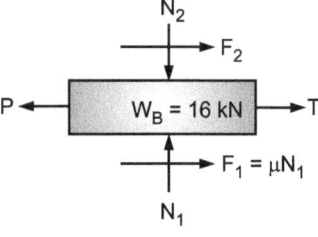

(b) F.B.D. of block A

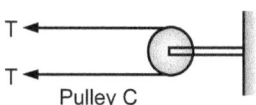

(c) F.B.D. of pulley C

Fig. 2.39

Now, consider F.B.D. of block B and applying condition of equilibrium,

$$T - \mu N_2 = 0 \quad \text{...(i)}$$
$$N_2 - W_B = 0 \quad \text{...(ii)}$$

Solving equations (i) and (ii), we get,

$N_2 - $ kN and $T = 0.25 \times 8 = 2$ kN

Now, applying condition of equilibrium to block B,

$$T + F_1 + F_2 - P_{min} = 0 \quad \ldots \text{(iii)}$$
$$N_1 - W_A - N_2 = 0 \quad \ldots \text{(iv)}$$
$$N_1 = 16 + 8 = 24 \text{ kN}$$
$$F_1 = \mu N_1 = 24 \times 0.25 = 6 \text{ kN}$$
$$F_2 = \mu N_2 = 8 \times 0.25 = 2 \text{ kN}$$

Substituting all values in equation (iii), we get,

$$P_{min} = T + F_1 + F_2 = 2 + 6 + 2 = 10 \text{ kN}$$
$$T = 2 \text{ kN}, \quad P_{min} = 10 \text{ kN} \quad \ldots \text{Ans.}$$

Example 2.22 :

A body of weight 1000 N is pulled upon inclined plane by a force of 600 N. The inclination of the plane is 27° to the horizontal and force is applied parallel to the plane. Determine the angle of friction.

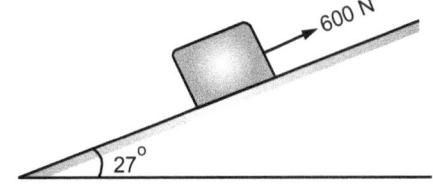

Fig. 2.40

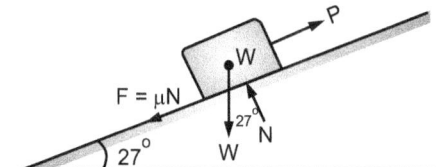

Fig. 2.41 : F.B.D. of body

Solution :

We know, angle of friction, $\theta = \tan^{-1}(\mu)$

Therefore, due to force (P = 600 N), applied to body parallel to the plane in upward direction, a frictional force F acting opposite to the force P. Now, consider free body diagram of block and applying condition of equilibrium.

Resolving forces along and normal to the plane,

$$P = W \sin 27° + F \quad \ldots \text{(i)}$$
$$N = W \cos 27°$$
$$= 1000 \cos 27° = 891 \text{ N} \quad \ldots \text{(ii)}$$

Putting $P = 600$, $W = 1000$ and $F = \mu N$ in equation (i),

$$\therefore \quad 600 = 453.9 + \mu \times 891$$
$$\therefore \quad \mu = \frac{146.1}{891} = 0.164$$
$$\therefore \quad \text{Angle of friction}, \theta = \tan^{-1}(0.164) = \mathbf{9.315°} \quad \ldots \text{Ans.}$$

Example 2.23 :

Two blocks A and B are connected by a string passing over a smooth pulley as shown in Fig. 2.42. The block A of weight 50 N, the angle of inclined plane with the horizontal is 30°. If the coefficient of friction between the plane and the block A is 0.4, find the maximum and minimum values of mass B for equilibrium of the system.

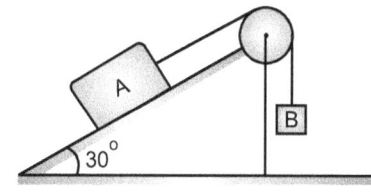

Fig. 2.42

Solution :

The possible motion of block is either downward or upward, it depends upon the magnitude of hanging mass B. At the stage when mass B has its minimum limit i.e. P_{min}. If $P < P_{min}$, block A slides down to plane. Similarly for $P > P_{max}$, block A moves up the plane.

Case 1 : Now consider the equilibrium of the system, for $(P = P_{min})$.

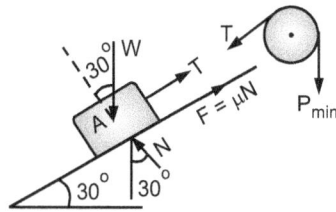 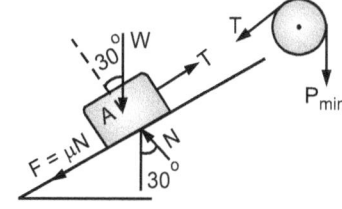

Fig. 2.43 (a) Fig. 2.43 (b)

Consider F.B.D. of smooth pulley.

$$P_{min} = T$$

For pulley, $P_{min} = T$ (because pulley is smooth) for block A. Resolving forces along and normal to the plane,

$T + F = W \sin 30° = 25$ N ... (i)

$N = W \cos 30° = 25\sqrt{3}$ ... (ii)

$N = 43.3$

Solving we get, $T = 25 - F = 25 - 0.4 \times 25\sqrt{3}$

∴ $T = 7.679$ N

$P_{min} \approx 7.68$ N

Case 2 : Motion of blocks up the plane.

$P_{max} = T$ (for pulley)

For equilibrium of the system, resolving forces along and normal to the plane,
$$T = F + W \sin 30° \qquad \text{... (iii)}$$
$$W \cos 30° = 43.3 \text{ N} \qquad \text{... (iv)}$$
Solving we get, $T = 0.4 \times 43.3 + 50 \sin 30° = 42.32$ N
$\therefore \quad P_{max} = 42.32$ N

Therefore range of mass B is **7.68 N to 42.32 N** ... Ans.

Example 2.24 :

Determine the maximum value of P which can be applied to the roller shown in Fig. 2.44 without causing it to rotate. The coefficient of friction for contact surfaces is 0.5.

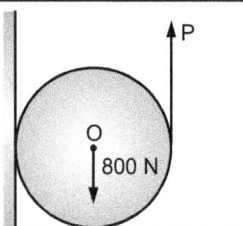

Fig. 2.44

Solution :

Consider F.B.D. of roller, as $P > P_{max}$, roller moves anticlockwise.

Thus, frictional force acting in such a direction will produce clockwise rotation.

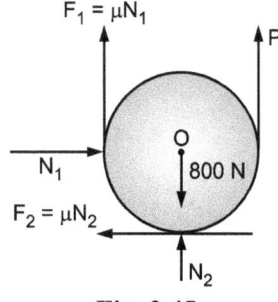

Fig. 2.45

Applying condition of equilibrium,
$$N_1 = F_2 = \mu N_2 \qquad \text{... (i)}$$
$$F_1 + N_2 + P = 800$$
$$\mu N_1 + N_2 + P = 800 \qquad \text{... (ii)}$$
$$\mu (\mu N_2) + N_2 + P = 800$$
$$1.25 N_2 + P = 800 \qquad \text{... (iii)}$$

Now taking moment of forces about O,
$$P \cdot R = \mu N_1 \cdot R + \mu N_2 \cdot R = (\mu N_1 + \mu N_2) \cdot R$$
$$P = \mu (\mu N_2) + \mu N_2 = 0.5 (0.5 N_2) + 0.5 N_2$$
$$P = 0.75 N_2$$

Substituting the value of P in equation (ii),

$2N_2 = 800 \quad \therefore \quad N_2 = 400$ and $P = 300$ N. Thus, $P_{max} = 300$ N ... Ans.

2.9 SUPPORTS

If a support prevents translation of a body in a given direction, then a force is developed on the body in that direction.

If a support prevents rotation of a body, then a couple moment is exerted on the body.

For drawing F.B.D., body is isolated from surrounding supports. Supports are replaced by reactions as shown in Table 2.1.

Table 2.1 : Types of Supports

Type of support	Sketch of support	Reactions of support	Remark
Pin or Hinge			It prevents translation along X and Y directions.
Roller			It prevents translation in the direction perpendicular to the roller surface.
Fixed			It prevents translation along X and Y directions. It also prevents rotation of a body.
Smooth surface			It prevents translation in the direction perpendicular to surface.
Cable			Tension force acts along direction of cable away from the body.
Link			Reaction acts along the link away or towards the body.
Member pin connected to collar on smooth rod			Reaction acts perpendicular to the rod.

2.10 BEAM

Beams are long and straight bars having a constant cross-sectional area. Beams are designed to support loads applied at various points.

Beams are classified according to the way in which they are supported.

(1) Determinate beams.

(2) Indeterminate beams.

1. Determinate Beams :

The beams which are supported by the minimum number of supports necessary to ensure equilibrium are called statically determinate beams.

Equilibrium equations i.e. $\sum F_x = 0$, $\sum F_y = 0$ and $\sum M$ at any point $= 0$ are sufficient to determine unknown reactions of beam.

Types of Determinate Beams :

(a) Simply supported beam :

It is hinged at one end and roller supported at other end.

(b) Overhanging beam :

The beam has a overhanging span on either or both sides of supports. One support is hinged and other is roller support.

(c) Cantilever beam :

It is fixed at one end and free at the other end.

(d) Compound beam :

Two or more beams are connected by hinges or pins to form a single continuous beam. Reactions at supports can be determined by considering F.B.D. of each beam separately as shown in Table 2.2.

Table 2.2 : Types of Determinate Beams

Table 9.2 : Types of Determinate Beams

Type beam	Sketch of beam	F.B.D. of beam	Unknown reactions of beam
Simply supported beam			R_{Ax}, R_{Ay} and R_B
Overhanging beam			R_{Ax}, R_{Ay} and R_B
Cantilever beam			R_{Ax}, R_{Ay} and M_A
Compound beam			R_{Ax}, R_{Ay}, M_A : Beam AP R_P, R_B : Beam PB
			R_{Ax}, R_{Ay}, R_B : Beam AP R_P, R_C : Beam PC.

2. Indeterminate Beams : Beams which have more external supports than necessary to maintain an equilibrium are called statically indeterminate.

Equilibrium equations are insufficient to determine unknown reactions.

Table 2.3 : Types of Loads

Type of load	Diagram	Load intensity	Equivalent load diagram
1. Point load or concentrated load	W_1, W_2, W_3	–	–
2. Uniformly distributed load (u.d.l.)	w per unit length, l	wL	Area under rectangle = wl; $l/2$, $l/2$
3. Uniformly varying load (u.v.l)	w per unit length, l	$\dfrac{(0+w)\,l}{2} = \dfrac{wl}{2}$	Area under triangle = $\dfrac{1}{2} \times w \times l$; $\dfrac{2l}{3}$, $l/3$
4. Trapezoidal load	w_1 / unit length, w_2 per unit length, w per unit length, l	$\dfrac{(w_1 + w_2)}{2} \times l$	Area under trapezoid = $\left(\dfrac{w_1 + w_2}{2}\right)l$; $\left(\dfrac{w_1 + 2w_2}{w_1 + w_2}\right)\left(\dfrac{w_2 + w_1 + 2}{w_1 + w_2}\right)\dfrac{l}{3}$
5. Load due to irregular shape	w per unit length, Area under curve, l	Area under curve	Area under total load curve; Centroidal area

NUMERICAL EXAMPLES ON BEAM

Example 2.25 :

Determine reactions at supports A and B.

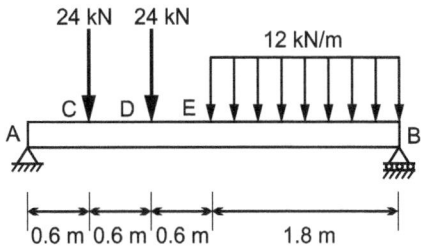

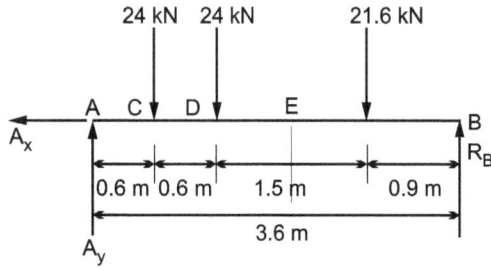

Fig. 2.46   **Fig. 2.46 (a) : Equivalent load diagram**

Solution :

Given data : Loads acting on the beam are :

Point loads : 24 kN and 24 kN

UDL : 12 kN/m on the span 1.8 m.

To find : Reaction at hinge support A (R_A)

Reaction at roller support B (R_B)

(a) Equivalent load diagram is as shown in Fig. 2.46 (a).

UDL can be replaced by equivalent point load = (12×1.8) = 21.6 kN acting at the centre of span EB as shown.

(b) Beam is in equilibrium.

Applying conditions of equilibrium,

$$\Sigma M_A = 0 \quad \therefore \quad 24 \times 0.6 + 24 \times 1.2 + 21.6 \times 2.7 - R_B \times 3.6 = 0$$

$$\therefore \quad R_B = \mathbf{28.2 \text{ kN}} \,(\circlearrowleft) \qquad \qquad \text{... Ans.}$$

$$\Sigma F_y = 0 \quad \therefore \quad A_y + R_B - 24 - 24 - 21.6 = 0$$

$$\therefore \quad A_y = 41.4 \text{ kN} \,(\circlearrowleft)$$

$$\Sigma F_x = 0 \quad \therefore \quad A_x = 0 \text{ kN}$$

$\therefore$ Reaction at A is $R_A = \mathbf{41.4 \text{ kN}} \,(\circlearrowleft)$ ... Ans.

Example 2.26 :

For the beam shown in Fig. 2.47 (a), find the reactions at supports.

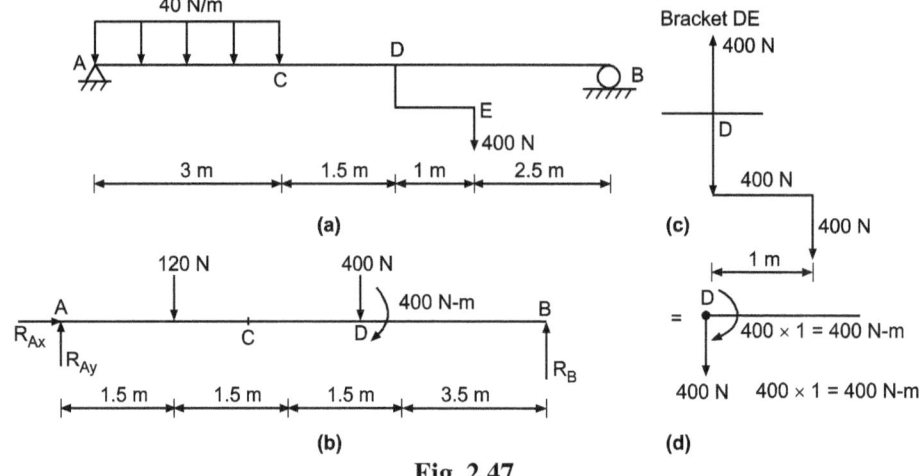

Fig. 2.47

Solution :

Given data : As shown in Fig. 2.47 (a).
To find : Reactions at supports.
Considering equilibrium of beam AB shown in Fig. 2.47 (c),

$$\Sigma M_A = 0$$
$$120 + 1.5 \times 400 \times 4.5 + 400 - R_B \times 7 = 0$$
$$\therefore \quad R_B = 340 \text{ N } (\circlearrowleft)$$
$$\Sigma F_y = 0$$
$$R_{Ay} + R_B = 120 + 400$$
$$R_{Ay} = 120 + 400 - 340 = 180 \text{ N } (\circlearrowleft)$$
$$\Sigma F_x = 0, \quad R_{Ax} = 0 \qquad \ldots \text{Ans.}$$

Example 2.27 :

For the beam shown in Fig. 2.48 (a), calculate the reactions at supports.

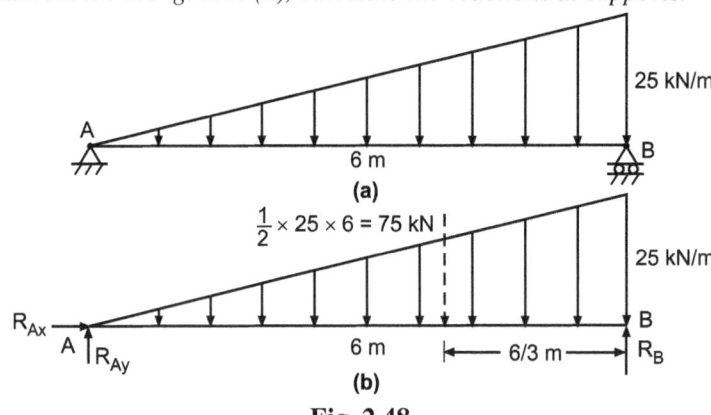

Fig. 2.48

Solution :

Given data : As shown in Fig. 2.48 (a).
To find : Reactions at support.

$$\Sigma M \text{ at } A = 0$$

$$\therefore \quad -R_B \times 6 + \frac{1}{2} \times 25 \times 6 \times \frac{2}{3} \times 6 = 0$$

$$\therefore \quad R_B = 50 \text{ kN} \qquad \text{... Ans.}$$

$$\Sigma F_y = 0$$

$$\therefore \quad R_{Ay} + R_B - \frac{1}{2} \times 25 \times 6 = 0$$

$$\therefore \quad R_{Ay} = 75 - 50 = 25 \text{ kN}$$

$$\Sigma F_x = 0$$

$$\therefore \quad R_{Ax} = 0 \quad \therefore \quad R_A = 25 \text{ kN} \qquad \text{... Ans.}$$

Example 2.28 :

Calculate the reactions for the trapezoidal load as shown in Fig. 2.49 (a).

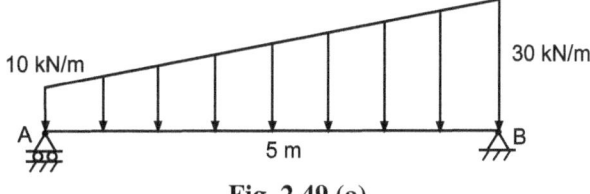

Fig. 2.49 (a)

Solution :

Given data : As shown in Fig. 2.49 (a).
To find : Reactions at support.
Method I :

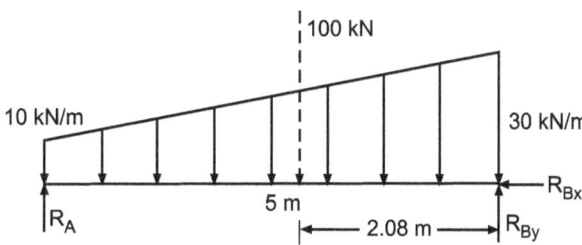

Fig. 2.49 (b)

$$\text{C.G. of trapezoid from A} = \left(\frac{10 + 2 \times 30}{10 + 30}\right) \times \frac{5}{3} = 2.92 \text{ m}$$

$$\text{C.G. of trapezoid from B} = \left(\frac{30 + 2 \times 10}{10 + 30}\right) \times \frac{5}{3} = 2.08 \text{ m}$$

$$\text{Area of load} = \frac{1}{2}(10+30) \times 5 = 100 \text{ kN}$$

$$\sum M \text{ at } A = 0$$

$\therefore \quad -R_{By} \times 5 + 100 \times 2.92 = 0$

$\therefore \quad R_{By} = 58.4 \text{ kN}$

$\quad R_B = 58.4$ ... **Ans.**

$$\sum F_y = 0$$

$\therefore \quad R_A + R_{By} - 100 = 0$

$\therefore \quad R_A = 100 - 58.4 = 41.6 \text{ kN} \quad \therefore R_A = \mathbf{41.6 \text{ kN}}$ ... **Ans.**

Method II : Divide trapezoid into rectangle (UDL) and triangle (UVL) :

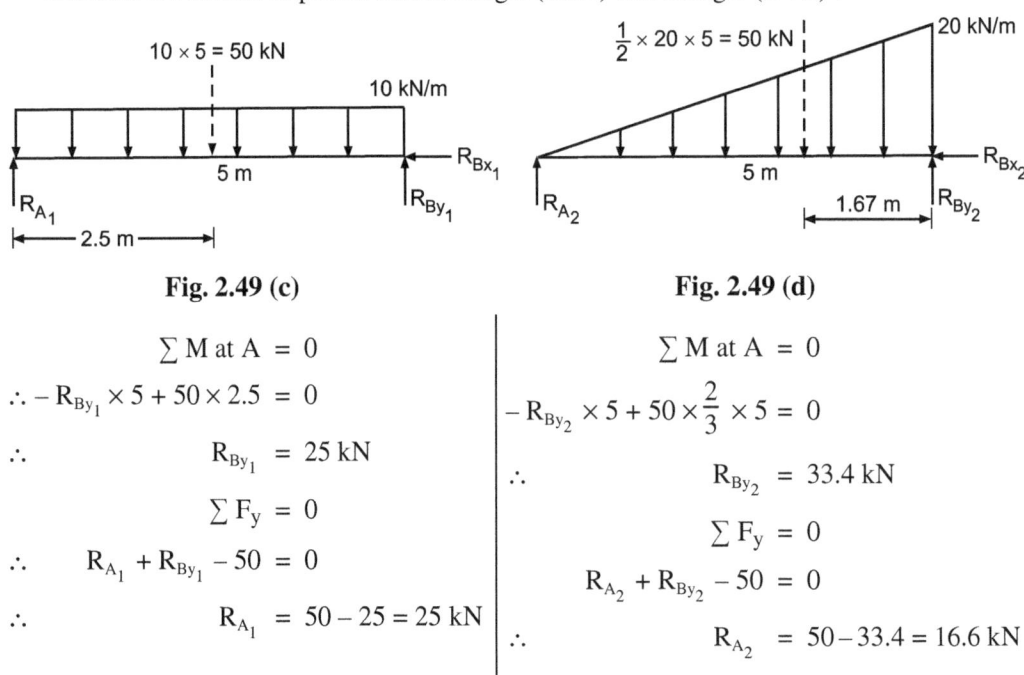

Fig. 2.49 (c)   **Fig. 2.49 (d)**

$$\sum M \text{ at } A = 0 \quad\bigg|\quad \sum M \text{ at } A = 0$$

$\therefore -R_{By_1} \times 5 + 50 \times 2.5 = 0 \quad\bigg|\quad -R_{By_2} \times 5 + 50 \times \frac{2}{3} \times 5 = 0$

$\therefore \quad R_{By_1} = 25 \text{ kN} \quad\bigg|\quad \therefore \quad R_{By_2} = 33.4 \text{ kN}$

$\quad \sum F_y = 0 \quad\bigg|\quad \sum F_y = 0$

$\therefore \quad R_{A_1} + R_{By_1} - 50 = 0 \quad\bigg|\quad R_{A_2} + R_{By_2} - 50 = 0$

$\therefore \quad R_{A_1} = 50 - 25 = 25 \text{ kN} \quad\bigg|\quad \therefore \quad R_{A_2} = 50 - 33.4 = 16.6 \text{ kN}$

$\therefore \quad R_A = R_{A_1} + R_{A_2} = 25 + 16.6 = 41.6 \text{ kN}$

$R_A = \mathbf{41.6 \text{ kN}}$ ... **Ans.**

$R_B = R_{By_1} + R_{By_2} = 25 + 33.4 = 58.4 \text{ kN}$

$R_B = \mathbf{58.4 \text{ kN}}$ ... **Ans.**

As no horizontal load is there, therefore, $R_{Bx \times 1}$ and $R_{By \times 2}$ are zero.

Example 2.29 :

For the beam shown in Fig. 2.50 (a), calculate the reactions at A and C.

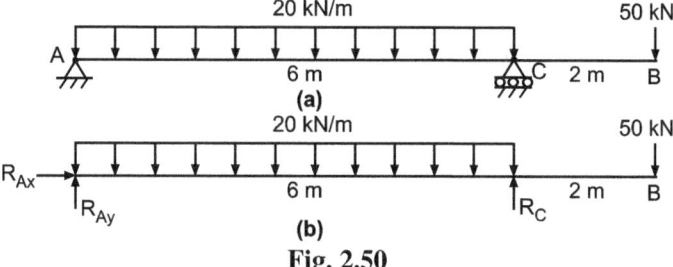

Fig. 2.50

Solution :
Given data : As shown in Fig. 2.50 (a).
To find : Reactions at support.

$$\Sigma M @ \text{ point A} = 0$$
$$20 \times 6 \times 3 - R_C \times 6 + 50 \times 8 = 0$$
∴ $\qquad R_C = \mathbf{126.67 \text{ kN}}$ (↻) ... Ans.

$$\Sigma F_y = 0$$
$$R_{Ay} - 20 \times 6 + R_C - 50 = 0$$
∴ $\qquad R_{Ay} = 120 + 50 - R_C = 170 - 126.67 = 43.33 \text{ kN}$ (↻)

$\Sigma F_x = 0 \quad \therefore R_{Ax} = 0 \quad \therefore R_A = \mathbf{43.33 \text{ kN}}$ (↻) ... Ans.

Example 2.30 :

Determine reactions at A and B.

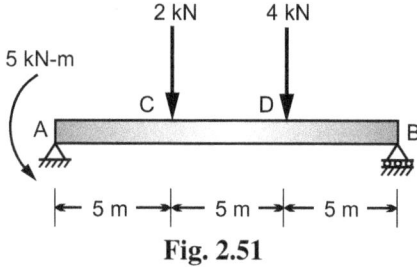

Fig. 2.51

Solution :
Given data : Loads acting on the beam are point loads 2 kN and 4 kN, couple and moment 5 kNm (↻).
To find : Reaction at hinge support A (R_A)
Reaction at roller support B (R_B).

(a) Beam is in equilibrium.
Applying conditions of equilibrium,
$$\Sigma M_A = 0 \therefore -5 + 2 \times 5 + 4 \times 10 - R_B \times 15 = 0$$
$\qquad \therefore R_B = \mathbf{3 \text{ kN}}$ (↻) ... Ans.

$\Sigma F_y = 0 \quad \therefore R_A + R_B - 2 - 4 = 0$
$\qquad \therefore R_A = \mathbf{3 \text{ kN}}$ (↻) ... Ans.

Example 2.31 :

Determine reactions at A and D.

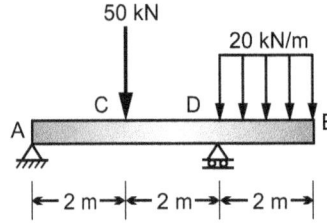

Fig. 2.52

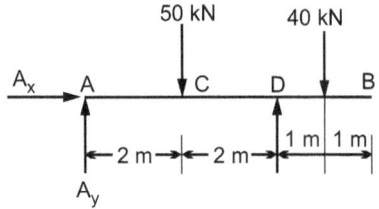

Fig. 2.52 (a) : Equivalent load diagram

Solution :

Given data : Loads acting on the beam are :

Point load : 50 kN

UDL : 20 kN/m on the span 2 m.

To find : Reaction at hinge A (R_A).

Reaction at roller support D (R_D).

(a) Equivalent load diagram is as shown in Fig. 2.52 (a).

UDL can be replaced by equivalent point load = $(20 \times 2) = 40$ kN acting at centre of span DB.

(b) The beam is in equilibrium. Applying conditions of equilibrium,

$\Sigma M_A = 0$ ∴ $50 \times 2 - R_D \times 4 + 40 \times 5 = 0$

∴ $R_D = \mathbf{75}$ **kN** (↻) ... Ans.

$\Sigma F_y = 0$ ∴ $A_y - 50 - 40 + R_D = 0$

∴ $A_y = 15$ kN (↻)

$\Sigma F_x = 0$ ∴ $A_x = 0$

Reaction at A is $R_A = \mathbf{15}$ **kN** (↻) ... Ans.

Example 2.32 :

Determine reaction and moment at B.

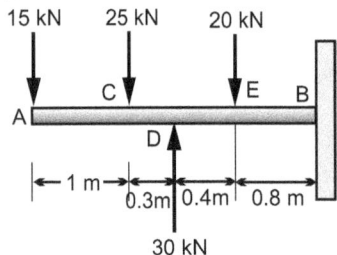

Fig. 2.53

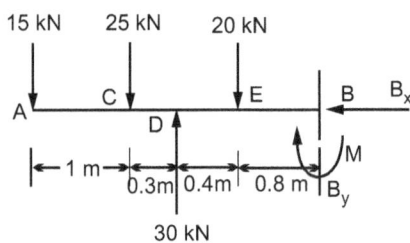

Fig. 2.53 (a) : Equivalent load diagram

Solution :

Given data : Loads acting on the beam are :

Point loads : 15 kN, 25 kN, 30 kN, 20 kN.

To find : Reactions at fixed support B i.e. B_x and B_y.

Moment at fixed support B i.e. M.

(a) Beam is in equilibrium. [Refer Fig. 2.53 (a)]

Applying conditions of equilibrium,

$\Sigma M_B = 0$ $\therefore$ $-15 \times 2.5 - 25 \times 1.5 - 20 \times 0.8 + M = 0$

$\therefore$ **M = 91 kNm** ($\circlearrowleft$) ... Ans.

$\Sigma F_y = 0$ $\therefore$ $-15 - 25 - 20 + B_y = 0$

$\therefore$ B_y = **60 kN** ($\circlearrowleft$) ... Ans.

$\Sigma F_x = 0$ $\therefore$ $B_x = 0$ ... Ans.

Example 2.33 :

Determine reactions at A and D for the beam as shown in Fig. 2.54 (a).

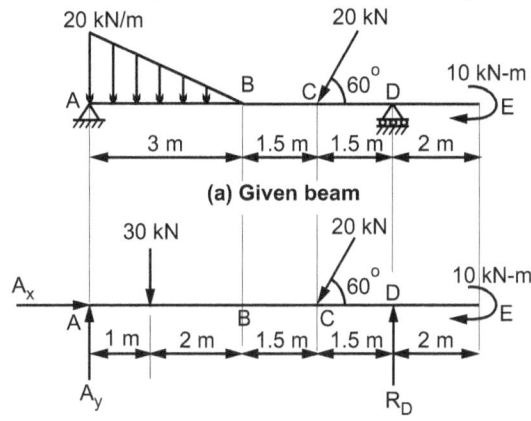

Fig. 2.54 (b) : FBD of beam

Solution :

Given data : Loads acting on the beam are :

Point load : 20 kN

Uniformly varying load (UVL) : 0 kN/m to 20 kN/m on 3 m span.

Moment of couple : 10 kNm ($\circlearrowleft$)

To find : Reaction at hinge A.

Reaction at roller support D.

(a) Equivalent load diagram is as shown in Fig. 2.54 (b).

UVL can be replaced by equivalent point load $= \frac{1}{2} \times 20 \times 3 = 30$ kN acting at $\left(\frac{1}{3} \times 3 = 1 \text{ m}\right)$ from end A.

(b) The beam is in equilibrium.
Applying conditions of equilibrium,

$\Sigma M_A = 0 \therefore 30 \times 1 + 20 \sin 60° \times 4.5 - R_D \times 6 + 10 = 0$

$\therefore R_D = \mathbf{19.66 \text{ kN}} (\circlearrowleft)$ ... Ans.

$\Sigma F_y = 0 \therefore A_y - 30 - 20 \sin 60° + R_D = 0$

$\therefore A_y - 30 - 20 \sin 60° + 19.66 = 0$

$\therefore A_y = 27.66 \text{ kN} (\circlearrowleft)$

$\Sigma F_x = 0 \therefore A_x - 20 \cos 60° = 0$

$\therefore A_x = 10 \text{ kN} (\rightarrow)$

Refer Fig. 2.54 (a).

Reaction at A, $R_A = \sqrt{A_x^2 + A_y^2} = \sqrt{(10)^2 + (27.66)^2} = \mathbf{29.41 \text{ kN}}$ ... Ans.

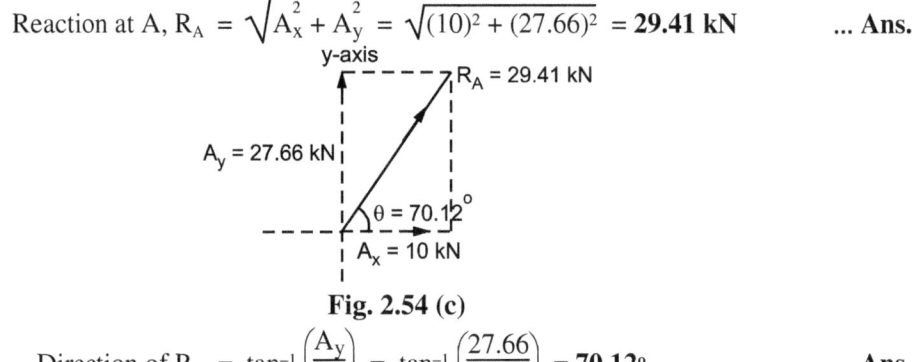

Fig. 2.54 (c)

Direction of $R_A = \tan^{-1}\left(\frac{A_y}{A_x}\right) = \tan^{-1}\left(\frac{27.66}{10}\right) = \mathbf{70.12°}$ ... Ans.

Example 2.34 :
Determine reactions at C and G.

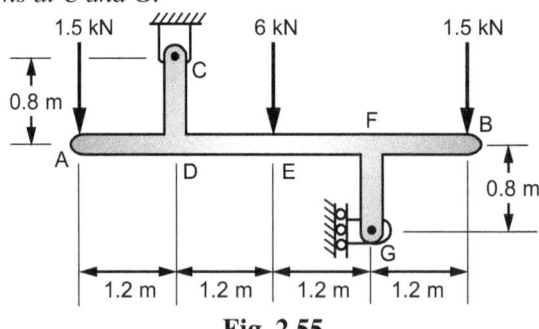

Fig. 2.55

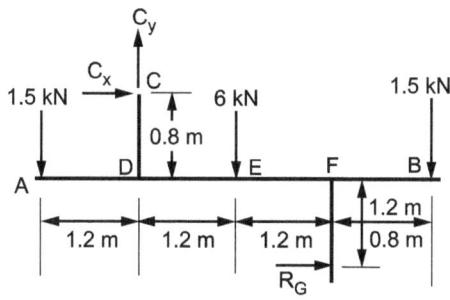

Fig. 2.55 (a)

Solution :

Given data : Loads acting on the beam AB are :
Point loads 1.5 kN, 6 kN, 1.5 kN.
To find : Reaction at hinge C (R_C)
Reaction at roller G (R_G).

(a) Beam AB is in equilibrium. [Refer Fig. 2.55 (a)]
Applying conditions of equilibrium,

$\Sigma M_C = 0$ ∴ $-1.5 \times 1.2 + 6 \times 1.2 - R_G \times 1.6 + 1.5 \times 3.6 = 0$

∴ $R_G = $ **6.75 kN (→)** ... Ans.

$\Sigma F_y = 0$ ∴ $-1.5 + C_y - 6 - 1.5 = 0$

∴ $C_y = 9$ kN (↻)

$\Sigma F_x = 0$ ∴ $C_x + R_G = 0$

∴ $C_x = -6.75$ kN

(Since the value of C_x is negative, assumed direction is wrong)

$C_x = 6.75$ kN (←)

Refer Fig. 2.55 (b).

Reaction at C = $R_C = \sqrt{C_x^2 + C_y^2} = \sqrt{(6.75)^2 + (9)^2} = $ **11.25 kN** ... Ans.

Fig. 2.55 (b)

Direction of $R_C = \theta = \tan^{-1}\left(\dfrac{C_y}{C_x}\right) = \tan^{-1}\left(\dfrac{9}{6.75}\right) = $ **53.13°** ... Ans.

Example 2.35 :

If rope BC fails when tension becomes 50 kN, determine greatest vertical load F that can be applied to the beam at B. What is the magnitude of reaction at A ?

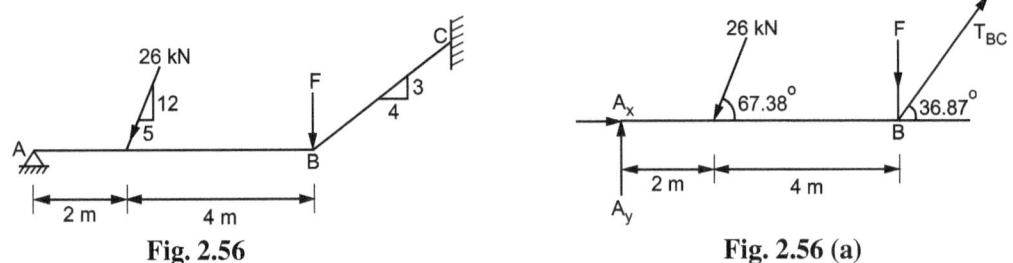

Fig. 2.56   Fig. 2.56 (a)

Solution :

Given data : Loads acting on the beam AB are :
Point load 26 kN, maximum tension in rope BC, $T_{BC} = 50$ kN and force F.

To find : (a) Greatest vertical load F.
(b) Magnitude of reaction at A.

(a) Beam is in equilibrium. Refer Fig. 2.56 (a) :

Applying conditions of equilibrium,

$\Sigma M_A = 0$ ∴ $26 \times \sin 67.38° \times 2 + F \times 6 - T_{BC} \sin 36.87° \times 6 = 0$

∴ **F = 22 kN (↓)**   ... Ans.

$\Sigma F_x = 0$ ∴ $A_x - 26 \cos 67.38° + T_{BC} \cos 36.87° = 0$

∴ $A_x - 26 \cos 67.38° + 50 \cos 36.87° = 0$

∴ $A_x = -30$ kN

∴ $A_x = 30$ kN (←)

$\Sigma F_y = 0$ ∴ $A_y - 26 \sin 67.38° - F + T_{BC} \sin 36.87° = 0$

∴ $A_y = 16$ kN (↺)

Refer Fig. 2.56 (a).

Reaction at A = $R_A = \sqrt{A_x^2 + A_y^2} = \sqrt{(30)^2 + (16)^2} =$ **34 kN**   ... Ans.

Fig. 2.56 (b)

Direction of $R_A = \alpha = \tan^{-1}\left(\dfrac{A_y}{A_x}\right) = \tan^{-1}\left(\dfrac{16}{30}\right) =$ **28°**   ... Ans.

Example 2.36 :

The compound beam is fixed at A and supported by a rocker at B and C. There are pins at D and E. Determine the reactions at the supports.

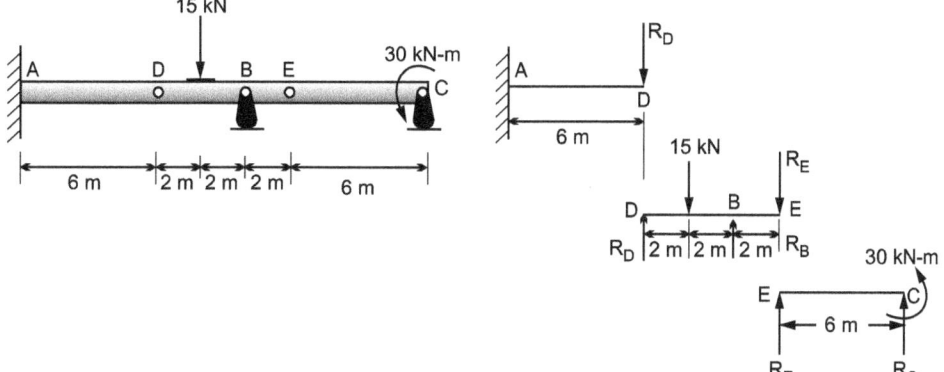

Fig. 2.57   **Fig. 2.57 (a) : Equivalent load diagram**

Solution :

Given data : Load acting on beam DE : Point load : 15 kN

Moment acting on beam EC : 30 kNm (↺)

To find : Reactions at the supports A, D, B, E and C.

(a) Three beams AD, DE and EC are connected by two internal hinges at D and E. Refer Fig. 2.57 (a).

(b) Beam EC is in equilibrium.

$\Sigma M_C = 0$ ∴ $R_E \times 6 - 30 = 0$

           ∴ $R_E = \mathbf{5\ kN\ (↺)}$ ... Ans.

$\Sigma F_y = 0$ ∴ $R_E + R_C = 0$

           ∴ $R_C = -5\ kN$

           ∴ $R_C = \mathbf{5\ kN\ (↓)}$ ... Ans.

(c) Beam DE is in equilibrium.

$\Sigma M_D = 0$ ∴ $15 \times 2 - R_B \times 4 + R_E \times 6 = 0$

           ∴ $R_B = \mathbf{15\ kN\ (↺)}$ ... Ans.

$\Sigma F_y = 0$ ∴ $R_D + R_B - 15 - R_E = 0$

           ∴ $R_D = -15 + 15 + 5$

           ∴ $R_D = \mathbf{5\ kN\ (↺)}$ ... Ans.

(d) Beam AD is in equilibrium. Let M be moment at fixed end A.

$\Sigma M_A = 0$ ∴ $-M + R_D \times 6 = 0$

           ∴ $M = 5 \times 6 = 30\ kNm\ (↺)$

$\Sigma F_y = 0$ ∴ $A_y - R_D = 0$

           ∴ $A_y = 5\ kN\ (↺)$

$\Sigma F_x = 0$ ∴ $A_x = 0$

     Reaction at A = **5 kN (↺)**   ... Ans.

     Moment at A = **30 kNm (↺)**   ... Ans.

2.11 VIRTUAL WORK METHOD FOR SUPPORT REACTIONS

Introduction :

We already know that whenever a body moves, under the action of force, work is said to be done by that force. But in statics, we are usually concerned with the equilibrium of rigid body under the system of forces. Now, consider if the body is in equilibrium under the action of a system of forces acting on it, therefore, net resultant force acting on it is zero and hence no displacement and also no work. But it has been found useful to imagine that the body has infinite small displacement even when it is in equilibrium, i.e. even when the resultant force acting on it is zero and also work of some nature is done. But obviously for a system in equilibrium, displacement should be zero and no work should be done. Hence equating the expression of work done by the different forces of the system during the small displacement to zero, the unknown force may be evaluated. This small displacement which a body is assumed to have even when it is in equilibrium is called the virtual displacement of the body and the resultant work done is virtual work.

2.12 WORK

We know that work is measured by the product of the force and the displacement in the direction of the force. Thus,

Work done, W = Force × Displacement in the direction of the force.

Refer to Fig. 2.58 (a), if a force, P acts along AB and causes the displacement of a particle at A to C such that displacement is in the direction of force, then

$$W = P \times AC \text{ (positive)}$$

Now, refer Fig. 2.58 (b), it is seen that the displacement of the particle at A is AC but in the direction opposite to that in which the force acts. It is possible, if the resultant of number of forces acting at A is acting opposite to force P (i.e. AB) and hence the displacement in the direction AC.

$$W = P \times (-AC) = P \times AC \text{ (negative)}$$

But if the displacement AC of the particle is not collinear with AB, the line of action of the force, then

$$W = P \times \text{Displacement in the direction of force}$$

Let CD be the perpendicular from C to AB, then

$$AD = AC \cos \theta$$

∴ $$W = P \times AC \cos \theta \text{ (positive)}$$

But if θ is an obtuse angle, as shown in Fig. 2.58 (d), cos θ is negative.

∴ $$W = P \times AC \cos \theta \text{ (negative)}$$

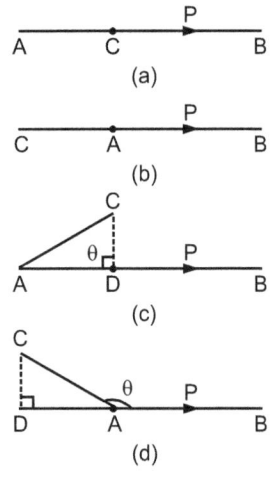

Fig. 2.58

Also if the displacement AC of the force at A is such that AC ⊥ AB as shown in Fig. 2.58 (e) then the displacement in the direction of force is zero and hence W is zero. Thus, *a force does not do any work in a direction at right angle to itself.*

If force system forming the couple is acting on a body, we have to find the work of the forces. So it is convenient to determine the work of a couple without considering separately the work of each of the two forces forming the couple. Refer Fig. 2.59.

Work of couple of moment M acting on a body is

$$W = M \cdot d\theta$$

If the magnitude of the force is varying with respect to displacement as shown in Fig. 2.60, then work done by the force P during an infinitesimal displacement is,

$$dw = \int_0^S dw = \int_0^S F \cdot ds$$

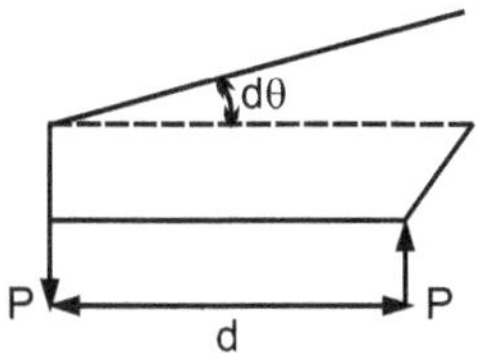

Fig. 2.59 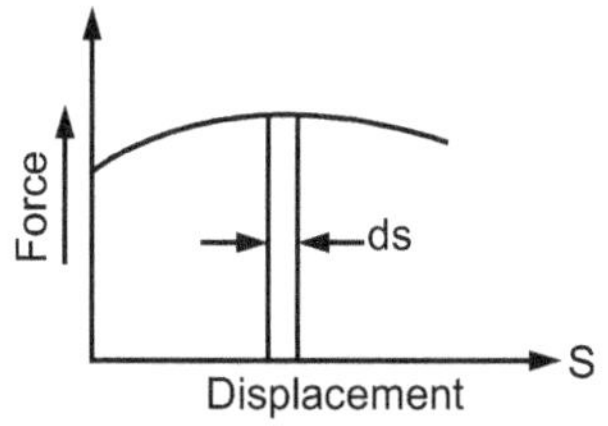   **Fig. 2.60**

As we have seen above that, work has a magnitude and a sign, but no direction, thus work is a scalar quantity.

Unit of work is obtained by multiplying units of force by units of length. In S.I. units, work is expressed in N-m.

2.13 THEOREM ON WORK

It states that "the work done by a force in moving a body from one position to another is equal to the sum of the work done by the components of that force".

2.14 PRINCIPLE OF VIRTUAL WORK

The principle of virtual work states that, if a particle or the rigid body are in equilibrium under the system of forces, then the virtual work of the force system acting on the rigid body or on a particle is zero for any virtual displacement of the particle or body.

This statement is expressed in two parts; firstly that if the system is to be in equilibrium. ΣW i.e. the sum of works done by the forces, during in any infinitesimal small displacement should be zero. The second part of the statement says that if the virtual work done by the forces is zero, this is a sufficient condition for the system to be in equilibrium. We shall now prove these aspects of the principle of virtual work.

Consider a system of forces P_1, P_2, P_3 acting on a particle at o, making angle θ_1, θ_2 and θ_3 with respect to ox (x-axis). ox and oy being two rectangular axes of reference through o, as shown in Fig. 2.61.

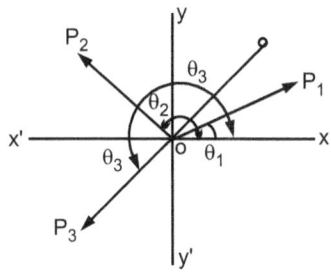

Fig. 2.61

Let the point o, have a virtual displacement to oo' such that the co-ordinates of o' are x and y. Thus, the point o has two virtual displacements x and y along ox and oy respectively. Let the components of P_1, P_2 and P_3 along ox and oy be Px_1, Px_2, Px_3 and Py_1, Py_2, Py_3 respectively.

Virtual work done along ox during the virtual displacement x

$$= Px_1 \cdot x + Px_2 \cdot x + Px_3 \cdot x = x(Px_1 + Px_2 + Px_3)$$
$$= x \Sigma Px_1$$

Similarly, the virtual work done along oy during the virtual displacement y

$$= y(Py_1 + Py_2 + Py_3) = y \cdot \Sigma Py_1$$

∴ Total work done, $W = x \Sigma Px_1 + y \Sigma Py_1$

Now, if the system is in equilibrium, the condition for system is in equilibrium,

$\Sigma Px_1 = 0$ and also $\Sigma Py_1 = 0$

Net virtual work done $= x \times 0 + y \times 0 = 0$

Hence, the necessary condition for the system to be in equilibrium is that the net virtual work done by the system of forces should be zero.

We have seen above that the net virtual work done during a small virtual displacement

$$= x \Sigma Px_1 + y \Sigma Py_1$$

If the point o is given only the displacement x along ox then y = 0, and hence

$$\Sigma W = x \Sigma Px_1$$

and if $\Sigma W = 0 \quad x \Sigma Px_1 = 0$

which is possible only if $\Sigma Px_1 = 0$ because x is finite quantity.

Similarly, for x = 0, $\Sigma W = y \Sigma Py_1$ and when $\Sigma W = 0$, then ΣPy is zero because again y being finite, cannot be equal to zero.

Thus from above when $\Sigma W = 0$, $\Sigma Px_1 = \Sigma Py_1 = 0$, this is a sufficient condition for the system to be in equilibrium, which proves the principle of virtual work.

2.15 FORCES WHICH CAN BE OMITTED FROM THE EQUATION OF VIRTUAL WORK

The following forces may be omitted while applying the principle of virtual work.

(a) Tension of a light inextensible string on the thrust in a rod, whose length is taken as constant even when the system has a virtual displacement.

(b) The action and reaction between any two bodies of a system if the same remains in contact during the displacement.
(c) The reaction of any smooth surface with which the body is in contact.
(d) The reaction of a rough surface on a body which rolls on it without slipping.
(e) Forces normal to the direction of motion.
(f) The reaction at a point or an axis, fixed in space, around which a body is constrained to turn.

2.16 APPLICATIONS OF THE PRINCIPLE OF VIRTUAL WORK

The following are the applications of "virtual work principle".
(a) For finding reaction of determinate structure i.e. simply supported and compound beam.
(b) It is also useful for solving framed structure and lifting machine.
(c) It may also be used to solve problems involving completely constrained structure.
(d) It may also be used to determine the configuration of a system in equilibrium under given force system.
(e) It may also be used to determine the forces necessary to maintain equilibrium.
(f) It may also be very useful for the investigation regarding the stability of equilibrium of the body.

2.17 POTENTIAL ENERGY AND EQUILIBRIUM

If any body or particle are acted on by forces (active) and these forces are expressed as a function of position. As we know when body undergoes some virtual displacement, active forces do some work. The work done by such forces is independent of the path taken and is dependent only on the end points.

Consider a body of mass m at A, its position is changed from A to B. Points A and B are at an elevation of h_A and h_B with respect to horizontal. Work done by weight W,

$$W_{A \to B} = -mg(h_B - h_A) \quad (W = mg)$$

(–ve sign due to direction of force and displacement are opposite.)

$$W_{A \to B} = -mgh_B + mgh_A$$

We know, the quantity mgh is called the potential energy.

$$\therefore W_{A \to B} = V_A - V_B$$

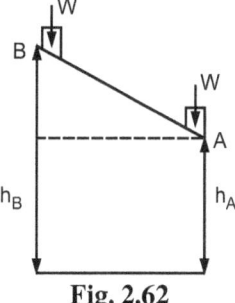

Fig. 2.62

where V, is the potential energy ($V_A < V_B$). Now, we conclude from above discussion, that the change in potential energy between two points equals the negative of the work done by the active force in moving between these points along any path.

In our case, if the potential energy is increase during displacement (from A to B) the work is negative. If work is positive (direction of force and displacement are same), the potential energy decreases (from B to A). The concept of potential energy is also useful for forces other than gravity force.

If we know the potential energy of the system, then principle of virtual work can be simplified. In the case of virtual displacement,

Total virtual work done = − Change in P.E.

If y be the virtual displacement of the system,

$$\delta w = -\delta v = \left(\frac{dv}{dy}\right) dy$$

Since dy is not equal to zero, for equilibrium condition, $\delta w = 0$. Thus,

$$\frac{dv}{dy} = 0$$

Now, principle of virtual work states that, for the equilibrium system, the derivative of its total potential energy is zero. If the position of the system depends upon more than one independent variables, then the partial derivatives of potential energy with respect to each variables must be zero.

2.18 STABILITY OF EQUILIBRIUM

We study the application of virtual work principle for establishing the conditions of equilibrium of a body under active forces. However, this principle is also very useful for making further investigation regarding the stability of equilibrium of the body whether it is stable or unstable.

We know that first derivative of potential energy is zero for equilibrium of the body. If further derivatives,

$$\frac{dv}{dy} = 0, \quad \frac{d^2v}{dy^2} > 0 \text{ Stable equilibrium}$$

$$\frac{dv}{dy} = 0, \quad \frac{d^2v}{dy^2} < 0 \text{ Unstable equilibrium}$$

$$\frac{dv}{dy} = 0, \quad \frac{d^2v}{dy^2} = 0 \text{ Neutral equilibrium}$$

Now, consider the position of body shown in Fig. 2.63 (a). The equilibrium is stable and the characteristics of this position (configuration) of equilibrium is that, if the small force which acts only momentarily produce a small displacement from this position, the system will return to the original position after the removal of force.

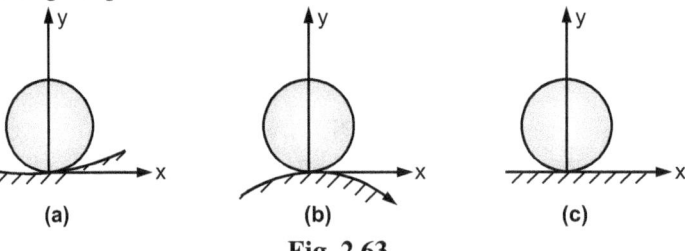

Fig. 2.63

The potential energy is at a minimum for this condition. Now consider Fig. 2.63 (b), ball is placed at the highest point on a smooth convex supporting surface. This position of equilibrium of the ball is unstable, since the slightest force may bring the ball into motion, and will not return to the original position after the removal of force. The potential energy is at a maximum for this condition. In case of Fig. 2.63 (c), the equilibrium is neutral. Due to any disturbance, ball will establish another equilibrium position. The potential energy is a constant for all possible positions of the body in the vicinity.

NUMERICAL EXAMPLES ON VIRTUAL WORK

Example 2.37 :

Using the principle of virtual work, determine the reaction of following beams.

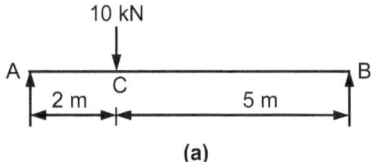
(a)

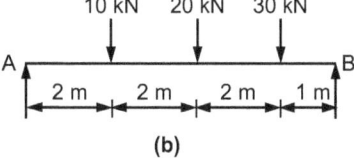
(b)

Fig. 2.64

Solution :

As we know from principle of virtual work, that total work done by the system which is in equilibrium, is zero.

$$\text{Virtual work done} = \text{Force} \times \text{Displacement}$$

(A) Let the beam AB undergo a virtual angular displacement θ. Then, virtual displacement of the reaction R_B is $BB' = AB \cdot \theta$

Similarly, the virtual displacement of 10 kN at C is $CC' = AC \cdot \theta$

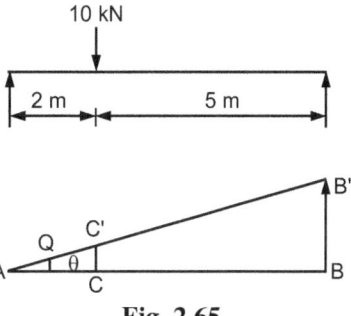

Fig. 2.65

Virtual work done by reaction R_A

$$= R_A \times 0 = 0$$

Virtual work done by reaction R_B

$$= R_B \times BB' = R_B \times AB \cdot \theta$$
$$= 7 R_B \theta \; (\because BB = AB \cdot \theta)$$

Virtual work done by force 10 kN

$$= -10 \times CC'$$
$$= -10 \times AC \cdot \theta \; (\because CC' = AC \cdot \theta)$$
$$= -20 \theta$$

–ve sign indicates that the work is done in opposite direction.

$\therefore$ Total work done $= 7 R_B \theta - 20 \theta$

By using the principle of virtual work, $\Sigma W = 0$

$\therefore \qquad 7 R_B \theta - 20 \theta = 0 \quad$ or $\quad R_B = 2.857$ kN

and $\qquad R_A = 10 - R_B = 10 - 2.857 = 7.143$ kN

(B) Let the beam AB undergo a virtual angular displacement θ in clockwise direction. Then the virtual displacement of the reaction R_A is

$$AA' = AB \cdot \theta = 7\theta$$

Similarly, virtual displacement under loads

$$CC' = CB \cdot \theta = 5\theta$$
$$DD' = DB \cdot \theta = 3\theta$$
$$EE' = EB \cdot \theta = \theta$$

Virtual work done by the reaction R_A

$$= R_A \times AA' = 7R_A\, \theta$$

Virtual work done by the reaction R_B

$$= R_B \times 0 = 0$$

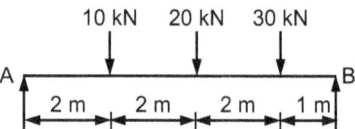

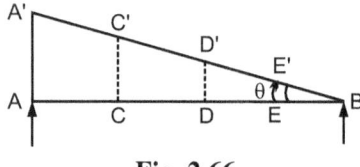

Fig. 2.66

and virtual work done by forces

$$= -(10 \times CC' + 20 \times DD' + 30 \times EE')$$
$$= -(10 \times 5\theta + 20 \times 3\theta + 30 \times \theta)$$
$$= -140\,\theta \quad (\text{–ve sign due to negative work done})$$

Using principle of virtual work,

$$7R_A\theta - 140\,\theta = 0$$

∴ $R_A = 20$ kN, and similarly, $R_B = 40$ kN ... **Ans.**

Example 2.38 :

Find the reaction of beam by principle of virtual work. (Refer Fig. 2.67)

Solution :

Let us assume beam AB undergo a virtual angular displacement θ anticlockwise. Then the virtual displacements

$$BB' = AB \cdot \theta = 6\theta$$
$$CC' = AC \cdot \theta = \theta$$
$$DD' = AD \cdot \theta = 2\theta$$
$$EE' = AE \cdot \theta = 5\theta$$

Virtual work done by the reaction R_A

$$= R_A \times 0 = 0$$

and by $R_B = R_B \times BB' = 6R_B \cdot \theta$

Fig. 2.67

Fig. 2.67 (a)

Virtual work done by the load 15 kN = $-15 \times CC' = -15 \cdot \theta$

Virtual work done by U.D.L. $= 20 \times \left[\left(\dfrac{DD' + EE'}{2}\right) \times DE\right]$

$$= -20 \times \left[\left(\dfrac{2\theta + 5\theta}{2}\right) \times 3\right] = -210\,\theta$$

(Work done by U.D.L. = Intensity of load × Area under loading of displacement diagram.)

Using principle of virtual work,
$$6R_B \cdot \theta - 15\theta - 210\theta = 0$$

or $\quad R_B = \dfrac{225}{6} = 37.5$ kN ... **Ans.**

and similarly, reaction at support A' can be found.

∴ $\quad R_A = 37.5$ kN ... **Ans.**

Note : Work done by U.D.L. may also be calculated by the work done of its equivalent point load.

$$W = wl = 20 \times 3 = 60 \text{ kN} \quad \text{(acting at F)}$$
$$\text{Virtual work done} = 60 \times FF' = -60 \times 3.5\theta = -210\theta$$

(which is same as work done by U.D.L.)

Example 2.39 :

An overhanging beam ABC of span 3 m is loaded as shown in Fig. 2.68. Find the reactions at A and B using principle of virtual work.

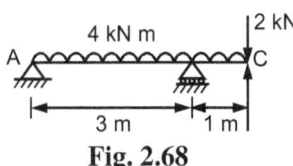

Fig. 2.68

Fig. 2.68 (a)

Solution :

Let Δ be the virtual displacement at support B. Refer Fig. 2.68 (a). From the similar triangle, $\dfrac{4}{3}\Delta$ will be the virtual displacement at C.

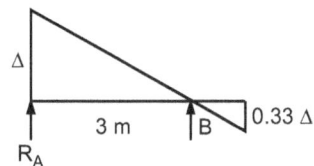

Fig. 2.68 (b)

Now, applying principle of virtual work,
i.e. Total virtual work done is zero.

$$R_A \times 0 + R_B \times \Delta - 2 \times 1.33\Delta - 4 \times \left[\dfrac{0 + 1.33\Delta}{2} \times 4\right] = 0$$

Solving, we get
$$R_B = 13.3 \text{ kN } (\uparrow) \quad \text{... Ans.}$$

Similarly, if Δ be the virtual displacement at support A.
Total virtual work done,

$$R_A \times \Delta - 4 \times \left(\dfrac{0+\Delta}{2}\right) \times 3 + 4 \times \left(\dfrac{0+0.33\Delta}{2}\right) \times 1 + 2 \times 0.33\Delta = 0$$
$$R_A = 4.70 \text{ kN } (\uparrow) \quad \text{... Ans.}$$

Example 2.40 :

By the principle of virtual work, determine the reaction for the beam as shown in Fig. 2.69.

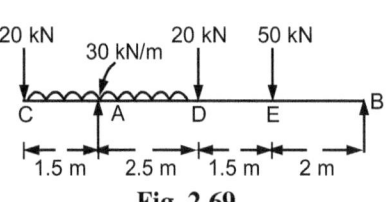
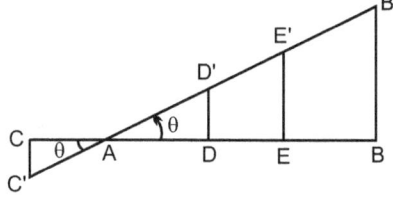

Fig. 2.69   **Fig. 2.69 (a)**

Solution :

Let us assume beam AB rotate through θ virtual angular displacement in anticlockwise direction, keeping the end A intact. All the points lying on right of A, have upward virtual displacement whereas the points lying on left of A have downward virtual displacement.

$$BB' = AB \cdot \theta = 6\theta$$
$$EE' = AE \cdot \theta = 4\theta$$
$$DD' = AD \cdot \theta = 2.5\theta$$
$$CC' = AC \cdot \theta = 1.5\theta$$

Virtual work done by the reaction R_A

$$= R_A \times 0 = 0$$

and by $R_B \ = \ R_B \times BB' = 6R_B \cdot \theta$

Virtual work done by the load $= (-20) \times (-CC')$

(–ve sign is for force acting downward as well as for displacement, which is also downward.)

$$= 20 \times CC' = 20 \times 1.5\theta = 30 \cdot \theta$$

Virtual work done by U.D.L. on left side of A

$$= (-30) \times \frac{1}{2} \times 1.5 \times (-CC') = 15 \times 1.5 \times 1.5\theta$$
$$= 33.75\theta$$

and virtual work done by U.D.L. on right side of A

$$= -30 \times \frac{1}{2} \times 2.5 \times DD'$$
$$= -15 \times 2.5 \times 2.5\theta = -93.75\theta$$

Similarly, the virtual work by point loads of 10 kN and 50 kN are,

$$= -(20 \times DD' + 50 \times EE')$$
$$= -(20 \times 2.5\theta + 50 \times 4\theta) = -250\theta$$

Using principle of virtual work,

$$6R_B\theta + 30\theta + 33.75\theta - 93.75\theta - 250\theta = 0$$

$$\therefore \quad 6R_B\theta = 280\,\theta$$
$$\therefore \quad R_B = 46.67 \text{ kN}$$
and $\quad R_A + R_B = 20 + 20 + 50 + 30 \times 4$
$$R_A + R_B = 210$$
$$\therefore \quad R_A = 163.33 \text{ kN} \quad \text{... Ans.}$$

Example 2.41 :

A rigid beam AB of length 5 m is hinged at the end A and supported on a roller at C, 3 m away from the end A.

The beam is subjected to a point load of 400 N at a distance of 2 m from the end A. Using virtual work method, determine the reaction at C.

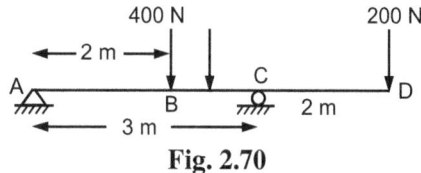

Fig. 2.70

Solution :

Let Δ be the virtual displacement at support C.

The corresponding displacement at points B and D will be 0.67 Δ and 1.67 Δ respectively.

Using principle of virtual work,

$$R_C \cdot \Delta - 400 \times \frac{2}{3} \Delta - 200 \times \frac{5}{3} \Delta = 0$$

Solving, we get
$$R_C = 600 \text{ N} \quad \text{... Ans.}$$

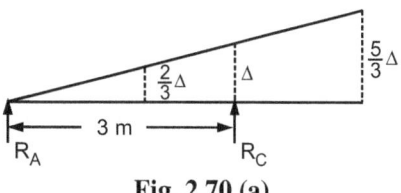

Fig. 2.70 (a)

Example 2.42 :

A compound beam ABCD supported and loaded as shown in Fig. 2.71. Using the principle of virtual work, determine the reaction at the hinge C and the support B.

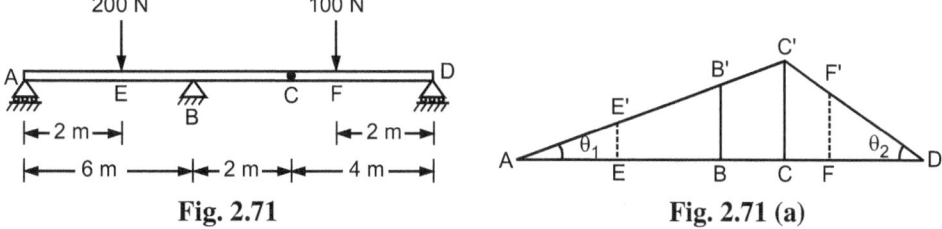

Fig. 2.71   Fig. 2.71 (a)

Solution :

Let a virtual displacement at hinge C is given in the upward direction, such that both supported A and D are intact as shown in Fig. 2.71 (a).

Let us assume virtual displacement C. Beam AC rotate by angular displacement θ_1 and beam BC by θ_2, and reactions at B and C be R_B and R_C.

From $\triangle$ ACC', $\quad$ CC' = AC·θ_1 = 8θ_1
and from $\triangle$ DCC', $\quad$ CC' = DC·θ_2 = 4θ_2
$\therefore \quad 8\theta_1 = 4\theta_2$ or $\theta_2 = 2\theta_1$

Consider part CD, reaction at C for part CD is acting vertically upward for maintaining condition of equilibrium.

Virtual displacement, $\quad$ FF' = DF·θ_2 = 2θ_2
Virtual work done by reaction R_D = $R_D \times 0$ = 0
Virtual work done by reaction,
$$R_C = R_C \times CC'$$
or $\quad R_C = 4 R_C \cdot \theta_2$

Virtual work done by load = $-100 \times$ FF' = $-100 \times 2\theta_2$ = $-200\, \theta_2$

(Virtual work will be $-$ve, as load is acting downward and displacement is in upward direction.)

Using principle of virtual work i.e. sum of total work should be zero.
$$4R_C\, \theta_2 - 200\, \theta_2 = 0$$
or $\quad R_C = 50$ N $\hfill$ ... Ans.

Now consider part AC, the reaction at C is acting downward.

Virtual displacements, BB' = AB·θ_1 = 6θ_1 and EE' = AE·θ_1 = 2θ_1

Virtual work by reaction R_A = $R_A \times 0$ = 0
Virtual work by reaction R_B = $R_B \cdot$ BB$_1$ = 6$R_B \cdot \theta_1$
Virtual work by reaction R_C = $R_C \times$ CC' = $-8R_C\, \theta_1$ $\quad$ ($\because$ CC' = 8θ_1)
Virtual work by load 200 N = -200 EE' = $-400\, \theta_1$ $\quad$ ($\because$ EE' = 2θ_1)

Using principle of virtual work, total work should be zero.
$$6R_B\, \theta_1 - 8R_C\, \theta_1 - 400\, \theta_1 = 0$$
Substitute $R_C = 50$ $\quad \therefore \quad R_B = 133.33$ N $\hfill$ ... Ans.

We can also solve by considering whole beam. As the beams AC and CD are supported on rollers at A and D, the virtual work done by reaction at these supports would be zero. (In this case, work done by internal hinge is zero.)

Virtual work by reaction R_B = $R_B \cdot$ BB' = 6$R_B\, \theta_1$
Virtual work by load 200 N = $-200 \times$ EE' = $-400\, \theta_1$ $\quad$ ($\because$ EE' = 2θ_1)
Virtual work by load 100 N = $-100 \times$ FF' = $-200\, \theta_2$ $\quad$ ($\because$ FF' = 2θ_2)

By using principle of virtual work, sum of work = 0
$$6R_B\, \theta_1 - 400\, \theta_1 - 200\, \theta_2 = 0$$
or $\quad 6R_B\, \theta_1 = 800\, \theta_1$
Solving ($\theta_2 = 2\theta_1$), we get, $\quad R_B = 133.33$ N $\hfill$ ... Ans.

Example 2.43 :

By using principle of virtual work, calculate the reaction at C and D of compound beam, supported and loaded as shown in Fig. 2.72.

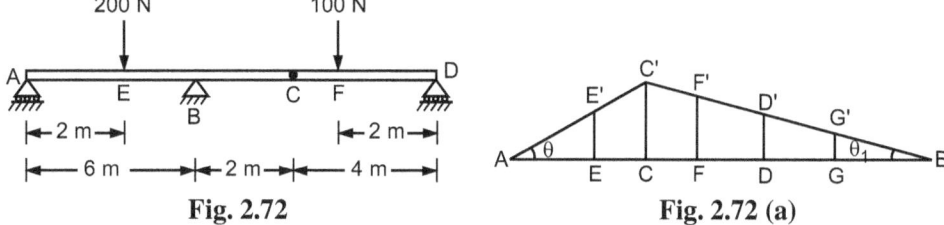

Fig. 2.72   Fig. 2.72 (a)

Solution :

Let us assume θ and θ_1 be the virtual angular displacements of beams AC and BC respectively.

From $\triangle$ ACC' and $\triangle$ BCC',

$$CC' = AC \cdot \theta = BC \cdot \theta_1$$

$$4\theta = 7\theta_1 \quad \text{or} \quad \theta = \frac{7}{4}\theta_1$$

Virtual displacements, $EE' = 1.5\,\theta$ $FF' = 6\,\theta_1$

$DD' = 5\,\theta_1$ $GG' = 3\,\theta_1$

Now consider beam AC, for equilibrium of beam, reaction at C must act vertically upward.

Virtual work by reaction $R_C = R_C \times CC' = 4R_C\,\theta$

Virtual work by load 60 kN $= -60 \times EE' = 90\,\theta$

Using principle of virtual work, $\Sigma W = 0$

$$4R_C\,\theta - 90\,\theta = 0 \quad \text{or} \quad R_C = 22.5\,N$$

Now, consider whole beam.

Virtual work by reaction D $= R_D \times DD' = 5R_D\,\theta_1$

Virtual work by load 50 kN $= -50 \times FF' = -300\,\theta_1$

Virtual work by U.D.L. $= -40 \times \frac{1}{2} \times 3 \times GG' = -180\,\theta_1$

Virtual work by load 60 kN $= -60 \times EE' = -90\,\theta$

or $\qquad = -90 \times \frac{7}{4}\theta_1 = -157.5\,\theta_1 \quad \left(\because \theta = \frac{7}{4}\theta_1\right)$

Using principle of virtual work, $\Sigma W = 0$

$5R_D\,\theta_1 - 300\,\theta_1 - 180\,\theta_1 - 157.5\,\theta_1 = 0$

$5R_D\,\theta_1 = 637.5\,\theta_1 \quad \text{or} \quad R_D = 127.5\,N$ ... **Ans.**

(Reaction at D may also be found by taking beam BC.)

Example 2.44 :

Find the moment and vertical reaction at fixed end of the beam shown in Fig. 2.73, by virtual work method.

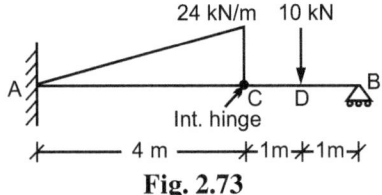

Fig. 2.73

Solution :

Consider CB portion of the beam, let Δ_C be the virtual displacement at C,

if $\Delta_C = \Delta$, then $\Delta_D = \dfrac{\Delta}{2}$

Using principle of virtual work
$$\sum W = 0$$

$$R_C \cdot \Delta - 10 \cdot \dfrac{\Delta}{2} = 0$$

$\therefore \quad R_C = 5 \text{ kN } (\uparrow)$ ... **Ans.**

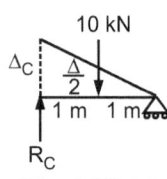

Fig. 2.73 (a)

Equivalent point load of given U.V.L.

$= \dfrac{1}{2} \times 24 \times 4 = 48 \text{ kN}$,

acting at a distance $\dfrac{2}{3} \times 4 = 2.67$ m from A

Now, consider the portion AC, if Δ_A be the virtual displacement at A.

From similar triangle, displacement under equivalent point load,

$$\Delta = \dfrac{\Delta_A}{4} \times 1.33$$

$$\Delta = \dfrac{\Delta_A}{3}$$

and rotation of portion,

$$\theta_C = \dfrac{\Delta_A}{4}$$

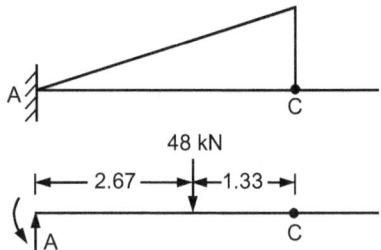

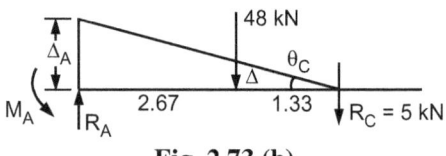

Fig. 2.73 (b)

Using principle of virtual work,

$$R_A \times \Delta_A - M_A \times \theta_C - 48 \times \dfrac{\Delta_A}{3} = 0$$

$$R_A \times \Delta_A - M_A \times \dfrac{\Delta_A}{4} - 48 \times \dfrac{\Delta_A}{3} = 0$$

$$M_A = 4 R_A - 64 \qquad \qquad \text{... (i)}$$

Now consider virtual displacement Δ at C.
Then virtual displacement under equivalent point load = $\frac{2}{3} \times \Delta$ and $\theta_A = \frac{\Delta}{4}$

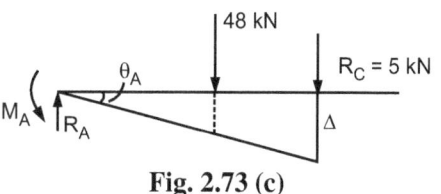

Fig. 2.73 (c)

Using principle of virtual work,
$$-M_A \theta_A + 48 \times \frac{2}{3} \Delta + 5 \cdot \Delta = 0$$
$$M_A = 148 \text{ kN-m } (\circlearrowleft) \quad \ldots \text{ Ans.}$$
Substituting in equation (i),
$$R_A = 53 \text{ kN } (\uparrow) \quad \ldots \text{ Ans.}$$

Example 2.45 :
Using the principle of virtual work, find the reaction R_D for the system shown in Fig. 2.74.

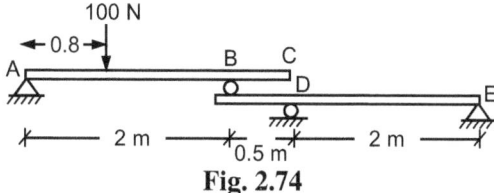

Fig. 2.74

Solution :
Consider upper beam ABC.
Let Δ_B be the virtual displacement at 'B'.
Virtual displacement at point load
$$\Delta = \frac{\Delta}{2} \times 0.8$$
$$= 0.4 \Delta_B$$

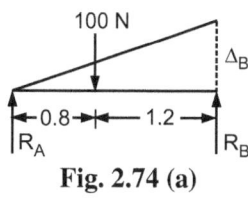

Fig. 2.74 (a)

Using principle of virtual work,
$$R_A \times 0 - 100 \times 0.4 \Delta_B + R_B \times \Delta_B = 0$$
$$R_B = 40 \text{ N}$$

Now, consider lower beam BDE, if Δ_B be the virtual displacement at B, then
$$\Delta_D = \frac{\Delta_B}{2.5} \times 2$$
$$\Delta_D = 0.8 \Delta_B$$

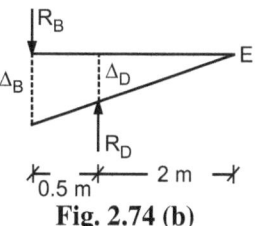

Fig. 2.74 (b)

Using principle of virtual work,
$$R_B \cdot \Delta_B - R_D \cdot \Delta_D = 0$$
$$40 \cdot \Delta_B - 0.8 \Delta_D \cdot R_D = 0$$
$$\therefore \quad R_D = 50 \text{ N } (\uparrow) \quad \ldots \text{ Ans.}$$

Similarly, reaction at other support can be obtained.
$$R_A = 60 \text{ N } (\uparrow)$$
$$R_E = 10 \text{ N } (\downarrow)$$

Example 2.46 :

Using virtual work method, find support reactions at A and B for the beam system connected by an internal hinge at C as shown in Fig. 2.75.

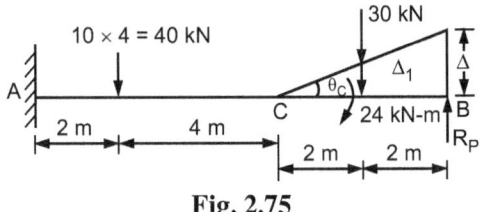

Fig. 2.75

Solution :

Equivalent point load of U.D.L. of 10 kN/m is $(10 \times 4) = 40$ kN, acting at a distance 2 m from A as shown in Fig. 2.75 (a).

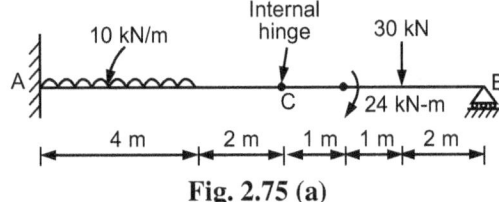

Fig. 2.75 (a)

Consider portion CB.

Let Δ be the upward virtual displacement at B, due to portion rotate anticlockwise (θ_C).

Using principle of virtual work,

$$R_B \cdot \Delta - 30 \times \Delta_1 - M \cdot \theta_C = 0$$

$$\therefore \quad R_B \cdot \Delta - 30 \cdot \frac{\Delta}{2} - 24 \frac{\Delta}{4} = 0 \qquad \left[\because \Delta_1 = \frac{\Delta}{2}, \ \theta_C = \frac{\Delta}{4}\right]$$

$$R_B = 21 \text{ kN } (\uparrow)$$

Now, consider Δ be the upward virtual displacement at A as shown in Fig. 2.75 (b).

$$\Delta_1 = \frac{4}{6} \Delta,$$

$$\Delta = 6 \, \theta_C.$$

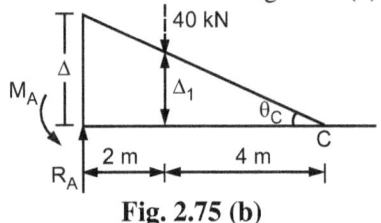

Fig. 2.75 (b)

Using principle of virtual work,

$$R_A \cdot \Delta - 40 \times \Delta_1 - M_A \cdot \theta_C$$

$$R_A \cdot \Delta - 40 \times \frac{4}{6} \Delta - M_A \cdot \frac{\Delta}{6} \qquad \ldots \text{(i)}$$

$$\therefore \qquad R_A = \frac{80}{3} + \frac{M_A}{6}$$

Now, consider whole beam with Δ be the vertical virtual displacement at internal hinge C as shown in Fig. 2.75 (c).

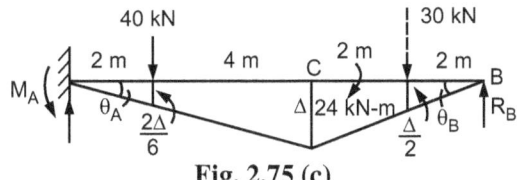

Fig. 2.75 (c)

$$\Delta = 6\theta_A = 4\theta_B$$

Using principle of virtual work,

$$-M_A \cdot \theta_A + 40 \cdot \frac{2\Delta}{6} + 30 \frac{\Delta}{2} - 24 \cdot \theta_B = 0$$

$$\therefore -M_A \cdot \frac{\Delta}{6} + 40 \cdot \frac{2\Delta}{6} + 30\frac{\Delta}{2} - 24 \cdot \frac{\Delta}{4} = 0$$

$$\therefore M_A = 134 \text{ kN-m } (\circlearrowleft)$$

Substituting the value of M_A in equation (i), we get,

$$R_A = \frac{80}{3} + \frac{134}{6} = 49 \text{ kN} (\uparrow) \qquad \ldots \text{ Ans.}$$

PROBLEMS FOR PRACTICE

Problem No. 1 : A bar AB is hinged at 'A' and supported by rod CD. Force of 5 N is acting on the bar AB as shown. Find tensile force T in rod CD and reaction R_A at A.

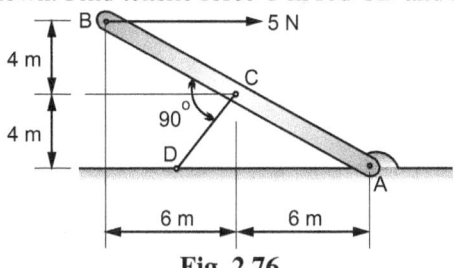

Fig. 2.76

Answer : T = 5.55 N, α = 67.43°, R_A = 5 N

Problem No. 2 : A bar AB of weight W = 2 N is hinged to the vertical wall at A and supported at B by a cable BC. Determine the magnitude and direction of the reaction R_A at the hinge A and tensile force T in the cable BC.

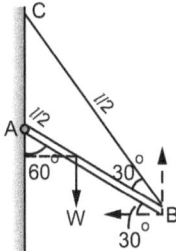

Fig. 2.77

Answer : T = 1.73 N.
Direction of reaction at hinge A = 30° with horizontal.
Magnitude of R_A = 1 N

Problem No. 3 : The boom supports two vertical loads F_1 and F_2. If cable CB can sustain a maximum load of 1500 N before it fails, determine the critical loads if $F_1 = 2 F_2$. What is the magnitude of maximum reaction at pin A ?

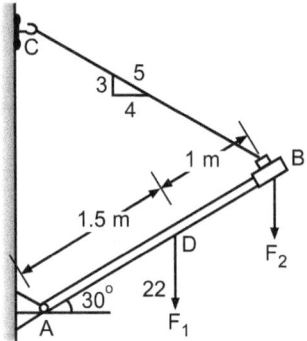

Fig. 2.78

Answer : $F_2 = 723.66$ N, $F_1 = 1447.32$ N

Problem No. 4 : The lever BCD is hinged at C and attached to the rod at B.
(i)   If P = 400 N, determine (a) tension in the rod AB, (b) reaction at C.
(ii) If maximum allowable reaction at C is 1000 N, determine the maximum force P which can be safely applied at D.

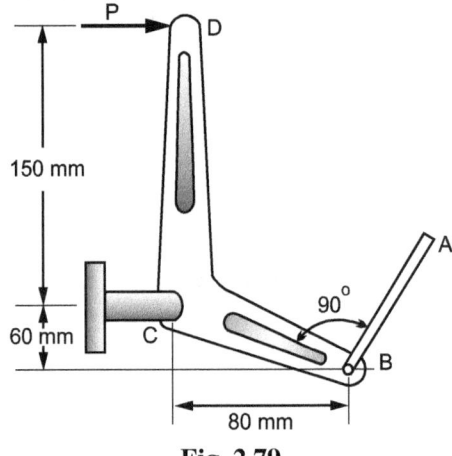

Fig. 2.79

Answer : (i) (a) $T_{AB} = 600$ N, (b) Reaction at C = 899 N, Direction of $R_C = \alpha = 32.27°$

(ii) Maximum force P = 445 N can be safely applied at D, if maximum allowable reaction at C is 1000 N.

Problem No. 5 : (i) Determine reaction at the fixed support C of the frame shown, if tension in the wire BD is 1300 N. (ii) Determine range of allowable values of tension in the wire if magnitude of couple at fixed support C does not exceed 100 Nm.

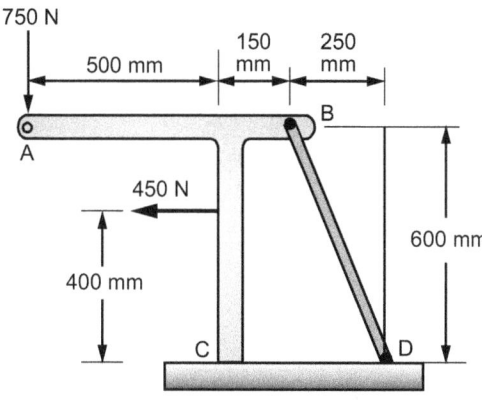

Fig. 2.80

Answer : (i) Reaction at C = R_C = 1950.64 N

(ii) Range of T = 655 N to 1232 N i.e. $655 \leq T \leq 1775$ N

Problem No. 6 : Bar AC supports two 400 N loads as shown. Rollers at A and C are again frictionless surfaces and cable BD is attached at B.
(a) Determine the tension in the cable BD.
(b) Reaction at A.
(c) Reaction at C.

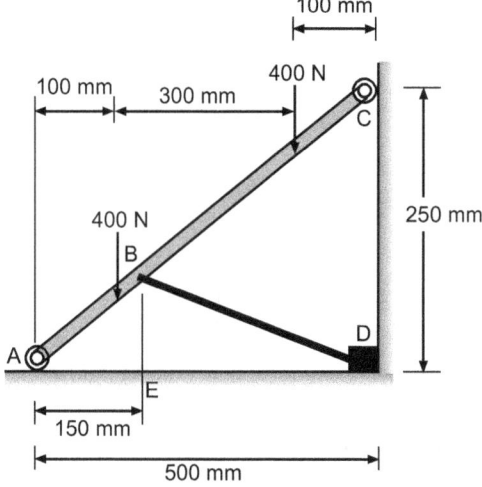

Fig. 2.81

Answer : (a) T = 1434.10 N, (b) R_A = 1101.16 N, (c) R_C = 1402.24 N

Problem No. 7 : For the frame and loading, determine the reactions at A and E when $\alpha = 30°$.

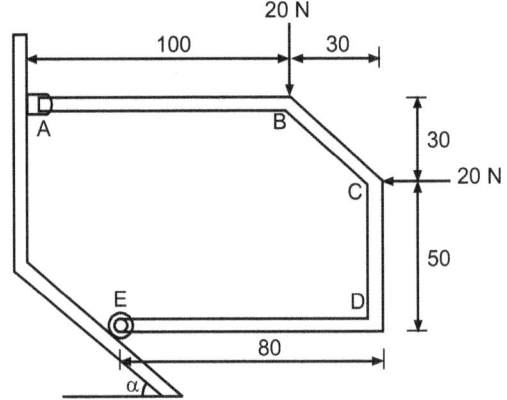

All dimensions in mm
Fig. 2.82

Answer : $R_E = 45.36$ N, $R_A = 19.48$ N,
Direction of $R_A = \theta = 82.1°$

Problem No. 8 : Rod AC is supported by a pin and bracket at A and rests against a peg at B. Determine the reactions at A and B.

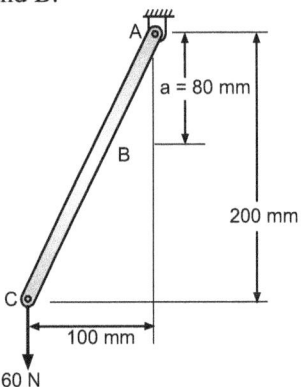

Fig. 2.83

Answer : Reaction at A, $R_A = 67.08$ N, Direction of R_A, $\alpha = 26.56°$
Reaction at B = R_B (Perpendicular to rod AC), Direction of R_B, $\alpha = 26.57°$

Problem No. 9 : Determine whether the block shown is in equilibrium and find the magnitude and direction of the friction force when $\theta = 35°$ and P = 200 N.

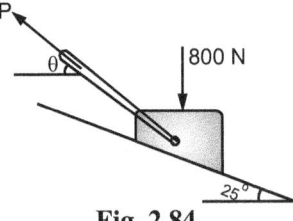

Fig. 2.84

Answer : $F_r = 141.13$ N and $F_m = 138.06$ N i.e. $F_r > F_m$ ∴ block is not in equilibrium. $F_{actual} = 103.55$ N

Problem No. 10 : Considering only value of θ less than 90°, determine the smallest value of θ required to start the block moving to the right when W = 100 N.

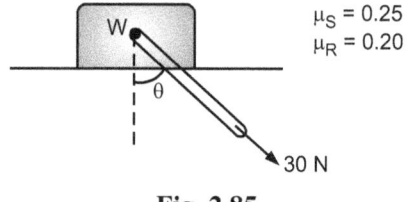

Fig. 2.85

Answer : θ = 67.73°

Problem No. 11 : A block of weight 1000 N rests on a horizontal surface and supports on top of it another block of weight 250 N as shown in Fig. 2.86. The upper block is attached to a vertical wall by an inclined string AB. Find the magnitude of the horizontal force P applied to the lower block as shown, that will be necessary to cause slipping to impend. The coefficient of static friction for all the surfaces is µ = 0.3.

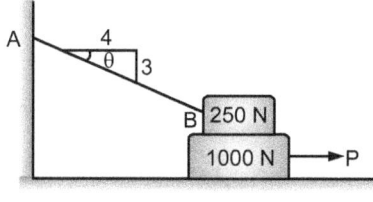

Fig. 2.86

Answer : P = 422.45 N

Problem No. 12 : What force 'P' is required to move the block A of weight 0.5 kN as shown in Fig. 2.87. If the coefficient of friction for all contact surfaces is 0.2, also calculate the tension in the cord OD.

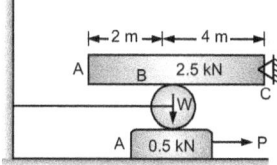

Fig. 2.87

Problem No. 13 : A 500 N cylinder shown in Fig. 2.88 is held at rest by a weight P suspended from a chord wrapped around the cylinder. If the slipping impends between cylinder and the incline, determine the value of P and the coefficient of friction. The diameter of the cylinder is 0.8 m.

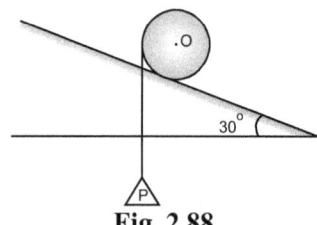

Fig. 2.88

Answer : P = 500 N and μ = 0.573

Problem No. 14 : Determine the necessary force P acting parallel to the plane to cause motion to impend. Assume coefficient of friction is 0.25 and pulley is smooth.

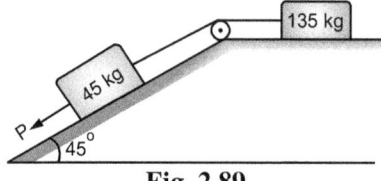

Fig. 2.89

Answer : P = 96.97 N

Problem No. 15 : Two bodies of weight W_1 and W_2 rest on a rough inclined plane and are connected by a short piece of string as shown in Fig. 2.90. If μ_1 = 0.2 and μ_2 = 0.3, find the angle of inclination of the plane for which the sliding will impend. Assume $W_1 = W_2$.

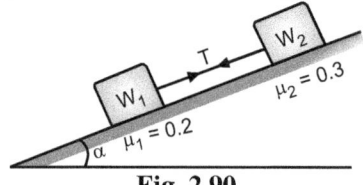

Fig. 2.90

Answer : α = 14.04°

Problem No. 16 : Two blocks connected by a horizontal link AB are supported on two rough planes as shown in Fig. 2.91. μ_s for block A = 0.40, ϕ_s for block B is 15°. What is the smallest weight W_A of the block A for which the equilibrium of the system can exist ?

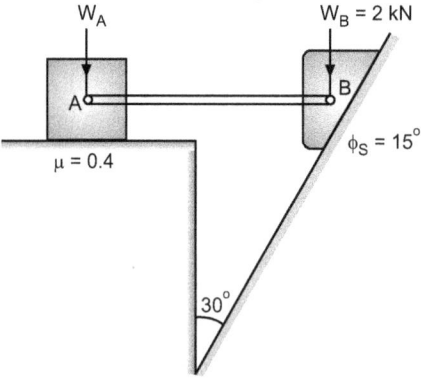

Fig. 2.91

Answer : W_A = 5.00 kN

Problem No. 17 : A rigid U-pin bracket ABC is hinged at B. Its end C rests on a 15° wedge as shown in Fig. 2.92. If the vertical load acting on the bracket at A is 500 N downwards, determine the minimum horizontal force P required to push the wedge to the left. Neglect the weight of the wedge and the bracket. Assume coefficient of friction at all surfaces of contact as 0.2.

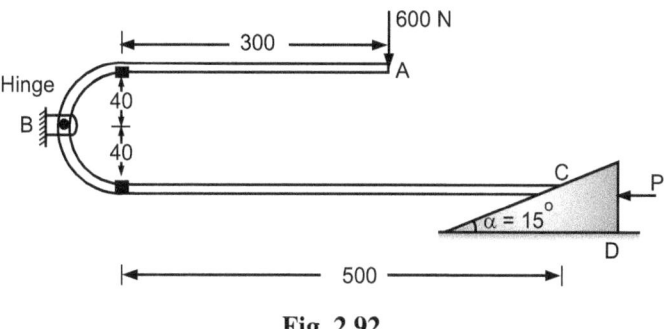

Fig. 2.92

Answer : $P_{min} = 217.19$ N

Problem No. 18 : Determine the horizontal force P needed to just moving the 300 N block up the plane. Take $\mu_s = 0.3$ and refer Fig. 2.93.

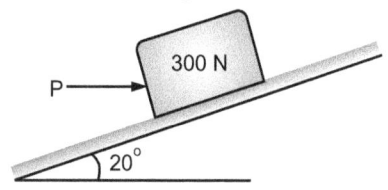

Fig. 2.93

Answer : P = 223.62 N

Problem No. 19 : Determine the reactions at support for the beam loaded and supported as shown in Fig. 2.94.

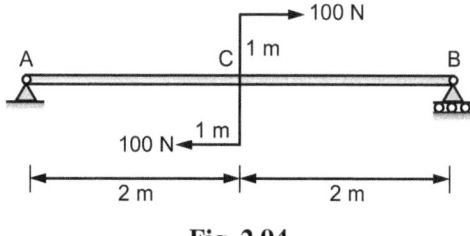

Fig. 2.94

Answer : $R_A = -50$ N, $R_B = 50$ N

Problem No. 20 : The rope BC will fail when the tension becomes 50 kN as shown in Fig. 2.95. Determine the greatest load P that can be applied to the beam at B and reaction at A for equilibrium.

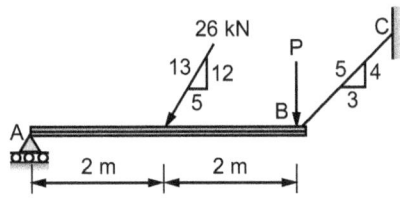

Fig. 2.95

Answer : T = 16.67 kN, P = 1.34 kN, R_A = 12 kN

CHAPTER THREE

ANALYSIS OF TRUSS

3.1 INTRODUCTION

In this chapter, we will study the analysis of any structure like truss, frame, cable.

Analysis is done based on the assumption that structure is in equilibrium. When the structure is in equilibrium, any part of the structure is also in equilibrium.

Hence, analysis includes application of equilibrium conditions i.e. $\sum F_x = 0$, $\sum F_y = 0$ and $\sum$ Moment at any point = 0 to determine unknown forces in the members of the structure.

3.2 TWO FORCE MEMBER

When a member is in equilibrium under only two forces, it is called as two force member. The two forces must be collinear, equal in magnitude and opposite in direction.

If two forces tend to elongate the member, then the forces are Tensile forces (T).

If two forces tend to compress the member, then the forces are Compressive forces (C).

3.3 TRUSS

A truss is a structure made up of several bars riveted or welded together only at their ends. Plane truss lies in a single plane. It is used to support roofs and bridges.

A truss is classified depending upon number of members required for stability. The following equation is used to determine number of members in the truss.

$$\boxed{n = 2j - 3}$$

where, n = number of members

j = number of joints.

1. Perfect Truss : A perfect truss is composed of minimum number of members required to keep it stable.

∴   n = 2j − 3

n = 3, j = 3

∴   n = 2j − 3

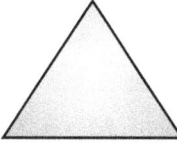

Fig. 3.1 (a)

2. Deficient Truss : A deficient truss is composed of number of members less than that required to keep the truss stable.

$\therefore$ $n < 2j - 3$
$n = 6$
$j = 5$
$n < 2j - 3$
$6 < 2(5) - 3$ i.e. 7

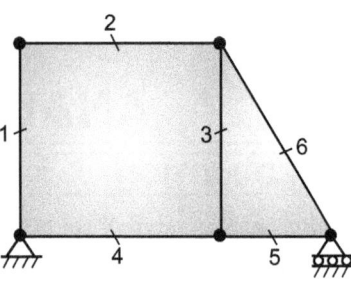

Fig. 3.1 (b)

3. Redundant Truss : A redundant truss is composed of number of members more than that required to keep the truss stable.

$n > 2j - 3$
$n = 6$
$j = 4$
$n > 2j - 3$
$6 > 2(4) - 3$ i.e. 5

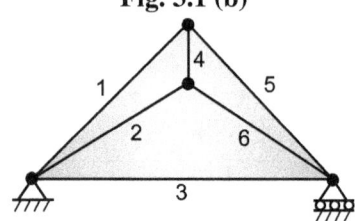

Fig. 3.1 (c)

3.3.1 Analysis of Truss

Analysis of truss includes determination of magnitude and direction of axial forces developed in members of truss due to loading. It also includes determination of magnitude and direction of support reactions of the truss.

The following assumptions are made for analysis as well as design of truss :

(1) A truss is a perfect truss.
(2) External loading is applied only at joints of the truss.
(3) Members of the truss are joined by pins.

Since loading is only at the joints, members of truss must be 'two force members' and forces must be axial forces acting at the ends of members, compressive or tensile. Refer Fig. 3.2 (a) and (b).

Since members are pin-jointed at ends, centre line of joining members are concurrent and hence axial forces in joining members are also concurrent forces.

When the whole truss is in equilibrium, any member or any part of truss or any joint of truss must be in equilibrium. Refer Fig. 3.2 (a) and (b).

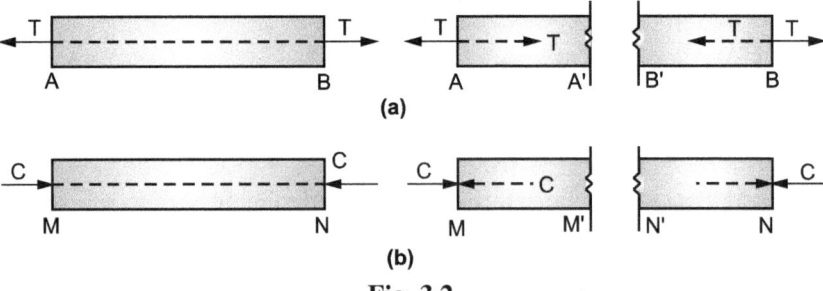

Fig. 3.2

Analysis of truss may be done by two methods :
(1) Method of joints.
(2) Method of sections.

Sign conventions used for truss analysis are as follows :

For forces

$$\rightarrow (+) \quad \uparrow (+) \quad \downarrow (-)$$
$$\leftarrow (-)$$

For moments

$$\circlearrowleft (+) \quad \circlearrowright (-)$$

1. Method of Joints

Since whole truss is in equilibrium, each joint of truss is also in equilibrium. Forces exerted at each joint are axial forces i.e. tension or compression. The conditions of equilibrium i.e. $\sum F_x = 0$ and $\sum F_y = 0$ are applied to each joint.

The joint having maximum two number of unknown forces can be selected initially for analysis as only two conditions of equilibrium are available. The result of analysis is represented in a tabular form.

Member	Force (Magnitude)	Nature of force (C/T)

Illustrative Example :

A truss ABC is supported by a roller at A and hinged at C. It is loaded by horizontal force 10 N. The lengths of members and directions are as shown in Fig. 3.3.

Let F_{AB}, F_{BC} and F_{AC} be axial forces in respective members.

Joint B has two unknown axial forces viz. F_{AB} and F_{BC}, it is selected initially for the analysis.

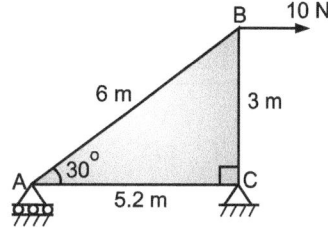

Fig. 3.3

F.B.D. of joint B is drawn as shown in Fig. 3.3 (a). F_{AB} and F_{BC} are assumed to be tensile forces (i.e. showing arrow away from the joint).

Applying conditions of equilibrium,

$$\sum F_x = 0 \left(\begin{array}{c} \rightarrow + \\ \leftarrow - \end{array} \right)$$

$$+ 10 - F_{AB} \sin 60° = 0$$

$$\therefore \quad F_{AB} = 11.55 \text{ N}$$

Force F_{AB} is a tensile axial force.

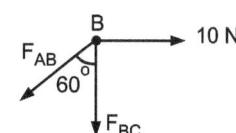

Fig. 3.3 (a) : F.B.D. of joint B

Since F_{AB} is positive, assumed direction is correct.
$$\Sigma F_y = 0 \quad (\uparrow +, \downarrow -)$$
$$-F_{BC} - F_{AB} \cos 60° = 0$$
$$\therefore \quad -F_{BC} - (11.55) \cos 60° = 0$$
$$\therefore \quad F_{BC} = -5.775 \text{ N}$$

Since F_{BC} is negative, assumed direction of force is incorrect. Force F_{BC} is a compressive axial force.

Consider joint A. At A, let A_y be the support reaction due to roller.

By inspection, it can be stated, to balance the effect of horizontal component of F_{AB} ($\rightarrow$), F_{AC} can be assumed as compressive force ($\leftarrow$).

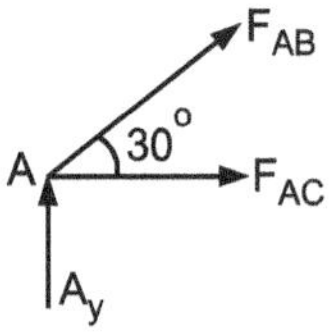

Applying conditions of equilibrium,
$$\Sigma F_x = 0$$
$$\therefore \quad +F_{AB} \cos 30° - F_{AC} = 0$$
$$\therefore \quad F_{AC} = 11.55 \cos 30° = 10 \text{ N}$$

Fig. 3.3 (b)

Since F_{AC} is positive, assumed direction is correct. F_{AC} is compressive force.
$$\Sigma F_y = 0$$
$$+F_{AB} \sin 30° + A_y = 0$$
$$\therefore \quad A_y = -F_{AB} \sin 30° = -11.55 \sin 30° = -5.77 \text{ N} = 5.77 \text{ N} (\downarrow)$$

Member	Magnitude of force	Nature of force
AB	11.55 N	Tension
BC	5.77 N	Compression
AC	10 N	Compression

2. Method of Section

Generally, method of section is used when axial forces of a few number of members are required.

A section is passed through members of truss (whose axial forces are to be found out). A truss is divided into two portions at cut section. The conditions of equilibrium are applied to either portion of the truss. i.e. $\Sigma F_x = 0$, $\Sigma F_y = 0$, $\Sigma M = 0$. F.B.D. of this portion includes external loads, support reaction (if present) and internal axial forces in cut members.

A section cutting maximum three number of members, is selected as only three conditions of equilibrium are available.

In both the methods of analysis, support reactions of truss are found out initially, if required.

Illustrative Example :

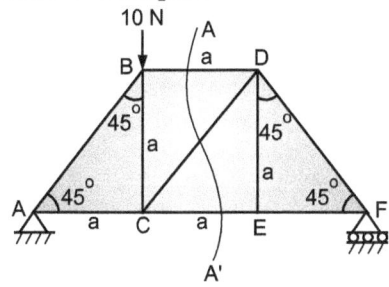

Fig. 3.4

A truss ABCDEF is supported by hinge at A and roller at F. It is loaded by 10 N at B. Length of members and their directions are as shown. Determine axial forces in members BD, CD and CE. Let F_{BD}, F_{CD} and F_{CE} be the axial forces in respective members.

Support reactions at hinge and roller are determined by applying conditions of equilibrium to the whole truss.

$\sum F_x = 0 \Rightarrow A_x = 0$, $\sum F_y = 0 \Rightarrow A_y + F_y = 10$, $\sum M_F = 0 \Rightarrow$
$A_y \times 3a - 10 \times 2a = 0 \Rightarrow A_y = 6.67$ N ($\uparrow$).

Let AA' be the section cutting three members, viz. BD, CD and CE.

Assume axial forces in three members be tensile.

Let us consider L.H.S. of cut section of truss.

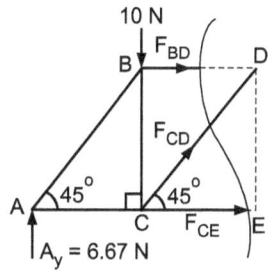

Fig. 3.4 (a)

Applying conditions of equilibrium to L.H.S. part of truss,

$\sum M$ at point D $= 0 \Rightarrow -F_{CE} \times a + 6.67 \times 2a - 10 \times a = 0$

∴ $F_{CE} = 3.34$ N

∴ $F_{CE} = 3.34$ N (Tensile)

$\sum M$ at point B $= 0 \Rightarrow a \times 6.67 + 23.34$ (a)
$= 0 \Rightarrow -10 \times a + A_y \times 2a$

$\sum M$ at point E $= 0$

$\sum M$ at C $= 0 \Rightarrow F_{BD} \times a + A_y \times a = 0 \Rightarrow F_{BD} = -A_y = -6.67$

∴ $F_{BD} = 6.67$ N (Compression)

$\sum M_{\text{at point B}} = 0 \Rightarrow A_y \times a - F_{CE} \times a - F_{CD} \cos 45° \times a = 0$

$\Rightarrow 6.67 - 3.34 - F_{CD} \cos 45° = 0$

$\Rightarrow F_{CD} = 4.71$ N (Tension)

Member	Magnitude of force	Nature of force
BD	6.67 N	Compression
CD	4.71 N	Tension
CE	3.34 N	Tension

3.3.2 Zero Force Members

The members having no axial force are called **zero force members**. These members do not support loading, but increase stability of truss during construction.

Analysis of truss is simplified, if zero force members are found by inspection initially. Generally, the following rules may be followed to find zero force members.

(1) If there are only two members at a joint without external load as well as support reaction, then the members are zero force members.

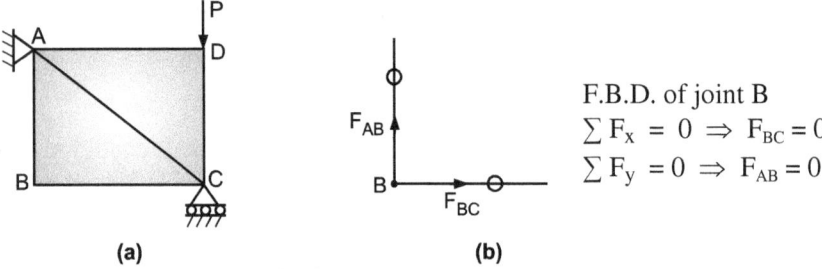

F.B.D. of joint B
$\sum F_x = 0 \Rightarrow F_{BC} = 0$
$\sum F_y = 0 \Rightarrow F_{AB} = 0$

(a)   (b)

Fig. 3.5

(2) If there are only three members at a joint without external load as well as support reaction and out of three members, two are collinear then third member is a zero force member.

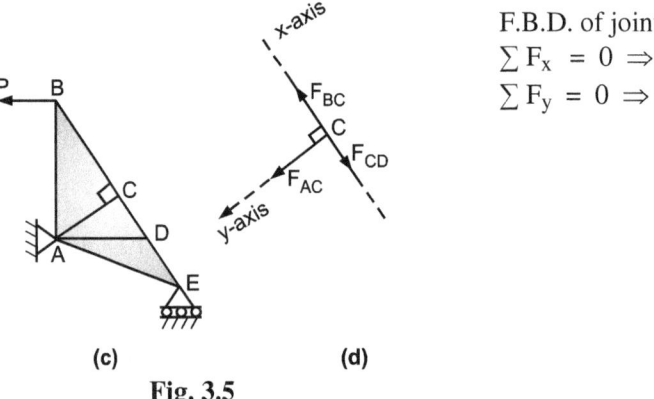

F.B.D. of joint C
$\sum F_x = 0 \Rightarrow F_{BC} = F_{CD}$
$\sum F_y = 0 \Rightarrow F_{AC} = 0$

(c)   (d)

Fig. 3.5

NUMERICAL EXAMPLES ON METHOD OF JOINT & METHOD OF SECTION

Example 3.1 :

Identify zero force members in the truss.

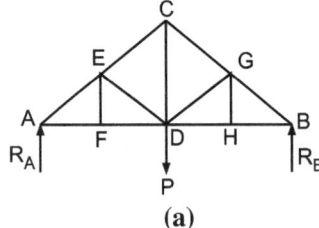   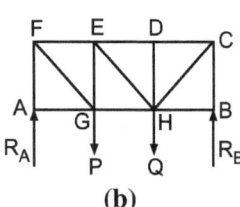

(a)   (b)

Fig. 3.6

Applied Mechanics — Analysis of Truss

Solution :

Zero force members : EF, ED, HG, GD.

Zero force members : BH, AG, DH.

Example 3.2 :

Determine magnitude and nature of axial forces in the members of given truss.

Fig. 3.7 **Fig. 3.7 (a)**

Solution :

Given data : Forces acting on the truss are :

10.8 kN at B and 10.8 kN at C acting vertically downward.

Dimensions are as shown in Fig. 3.7.

To find : Magnitude and nature of axial force in members AB, AD, BC, BD and CD.

(a) To find reactions at hinge and roller support i.e. R_A (A_x and A_y) and R_D :

Since truss is in equilibrium,

Applying conditions of equilibrium,

$\Sigma M_A = 0 \Rightarrow 10.8 + 22.5 + 10.8 \times 57.5 - R_D \times 22.5 = 0$

$\Rightarrow R_D = 38.4 \text{ kN } (\uparrow)$

$\Sigma F_y = 0 \Rightarrow A_y - 10.8 - 10.8 + R_D = 0$

$\Rightarrow A_y = -16.8 \text{ kN}$

$\Rightarrow A_y = 16.8 \text{ kN } (\downarrow)$

$\Sigma F_x = 0 \Rightarrow A_x = 0$

Reaction at hinge support = $R_A = 16.8 \text{ kN } (\downarrow)$

Reaction at roller support = $R_D = 38.4 \text{ kN } (\uparrow)$

(b) Joint A : Assumed directions of axial forces are as shown in Fig. 3.7 (b).

$\Sigma F_y = 0 \Rightarrow -A_y + F_{AD} \sin 28° = 0$

$\Rightarrow F_{AD} = 35.78 \text{ kN (C)}$

$\Sigma F_x = 0 \Rightarrow F_{AB} - F_{AD} \cos 28° = 0$

$\Rightarrow F_{AB} = 31.6 \text{ kN (T)}$

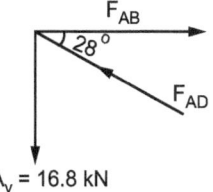

Fig. 3.7 (b) : Joint A

(c) Joint B : Assumed directions of axial forces are as shown in Fig. 3.7 (c).

$$\Sigma F_x = 0 \Rightarrow -F_{AB} + F_{BC} = 0$$
$$\Rightarrow F_{BC} = 31.6 \text{ kN (T)}$$
$$\Sigma F_y = 0 \Rightarrow -10.8 + F_{BD} = 0$$
$$\Rightarrow F_{BD} = 10.8 \text{ kN (C)}$$

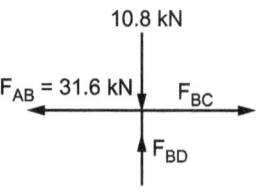

Fig. 3.7 (c) : Joint B

(d) Joint C : Assumed directions of axial forces are as shown in Fig. 3.7 (d).

$$\Sigma F_y = 0 \Rightarrow -10.8 + F_{CD} \sin 19° = 0$$
$$\Rightarrow F_{CD} = 33.17 \text{ kN (C)}$$

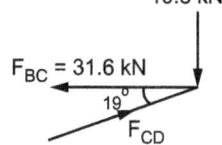

Fig. 3.7 (d) : Joint C

(e)

Sr. No.	Member	Force (kN)	Nature (C/T)
1	AB	31.6	T
2	AD	35.78	C
3	BC	31.6	T
4	BD	10.8	C
5	CD	33.17	C

Example 3.3 :

Determine magnitude and nature of axial forces in the members of given truss.

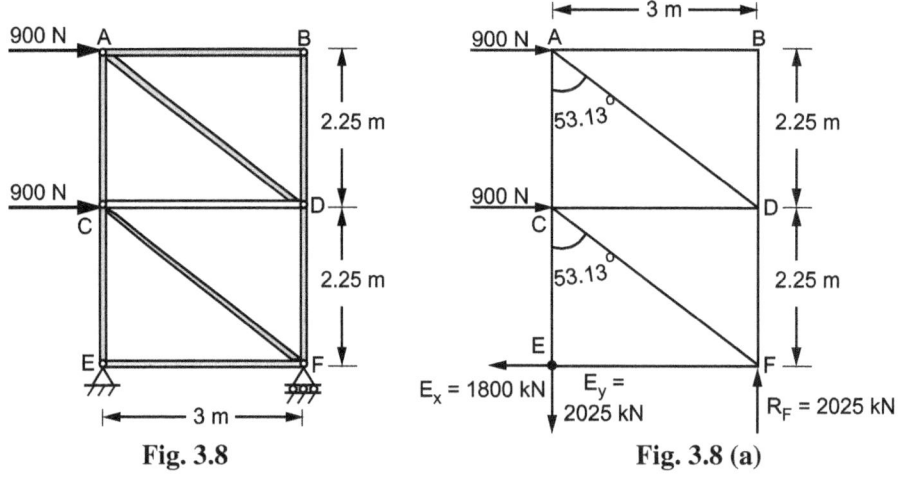

Fig. 3.8   Fig. 3.8 (a)

Solution :

Given data : Forces acting on the truss : 900 N each at A and C horizontally. Dimensions are as shown in Fig. 3.8.

To find : Magnitude and nature of axial forces in members AB, BD, AD, AC, CD, CE, CF, DF and EF.

(a) To find reactions at hinge and roller supports i.e. R_E (i.e. E_x and E_y) and R_F :

Since truss is in equilibrium, applying conditions of equilibrium,

$\Sigma M_E = 0 \Rightarrow 900 \times 2.25 + 900 \times 4.5 - R_F \times 3 = 0$

$\Rightarrow R_F = 2025 \text{ N } (\uparrow)$

$\Sigma F_y = 0 \Rightarrow -E_y + R_F = 0$

$\Rightarrow E_y = 2025 \text{ N } (\downarrow)$

$\Sigma F_x = 0 \Rightarrow -E_x + 900 + 900 = 0$

$\Rightarrow E_x = 1800 \text{ N } (\leftarrow)$

Reaction at hinge support = R_E = 2709 N

Reaction at roller support = R_F = 2025 kN ($\uparrow$)

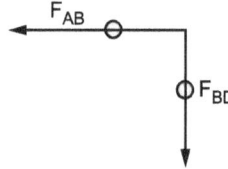

(b) Zero force members :

(i) Joint B :

$\Sigma F_x = 0 \Rightarrow F_{AB} = 0$

$\Sigma F_y = 0 \Rightarrow F_{BD} = 0$

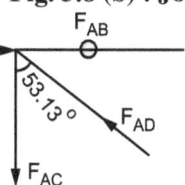

Fig. 3.8 (b) : Joint B

(c) Joint A : Assumed directions of axial forces are as shown in Fig. 3.8 (c).

$\Sigma F_x = 0 \Rightarrow 900 - F_{AD} \sin 53.13° = 0$

$\Rightarrow F_{AD} = 1125 \text{ N (C)}$

$\Sigma F_y = 0 \Rightarrow F_{AD} \cos 53.13° - F_{AC} = 0$

$\Rightarrow F_{AC} = 675 \text{ N (T)}$

Fig. 3.8 (c) : Joint A

(d) Joint E : Assumed directions of axial forces are as shown in Fig. 3.8 (d).

$\Sigma F_x = 0 \Rightarrow -E_x + F_{EF} = 0$

$\Rightarrow F_{EF} = 1800 \text{ N (T)}$

$\Sigma F_y = 0 \Rightarrow F_{EC} - E_y = 0$

$\Rightarrow F_{EC} = 2025 \text{ kN (T)}$

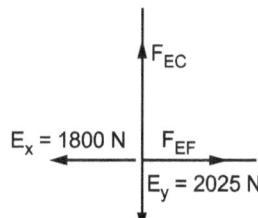

Fig. 3.8 (d) : Joint E

(e) Joint F : Assumed directions of axial forces are as shown in Fig. 3.8 (e).

$\Sigma F_x = 0 \Rightarrow -F_{EF} + F_{CF} \sin 53.13° = 0$

$\Rightarrow F_{CF} = 2250 \text{ N (C)}$

$\Sigma F_y = 0 \Rightarrow -F_{CF} \cos 53.13° + R_F - F_{FD} = 0$

$\Rightarrow F_{FD} = 700 \text{ N (C)}$

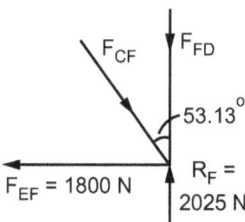

Fig. 3.8 (e) : Joint F

(f) Joint D : Assumed directions of axial forces are as shown in Fig. 3.8 (f).

$$\Sigma F_x = 0 \Rightarrow +F_{DA} \sin 53.13° + F_{DC} = 0$$
$$\Rightarrow F_{DC} = 900 \text{ N (T)}$$

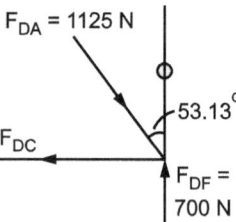

Fig. 3.8 (f) : Joint D

(g)

Sr. No.	Member	Force (N)	Nature (C/T)
1	AB	0	
2	DB	0	
3	AD	1125	C
4	AC	675	T
5	EF	1800	T
6	EC	2025	T
7	CF	2250	C
8	FD	700	C
9	DC	900	T

Example 3.4 :

Determine magnitude and nature of axial forces in the members of given truss.

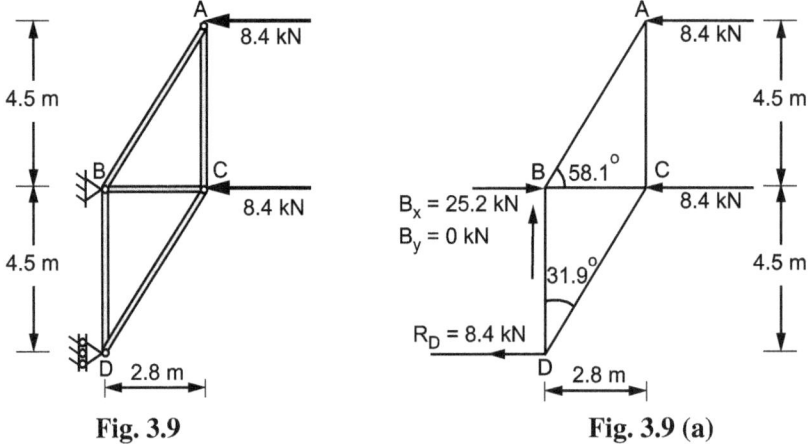

Fig. 3.9   Fig. 3.9 (a)

Solution :

Given data : Forces acting on the truss : 8.4 kN and 8.4 kN at A and C horizontally. Dimensions are as shown in Fig. 3.9 (a).

To find : Magnitude and nature of axial forces in members AC, AB, BC, CD, BD.

(a) To find reactions at hinge and roller supports i.e. R_B (B_x and B_y) and R_D :

Since truss is in equilibrium, applying conditions of equilibrium,

$\Sigma M_B = 0 \Rightarrow -8.4 \times 4.5 + R_D \times 4.5 = 0 \Rightarrow R_D = +8.4$ kN

$\Rightarrow R_D = 8.4$ kN ($\leftarrow$)

$\Sigma F_x = 0 \Rightarrow -8.4 - 8.4 - R_D + B_x$

$\Rightarrow B_x = 25.2$ kN ($\rightarrow$)

$\Sigma F_y = 0 \Rightarrow B_y = 0$

Reaction at hinge support = R_B = 25.23 kN ($\rightarrow$)

Reaction at roller support = R_D = 8.4 kN ($\leftarrow$)

(b) Joint A : Assumed directions of axial forces are as shown in Fig. 3.9 (b).

$\Sigma F_x = 0 \Rightarrow F_{AB} \sin 31.9° - 8.4 = 0$

$\Rightarrow F_{AB} = 15.9$ kN (C)

$\Sigma F_y = 0 \Rightarrow F_{AB} \cos 31.9° - F_{AC} = 0$

$\Rightarrow F_{AC} = 13.5$ kN (T)

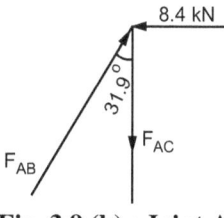

Fig. 3.9 (b) : Joint A

(c) Joint D : Assumed directions of axial forces are as shown in Fig. 3.9 (c).

$\Sigma F_x = 0 \Rightarrow -R_D + F_{DC} \sin 31.9° = 0$

$\Rightarrow F_{DC} = 15.9$ kN (T)

$\Sigma F_y = 0 \Rightarrow -F_{DB} + F_{DC} \cos 31.9° = 0$

$\Rightarrow F_{DB} = 13.50$ kN (C)

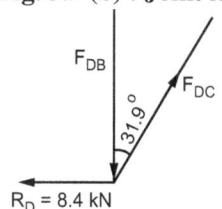

Fig. 3.9 (c) : Joint D

(d) Joint B : Assumed directions of axial forces are as shown in Fig. 3.9 (d).

$\Sigma F_x = 0 \Rightarrow +B_x - F_{AB} \sin 31.9° - F_{BC} = 0$

$\Rightarrow F_{BC} = 16.8$ kN (C)

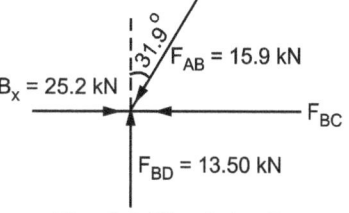

Fig. 3.9 (d) : Joint B

(e)

Sr. No.	Member	Force (kN)	Nature (C/T)
1	AB	15.9	C
2	AC	13.5	T
3	DC	15.9	T
4	DB	13.50	C
5	BC	16.8	C

Example 3.5 :

Determine the force in each member of the truss and state if the members are in tension or compression.

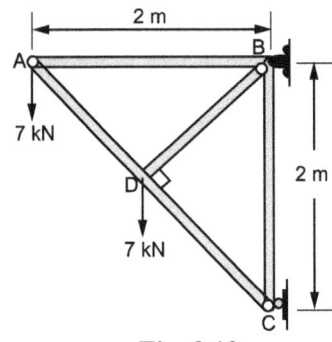

Fig. 3.10

Solution :

Given data : Forces acting on the truss : 7 kN each at A and D vertically downward. Dimensions are shown in Fig. 3.10.

To find : Magnitude and nature of axial forces in members AB, DB, BC, AD and DC.

(a) To find reactions at hinge and roller supports i.e. R_B (B_x and B_y) and R_C :

Since truss is in equilibrium, applying conditions of equilibrium,

$\Sigma M_B = 0 \Rightarrow -7 \times 2 - 7 \times 1 + R_C \times 2 = 0$

$\Rightarrow R_C = 10.5$ kN ($\leftarrow$)

$\Sigma F_x = 0 \Rightarrow -R_C + B_x = 0$

$\Rightarrow B_x = 10.5$ kN ($\rightarrow$)

$\Sigma F_y = 0 \Rightarrow -7 - 7 + B_y = 0$

$\Rightarrow B_y = 14$ kN ($\uparrow$)

Reaction at hinge support = R_B = 17.5 kN

Reaction at roller support = R_C = 10.5 kN ($\leftarrow$)

R_B = 17.5 kN

53.13°

Fig. 3.10 (a)

(b) From geometry :

Consider $\triangle$ ABC.

Since AB = BC $\therefore$ $\angle$ BAC = $\angle$ BCA = 45°

Consider $\triangle$ BDC.

$\angle$ DBC = $\angle$ DCB = 45°

Consider $\triangle$ ABD.

$\angle$ DBA = $\angle$ BAD = 45°

(c) Joint C : Assumed directions of axial forces are as shown in Fig. 3.10 (b).

$\Sigma F_x = 0 \Rightarrow F_{CD} \sin 45° - R_C = 0$

$\Rightarrow F_{CD} = 14.85$ kN (C)

$\Sigma F_y = 0 \Rightarrow F_{CB} - F_{CD} \cos 45° = 0$

$\Rightarrow F_{CB} = 10.5$ kN (T)

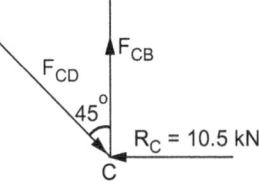

Fig. 3.10 (b) : Joint C

(d) Joint A : Assumed directions of axial forces are as shown in Fig. 3.10 (c).

$\Sigma F_y = 0 \Rightarrow -7 + F_{AD} \sin 60° = 0$

$\Rightarrow F_{AD} = 8.08$ kN (C)

$\Sigma F_x = 0 \Rightarrow F_{AB} - F_{AD} \cos 60° = 0$

$\Rightarrow F_{AB} = 4.04$ kN (T)

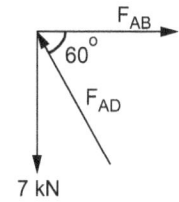

Fig. 3.10 (c) : Joint A

(e) Joint B : Assumed directions of axial forces are as shown in Fig. 3.10 (d).

$\Sigma F_y = 0 \Rightarrow +B_y - F_{BC} - F_{BD} \sin 45° = 0$

$\Rightarrow F_{BD} = 4.95$ kN (T)

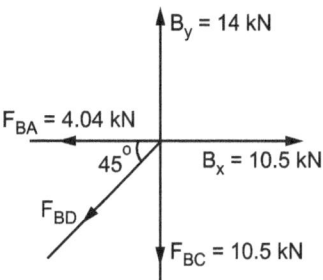

Fig. 3.10 (d) : Joint B

(f)

Sr. No.	Member	Force (kN)	Nature (C/T)
1	AB	4.04	T
2	AD	8.08	C
3	CD	14.85	C
4	CB	10.5	T
5	BD	4.95	T

Example 3.6 :

Determine the force in each member of the truss and state if the members are in tension or compression.

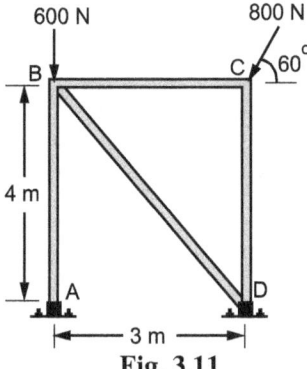

Fig. 3.11

Solution :

Given data : Forces acting on the truss :
600 N acting vertically downward.
800 N acting at 60° with horizontal.
Dimensions are as shown in Fig. 3.11.

To find : Magnitude and nature of force in members AB, BC, BD and CD.

(a) Joint C :

$\Sigma F_x = 0 \Rightarrow -800 \cos 60° + F_{CB} = 0$
$\Rightarrow F_{CB} = 400 \text{ N (C)}$
$\Sigma F_y = 0 \Rightarrow F_{CD} - 800 \sin 60° = 0$
$\Rightarrow F_{CD} = 692.82 \text{ N (C)}$

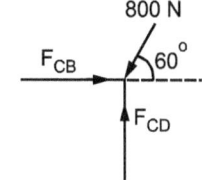

Fig. 3.11 (a) : Joint C

(b) Joint B :

$\Sigma F_x = 0 \Rightarrow -F_{BC} + F_{BD} \sin 36.87° = 0$
$\Rightarrow F_{BD} = 666.67 \text{ N (T)}$
$\Sigma F_y = 0 \Rightarrow -600 + F_{BA} - F_{BD} \cos 36.87° = 0$
$\Rightarrow F_{BA} = 1133.33 \text{ N (C)}$

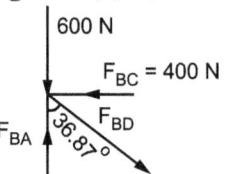

Fig. 3.11 (b) : Joint B

(c)

Sr. No.	Member	Force (N)	Nature (C/T)
1.	CB	400	C
2.	CD	692.82	C
3.	BD	666.67	T
4.	BA	1133.33	C

Example 3.7 :

Determine the force in members BC, CK and KJ and state if these members are in tension or compression.

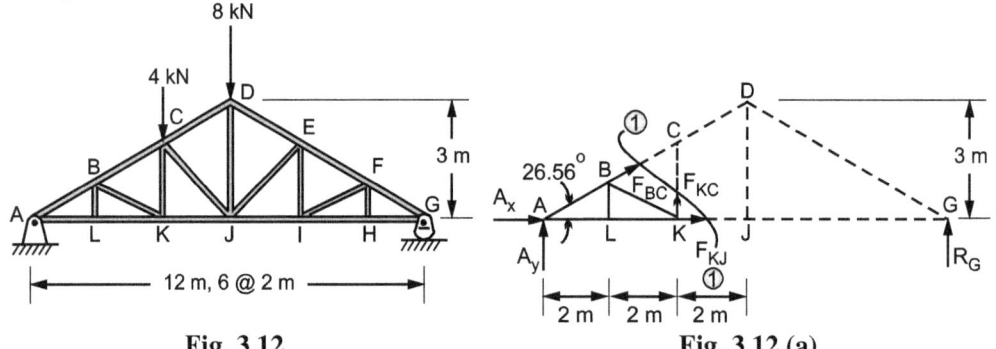

Fig. 3.12   Fig. 3.12 (a)

Solution :

Given data : Forces acting on the truss are as shown.
Dimensions are as shown in Fig. 3.12 (a).
To find : Forces in members BC, CK and KJ.

(a) To find support reaction :
Applying conditions of equilibrium,

$\Sigma M_A = 0 \Rightarrow 4 \times 4 + 8 \times 6 - R_G \times 12 = 0$
$\Rightarrow R_G = 5.33 \text{ kN } (\uparrow)$

$\Sigma F_y = 0 \Rightarrow A_y + R_G - 4 - 8 = 0$

$\Rightarrow A_y = 6.67 \text{ kN} (\uparrow)$

$\Sigma F_x = 0 \Rightarrow A_x = 0$

(b) Section 1-1 cuts the members BC, CK and KJ as shown in Fig. 3.12 (a).
Consider L.H.S. of truss.
Assume tension in members BC, CK and KJ.
Applying conditions of equilibrium to L.H.S. part of truss,

$\Sigma M_A = 0 \Rightarrow F_{CK} \times 4 = 0$

$\Rightarrow \mathbf{F_{CK} = 0}$ ... Ans.

$\Sigma F_y = 0 \Rightarrow F_{BC} \sin 26.56° + 6.67 = 0$

$\Rightarrow F_{BC} = -14.9 \text{ kN}$

$\Rightarrow \mathbf{F_{BC} = 14.9 \text{ kN (Compression)}}$ ... Ans.

$\Sigma F_x = 0 \Rightarrow F_{KJ} + F_{BC} \cos 26.56° = 0$

$\Rightarrow F_{KJ} + (-14.9) \cos 26.56° = 0$

$\Rightarrow \mathbf{F_{KJ} = 13.3 \text{ kN (Tension)}}$ ... Ans.

Example 3.8 :

Identify zero force members and find magnitude and nature of forces in remaining members of the truss as shown in Fig. 3.13.

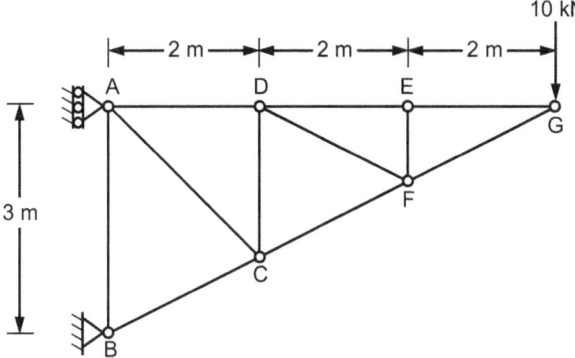

Fig. 3.13

Solution :

From geometry of truss $\angle AGB = \tan^{-1}\left(\dfrac{3}{6}\right) = 26.56°$

(a) Zero force members in the given truss are : EF, DE, CD, AC.

(b) Joint G.

$\Sigma F_y = -10 + F_{FG} \sin 26.56° = 0$

$\Rightarrow F_{FG} = 22.36 \text{ kN (C)}$

$\Sigma F_x = -F_{EG} + 22.36 \cos 26.36° = 0$

$\Rightarrow F_{EG} = 20.03 \text{ kN (T)}$

Fig. 3.13 (a)

(c) Joint E : $F_{ED} = E_{EG} = 20.03$ kN (T)
(d) Joint D : $F_{DE} = F_{DA} = 20.03$ kN (T)
(c) Joint F : $F_{FG} = F_{FC} = 22.36$ kN (C)
(d) Joint C : $F_{CB} = F_{CF} = 22.36$ kN (C)

At Joint A : Reaction at roller support is horizontal with magnitude 20.03 kN.

Hence, $F_{AB} = 0$

Sr. No.	Member	Force (kN)	Nature (C/T)
1.	AB, EF, DF, CD, AC	0	–
2.	ED, EG, DA	20.03	T
3.	FG, FC, CB	22.36	C

Example 3.9 :

Determine the force in each member of the truss and state if the members are in tension or compression. Assume L = 2 m and P = 10 kN.

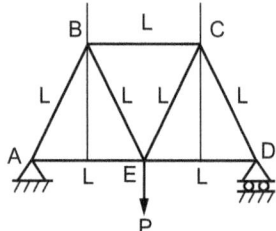

Fig. 3.14

Solution :

(a) **To find support reactions at A and D :**

$$R_A = 5 \text{ kN} \uparrow \qquad (\because A_x = 0)$$
$$R_D = 5 \text{ kN} \uparrow$$

(b) **Joint A :**

$$\Sigma F_y = +5 - F_{AB} \sin 60° = 0$$
$$\Rightarrow F_{AB} = 5.77 \text{ kN (C)}$$
$$\Sigma F_x = -F_{AE} - F_{AB} \cos 60° = 0$$
$$\Rightarrow F_{AE} = 2.885 \text{ kN (T)}$$

Fig. 3.14 (a)

Due to symmetry of truss,

$$F_{AB} = F_{CD} = \mathbf{5.77 \text{ kN (C)}} \qquad \text{... Ans.}$$
$$F_{AE} = F_{DE} = \mathbf{2.885 \text{ kN (T)}} \qquad \text{... Ans.}$$

(C) Joint B :

$\Sigma F_y = -F_{BE} \sin 60° + 5.77 \sin 60° = 0$
$\therefore F_{BE} = 5.77$ kN (T)
$\Sigma F_x = -F_{BC} + 5.77 \cos 60° + 5.77 \cos 60°$
$\therefore F_{BC} = \mathbf{5.77}$ **kN (C)** ... Ans.

Fig. 3.14 (b)

Due to symmetry, $F_{BE} = F_{CE} = \mathbf{5.77}$ **kN (T)** ... Ans.

Example 3.10 :

A plane truss is loaded and supported as shown in Fig. 3.15. Determine the magnitude and nature of forces in all the members.

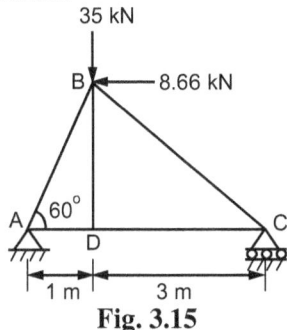

Fig. 3.15

Solution :

(a) To find support reactions at A and C : By applying conditions at equilibrium to the truss.

$\Sigma F_x = 0, \ \Sigma F_y = 0, \ \Sigma M_A = 0, \ A_x = 8.66$ kN ($\rightarrow$), $A_y = 30$ kN ($\uparrow$), $R_C = 5$ kN ($\uparrow$)

(b) Zero force member : BD ... Ans.

(c) Joint B :

$\Sigma F_x = -8.66 - F_{BC} \cos 30° + F_{BA} \cos 60° = 0$ ... (i)
$\Sigma F_y = -35 + F_{BA} \sin 60° + F_{BC} \sin 30° = 0$ ... (ii)

Fig. 3.15 (a)

From equations (i) and (ii),

$F_{BA} = \mathbf{34.64}$ **kN (C)** ... Ans.
$F_{BC} = \mathbf{10}$ **kN (C)** ... Ans.

(d) Joint A :

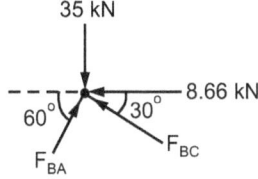

$\Sigma F_x = F_{AD} - 34.64 \cos 60°$
$\Rightarrow F_{AD} = \mathbf{17.32}$ **kN (T)** ... Ans.

Fig. 3.15 (b)

PROBLEMS FOR PRACTICE

Problem No. 1 : Determine the force in each member of the truss.

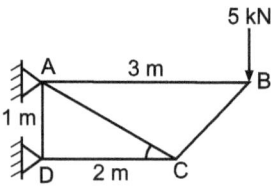

Fig. 3.16

Answer : F_{DC} = 15 kN (C), F_{AC} = 11.18 kN (T), F_{AB} = 5 kN (T), F_{BC} = 7.07 kN (C).

Problem No. 2 : Determine the force in each member of the truss.

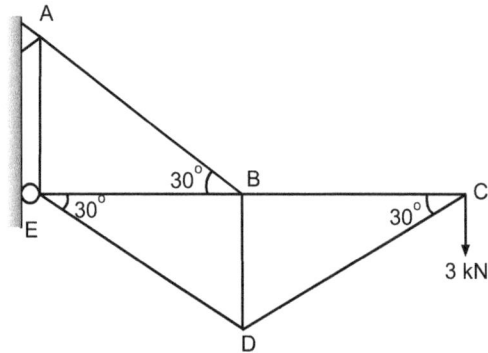

Fig. 3.17

Answer : F_{AB} = 12 kN (T), F_{AE} = 3 kN (C), F_{FD} = 6 kN (C), F_{EB} = 5.2 kN (C), F_{CD} = 6 kN (C), F_{CB} = 5.19 kN (T), F_{DB} = 6 kN (T).

Problem No. 3 : Calculate the force in each number of truss.

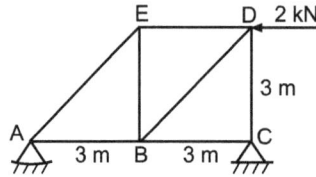

Fig. 3.18

Answer : (a) F_{AE} = 1.414 kN (C), F_{AB} = 1 kN (T); (b) F_{EB} = 1 kN (T)

(c) F_{CB} = 2 kN (T), F_{CD} = 1 kN (T); (d) F_{BD} = 1.414 kN (C)

Problem No. 4 : Determine the force in each member of the truss and state if the members are in tension or compression.

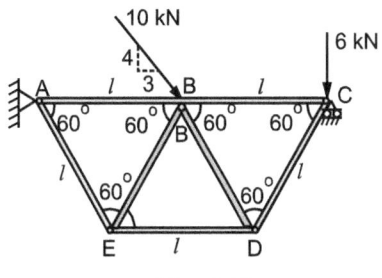

Fig. 3.19

Answer : (a) Reaction at hinge support, $R_A = 15.23$ kN

Reaction at roller support, $R_C = 10$ kN (↑), (b) $F_{AE} = 16.16$ kN (T), $F_{AB} = 2.08$ kN (C)

(c) $F_{CD} = 4.62$ kN (T), $F_{BC} = 2.31$ kN (C),

(d) $F_{EB} = 16.16$ kN (C), $F_{ED} = 16.16$ kN (T), (e) $F_{DB} = 4.62$ kN (C)

Problem No. 5 : Determine the force in each member of the truss. State if the members are in tension or compression.

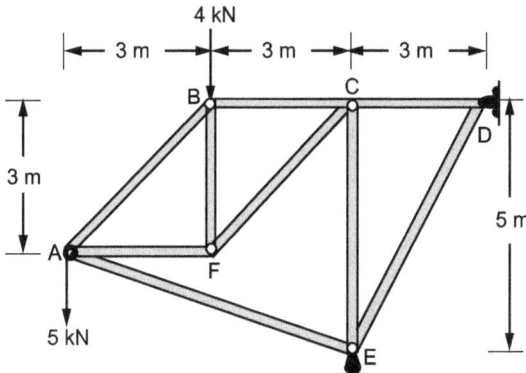

Fig. 3.20

Answer : (a) Reaction at hinge support D = $R_D = 14$ kN (↓)

Reaction at roller support E = $R_E = 23$ kN (↑),

(b) $F_{DE} = 16.33$ kN (C), $F_{CD} = 8.41$ kN (T), (c) $F_{AE} = 8.86$ kN (C), $F_{EC} = 6.20$ kN (C),

(d) $F_{CF} = 8.76$ kN (T), $F_{CB} = 2.21$ kN (T)

(e) $F_{BA} = 3.12$ kN (T), $F_{BF} = 6.20$ kN (C), (f) $F_{FA} = 6.19$ kN (T)

Problem No. 6 : Calculate axial forces in each bar of simple truss supported and loaded as shown. Triangle ACB is isosceles with 30° angles at A and B, and P = 5 kN.

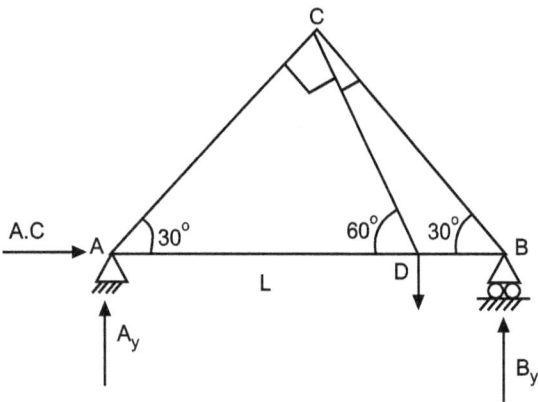

Fig. 3.21

Answer : (a) $\Sigma F_x = A_x = 0$, Reaction at hinge support $R_A = 1.67$ kN (↑),

(b) $F_{AC} = 3.34$ kN (C), $F_{AD} = 2.89$ kN (T), $F_{BC} = 6.66$ kN (C), $F_{BD} = 5.77$ kN (T), $F_{CD} = 5.77$ kN (T)

Problem No. 7 : Determine the forces in each member of the truss and state if member is in tension or compression. All the members are inclined at 45° with the horizontal.

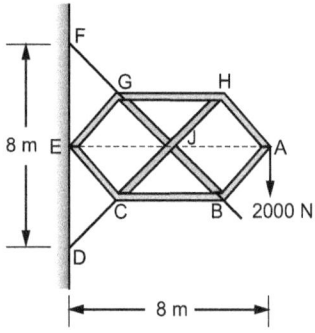

Fig. 3.22

Answer : (a) $F_{AB} = 1414.21$ N (C), $F_{AH} = 1414.21$ N (C), (b) $F_{GH} = 2000$ N (C),

$F_{HJ} = 1414.21$ N (C), (c) $F_{BJ} = 1414.21$ N (T), $F_{BC} = 2000$ N (C),

(d) $F_{CJ} = 1414.21$ N (C), $F_{GJ} = 1414.21$ N (T), (e) $F_{GE} = 1414.42$ N (C), $F_{GF} = 0$ N

(f) $F_{CE} = 1414.21$ N (C), $F_{CD} = 2828.42$ N (C)

Problem No. 8 : The maximum allowable tensile force in the member of the truss is 2 kN and the maximum allowable compressive force is 1.2 kN. Determine the maximum magnitude P of the two loads that can be applied to the truss.

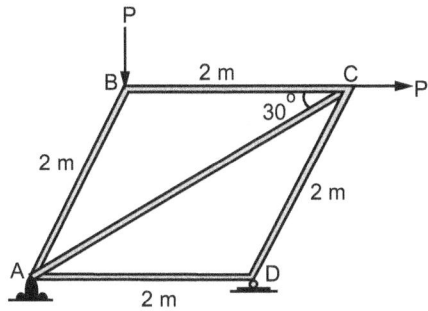

Fig. 3.23

Answer : Maximum magnitude of force P = 0.76 kN.

Problem No. 9 : Calculate the forces in members BC, BE and EF.

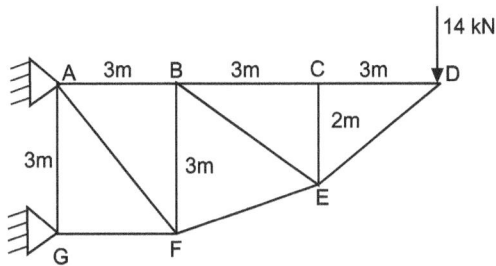

Fig. 3.24

Answer : F_{EF} = 29.53 kN (C), F_{BC} = 21 kN (T), F_{BE} = 8.43 kN (T)

Problem No. 10 : Calculate the forces in the members DF, DE and CE.

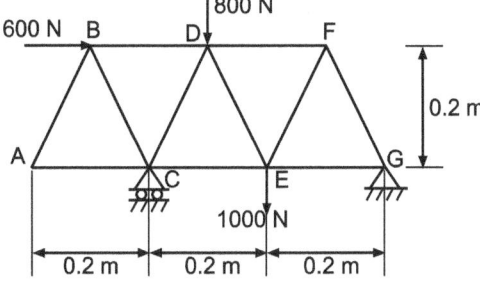

Fig. 3.25

Answer : F_{EC} = 400 N (T), F_{DF} = 1000 N (C), F_{ED} = 0.

Problem No. 11 : Calculate the forces in the members DF, DG, EG.

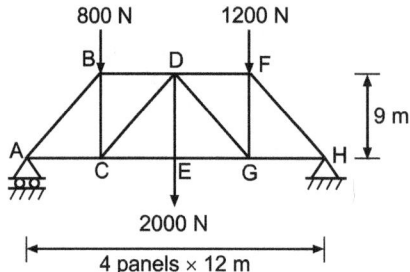

Fig. 3.26

Answer : $F_{EG} = 4000$ N (T), $F_{DF} = 2800$ N (C), $F_{DG} = 1500$ N (C)

SECTION-II

CHAPTER FOUR

CENTROID AND MOMENT OF INERTIA

CENTROID

4.1 INTRODUCTION

We all know that every particle of a rigid body is attracted by the earth towards its centre. The force of attraction which is proportional to the mass of the particle and acts vertically downward is called the **weight of the particle**. As we assume that the distance between the different particles of a body and the centre of the earth is the same (because of the very small size of the body compared with that of the earth), these weights may be taken to act along the parallel lines thus reducing the system to a system of parallel forces. We know that, a point may be found in the body through which the resultant of all such parallel forces acts. The point through which the whole weight of the body acts, whatever may be the position of the body, is called the **centre of gravity** of the body. It always lies in a plane of symmetry.

4.2 CENTRE OF GRAVITY

The centre of gravity can, therefore be defined as follows. "The centre of gravity of a body is the point at which the resultant gravitational force of the body acts, irrespective of and the orientation of the body". It is represented by C.G. or simply G.

As the C.G. of a body is the point at which the resultant of the gravity forces act. The problem of locating the C.G. reduces to finding the resultant of a system of parallel forces. So before attempting such a problem, we will first have to look to a concept known as "Centroid and its location" which is a two-dimensional problem and is much easier to solve. This also helps in the location of C.G. of solids.

4.3 CENTROID

The term centroid is analogous to the centre of gravity, while the centre of gravity refers to the point at which the resultant gravitational forces act, the centroid refers to a point (or outside) an area at which the whole area may be assumed to be concentrated.

Centroid is simply the centre of area of the body. The concept of centroid is very useful in many engineering problems. It also helps in locating the C.G. of bodies. The centroid of an area always lies on an axis of symmetry of area (if any).

4.4 CENTROIDS OF BASIC FIGURES

Table 4.1

Shape	Area	$\bar{x}$	$\bar{y}$
1. Line	$l = \sqrt{a^2 + b^2}$	$\dfrac{a}{2}$	$\dfrac{b}{2}$
2. Rectangle	$A = bd$	$\dfrac{b}{2}$	$\dfrac{d}{2}$
3. Isosceles triangle	$A = \dfrac{1}{2} bh$	$\dfrac{b}{2}$	$\dfrac{h}{3}$
4. Right angled triangle	$A = \dfrac{1}{2} bh$	$\dfrac{b}{3}$	$\dfrac{h}{3}$
5. Circle	$A = \pi r^2$	r	r
6. Semicircle	$A = \dfrac{\pi r^2}{2}$	r	$\dfrac{4r}{3\pi}$

7. Quarter circle	$A = \dfrac{\pi r^2}{4}$	$\dfrac{4r}{3\pi}$	$\dfrac{4r}{3\pi}$
8. Circular sector	$A = r^2 \alpha$	$\dfrac{2r \sin \alpha}{3\alpha}$	0
9. Semicircular arc :	$l = \pi r$	r	$\dfrac{2r}{\pi}$
10. Quarter circular arc :	$l = \dfrac{\pi r}{2}$	$\dfrac{2r}{\pi}$	$\dfrac{2r}{\pi}$
11. Segment of an arc :	$l = 2r\alpha$	$\dfrac{r \sin \alpha}{\alpha}$	0

NUMERICALS ON CENTROID

Example 4.1 :

Find the centroid of thin homogeneous wire ABCA as shown in Fig. 4.1.

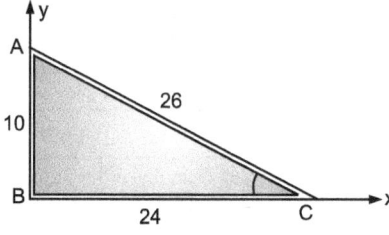

Fig. 4.1

Solution :

Given data : As shown in Fig. 4.1.
To find : Centroid of the thin wire.

Part	l	x̄	ȳ	lx̄	lȳ
AB	10	0	5	0	50
BC	24	12	0	288	0
AC	26	12	5	312	130
	Σl = 60			Σlx̄ = 600	Σlȳ = 180

$$\bar{x} = \frac{\Sigma l\bar{x}}{\Sigma l} = \frac{600}{60} = 10$$

$$\bar{y} = \frac{\Sigma l\bar{y}}{\Sigma l} = \frac{180}{60} = 3$$

∴ **Centroid = (10, 3)** ... **Ans.**

Example 4.2 :

A homogeneous wire AB is bent into the shape as shown in Fig. 4.2. Determine x co-ordinate of centroid.

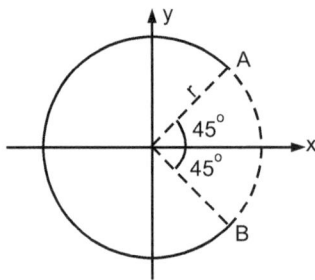

Fig. 4.2

Solution :

Given data : As shown in Fig. 4.2.
To find : x co-ordinate of centroid.

Since Fig. 4.2 is symmetrical with x-axis, therefore, ȳ = 0.

Sr. No.	l	x̄	lx̄
1.	2πr	0	0
2.	− 2r sin α = 1.57 r	$\frac{r \sin \alpha}{\alpha}$ = 0.9r	− 1.41 r²
	4.71 r		− 1.41 r²

$$\therefore \quad \bar{x} = \frac{\Sigma l\bar{x}}{\Sigma l} = \frac{-1.41 \, r^2}{4.71 \, r}$$

$$= -0.3 \, r$$

∴ **x co-ordinate of centroid is (− 0.3 r).** ... **Ans.**

Example 4.3 :

Locate the centroid of the shaded area with respect to the given axis.

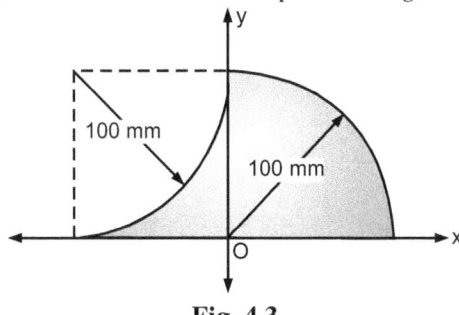

Fig. 4.3

Solution :

Given data : As shown in Fig. 4.3.
To find : Centroid of the shaded area.

Sr. No.	A	$\bar{x}$	$\bar{y}$	$A\bar{x}$	$A\bar{y}$
1.	$+\dfrac{\pi r^2}{4}$	$+\dfrac{4r}{3\pi}$	$+\dfrac{4r}{3\pi}$	$+0.3333\,r^3$	$+0.3333\,r^3$
2.	$+r^2$	$-\dfrac{r}{2}$	$+\dfrac{r}{2}$	$-0.5\,r^3$	$+0.5\,r^3$
3.	$-\dfrac{\pi r^2}{4}$	$-\left[r-\dfrac{4r}{3\pi}\right]$	$+\left[r-\dfrac{4r}{3\pi}\right]$	$+0.4515\,r^3$	$-0.4515\,r^3$
	$\Sigma A = (+r^2)$			$\Sigma A\bar{y} =$ $(+0.2848\,r^3)$	$\Sigma A\bar{x} =$ $(+0.3818\,r^3)$

$$\bar{x} = \frac{\Sigma A\bar{x}}{\Sigma A} = \frac{0.2848\,r^3}{r^2} = [0.2848\,r] = 28.48 \text{ mm}$$

$$\bar{y} = \frac{\Sigma A\bar{y}}{\Sigma A} = \frac{0.3818\,r^3}{r^2} = [0.3818\,r] = 38.18 \text{ mm}$$

∴ **Centroid = (28.48, 38.18)** ... Ans.

Example 4.4 :

A circular disc has a radius of 120 mm and portion above the line AB is removed. Locate the centroid of the remaining area.

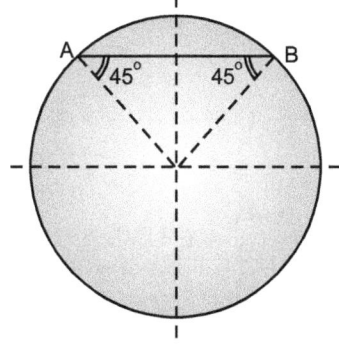

Fig. 4.4 (a)

Solution : **Given data :** Radius = 120 mm, as shown in Fig. 4.4 (a).
To find : Centroid.

(a) Area of quarter circle, $A = \dfrac{\pi r^2}{4} = 11309.4$ mm²

$$\bar{x} = \bar{y} = \dfrac{4r}{3\pi}$$

$(OP)^2 = (\bar{x})^2 + (\bar{y})^2$

$(OP)^2 = \left[\dfrac{4r}{3\pi}\right]^2 + \left[\dfrac{4r}{3\pi}\right]^2$

$(OP) = 72$ mm

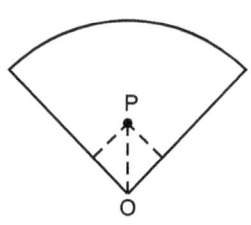

Fig. 4.4 (b)

(b) $\cos 45 = \dfrac{x_1}{r}$

$x_1 = 0.707\, r$

$AB = 2x_1 = (1.414)\, r$

Area of triangle $ABC = \dfrac{1}{2} \times$ base $\times$ height

$A = \dfrac{1}{2} \times (AB) \times (OQ)$

$A = \dfrac{1}{2} \times (1.414\, r)(0.707\, r)$

$A = 0.5\, r^2$

$A = 0.5 \times (120)^2$

$A = 7200$

$\bar{y} = \dfrac{2}{3} h$ from $O = \dfrac{2}{3}(0.707\, r) = (0.4713\, r) = 56.56$ mm

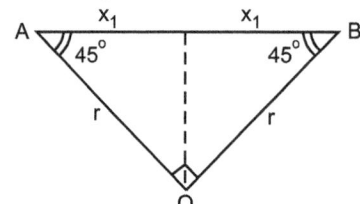

Fig. 4.4 (c)

Sr. No.	A	$\bar{x}$	$\bar{y}$	$A\bar{x}$	$A\bar{y}$
1.	$(\pi r^2) = 45237.6$	0	0	0	0
2.	$\left(-\dfrac{\pi r^2}{4}\right) = (-11309.4)$	0	72	0	– 814276.8
3.	$\left(\dfrac{1}{2} bh\right) = (7200)$	0	56.56	0	+ 407232
	$\Sigma A = +41128.2$				$\Sigma A\bar{y} = - 407044.8$

$$\therefore \quad \bar{y} = \frac{\Sigma A \bar{y}}{\Sigma A} = \frac{-407044.8}{+41128.2} = -9.897 \text{ mm}$$

$$\therefore \quad \text{Centroid} = (0, -9.897) \quad \text{... Ans.}$$

∴ **The centroid lies on y-axis at a distance of (9.897) mm below the original centre.**
... Ans.

Example 4.5 :

A slender homogeneous wire is bent into shape shown in Fig. 4.5 (a) and suspended from point A. Find the angle which the neck of the hook makes with vertical.

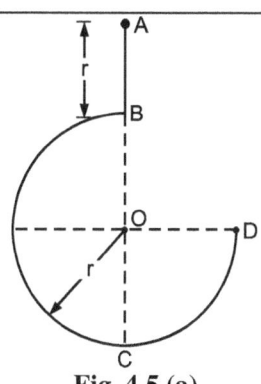

Fig. 4.5 (a)

Solution :

Given data : As shown in Fig. 4.5 (a).
To find : Angle of neck (θ).

Sr. No.	l	$\bar{x}$	$\bar{y}$	$l\bar{x}$	$l\bar{y}$
1.	r	0	$\left(r + \dfrac{r}{2}\right)$	0	$+1.5\, r^2$
2.	πr	$-\dfrac{2r}{\pi}$	0	$-2r^2$	0
3.	$\dfrac{\pi r}{2}$	$+\dfrac{2r}{\pi}$	$-\dfrac{2r}{\pi}$	$+r^2$	$-r^2$
	$\Sigma l = 5.71\, r$			$\Sigma l\bar{x} = (-r^2)$	$\Sigma l\bar{y} = +0.5\, r^2$

$$\bar{x} = \frac{\Sigma l \bar{x}}{\Sigma l} = \frac{-r^2}{5.71\, r} = (-0.175\, r)$$

$$\bar{y} = \frac{\Sigma l \bar{y}}{\Sigma l} = \frac{+0.5\, r^2}{5.71\, r} = (+0.0875\, r)$$

$$\tan \theta = \frac{\bar{x}}{(2r - \bar{y})}$$

$$\tan \theta = \frac{0.175\, r}{(2r - 0.0875\, r)}$$

$$\tan \theta = 0.915$$

$$\boldsymbol{\theta = 5.23°} \quad \text{... Ans.}$$

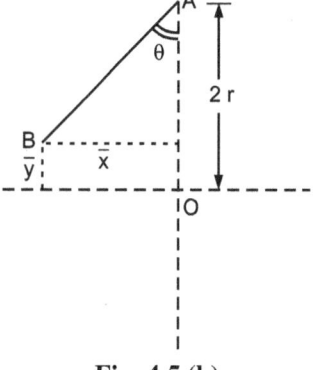

Fig. 4.5 (b)

Example 4.6 :

Locate the centroid of the shaded area.

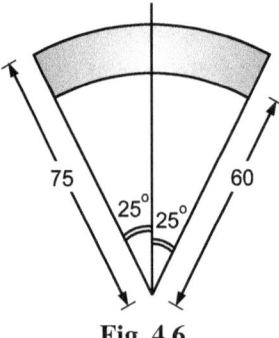

Fig. 4.6

Solution :

Given data : As shown in Fig. 4.6.

To find : Centroid of shaded area.

(a) $\quad A_1 = r^2 \alpha = (75)^2 \times (0.436) = 2454.37$

$$y_1 = \frac{2r \sin \alpha}{3\alpha} = \frac{2 \times 75 \times \sin 25}{3 \times (0.436)} = 48.465$$

(b) $\quad A_2 = r^2 \alpha = (60)^2 \times (0.436) = 1569.6$

$$y_2 = \frac{2r \sin \alpha}{3\alpha} = \frac{2 \times 60 \times \sin 25}{3 \times (0.436)} = 38.77$$

Now, $\quad \bar{y} = \dfrac{A_1 y_1 - A_2 y_2}{A_1 - A_2} = \dfrac{(2454.37)\,(48.465) - (1569.6)\,(38.77)}{(2454.37 - 1569.6)}$

$\bar{y} = 65.66 \qquad \therefore$ **Centroid = (0, 65.66)** ... **Ans.**

Example 4.7 :

Locate the centroid of the shaded lamina as shown in Fig. 4.7.

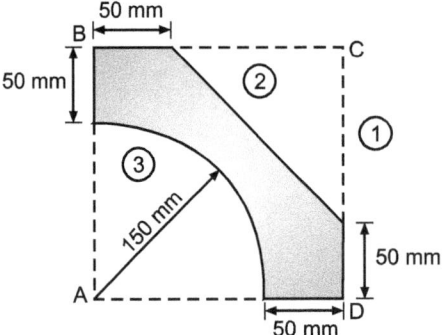

Fig. 4.7

Solution :

Given data : As shown in Fig. 4.7.
To find : Centroid of the shaded area.

Sr. No.	A	$\bar{x}$ (from A)	$\bar{y}$ (from A)	$A\bar{x}$	$A\bar{y}$
1.	200×200	100	100	4×10^6	4×10^6
2.	$-\dfrac{150 \times 150}{2}$	150	150	-1.69×10^6	-1.69×10^6
3.	$-\dfrac{1}{4}\left(\dfrac{\pi}{4} \times 300^2\right)$	$\dfrac{4 \times 150}{3\pi}$	$\dfrac{4 \times 150}{3\pi}$	-1.12×10^6	-1.12×10^6
	$\sum A = 11078.54$			$\sum A\bar{x} = 1.19 \times 10^6$	$\sum A\bar{y} = 1.19 \times 10^6$

$$\therefore \quad \bar{x} = \frac{\sum A \bar{x}}{\sum A} = \frac{1.19 \times 10^6}{11078.54} = 107.41 \text{ mm from A}$$

$$\bar{y} = \frac{\sum A \bar{y}}{\sum A} = \frac{1.19 \times 10^6}{11078.54} = 107.41 \text{ mm from A}.$$

$$\therefore \quad \textbf{Centroid = (107.41, 107.41)} \quad \ldots \textbf{Ans.}$$

Example 4.8 :

Locate centroid of the plate as shown in Fig. 4.8.

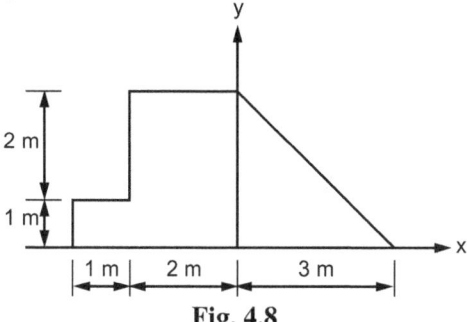

Fig. 4.8

Solution :

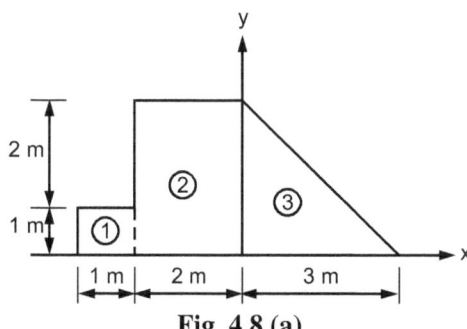

Fig. 4.8 (a)

Composite area is divided into 3 elementary shapes. Refer Fig. 4.8 (a).

Centroid locations of all these shapes are obtained.

Part	A (m²)	$\bar{x}$ (m)	$\bar{y}$ (m)	$\bar{x}$ A (m³)	$\bar{y}$ A (m³)
1	1	– 2.5	0.5	– 2.5	0.5
2	6	– 1	1.5	– 6	9.0
3	4.5	1	1	4.5	4.5
Total	11.5			– 4	14

Thus, $\bar{X} = \dfrac{\Sigma \bar{x} A}{\Sigma A} = \dfrac{-4}{11.5} = -0.3478$ m

$\bar{Y} = \dfrac{\Sigma \bar{y} A}{\Sigma A} = \dfrac{14}{11.5} = 1.2174$ m

Centroid = (**– 0.3478 m, 1.2174 m**) ... Ans.

Example 4.9 :

Determine the position of centroid of the shaded area as shown in Fig. 4.9 with respect to origin O.

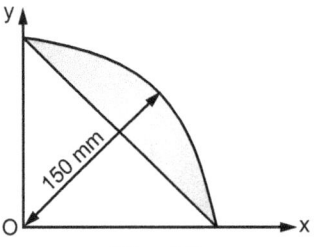

Fig. 4.9

Solution :

Composite area is divided into quarter circle and triangle. The area of triangle is indicated as negative, since it is to be subtracted from other area.

Part	A (mm²)	$\bar{x}$ (mm)	$\bar{y}$ (mm)	$\bar{x}$ A (mm³)	$\bar{y}$ A (mm³)
Quarter circle	$\dfrac{\pi r^2}{4} = 17671.46$	$\dfrac{4r}{3\pi} = 63.66$	$\dfrac{4r}{3\pi} = 63.66$	1125×10^3	1125×10^3
Triangle	– 11250	$\dfrac{150}{3} = 50$	$\dfrac{150}{3} = 50$	$- 562.5 \times 10^3$	$- 562.5 \times 10^3$
Total	6421.46			562.5×10^3	562.5×10^3

$\bar{X} = \dfrac{\Sigma \bar{x} A}{\Sigma A} = 87.59$ mm

$\bar{Y} = \bar{X} = 87.59$ mm

Centroid = (**87.59, 87.51**) ... Ans.

Example 4.10 :

Two quarter circular areas are removed from a rectangular plate AEFG as shown in Fig. 4.10. Locate the centroid of the remaining area.

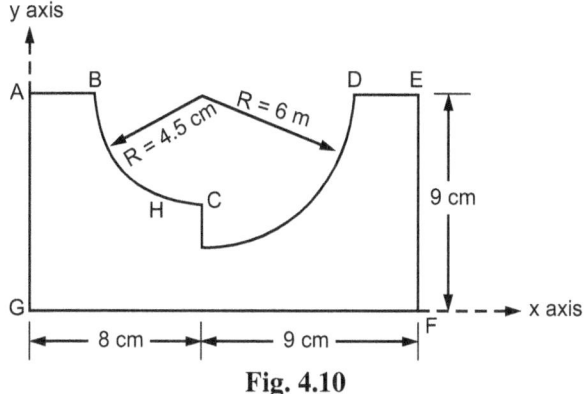

Fig. 4.10

Solution :

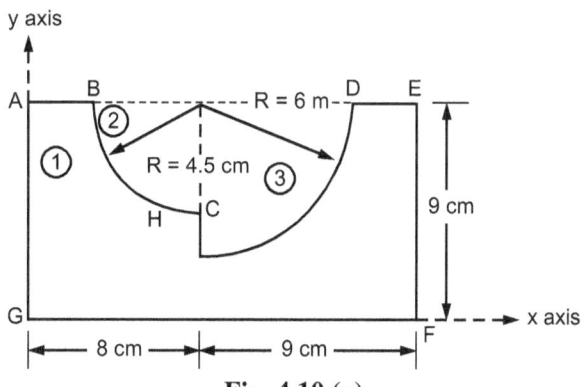

Fig. 4.10 (a)

Composite area is obtained by subtracting area of two quarter circles from rectangle. Origin is 'G'. Refer Fig. 4.34 (a).

Part	A (cm²)	$\bar{x}$ (cm)	$\bar{y}$ (cm)	$\bar{x}$A (cm³)	$\bar{y}$A (cm³)
Rectangle 1	9 × 17 = 153	8.5	4.5	1300.5	688.5
Quarter circle 2	$-\dfrac{\pi r^2}{4} = -15.90$	$8 - \dfrac{4r}{3\pi} = 6.091$	$9 - \dfrac{4r}{3\pi}$ $= 7.091$	− 96.8469	− 112.7469
Quarter circle 3	$-\dfrac{\pi r^2}{4}$ $= -28.2743$	$8 + \dfrac{4r}{3\pi}$ $= 10.546$	$9 - \dfrac{4r}{3\pi}$ $= 6.453$	− 298.180	− 182.454
Total	108.8257			905.4731	393.299

$$\bar{X} = \frac{\Sigma \bar{x} A}{\Sigma A} = 8.32 \text{ cm} \qquad \text{... Ans.}$$

$$\bar{Y} = \frac{\Sigma \bar{y} A}{\Sigma A} = 3.614 \text{ cm} \qquad \text{... Ans.}$$

Example 4.11 :

Determine the distance 'y' to the centroid of the trapezoidal area in terms of the dimensions shown in Fig. 4.11.

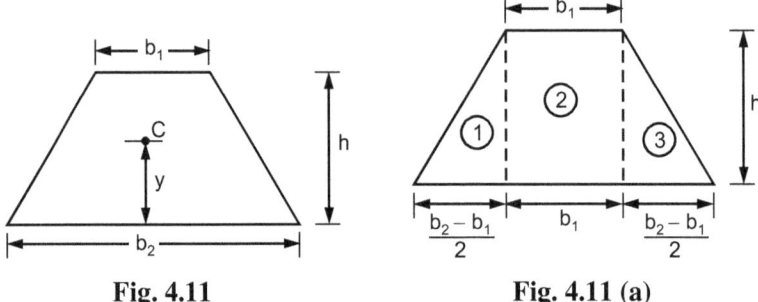

Fig. 4.11   **Fig. 4.11 (a)**

Solution :

Trapezoid area is divided into triangle and rectangle as shown in Fig. 4.11 (a).

Part	A (unit²)	$\bar{y}$ (unit)	$\bar{y}$ A (unit³)
1 and 3	$\dfrac{1}{2} \dfrac{(b_2 - b_1)}{2} h$	$\dfrac{1}{3} h$	$\dfrac{1}{12} h^2 \dfrac{(b_2 - b_1)}{2}$
2	$b_1 h$	$\dfrac{h}{2}$	$\dfrac{b_1 h^2}{2}$

$$\Sigma A = \left[\left(\frac{b_2 - b_1}{2}\right) h\right] + [b_1 h] = \frac{h}{2}(b_2 - b_1 + 2b_1) = \frac{h}{2}(b_2 + b_1)$$

$$\Sigma A \bar{y} = \left[\frac{2h^2}{12}(b_2 - b_1) + \frac{b_1 h^2}{2}\right] = \frac{h^2}{2}\left[\frac{b_2 - b_1}{3} + b_1\right] = \frac{h^2}{2}[b_2 + 2b_1]$$

$$\bar{Y} = \frac{\Sigma \bar{y} A}{\Sigma A} = \frac{\dfrac{h^2}{2}(b_2 + 2b_1)}{\dfrac{h}{2}(b_2 + b_1)}$$

$$\therefore \quad \bar{Y} = \frac{(b_2 + 2b_1)}{(b_2 + b_1)} h \qquad \text{... Ans.}$$

Example 4.12 :

Determine the position of centroid of the shaded area as shown in Fig. 4.12 w.r.t. origin O.

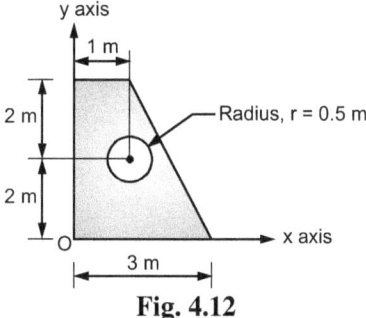

Fig. 4.12

Solution :

Composite area is divided into rectangle, triangle and circle. Area of circle is indicated as negative since it is to be subtracted from other area.

Part	A (m²)	$\bar{x}$ (m)	$\bar{y}$ (m)	$\bar{x}$ A (m²)	$\bar{y}$ A (m²)
Rectangle	$4 \times 1 = 4$	0.5	2	2	8
Triangle	$\frac{1}{2} \times 2 \times 4 = 4$	$1 + \frac{1}{3} \times 2$ = 1.667	$\frac{1}{3} \times 4 = 1.333$	6.668	5.332
Circle	$-\pi r^2 = -0.7854$	1	2	-0.7854	-1.5708
Total	7.2146			7.8826	11.7612

$$\bar{X} = \frac{\Sigma \bar{x} A}{\Sigma A} = 1.0926 \text{ m} \quad \text{... Ans.}$$

$$\bar{Y} = \frac{\Sigma \bar{y} A}{\Sigma A} = 1.6302 \text{ m} \quad \text{... Ans.}$$

Example 4.13 :

Determine the Y co-ordinate of centroid of the shaded area as shown in Fig. 4.13.

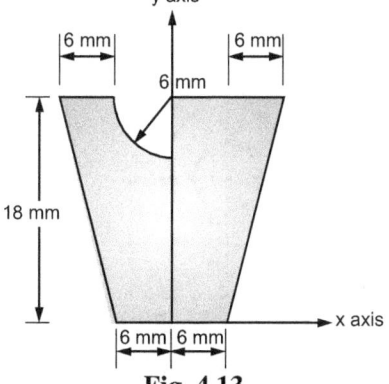

Fig. 4.13

Solution :

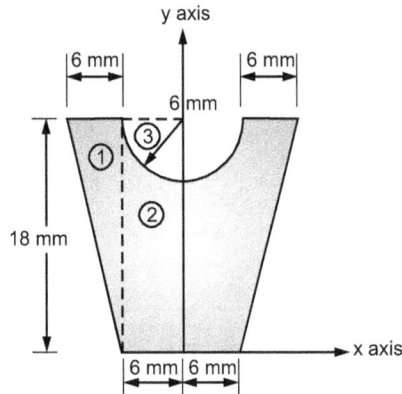

Fig. 4.13 (a)

Composite area is symmetrical about Y-axis.

Half part of composite area is considered to find $\bar{y}$ as shown in Fig. 4.13 (a).
Area of quarter circle is indicated negative since it is to be subtracted from other area.

Part	A (mm²)	$\bar{y}$ (mm)	$\bar{y}$ A (mm³)
Triangle	$\frac{1}{2} \times 6 \times 18 = 54$	$\frac{2}{3} \times 18 = 12$	648
Rectangle	$6 \times 18 = 108$	$\frac{1}{12} \times 18 = 9$	972
Quarter circle	$-\frac{\pi r^2}{4} = -28.27$	$18 - \frac{4r}{3\pi} = 15.45$	– 436.87
Total	133.73		1183.13

$$\bar{Y} = \frac{\Sigma \bar{y} A}{\Sigma A} = 8.847 \text{ mm} \qquad \text{... Ans.}$$

Example 4.14 :

Determine y-co-ordinate of centroid of shaded area as shown in Fig. 4.14.

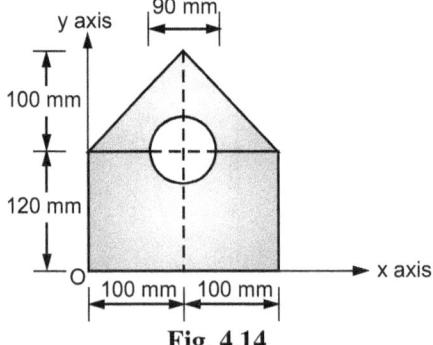

Fig. 4.14

Solution :

Composite area is divided into rectangle, triangle and circle. Area of circle is indicated negative since it is to be subtracted from other area.

Area	A (mm²)	$\bar{y}$ (mm)	$\bar{y}$ (A)
Rectangle	120 × 200 = 24000	$\frac{1}{2} \times 120 = 60$	1440000
Triangle	$\frac{1}{2} \times 100 \times 200 = 10000$	$120 + \frac{1}{3} \times 100 = 153.33$	1533333.333
Circle	$\pi r^2 = -6361.725$	120	– 763407.0148
Total	27638.275		2209926.318

$$\bar{Y} = \frac{\Sigma \bar{y} A}{\Sigma A} = 79.9589 \text{ mm} \qquad \ldots \text{Ans.}$$

Example 4.15 :

Locate the centroid of arc AB as shown in Fig. 4.15 (a).

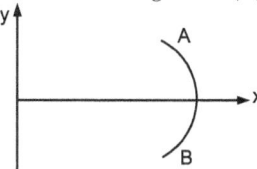

Fig. 4.15 (a)

Solution :

Given data : As shown in Fig. 4.15 (a).

To find : $\bar{x}$ of arc.

As arc is symmetrical with x-x axis, therefore, $\bar{y} = 0$.
Consider a small length dl.

∴ $\qquad dl = r \, d\theta$

∴ $\qquad l = 2 \int_0^\alpha dl = 2 \int_0^\alpha r \, d\theta$

$\qquad = 2 r\alpha$

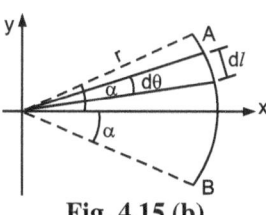

Fig. 4.15 (b)

$\qquad dl \cdot \bar{x} = r \, d\theta \, (r \cos \theta) = r^2 \cos \theta \cdot d\theta$

∴ $\qquad l\bar{x} = \int_0^\alpha dl \cdot \bar{x} = 2 \int_0^\alpha r^2 \cos \theta \cdot d\theta$

∴ $\qquad l\bar{x} = 2r^2 \sin \alpha$

∴ $\qquad \bar{x} = \frac{l\bar{x}}{l} = \frac{2r^2 \sin \alpha}{2r\alpha} = \frac{r \sin \alpha}{\alpha}$

∴ $\qquad \textbf{Centroid} = \left(\frac{r \sin \alpha}{\alpha}, 0 \right) \qquad \ldots \text{Ans.}$

MOMENT OF INERTIA

4.5 INTRODUCTION

We know that the moment of a force is the product of its magnitude and perpendicular distance between the line of action of the force and the point or line about which the moment is taken.

Referring to Fig. 4.16, this moment called the first moment about AB = Px. If this quantity (Px) is again multiplied by x, the product Px^2 is called the *moment of a force* or the *second moment of a force* or the *moment of inertia*. If instead of force, the area or the mass is under consideration, the second moment is known as the *second moment of area* or the *mass moment of inertia*.

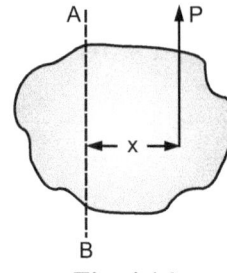

Fig. 4.16

As per Newton's first law of motion, "A body will continue in its state of rest or of uniform motion in a straight line unless it is compelled by the external forces to change that state".

This property of a body by virtue of which it resists any change of motion is called inertia and the mass of a body is a measure of its inertia when dealing with linear motion as well as rotatory motion.

Moment of inertia is a purely mathematical term. It is one of the important properties of areas. It is of prime consideration when dealing with the determination of stress under bending which depends upon its moment of inertia of its cross-section.

4.6 MOMENT OF INERTIA

Consider the plane area, shown in Fig. 4.17 (a) of elemental area dA.

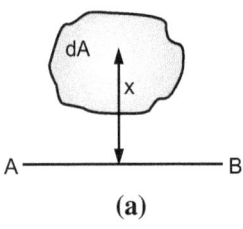
(a)

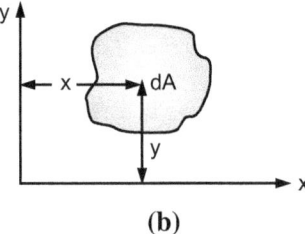
(b)

Fig. 4.17

We have to find the moment of inertia of plane figure about an axis AB. If r is the distance of elemental area dA from the axis AB in Fig. 4.17 (a), then,

$$\text{Moment of inertia} = \Sigma r^2 \, dA \quad \text{or} \quad I_{AB} = \Sigma r^2 \, dA = \int r^2 \, dA$$

The term rdA may be called as moment of area, similar to moment of a force and hence $r^2 dA$ be called second moment of area or moment of inertia.

Similarly, the moment of inertia of an area about x and y axes is [See Fig. 4.17 (b)]

$$I_{xx} = \Sigma y^2 \, dA, \quad I_{yy} = \Sigma x^2 \, dA$$

The moment of inertia is a fourth dimensional term since it is a term obtained by multiplying area by the square of the distance. In S.I. units, m⁴ is the unit of moment of inertia.

4.7 POLAR MOMENT OF INERTIA

Moment of inertia about an axis perpendicular to the plane of an area is called polar moment of inertia. It may be denoted by I_p, J or I_{zz}. Refer Fig. 4.18.

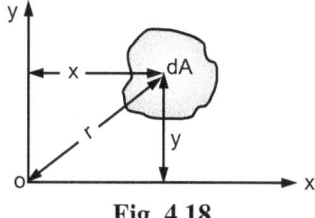

Fig. 4.18

The moment of inertia about an axis perpendicular to the plane of the area at o,

$$I_p = \Sigma r^2 \, dA$$

4.8 RADIUS OF GYRATION

The radius of gyration of a body may be defined as 'the distance at which the whole area, (or mass) of a body may be supposed to be concentrated with respect to an axis of reference'. It is denoted by letter K or r.

$$\therefore \quad I = AK^2 \quad \text{and} \quad K = \sqrt{\frac{I}{A}}$$

where, K - radius of gyration
I - moment of inertia
and A - the cross-sectional area

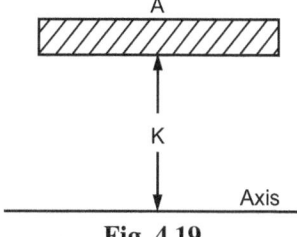

Fig. 4.19

The radius of gyration of a composite section is equal to square root of ratio of M.I. of composite section to the total area.

$$K = \sqrt{\frac{I'}{A'}}$$

where I' is the M.I. of composite section area and A' is the area of composite section. (It should be noted that radius of gyration of a composite section is not equal to the sum of the radius of gyration of the component part.)

4.9 THEOREM OF MOMENT OF INERTIA

There are two theorems of moment of inertia :

(1) Theorem of parallel axis,

(2) Theorem of perpendicular axis.

4.9.1 Theorem of Parallel Axis

It states "The moment of inertia of an area (or a body) about any axis in its plane is equal to the sum of its moment of inertia about a parallel axis through its centre of gravity and the product of its area (or mass) and the square of the distance between the two axes".

Mathematically, $I_{AB} = I_G + Ah^2$

where, I_{AB} - M.I. of the area about the line AB

I_G - M.I. of the area about its C.G.

A - Area of the section

h - Distance between C.G. of the section and the axis AB

Proof : Consider an elemental parallel strip of area dA of the body shown in Fig. 4.20 at a distance y from the C.G., then,

$I_{AB} = \Sigma\, dA\, [y + h]^2$

$= \Sigma\, dA\, [y^2 + h^2 + 2yh]$

$= \Sigma\, dA \cdot y^2 + \Sigma\, dA \cdot h^2 + \Sigma\, dA \cdot 2yh$

Now, $\Sigma\, dA \cdot y^2 = I_G$

$\Sigma\, dA \cdot h^2 = Ah^2$

and $\Sigma\, dA \cdot 2hy = 2h\, \Sigma\, dA \cdot y$

$= 2hA \dfrac{\Sigma\, dA \cdot y}{A}$

$= 2Ahy \left(\because \dfrac{\Sigma\, dA \cdot y}{A} = y \right)$

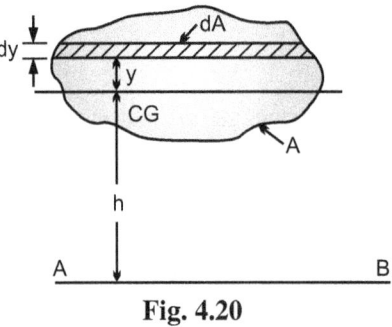

Fig. 4.20

Here, y is the distance of the whole area A from C.G. Since we have already considered C.G. itself as a reference axis, thus y is zero and hence the term $2h\, \Sigma\, dAy$ is zero.

$\therefore\quad I_{AB} = I_G + Ah^2$ Hence proved.

4.9.2 Theorem of Perpendicular Axis

It states "The moment of inertia of a plane area about an axis perpendicular to its plane is equal to the sum of its moments of inertia about two axes at right angles to each other, in its own plane intersecting each other at the point where the perpendicular axis passes through it.

$I_{zz} = I_{xx} + I_{yy}$

Proof : Let us consider an elemental area dA at a distance r from o. Let the co-ordinate of dA be x and y such that $r^2 = x^2 + y^2$.

Thus, $I_{zz} = \Sigma\, r^2 \cdot dA$

$= \Sigma\, (x^2 + y^2) \cdot dA\, (\because r^2 = x^2 + y^2)$

$= \Sigma\, x^2 \cdot dA + \Sigma\, y^2 \cdot dA$

But, $\Sigma\, r^2\, dA = \Sigma\, x^2\, dA = I_{yy}$

and $\Sigma\, y^2\, dA = I_{xx}$

$\therefore\quad I_{zz} = I_{xx} + I_{yy}$

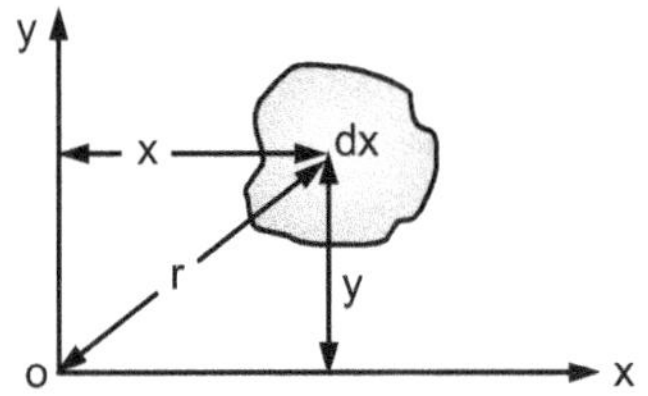

Fig. 4.21

Here, I_{xx} and I_{yy} are called the rectangular moments of inertia and I_{zz} is called polar moment of inertia.

4.10 METHODS FOR FINDING OUT THE M.I.

The moment of inertia of a plane figure (or a body) may be found out by any of the following methods.

(I) Using Routh's Rule, (II) By the method of integration.

(I) Routh's Rule :

If a body is symmetrical about three mutually perpendicular axes, then the moment of inertia of the body, as per this rule about an axis passing through its centre of gravity is given by,

(a) $\quad I = \dfrac{A \text{ (or M)} \times S}{3} \quad$ (for a square or rectangular lamina)

(b) $\quad I = \dfrac{A \text{ (or M)} \times S}{4} \quad$ (for a circular elliptical lamina)

(c) $\quad I = \dfrac{A \text{ (or M)} \times S}{5} \quad$ (for a spherical body)

where A - Area of the body
       M - Mass of the body
       S - Sum of the squares of the two semi-axes other than the axis, about which the moment of inertia has to be calculated.

We shall now find the moment of inertia of a few bodies of simple geometrical shapes using this rule.

(a) Moment of inertia of thin uniform rod :
Consider a thin uniform rod AB of length such that AC = CB = 0.5, we have to find M.I. about y-axis.

Using Routh's rule,
$$I_{yy} = \dfrac{MS}{3}$$

where, S - Sum of squares of the semi-axes xx and zz
and   M - Mass of the rod.

$\therefore \quad I_{yy} = \left(\dfrac{L}{2}\right)^2 + 0 = \dfrac{L^2}{4}$

$\therefore \quad I_{yy} = \dfrac{M}{3}\left(\dfrac{L^2}{4}\right) = \dfrac{ML^2}{12}$

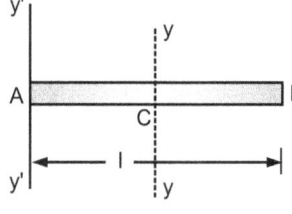

Fig. 4.22

(b) Moment of inertia of a rectangle :
Let b - Width of the rectangle parallel to the x-axis
    d - Depth of the rectangle perpendicular the to x-axis
    A - Area of the section = b × d
Using Routh's rule,
$$I_{xx} = \dfrac{AS}{3}$$

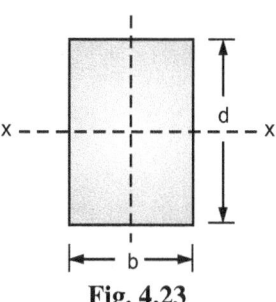

Fig. 4.23

where S - Sum of the squares of the semi-axis yy and zz

$$\therefore \quad I_{xx} = \left(\frac{d^2}{2}\right) + 0 = \frac{d^2}{4}$$

$$I_{xx} = \frac{b \cdot d}{3} \times \frac{d^2}{4} \quad \therefore \quad I_{xx} = \frac{bd^3}{12}$$

(c) Moment of inertia of a circular section :

Let D = Diameter of the circle

$$A = \frac{\pi}{4} D^2$$

Using Routh's rule,

$$I_{xx} = \frac{AS}{4}$$

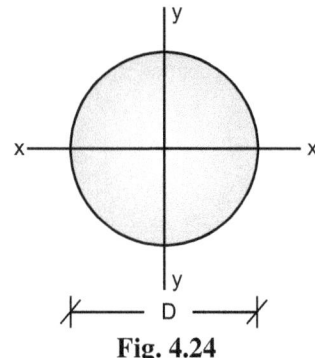

Fig. 4.24

where A - Area of the circle
and   S - Sum of the squares of the semi-axes yy and zz.

$$\therefore \quad S = \left(\frac{D}{2}\right)^2 + 0 = \frac{D^2}{4}$$

$$\therefore \quad I_{xx} = \frac{\pi}{4} \cdot \frac{D^2}{4} \times \frac{D^2}{4} = \frac{\pi D^4}{64} \text{ or } \frac{\pi R^4}{4}$$

(II) Moment of Inertia by the Method of Integration :

The moment of inertia of an area (or mass) may also be found out by the method of integration as discussed below.

(a) Moment of inertia of a rectangular section : Let a rectangle of width 'b' and depth 'd' whose moment of inertia is to be found about x-axis. Consider a strip of thickness dy at a distance y from the axis.

$$\text{Area of the strip} = b \cdot dy$$
$$\text{M.I. of the strip about xx axis} = \text{Area} \times (\text{Distance})^2$$
$$= b \cdot dy \cdot y^2 = b \cdot y^2 \cdot dy$$

Now, moment of inertia of the whole section may be found out by integration from $-d/2$ to $d/2$.

$$\therefore \quad I_{xx} = \int b y^2 \cdot dy$$

$$= b \left(\frac{y^3}{3}\right)^{d/2}$$

$$= b \left(\frac{d^3}{24} + \frac{d^3}{24}\right) = \frac{bd^3}{12}$$

Similarly, $I_{yy} = \dfrac{db^3}{12}$

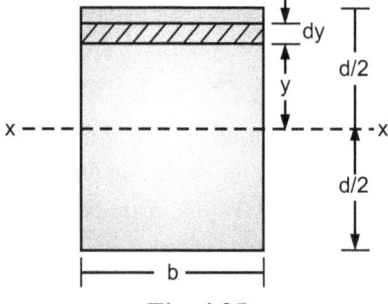

Fig. 4.25

(b) Moment of inertia of a triangle : Let ABC be a triangle of width 'b' and height 'h' whose moment of inertia is to be found.

(i) Moment of inertia about the base AB : Consider a small strip of width b_1 and thickness dy parallel to the base AB at a distance of y from the base. From the similar triangles DEC and ABC,

$$\frac{DE}{AB} = \frac{h-y}{h}$$

or $\frac{b_1}{b} = \frac{(h-y)}{h}$; $b_1 = \frac{b(h-y)}{h}$

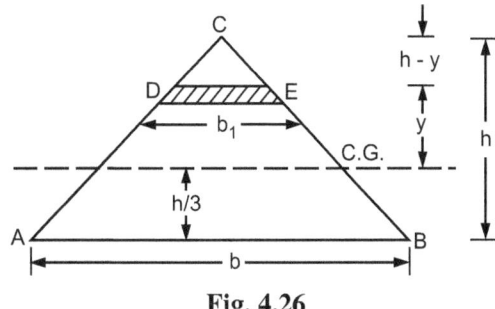

Fig. 4.26

∴ Area of the strip DE, $dA = b_1 \cdot dy$

M.I. of this strip about AB $= y^2 \cdot dA = b_1 y^2 \cdot dy = \frac{b(h-y)}{h} y^2 \cdot dy$

∴ M.I. of the section about AB,

$$I_{AB} = \int \frac{b(h-y)}{h} y^2 \cdot dy = \int_0^h \left(y^2 - \frac{y^3}{h}\right) b \cdot dy$$

$$= b\left[\frac{y^3}{3} - \frac{y^4}{4h}\right]_0^h = b\left(\frac{h^3}{3} - \frac{h^4}{4h}\right) = \frac{bh^3}{12}$$

(ii) Moment of inertia about the centroidal axis x-x : Using theorem of parallel axis,

$$I_{AB} = I_G + Ah^2$$

where   h - distance between the axes AB and x-x $= \frac{h}{3}$

∴ $I_G = I_{AB} - A\left(\frac{h}{3}\right)^2$

$$= \frac{bh^3}{12} - \frac{bh}{2}\left(\frac{h}{3}\right)^2 = \frac{bh^3}{36}$$

(c) Moment of inertia of a circular section : Consider a circular section with O as centre and radius r as shown in Fig. 4.27.

Now, consider an elementary ring of radius x and thickness dx.

Area of the ring, $dA = 2\pi x \cdot dx$

M.I. of the ring about x-x axis or y-y axis
$= dA \cdot x^2 = 2\pi x \cdot dx \cdot x^2 = 2\pi x^3 \, dx$

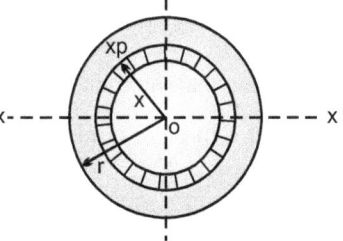

Fig. 4.27

Now, the M.I. of the whole section about the central axis,

$$I_{zz} = \int_0^r 2\pi x^3 \, dx = 2\pi \int_0^r x^3 \, dx$$

$$= 2\pi \left[\frac{x^4}{4}\right]_0^r = \frac{\pi r^4}{2}$$

$$\therefore \quad I_{zz} = \frac{\pi D^4}{32} \qquad \left[\because r = \frac{D}{2}\right]$$

We know from the theorem of perpendicular axis,

$$I_{xx} + I_{yy} = I_{zz}$$

Because section is symmetrical about both axes,

$$\therefore \quad I_{xx} = I_{yy}$$

$$\therefore \quad \frac{I_{zz}}{2} = \frac{\pi D^4}{64} = \frac{\pi R^4}{4}$$

(d) Moment of inertia of hollow section :

(i) Hollow rectangular section :

Moment of inertia of hollow rectangular section

= M.I. of large rectangle – M.I. of small rectangle

$$= I_{xx} = \frac{BD^3}{12} - \frac{bd^3}{12} = \frac{1}{12}[BD^3 - bd^3]$$

Similarly, $I_{yy} = \frac{DB^3}{12} - \frac{db^3}{12} = \frac{1}{12}[DB^3 - db^3]$

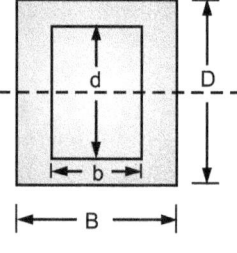

Fig. 4.28

(ii) Hollow circular section :

Let d and D be the inner and outer diameter of the circle.

We know that, moment of inertia,

I_{xx} = M.I. of outer circle – M.I. of inner circle

$$\therefore \quad I_{xx} = \frac{\pi D^4}{64} - \frac{\pi d^4}{64} = \frac{\pi}{64}(D^4 - d^4)$$

Similarly, $I_{yy} = \frac{\pi}{64}(D^4 - d^4)$

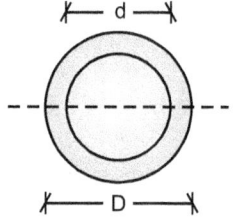

Fig. 4.29

4.11 MOMENT OF INERTIA OF STANDARD SECTIONS

The moment of inertia of common standard sections are given in Table 4.2.

Table 4.2

Shape	Figure	Moment of Inertia
1. Rectangle		$I_{xx} = \dfrac{bd^3}{12}$, $\quad I_{yy} = \dfrac{db^3}{12}$ $I_{AB} = \dfrac{bd^3}{3}$, $\quad I_{AC} = \dfrac{db^3}{3}$
2. Triangle		$I_{xx} = \dfrac{bd^3}{36}$, $\quad I_{AB} = \dfrac{bd^3}{12}$
3. Circle		$I_{xx} = I_{yy} = \dfrac{\pi d^4}{64}$
4. Hollow rectangle		$I_{xx} = \dfrac{BD^3 - bd^3}{12}$ $I_{yy} = \dfrac{DB^3 - db^3}{12}$
5. Hollow circle		$I_{xx} = I_{yy} = \dfrac{\pi}{64}(D^4 - d^4)$
6. Semi-circle		$I_{AB} = \dfrac{\pi d^4}{128}$, $\quad I_{yy} = \dfrac{\pi d^4}{128}$ $I_{xx} = \dfrac{\pi d^4}{128} - \dfrac{d^4}{18\pi} = 0.0068598\, d^4$
7. Quarter of a circle		$I_{AB} = I_{AC} = \dfrac{\pi d^4}{256} - \dfrac{d^4}{36\pi} = 0.000343\, d^4$

4.12 MOMENT OF INERTIA OF COMPOSITE SECTION

A composite section consists of a number of simple sections combined together.
The following steps are applied for finding moment of inertia of the composite section.
(1) Divide the given composite section into simple shapes (triangles, rectangles, rods or circle or their portions etc.)
(2) Locate the centroid of each simple figure with respect to reference axis.
(3) Find moment of inertia of each figure about its own centroidal axis. Then moment of inertia of composite section can be found by two methods.

Method 1 : In this method, we locate the centroid of composite section.

Then M.I. of composite section, $I_{xx} = I_G + Ah^2$

h is the distance between the centroid of individual figure to the centroid of the composite section.

Consider a composite section, consisting of three rectangles.

Let us name the rectangles as 1, 2 and 3, and y_1, y_2 and y_3 be the distances of their centroid with respect to reference axis AB. Locate the centroid as

$$y = \frac{\Sigma Ay}{\Sigma A} \text{ and find 'h'}$$

M.I. of section 1,

$$I_1 = I_{G1} + A_1 h_1^2 \quad (\text{as } h_1 = y - y_1)$$

Similarly for sections 2 and 3,

$$I_2 = I_{G2} + A_2 h_2^2 \quad (\text{as } h_2 = y - y_2)$$

and $\quad I_3 = I_{G3} + A_3 h_3^2 \quad (\text{as } h_3 = y - y_3)$

I_{G1}, I_{G2} and I_{G3} be the M.I. of part about its own centroid.

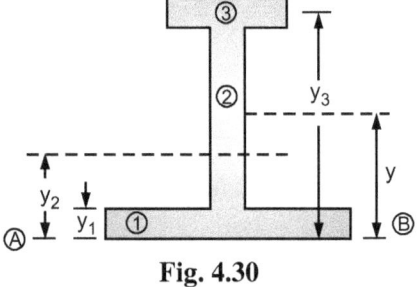

Fig. 4.30

$\therefore$ M.I. of composite section, $I_{xx} = I_1 + I_2 + I_3$

Method 2 : Considering same composite section (Fig. 4.30), find the moment of inertia of each part about its centroidal axis (I_{G1}, I_{G2} and I_{G3}).

Add the term Ay^2, where A is the area of the part and y is the distance of its centroid from the reference axis, get the moment of inertia about the axis AB as

$$I_1 = I_{G1} + A_1 y_1^2$$
$$I_2 = I_{G2} + A_2 y_2^2$$
and $\quad I_3 = I_{G3} + A_3 y_3^2$

Moment of inertia of the composite section about AB is

$$I_{AB} = I_1 + I_2 + I_3$$

Now, using parallel axis theorem, the moment of inertia about centroidal axis is found.

$$I_{AB} = I_{xx} + Ay^2 \qquad \therefore \quad I_{xx} = I_{AB} - Ay^2$$

where y is the centroid of the composite section from reference axis AB and A is the area of the composite section.

$$\bar{y} = \frac{\Sigma Ay}{\Sigma A} \text{ is calculated as usual.}$$

If we arrange in tabular form,

Component	Area	Centroidal distance from the axis AB	Ay	Ay²	I_{self}
1	A_1	y_1	$A_1 y_1$	$A_1 y_1^2$	I_{G1}
2	A_2	y_2	$A_2 y_2$	$A_2 y_2^2$	I_{G2}
3	A_3	y_3	$A_3 y_3$	$A_3 y_3^2$	I_{G3}
	ΣA		ΣAy	ΣAy^2	ΣI_{self}

and M.I. about AB,
$$I_{AB} = \Sigma I_{self} + \Sigma Ay^2$$
and distance of centroidal axis I_{xx} from AB is
$$\bar{y} = \frac{\Sigma Ay}{\Sigma A}$$
and the moment of inertia about the centroidal axis xx is given by parallel axis theorem
$$I_{AB} = I_{xx} + \Sigma Ay^2$$
Therefore, $I_{xx} = I_{AB} - (\Sigma A) \cdot \bar{y}^2$

4.13 PRODUCT OF INERTIA

Consider the plane area shown in Fig. 4.31, of elemental area dA, we have to find the product of inertia of the plane figure. If (x, y) be the co-ordinate of the centroid of an elemental area then product of inertia is obtained by multiplying element area by its co-ordinates x and y and integrating over the area. It is denoted by I_{xy}.

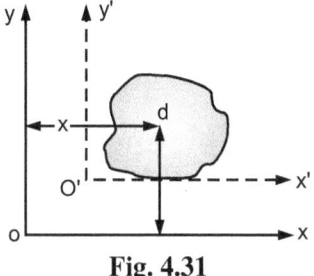

Fig. 4.31

$$\therefore \quad I_{xy} = \int xy\, dA$$

Product of inertia I_{xy} may be either positive or negative. Its value becomes zero, if any of two axis (one or both) are axes of symmetry.

The product of inertia of Tee, channel, beam (I), circular and rectangular section are zero about their own centroidal axis.

The parallel axis theorem for the product of inertia
$$I_{xy} = I_{x'y'} + xyA$$
where $I_{x'y'}$ be the product of inertia of the area 'A' with respect to the centroidal axes x' and y'.

4.14 MOMENT OF INERTIA OF A MASS

Mass moment of inertia of a body about an axis is defined as "The total sum of the product of its elemental masses and square of their distance from the axis". Consider a body of mass dm, r be the distance from reference axis AB.

The mass moment of the body about an axis AB,

$$I_{AB} = \Sigma\, dm\, r^2 = \int r^2\, dm$$

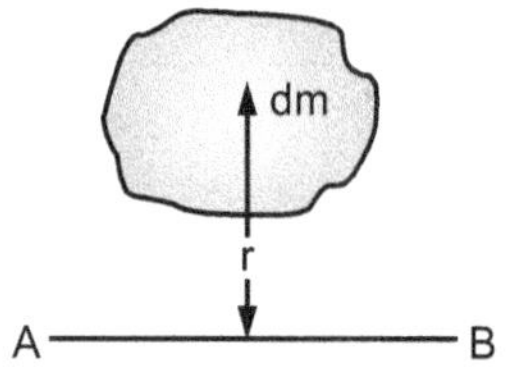

Since mass moment of inertia is product of mass and square of distance, its unit be N-m-sec^2.

The moment of inertia of a body with respect to a co-ordinate axes x, y and z. For example, if r be the distance of the elemental mass from z axis,

then $\quad r^2 = x^2 + y^2$

and $\quad I_z = \int r^2\, dm$

$$I_z = \int (x^2 + y^2)\, dm$$

Fig. 4.32

Similarly, the moments of inertia with respect to the x and y axes,

$$I_x = \int (y^2 + z^2)\, dm$$

$$I_y = \int (x^2 + z^2)\, dm$$

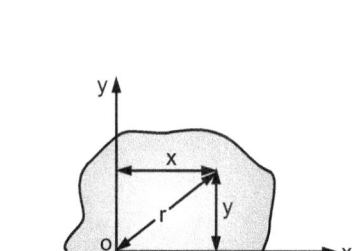

Fig. 4.33

4.14.1 Radius of Gyration

If I is the moment of inertia of a body of mass M about an axis, then radius of gyration K about that axis is given by the relation

$$I = MK^2$$

or $\quad K = \sqrt{\dfrac{I}{M}}$

Thus, this term is having some physical meaning. Radius of gyration is the distance at which entire mass is to be concentrated.

NUMERICAL EXAMPLES ON MOMENT OF INERTIA

Example 4.16 :

Determine the moment of inertia of a T section shown in Fig. 4.34 about x-x axis passing through the centre of gravity of the section. Also find out the radius of gyration.

Solution :

Method 1 : The given composite section can be divided into two rectangles viz. 1 and 2. Let y be the distance between centre of gravity of the section and the top face.

For rectangles (1) and (2),

$$A_1 = 120 \times 20 = 2400 \text{ mm}^2$$
$$y_1 = \frac{20}{2} = 10 \text{ mm}$$
$$A_2 = 100 \times 20 = 2000 \text{ mm}^2$$
$$y_2 = 20 + \frac{100}{2} = 70 \text{ mm}$$

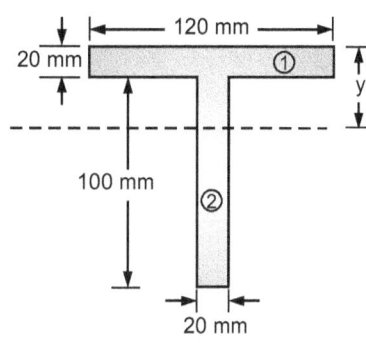

Fig. 4.34

Using the relation,
$$\bar{y} = \frac{A_1 y_1 + A_2 y_2}{A_1 + A_2}$$
$$= \frac{2400 \times 10 + 2000 \times 70}{2400 + 2000}$$
$$= 37.27 \text{ mm}$$

[Moment of inertia of the whole section about x-x axis] = [Sum of the moments of inertia of sections (1) and (2) about x-x axis].

Using parallel axis theorem,
$$I_x = I_G + Ah^2$$

For rectangle (1), $\quad I_{G1} = \dfrac{bd^3}{12} = \dfrac{120 \times (20)^3}{12} = 80000 \text{ mm}^4$

Distance of centre of gravity (C.G.) of rectangle (1) from x-x axis is
$$h_1 = \bar{y} - y_1 = 37.27 - 10 = 27.27 \text{ mm}$$

∴ M.I. of rectangle (1) about x-x axis is,
$$= I_{G1} + A_1 h_1^2 = 80000 + 2400 (27.27)^2$$
$$= 1,86,4767 \text{ mm}^4$$

Now, for rectangle (2),
$$I_{G2} = \frac{20 \times (100)^3}{12} = 1666666.67 \text{ mm}^4$$
$$h_2 = 70 - 37.27 = 32.73 \text{ mm}$$

∴ M.I. of rectangle (2) about x-x axis is,
$$= I_{G2} + A_2 h_2^2 = 1666666.67 + 2000 (32.73)^2$$
$$= 3,80,9172.5 \text{ mm}^4$$

Now, moment of inertia of whole section
$$= 1864767 + 3809172.5 = 5673939.5 \text{ mm}^4 \quad \text{... Ans.}$$

Method 2 : In this method, first we find the moment of inertia of the section about any axis (top or bottom of composite section) say 1-1 (top).
$$I_{1-1} = \Sigma I_G + \Sigma ay^2$$
(where y be the distance of component from axis 1-1)

Then using parallel axis theorem,
$$I_{1-1} = I_{xx} + Ay^2$$
∴ $$I_{xx} = I_{1-1} - A\bar{y}^2 \qquad (\because \Sigma a = A)$$

(where $\bar{y}$ be the distance of centroid from axis 1-1)

The whole calculation may be done in tabular form, considering same reference axis 1-1.

Sr. No.	Parts	Area	y	Ay	Ay²	I_self
1.	1	2400	10	24000	240000	$\dfrac{120 \times 20^3}{12} = 80000$
2.	2	2000	70	140000	9800000	$\dfrac{20 \times 100^3}{12} = 1666666.67$
Sum		4400		164000	10040000	1746666.67

Distance of the centroidal axis xx from the axis
$$\bar{y} = \frac{\Sigma Ay}{\Sigma A} = \frac{164000}{4400} = 37.27 \text{ mm}$$

∴ Moment of inertia about 1-1
$$I_{1-1} = \Sigma [I_{self} + Ay^2]$$
$$= 1746666.67 + 10040000 = 11786666.67 \text{ mm}^4$$

But $$I_{1-1} = I_{xx} + \Sigma A \bar{y}^2 \text{ (using parallel axis theorem)}$$
$$I_{xx} = I_{1-1} - \Sigma A\bar{y}^2$$
$$= 11786666.67 - 4400 \times (37.27)^2 = 5674833.91 \text{ mm}^4 \text{... Ans.}$$

And the radius of gyration is given by
$$K = \sqrt{\frac{I}{A}} = \sqrt{\frac{5674833.9}{4400}} = 35.91 \text{ mm}$$

Example 4.17 :

Determine the moment of inertia of the channel section shown in Fig. 4.35 about its centroidal axes x and y. Also find its polar moment of inertia.

Solution :

Consider 1-1, 2-2 as a reference axes parallel to y-y and x-x axes respectively. Divide whole section into rectangles 1, 2 and 3. As we have seen in previous example, method 2 is simple, thus we use same for solving this problem.

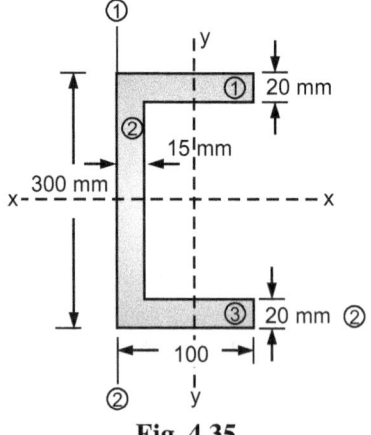

Fig. 4.35

Comp. parts	Area of part mm²	x	y	Ax	Ay	Ax²	Ay²	I_self	
								I_x	I_y
1	100 × 200 = 2000	50	290	100000	58×10^4	5×10^6	16.82×10^7	$100 \times \frac{20}{12}$ = 66666.67	$20 \times \frac{100}{12}$ = 1666666.7
2	260 × 15 = 3900	7.5	150	29250	58.5×10^4	219375	87.75×10^6	$15 \times \frac{260^3}{12}$ = 21.97×10^6	$60 \times \frac{15}{12}$ = 73125
3	100 × 20 = 2000	50	10	100000	20000	5×10^6	2×10^5	100×20^3 = 66666.67	20×100^3 = 1666666.7
	ΣA = 7900			229250	1185000	10219375	2.5615×10^8	2210333	3406458.3

Centroid of the section,

$$x = \frac{\Sigma Ax}{\Sigma A} = \frac{229250}{7900} = 29.02 \text{ mm}$$

$$y = \frac{\Sigma Ay}{\Sigma A} = \frac{1185000}{7900} = 150 \text{ mm}$$

Moment of inertia about 1-1 (parallel to y-axis)

$$I_{1-1} = \Sigma (I_{\text{self-y'}} + A\overline{y}^2)$$
$$= 340458.3 + 2.5615 \times 10^8 = 2.5955646 \times 10^8 \text{ mm}^4$$

But $\quad I_{1-1} = I_{yy} + \Sigma Ay^2$

∴ $\quad I_{yy} = I_{1-1} - \Sigma Ay^2$
$$= 2.5955646 \times 10^8 - 7900 \times 150^2 = 81806458 \text{ mm}^4 \quad \text{... Ans.}$$

Similarly, moment of inertia about 2-2 axis parallel to x-x axis is

$$I_{2-2} = \Sigma (I_{\text{self}} + \Sigma Ax^2)$$
$$= 22103333 + 10219375 = 32322708 \text{ mm}^4$$

∴ $\quad I_{xx} = I_{2-2} - \Sigma Ax^2 = 32322708 - 7900 \times (29.02)^2$
$$= 25669641 \text{ mm}^4 \quad \text{... Ans.}$$

Polar M.I. $= I_{xx} + I_{yy}$
$$= 25669641 + 81806458 = 107.476 \times 10^6 \text{ mm}^4 \quad \text{... Ans.}$$

Example 4.18 :

Determine the moment of inertia of the I-section shown in Fig. 4.36 about both axes passing through the centre of gravity of the section.

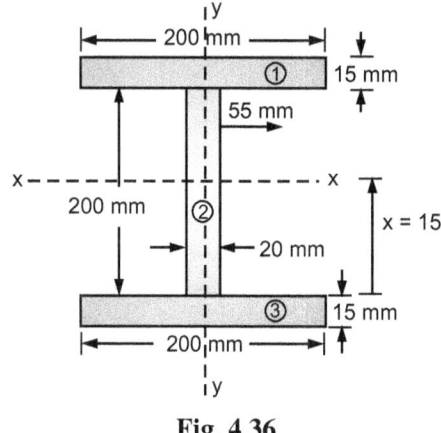

Fig. 4.36

Solution :

Given section is symmetrical about both axes. Thus, using parallel axis theorem, $I_{xx} = I_G + Ah^2$, where h is the distance between the centroid of individual component to the centroid of the composite section. Consider whole section is composite of three rectangles 1, 2 and 3. Due to symmetry, the centroid of I section will coincide with the centroid of rectangle 2.

$$\bar{x} = 115 \text{ mm and } \bar{y} = 0$$

$$I_{xx} = \frac{200 \times 15^3}{12} + 3000 \times (107.5)^2 + \frac{20 \times 200^3}{12} + 0$$

$$+ \frac{200 \times 15^3}{12} + 3000 \times (107.5)^2$$

$$= 82783333 \text{ mm}^4$$

Similarly, $I_{yy} = \frac{15 \times 200^3}{12} + \frac{200 \times 20^3}{12} + 0 + \frac{15 \times 200^3}{12}$

$$= 10 \times 10^6 + 133333.33 + 10 \times 10^6$$

$$= 20133333.3 \text{ mm}^4$$

Same problem can also be solved as :

Let us consider the section as a hollow, consisting of two rectangles of size (200×230) and (180×200) respectively.

$$\therefore \quad I_{xx} = \frac{1}{12} [BD^3 - bd^3]$$

$$= \frac{200 \times 230^3}{12} - \frac{180 \times 200^3}{12} = 82783333 \text{ mm}^4$$

Similarly, $I_{yy} = \frac{230 \times 200^3}{12} - 2 \times \left[\frac{200 \times 90^3}{12} + 200 \times 90 \times 55^2 \right]$

$$= 20133333.33 \text{ mm}^4$$

Example 4.19 :

Determine the moment of inertia of the inverted L-section shown in Fig. 4.37 about its centroidal axis parallel to the legs.

Solution :

Consider 1-1 and 2-2 as a reference axis, parallel to centroidal axes x-x and y-y respectively. Let the given section is divided into two rectangles (1) and (2).

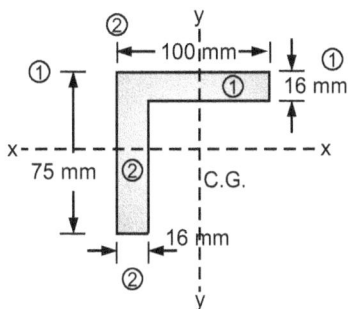

Fig. 4.37

Sr. No.	Parts A	x	y	Ax	Ay	Ax²	Ay²	I_{GX}	I_{GY}
1	84 × 16 = 1344	58	8	77952	10752	4521216	86016	$\frac{84 \times 16^3}{12}$ = 790272	$\frac{16 \times 84^3}{12}$
2	75 × 16 = 1200	8	37.5	9600	45000	76800	1687500	$\frac{16 \times 75^3}{12}$ = 562500	$\frac{75 \times 16^3}{12}$ = 25600
	ΣA = 2544			87552	55752	4598016	1773516	591172	815872

$$\bar{x} = \frac{\Sigma Ax}{\Sigma A} = \frac{87552}{2544} = 34.42 \text{ mm}$$

$$\bar{y} = \frac{\Sigma Ay}{\Sigma A} = \frac{55752}{2544} = 21.92 \text{ mm}$$

$$I_{1-1} = \Sigma (I_{GX} + Ay^2) = 591172 + 1773516 = 2364688.0 \text{ mm}^4$$

$$I_{xx} = I_{1-1} - A\bar{y}^2 = 2364688 - 2544 (21.92)^2$$
$$= 1142330.6 \text{ mm}^4 \quad \text{... Ans.}$$

Similarly,
$$I_{2-2} = \Sigma (I_G + Ax^2) = 815872 + 4598016$$
$$= 5413888.0 \text{ mm}^4$$

∴
$$I_{yy} = I_{2-2} - A\bar{x}^2 = 5413888.0 - 2544 \times (34.42)^2$$
$$= 2399918.6 \text{ mm}^4 \quad \text{... Ans.}$$

This problem can also be solved by other method.

$$I_{xx} = I_G + Ah^2$$
$$= \frac{84 \times 16^3}{12} + 1344 \times (21.92 - 8)^2 + \frac{16 \times 75^3}{12} + 1200 \times (37.5 - 21.92)^2$$
$$= 1142877.7 \text{ mm}^4 \quad \text{... Ans.}$$

$$I_{yy} = \frac{16 \times 84^3}{12} + 1344 \times (58 - 34.42)^2 + \frac{75 \times 16^3}{12} + 1200 \times (34.42 - 8)^2$$
$$= 2400777.7 \text{ mm}^4 \quad \text{... Ans.}$$

Example 4.20 :

Determine the M.I. of the Z-section given in Fig. Fig. 4.38, about its axis parallel to x-axis.

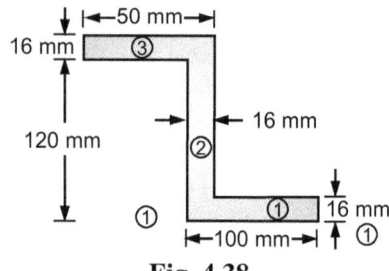

Fig. 4.38

Solution :

Method 1 : Consider (1)-(1) as a reference axis passing through bottom of the section. Whole section is divided into three rectangles (1), (2) and (3). All calculations are tabulated as shown in the following table.

Parts	A	y	Ay	Ay²	$I_{self\ x}$
1	100 × 16 = 1600	8	12800	102400	$\dfrac{100 \times 16^3}{12} = 34133.33$
2	104 × 16 = 1664	68	113152	7694336	$\dfrac{16 \times 104^3}{12} = 1499818.7$
3	50 × 16 = 800	128	102400	13107200	$\dfrac{50 \times 16^3}{12} = 17066.67$
	ΣA = 4064		228352	20903936	$\Sigma I_{self} = 1551018.7$

$$\bar{y} = \frac{\Sigma Ay}{\Sigma A} = \frac{228352}{4064} = 56.19$$

M.I. about 1-1,
$$I_{1-1} = I_{GX} + \Sigma (Ay^2)$$
$$= 1551018.7 + 20903936 = 22454955 \text{ mm}^4$$

∴ $\quad I_{xx} = I_{1-1} - \Sigma Ay^2$
$$= 22454955 - 4064 \times 56.19^2 = 9623622.1 \text{ mm}^4 \quad \text{... Ans.}$$

Method 2 : After knowing the centroid of the section, we can find M.I. by parallel axis theorem,

$$I_{xx} = I_G + Ah^2$$
$$h_1 = 56.19 - 8 = 48.19 \text{ mm}$$
$$h_2 = 68.0 - 56.19 = 11.81 \text{ mm}$$
$$h_3 = 128 - 56.19 = 71.81 \text{ mm}$$

∴ $\quad I_{xx} = \left(I_{G1} + A_1 h_1^2\right) + \left(I_{G2} + A_2 h_2^2\right) + \left(I_{G3} + A_3 h_3^2\right)$
$$= \frac{100 \times 16^3}{12} + 1600 \times 48.19^2 + \frac{16 \times 104^3}{12}$$
$$+ 1664 \times 11.81^2 + \frac{50 \times 16^3}{12} + 800 \times 71.81^2$$

∴ $\quad I_{xx} = 9624089.6 \text{ mm}^4 \quad \text{... Ans.}$

(Difference in value of M.I. by the two methods are due to decimal points taken in calculation.)

Example 4.21 :

Determine the M.I. of the composite section (Fig. 4.39) about the horizontal centroidal axis.

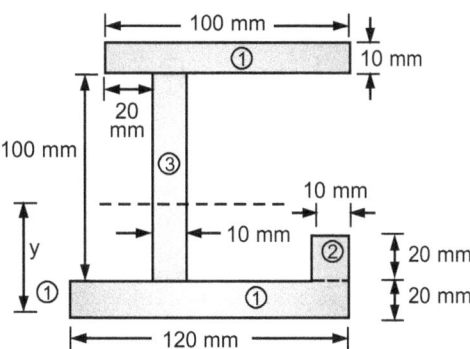

Fig. 4.39

Solution :

Method 1 : Consider 1-1 be the reference axis, whole composite section is divided into four rectangles 1, 2, 3 and 4.

Parts	A	y	Ay	Ay²	I_{self} x
1	120 × 20 = 2400	10	24000	240000	$\frac{120 \times 20^3}{12} = 8 \times 10^4$
2	10 × 20 = 200	30	6000	180000	$\frac{10 \times 20^3}{12} = 6666.67$
3	10 × 100 = 1000	70	70000	4900000	$\frac{10 \times 100^3}{12} = 833333.3$
4	100 × 10 = 1000	125	125000	15625000	$\frac{100 \times 10^3}{12} = 8333.3$
	ΣA = 4600		225000	20945000	ΣI_{self} = 921693.33

$$\bar{y} = \frac{\Sigma Ay}{\Sigma A} = \frac{225000}{4600} = 48.91 \text{ mm}$$

M.I. about reference axis,

$$I_{1-1} = \Sigma (I_G + Ay^2)$$
$$= 921693.33 + 20945000 = 21866693.33 \text{ mm}^4$$

∴ $I_{xx} = I_{1-1} - \Sigma A \bar{y}^2$
$$= 21866693.33 - 4600 \times (48.91)^2 = 10862628.33 \text{ mm}^4$$

Method 2 : Using formula, $I_{xx} = I_G + Ah^2$, distance between individual C.G. to C.G. of the composite member.

∴ $h_1 = 48.91 - 10 = 38.91$ mm
$h_2 = 48.91 - 30 = 18.91$ mm
$h_3 = 70 - 48.91 = 21.09$ mm
$h_4 = 125 - 48.91 = 76.09$ mm

∴ $I_{xx} = \frac{120 \times 20^3}{12} + 2400 \times 38.91^2 + \frac{10 \times 20^3}{12} + 200 \times 18.91^2$
$+ \frac{10 \times 100^3}{12} + 1000 \times 21.09^2 + \frac{100 \times 10^3}{12} + 1000 \times 76.09^2$

∴ $I_{xx} = 10861259.33$ mm⁴ ... **Ans.**

Example 4.22 :

Determine the polar moment of inertia of shaded area shown in Fig. 4.40 with respect to

(i) Point O

(ii) Centroid of the area

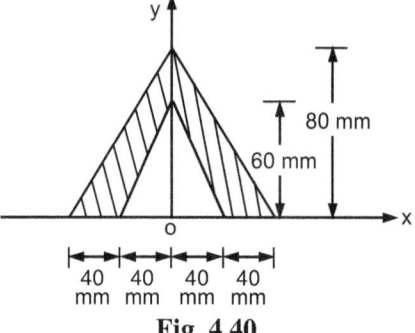

Fig. 4.40

Solution :

We know, polar moment of inertia

$$I_{oz} = I_{ox} + I_{oy}$$

Let us assume ox and oy be the axes along x and y direction.

$$I_{ox} = 2\left[\frac{1}{12} \times 80 \times 80^3 - \frac{1}{12} \times 40 \times 60^3\right] = 5386666.7 \text{ mm}^4$$

$$I_{oy} = 2\left[\frac{1}{12} \times 80 \times 80^3 - \frac{1}{12} \times 60 \times 40^3\right] = 6186666.7 \text{ mm}^4$$

∴ Polar moment of inertia about point O is

$$I_{oz} = I_{ox} + I_{oy}$$
$$= 5386666.7 + 6186666.7 = 11573333.4 \text{ mm}^4 \quad \text{... Ans.}$$

M.I. about centroid of the area : Section is symmetrical about y-axis. Let us again assume ox and oy be reference axes for locating centroid.

$$\bar{y} = \frac{A_1 y_1 - A_2 y_2}{A_1 - A_2}$$

$$A_1 = 0.5 \times 160 \times 80 = 6400 \text{ mm}^2, \quad y_1 = \frac{80}{3} = 26.67 \text{ mm}$$

$$A_2 = 0.5 \times 80 \times 60 = 2400 \text{ mm}^2, \quad y_2 = \frac{60}{3} = 20 \text{ mm}$$

∴ $$\bar{y} = \frac{6400 \times 26.67 - 2400 \times 20}{6400 - 2400} = \frac{122688}{4000} = 30.67 \text{ mm}$$

M.I. of the shaded area about centroidal x-axis is

$$I_{xx} = I_{ox} - \Sigma A\bar{y}^2$$
$$= 5386666.7 - 4000 \times 30.67^2 = 1623580.4 \text{ mm}^4$$

Similarly, M.I. of the area about y axis is

$$I_{yy} = I_{oy} = 6186666.7 \text{ mm}^4$$

∴ Polar M.I., $$I_{zz} = I_{xx} + I_{yy}$$
$$= 1623580.4 + 6186666.7 = 7810247.1 \text{ mm}^4 \quad \text{... Ans.}$$

Example 4.23 :

A built up section consists of two angles ISA 90 × 90 × 12 connected back to back and gusset plate (200 × 20) mm as shown in Fig. 4.41. Calculate M.I. about an axis parallel to and perpendicular to the gusset plate, passing through its centroid.

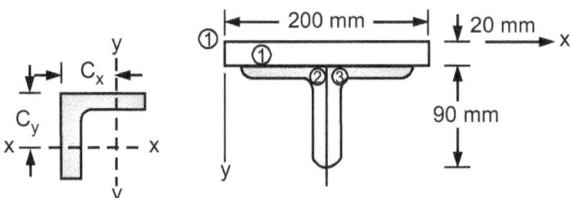

Fig. 4.41

Also find radius of gyration of the system. Property of ISA $90 \times 90 \times 12$:
$A = 2019$ mm²,
$C_x = C_y = 26.6$ mm,
$I_{xx} = I_{yy} = 14.79 \times 10^5$ mm⁴
for angle section.

Solution :

Consider ox and oy be the reference axes. Let us assume 1, 2 and 3 represent the plate and angles respectively.

	A	x	y	Ax	Ay	Ax²	Ay²	I_{GX}	I_{GY}
1.	4000	100	10	4 × 10⁵	4 × 10⁴	4 × 10⁷	4 × 10⁵	133333.3	1.3333333
2.	2019	73.4	46.6	148194.6	94085.4	10877484	4384379.6	14.79 × 10⁵	1479.10⁵
3.	2019	126.6	46.6	255605.4	94085.4	32359644	4384379.6	14.79 × 10⁵	
	8038			803800	228170.8	83237128	9168759	3091333.3	16291333

$$\bar{x} = \frac{\Sigma Ax}{\Sigma A} = \frac{803800}{8038} = 100 \text{ mm}$$

$$\bar{y} = \frac{\Sigma Ay}{\Sigma A} = \frac{228170.8}{8038} = 28.39 \text{ mm}$$

M.I. about ox axis, $\quad I_{ox} = \Sigma (I_{GX} + Ay^2)$
$\quad\quad\quad\quad\quad\quad\quad\quad = 3091333.3 + 9168759.2 = 12260093.5$ mm⁴

$\therefore \quad\quad\quad\quad\quad\quad I_{xx} = I_{ox} - \Sigma Ay^2$
$\quad\quad\quad\quad\quad\quad\quad\quad = 12260093.5 - 8038 \times (28.39)^2 = 5781528$ mm⁴

Radius of gyration about x-x axis,

$$K_{xx} = \sqrt{\frac{I_{xx}}{A}} = \sqrt{\frac{5781528}{8038}} = 26.82 \text{ mm}$$

M.I. about oy axis, $\quad I_{oy} = \Sigma (I_{GY} + Ax^2)$
$\quad\quad\quad\quad\quad\quad\quad\quad = 1629133 + 83237128 = 99528461$ mm⁴

$\therefore \quad\quad\quad\quad\quad\quad I_{yy} = (I_{oy} - \Sigma Ax^2)$
$\quad\quad\quad\quad\quad\quad\quad\quad = 99528461 - 8038 \times (100)^2 = 19148461$ mm⁴

Radius of gyration about y-y axis,

$$K_{yy} = \sqrt{\frac{I_{yy}}{A}} = \sqrt{\frac{19148461}{8038}} = 48.81 \text{ mm} \quad\quad\quad \text{... Ans.}$$

Example 4.24 :

Determine the M.I. of the section of a gantry girder about the horizontal and vertical centroidal axes. It is made up of a I-section and a channel section as shown in Fig. 4.42.

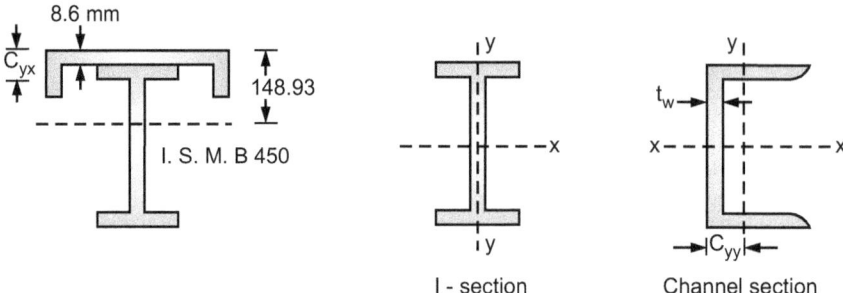

I - section   Channel section

Fig. 4.42

Properties of the section	ISMB 450	ISMC 400
Area of cross-section A	9227 mm²	6293 mm²
I_{xx}	30390.8 × 10⁴ mm⁴	15082.8 × 10⁴ mm⁴
I_{yy}	834 × 10⁴ mm⁴	504.8 × 10⁴ mm⁴
C_{yy}		24.2 mm
t_w		8.6 mm

Solution :

As section is symmetrical about y-axis, we have to locate centroid about x-axis.

$$A_1 = 6293 \text{ mm}^2 \quad y_1 = 24.2 \text{ mm}$$
$$A_2 = 9227 \text{ mm}^2 \quad y_2 = 8.6 + 225 = 233.6 \text{ mm}$$

$$y = \frac{A_1 y_1 + A_2 y_2}{A_1 + A_2}$$

or
$$y = \frac{6293 \times 24.2 + 9227 \times 233.6}{6293 + 9227} = \frac{2307717.8}{15520} = 148.93 \text{ mm}$$

M.I. of girder about centroidal x-axis is

$$I_{xx} = 30390.8 \times 10^4 + 504.8 \times 10^4 + 6293 \times (148.93 - 24.2)^2 + 9227 (84.67)^2$$
$$= 4.7300826 \times 10 \text{ mm}$$

$$I_{yy} = 834 \times 10^4 + 150828 \times 10^4$$
$$= 1.59168 \times 10^8 \text{ mm}^4 \qquad \text{... Ans.}$$

Example 4.25 :

Determine the moment of inertia of the shaded area shown in Fig. 4.43 about the axes OA and OB.

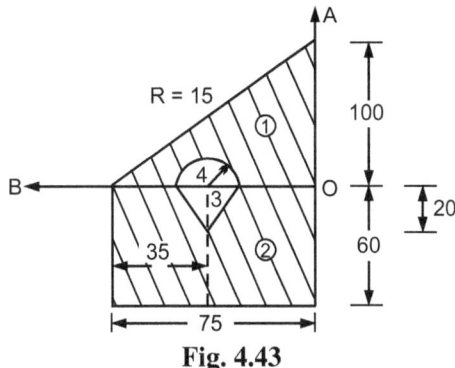

Fig. 4.43

Solution :

Section is divided into four parts 1, 2, 3 and 4 represented as shown in Fig. 4.43.

M.I. of the section about axis OB = M.I. of triangle and rectangle about OB
= M.I. of semi-circle and triangle about OB

$$I_{OB} = \frac{75 \times 100^3}{12} + \frac{75 \times 60^3}{3} - \frac{30 \times 20^3}{12} - \frac{\pi \times 30^4}{128}$$

= 11610120 mm⁴ ... Ans.

$$I_{OA} = \frac{100 \times 75^3}{12} + \frac{60 \times 75^3}{3} - \left[\frac{\pi \times 30^4}{128} + \frac{\pi}{8} \times 30^2 \times 40^2\right]$$

$$- \left[\frac{20 \times 15^3}{36} + \frac{20 \times 15}{2} \times \frac{(40-15)^2}{3} + \frac{20 \times 15^3}{36} + \frac{20 \times 15}{2} \times \frac{(40+15)^2}{3}\right]$$

= 10876508 mm⁴ ... Ans.

This problem can also be solved in tabular form because there is no need to find centroid of the section, thus omitting terms Ax and Ay.

	A	x	y	Ax²	Ay²	I_{GX}	I_{GY}
1	$\frac{75 \times 100}{2}$ = 3750	25	33.33	2343750	4165833.4	$\frac{75 \times 100^3}{36}$ = 2083333.3	$\frac{100 \times 75^3}{36}$ = 1171875
2	75×60	37.5	−30	6328125	4050000	$\frac{75 \times 60^3}{12}$ = 1350000	$\frac{60 \times 75^3}{12}$ = 2109375
3	$\frac{-1 \times 15 \times 20}{2}$	35	−6.67	−183750	−6673.335	$\frac{-15 \times 20^3}{36}$ = −3333.33	$\frac{-20 \times 15^3}{36}$ = −1875
4	$\frac{-\pi \times 30^2}{8}$	40	6.37	−565486.4	−14341.05	$\left[\frac{\pi}{128} - \frac{1}{18\pi}\right] \times 30^4$ = −5556.44	$\frac{\pi \times 30^4}{128}$ = 19880.39
				Σ Ax² = 7618888.6	Σ Ay² = 8188145.7	3421110.2	3257619.6

$\therefore I_{OA} = \Sigma(I_{GY} + Ax^2) = 3257619.6 + 7618888.6 = 10876508 \text{ mm}^4$

and $I_{OB} = \Sigma(I_{GX} + Ay^2)$
$= 3421110.2 + 8188145.7 = 11609256 \text{ mm}^4$

Example 4.26 :

Determine the M.I. of the shaded area about the axes OA and OB as shown in Fig. 4.44.

Solution :

M.I. of the section = M.I. of rectangle – M.I. of triangle – M.I. of quarter circle.

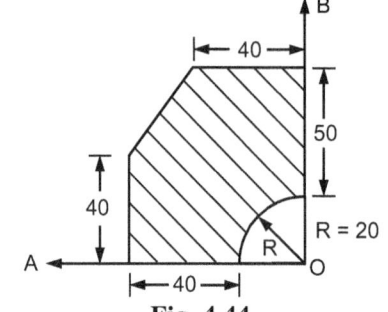

Fig. 4.44

$\therefore \quad I_{OA} = \dfrac{60 \times 70^3}{3} - \dfrac{\pi}{265}(40)^4 - \left[\dfrac{20 \times 30^3}{36} + \dfrac{20 \times 30}{2} \times (70-10)^2\right]$

$= 5733584.1 \text{ mm}^4$ ... **Ans.**

$I_{OB} = \dfrac{70 \times 60^3}{3} - \dfrac{\pi}{265}(40)^4 - \left[\dfrac{30 \times 20^3}{36} + \dfrac{30 \times 20}{2} \times \dfrac{(60-20)^2}{3}\right]$

$= 4148584.1 \text{ mm}^4$ ... **Ans.**

Example 4.27 :

Determine the product of moment of inertia of a rectangle with respect to the x and y axes shown in Fig. 4.45.

Solution :

Consider an elemental strip of dimension dx and d, elemental area dA = d·dx, its centroid with respect to given axes are (x, d/2).

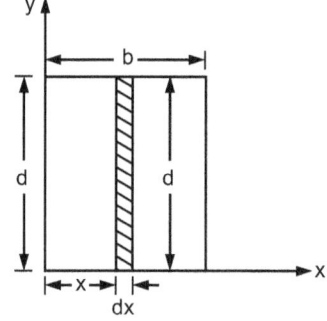

Fig. 4.45

$\therefore I_{xy} = \int_0^b x \cdot \left(\dfrac{d}{2}\right) dA$

$= \int_0^b x \cdot \left(\dfrac{d}{2}\right) d \cdot dx = \left(\dfrac{d^2}{2}\right) \int_0^b x \cdot dx$

$= \left(\dfrac{d^2}{2}\right)\left(\dfrac{x^2}{2}\right)_0^b = \dfrac{b^2 d^2}{4}$

Example 4.28 :

Determine the product of moment of inertia of a circular quadrant of radius r about given axes, as shown in Fig. 4.46.

Solution :

Consider a horizontal strip as shown in Fig. 4.46.

Area of element, $dA = x \cdot dy$

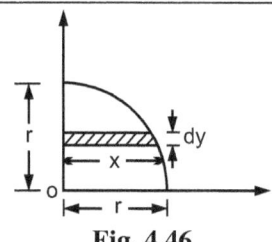

Fig. 4.46

and its centroid is (x/2, y). Thus, product of inertia with respect to two axes x and y,

$$I_{xy} = x\,dy \cdot \frac{x}{2} \cdot y = \left(\frac{1}{2}\right) x^2 y\,dy$$

for circle with centre at O.

$$x^2 + y^2 = r^2$$

∴
$$x^2 = r^2 - y^2 \quad I_{xy} = \left(\frac{1}{2}\right)(r^2 - y^2)\,y\,dy$$

∴ M.I. of whole section,

$$I_{xy} = \frac{1}{2}(r^2 y - y^3)\,dy$$

Solving we get, $\quad I_{xy} = \dfrac{r^4}{8}$

Example 4.29 :

Find product of inertia of given angle section about given axes. Also calculate product of inertia about its centroidal axis parallel to given axes, as shown in Fig. 4.47.

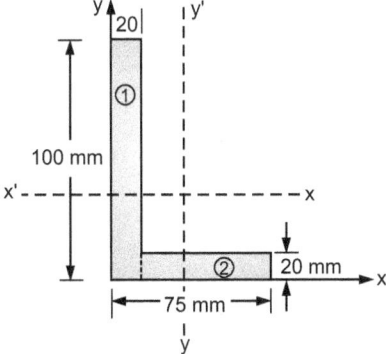

Fig. 4.47

Solution :

Section is divided into two rectangles 1 and 2.

	A	x	y	Ax	Ay	Axy
1.	100 × 20 = 2000	10	50	20000	100000	1 × 10⁶
2.	55 × 20 = 1100	47.5	10	52250	11000	522500
	3100			72250	111000	1522500

Product of M.I. about x and y axes,

$$I_{xy} = \Sigma A \cdot xy = 1522500 \text{ mm}^4$$

Product of M.I. about centroidal axes, using parallel axes theorem,

$$I_{x'y'} = I_{xy} + \Sigma A \cdot \bar{x}\,\bar{y}$$

Centroid of the section,

$$\bar{x} = \frac{\Sigma Ax}{\Sigma A} = \frac{72250}{3100} = 23.31 \text{ mm}$$

$$\bar{y} = \frac{\Sigma Ay}{\Sigma A} = \frac{111000}{3100} = 35.81 \text{ mm}$$

Substituting, $1522500 = I_{x'y'} + 3100 \times 23.31 \times 35.81$
∴ $I_{x'y'} = -1065166.4 \text{ mm}^2$

Example 4.30 :
Determine product M.I. of the section about given axes as shown in Fig. 4.48.

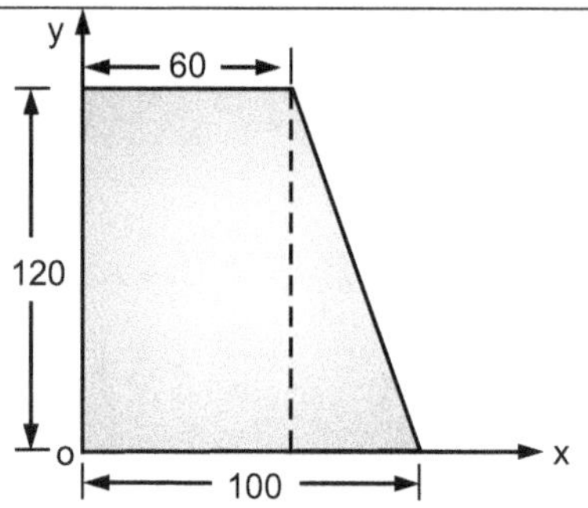

Solution :
Let us divide whole section into rectangle and triangle.

Area of rectangle, $A_1 = 60 \times 120 = 7200 \text{ mm}^2$
and its centroid, $x_1 = 30$, $y_1 = 60$

Area of triangle, $A_2 = \left(\dfrac{1}{2}\right) \times 120 \times 40 = 2400 \text{ mm}^2$

$x_2 = 73.33$, $y_2 = 40$

We know product M.I. of the section,
$$I_{xy} = \Sigma A \cdot xy = 7200 \times 30 \times 60 + 2400 \times 73.33 \times 40$$
$$I_{xy} = 19999680 \text{ mm}^4 \qquad \text{... Ans.}$$

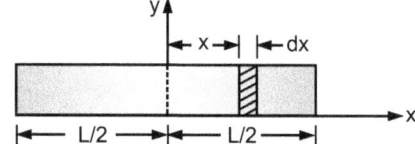

Fig. 4.48

Example 4.31 :
Determine the mass moment of inertia of a rod of mass M and length L about centroidal axis normal to rod.

Solution :
Consider an elemental length dx at a distance x from y-axis as shown in Fig. 4.49.

Let m be the mass per unit length of a rod.
∴ Mass of the element, $dm = m\,dx$

$$I = dm \cdot x^2 = x^2 m\,dx = m\left[\dfrac{x^3}{3}\right]_{-L/2}^{L/2} = \dfrac{mL^3}{12} = \dfrac{ML^2}{12}$$

where, $M = mL$ is the total mass of the rod

If we are interested to find mass moment of inertia about base (edges),

Moment of inertia of the rod about y-axis,

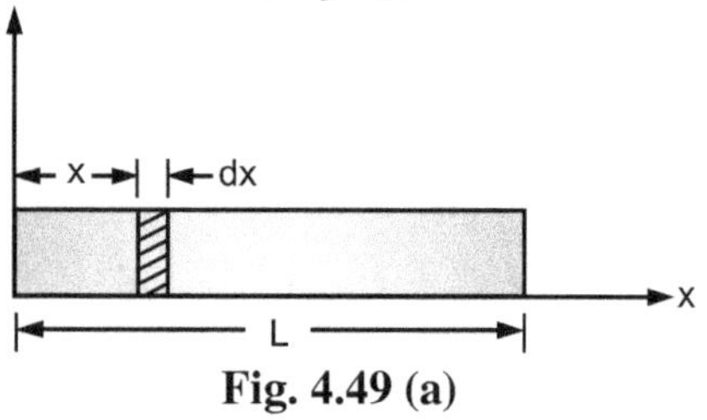

$$I_y = \int_0^L x^2 m\,dx$$
$$= m\left[\dfrac{x^3}{3}\right]_0^L = \dfrac{mL^3}{3}$$
$$I_y = \dfrac{ML^2}{3}$$

Fig. 4.49 (a)

Same also be found by theorem of parallel axes,
$$I_y = I_G + Mh^2$$
$$= \dfrac{ML^2}{12} + \dfrac{ML^2}{2^2} = \dfrac{ML^2}{12} + \dfrac{ML^2}{4} = \dfrac{ML^2}{3} \qquad \text{... Ans.}$$

Example 4.32 :

Determine the moment of inertia of a solid sphere of radius R about its diametral axis.

Solution :

Let a strip of thickness dy at a distance y from the axis. Mass of the elemental plate,

$$dm = w\pi x^2 \, dy$$

But $\quad r^2 = x^2 + y^2$

$\therefore \quad x^2 = r^2 - y^2$

$$dm = w\pi (r^2 - y^2) \, dy$$

We know, mass moment of inertia of this circular plate element about y-axis

$$= \left(\frac{1}{2}\right) \times mass \times square \text{ of radius}$$

$$= \frac{1}{2} w\pi x^2 \, dy \cdot x^2 = \frac{w\pi}{2} x^4 \, dy$$

$$= \frac{w\pi}{2} (r^2 - y^2)^2 \, dy$$

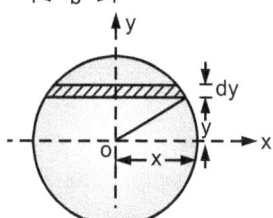

Fig. 4.50

$$\therefore \quad I_{yy} = 2 \int_0^R w\pi [r^4 + y^4 - 2r^2y^2] \, dy = w\pi r^4 y + \left[\frac{y^5}{5} - \frac{2r^2y^3}{3}\right]$$

$$= w\pi r \left[1 + \frac{1}{5} - \frac{2}{3}\right] = \frac{8}{15} [w\pi r^5]$$

But mass of the sphere, $m = \frac{4}{3} \pi r^3 w$

$\therefore \quad I_{yy} = \left(\frac{2}{5}\right) mr^2$

Example 4.33 :

Find the M.I. of circular plate of uniform thickness about its centroidal axis.

Solution :

Let r be the radius of the plate and M its mass. Consider a strip of the plate at a radius x and of width dx. Area of strip = $2\pi x \cdot dx$

Mass of the strip, $dm = 2\pi x \cdot t \cdot w \cdot dx$

$$= \frac{\pi r^2}{r^2} \, t \cdot w \cdot 2x \cdot dx$$

$$= \frac{M}{r^2} \cdot 2x \cdot dx$$

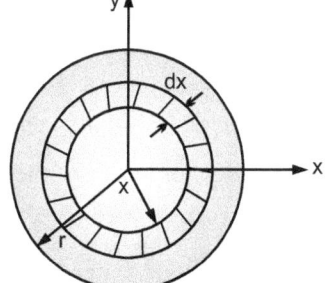

Fig. 4.51

M is the total mass of the plate = $\pi r^2 \cdot t \cdot w$

M.I. of the strip about the centroidal axis = $\frac{M}{r^2} \cdot 2x \cdot dx \cdot x^2$

M.I. of the whole plate, $I_{xx} = \int_0^R \frac{M}{r^2} \cdot 2x^3 \, dx = \frac{2M}{r^2} \left[\frac{x^4}{4}\right]_0^r = \frac{Mr^2}{2}$

Example 4.34 :

Calculate the product moment of inertia of the given section about given axis as shown in Fig. 4.52. Also find product M.I. of the section about its centroidal axis.

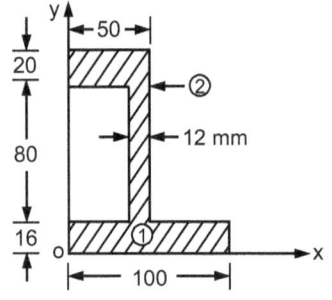

Fig. 4.52

Solution :

Let us divide whole section into three rectangles. All computational work is shown in tabular form.

Sr. No.	A	x	y	Ax	Ay	Axy
1.	1600	50	8	80000	12800	640000
2.	960	44	56	42240	53760	2365440
3.	1000	25	106	25000	106000	2650000
	3560			147240	172560	5655440

$$\bar{x} = \frac{\Sigma Ax}{\Sigma A} = \frac{147240}{3560} = 41.36 \text{ mm}$$

$$\bar{y} = \frac{\Sigma Ay}{\Sigma A} = \frac{172560}{3560} = 48.47 \text{ mm}$$

Product of M.I. of the section about x-y axis,

$$I_{x'y'} = I_{xy} + A \cdot \bar{x} \cdot \bar{y}$$

$$= 5655440 - 3560 \times 41.36 \times 48.47 = -1481634.6 \text{ mm}^4$$

Product moment of inertia of the section can also be calculated as

$$I_{x'y'} = \Sigma (A \cdot x' y')$$

where x' and y' is the distance between centroid of the individual parts and centroid of the whole section.

∴ $x_1' = 41.36 - 50 = -8.64$ $y_1' = 48.47 - 8 = 40.47$

   $x_2' = 41.36 - 44 = -2.64$ $y_2' = 48.47 - 56 = -7.53$

   $x_3' = 41.36 - 25 = 16.36$ $y_3' = 48.47 - 106 = -57.53$

$I_{xy} = 1600 \times (-8.64) \times 40.47 + 960 \times (-2.64) \times (-7.53) + 1000 \times (16.36) \times (-57.53)$

$= -148156 \text{ mm}^4$ ... **Ans.**

PROBLEMS FOR PRACTICE

Problem No. 1 : Find the centroid of the line AB shown in Fig. 4.53.

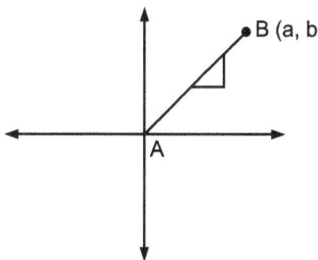

Fig. 4.53

Answer : Centroid $= \left(\dfrac{a}{2}, \dfrac{b}{2}\right)$

Problem No. 2 : Locate the centroid C of a cylindrical homogeneous wire of uniform cross-section is bent into shape as shown in Fig. 4.54. If dimension 'a' is fixed, find the dimension 'b' so that the centroid of wire will coincide with centre 'C' of the semicircular portion.

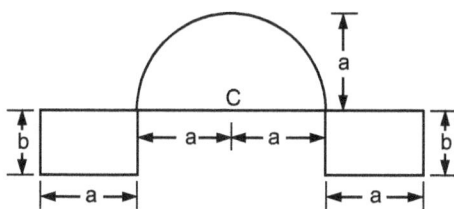

Fig. 4.54

Answer : $b = 0.618\ a$

Problem No. 3 : Locate the centroid of the shaded area shown in Fig. 4.55.

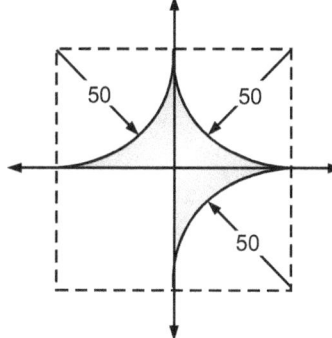

Fig. 4.55

Answer : Centroid = (3.72, 3.72)

Problem No. 4 : A homogeneous wire ABCD is bent as shown in Fig. 4.56 and is suspended at point C. Determine the length "l" for which

(a) portion BCD is horizontal, (b) portion AB is horizontal.

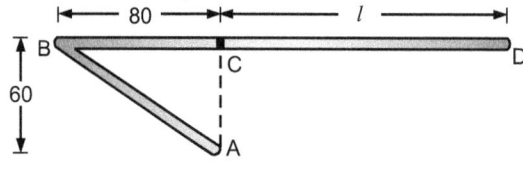

Fig. 4.56

Answer : (a) $l = 120$ mm, (b) $l = 99.5$ mm

Problem No. 5 : For the semi-annular area, determine the ratio of "a" to "b" for which the centroid of the area is located at the point of intersection of the inner circle and the y-axis.

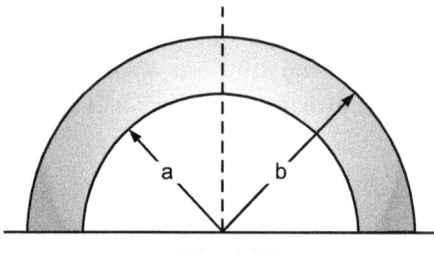

Fig. 4.57

Answer : $\dfrac{a}{b} = 0.495$

Problem No. 6 : Find the value of distance 'a' so that the centroid of the uniform lamina shown in Fig. 4.58 remains at the centre of rectangle ABCD.

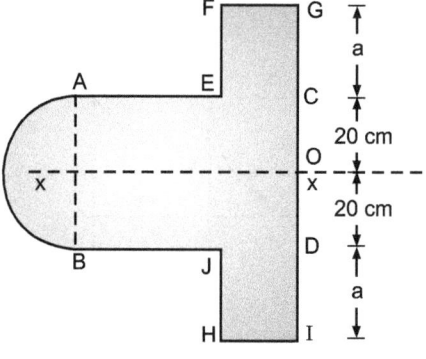

Fig. 4.58

Answer : Value of a = 21.58 cm

Problem No. 7 : Determine the moment of inertia of the following sections about an axis parallel to horizontal and vertical passing through its centroid, as shown in Fig. 4.59.

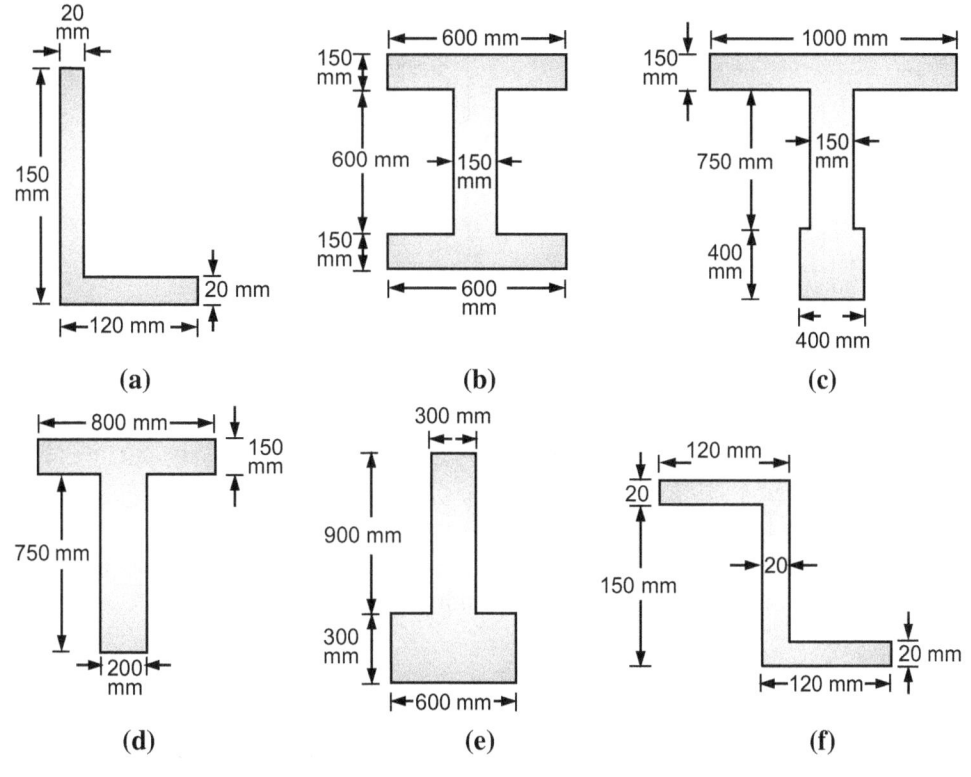

(All dimensions are in mm)

Fig. 4.59

Answers :

(a) $I_{xx} = 10761667$ mm^4 $I_{yy} = 6086666.7$ mm^4

(b) $I_{xx} = 2.835 \times 10^{10}$ mm^4 $I_{yy} = 5.569 \times 10^9$ mm^4

(c) $I_{xx} = 8.954 \times 10^{10}$ mm^4 $I_{yy} = 1.484 \times 10^{10}$ mm^4

(d) $I_{xx} = 2.0756 \times 10^{10}$ mm^4 $I_{yy} = 6.9 \times 10^9$ mm^4

(e) $I_{xx} = 5.8455 \times 10^{10}$ mm^4 $I_{yy} = 7.425 \times 10^9$ mm^4

(f) $I_{xx} = 32.785 \times 10^6$ mm^4 $I_{yy} = 17.86 \times 10^6$ mm^4

Problem No. 8 : Determine the moment of inertia of given built-up section, passing through the centroid of the section and parallel to the top plate. [See Fig. 4.60]

Answer : $I_{xx} = 20.46 \times 10^6$ mm^4

Problem No. 9 : Determine the moment of inertia of the section consisting of pair of angle placed back to back at a clear distance of 10 mm, about its centroidal axis parallel and perpendicular to the top edge. Also find its radii of gyration about both axes. [Fig. 4.61]

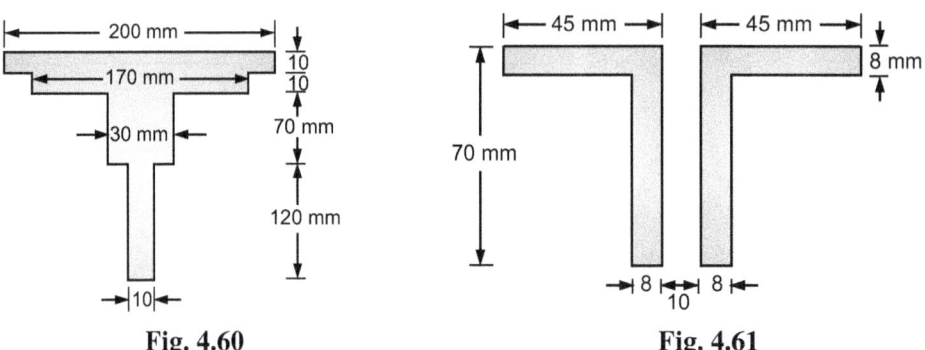

Fig. 4.60   Fig. 4.61

Answer : $I_{xx} = 82 \times 10^4$ mm^4, $I_{yy} = 73.486$ mm^4, $r_x = 21.9$ mm, $r_y = 20.69$ mm

Problem No. 10 : A hollow circular section has an external diameter 100 mm and internal diameter 80 mm. Find the M.I. of the section about an axis passing through its C.G.

Answer : $I_{xx} = I_{yy} = 2.898 \times 10^6$ mm^4

Problem No. 11 : Find the M.I. of a hollow rectangular section about its C.G. The external dimensions are depth 100 mm and breadth 80 mm and internal dimensions are depth 60 mm and breadth 40 mm.

Answers : $I_{xx} = 5.947 \times 10^6$ mm^4, $I_{yy} = 3.947 \times 10^4$ mm^4

Problem No. 12 : Determine the least radius of gyration of the built-up section of column as shown in Fig. 4.62.

Properties of ISHB 450 :

$I_{xx} = 39.211 \times 10^7$ mm^4, $I_{yy} = 2.985 \times 10^7$ mm^4, $A_1 = 11.14 \times 10^3$ mm^2

Answer : $r_{min} = 69$ mm

Problem No. 13 : Determine the least radii of gyration of the built-up section as shown in Fig. 4.63. The built-up section consists of two channels of ISMC 400 and one plate connected at top flange.

Properties of section : A = 6293 mm^2, C_{yy} = 24.2 mm

$I_{xx} = 15.08 \times 10^7$ mm^4, $I_{yy} = 50.48 \times 10^5$ mm^4

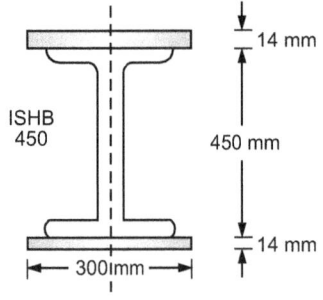

Fig. 4.62   Fig. 4.63

Answer : $r_{min} = 157.9$ mm

Problem No. 14 : Two channels of section ISMC 350 are used as a built-up section placed as shown in Fig. 4.64. Find the distance x between them, such that its M.I. about both centroidal axis are equal.

The properties of ISMC 350 :

A = 5366 mm², B = 100 mm, I_{xx} = 100.08 × 10⁶ mm⁴,

I_{yy} = 43.06 × 10⁵ mm⁴, C_y = 24.4 mm

Answer : (a) x = 218.3 mm, (b) x = 116 mm

Problem No. 15 : Determine the M.I. of the above section as shown in Fig. 4.65 about an x-x axis.

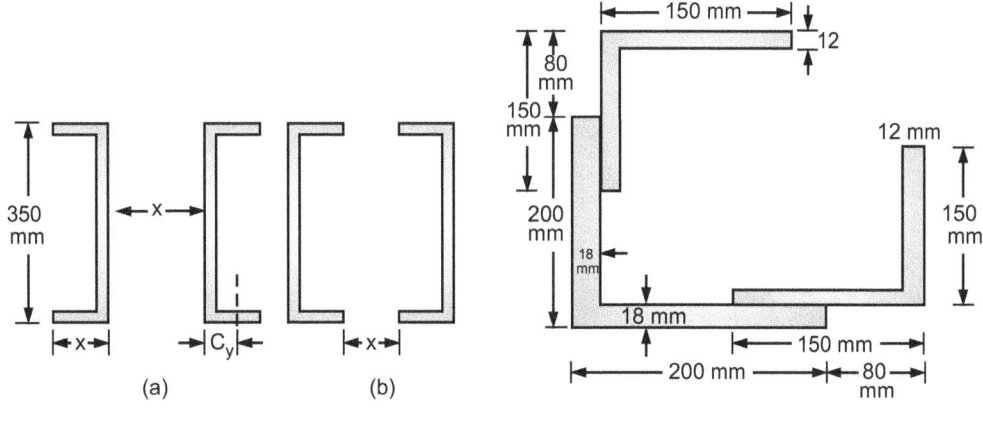

Fig. 4.64   Fig. 4.65

Answer : I_{xx} = 12.584 × 10⁷ mm⁴

Problem 16 : Determine the M.I. of the plate girder about horizontal and vertical centroidal axes. It is made up of a web plate of size 2600 mm × 10 mm, four angles of size 200 mm × 150 mm × 15 mm and cover plate of size 550 × 16 mm as shown in Fig. 4.66.

Properties of ISA 200 × 150 × 15 :

A = 5025 mm²

I_{xx} = 2005.6 × 10⁴ mm⁴

I_{yy} = 969.9 × 10⁴ mm⁴

C_{xx} = 62 mm

C_{yy} = 37.2 mm

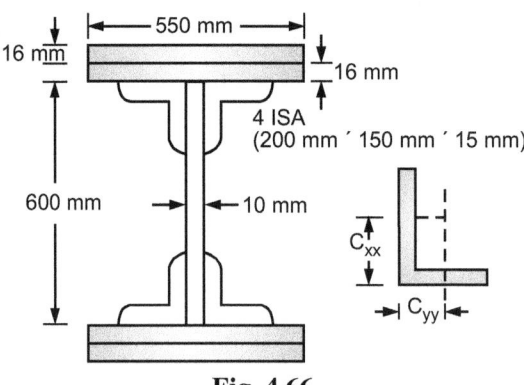

Fig. 4.66

Answer : $I_{xx} = 10.761879 \times 10^{10}$ mm^4, $I_{yy} = 10.580029 \times 10^8$ mm^4

CHAPTER FIVE
KINETICS OF LINEAR AND CIRCULAR MOTION

5.1 KINEMATICS OF LINEAR MOTION OF A PARTICLE

When a particle moves through space, it describes a curve which is known as path. The path of a particle may be either space curve or plane curve. In the simplest form, the path will be a straight line and the particle is said to be in rectilinear motion.

Position : The straight line path of the particle can be defined using a single co-ordinate axis s as shown in Fig. 5.1 (a).

The origin O on the path is fixed point and position vector $\bar{r}$ is used to specify the position of particle P at any given instant. For analytical calculation it is convenient to represent $\bar{r}$ by an algebraic scalar s, representing the position co-ordinate of the particle.

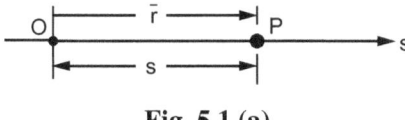

Fig. 5.1 (a)

Displacement : The change in position of a particle is known as displacement. If the particle moves from P to P_1, the displacement is $\Delta s = s_1 - s$, as shown in Fig. 5.1 (b).

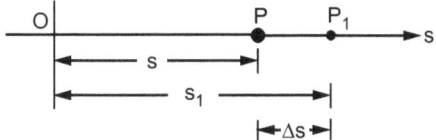

Fig. 5.1 (b)

Displacement is positive when the final position of particle is to the right of its initial position.

If the final position of the particle is to the left of its initial position, the displacement is negative.

Displacement of the particle is the vector quantity which gives magnitude as well as direction.

Distance travelled is a scalar quantity which represents total length of path travelled by the particle.

For example, particle moves from O to A and A to B as shown in Fig. 5.1 (c).

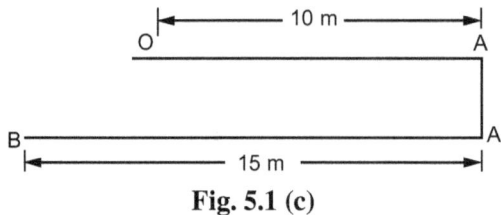

Fig. 5.1 (c)

Displacement = 10 − 15 = − 5 m
= 5 m (←)
Distance travelled = 10 + 15 = 25 m

Velocity : If the particle moves from P to P_1 through a displacement $\Delta \bar{r}$ in time interval Δt, then the average velocity of the particle during the time interval Δt is

$$v_{avg.} = \frac{\Delta \bar{r}}{\Delta t}$$

For a smaller value of Δt, the magnitude of $\Delta \bar{r}$ becomes smaller, the instantaneous velocity is defined as,

$$v = \lim_{\Delta t \to 0} \left(\frac{\Delta \bar{r}}{\Delta t} \right)$$

or $$v = \frac{dr}{dt}$$

Considering v as a algebraic scalar, we can write,

$$v = \frac{ds}{dt} \qquad \ldots (5.1)$$

Since, dt is always positive, the sign or direction of velocity depends on ds or Δs.

When Δs is positive, the particle is moving towards right and the velocity is positive.

When Δs is negative, it indicates that the position of particle is towards left and the velocity is negative.

The magnitude of the velocity is known as speed and its SI unit is m/s.

The average speed is a scalar quantity which is given by the total distance travelled by the particle during time interval Δt.

$$\text{Average speed} = \frac{s}{\Delta t}$$

Fig. 5.1 (d)

Acceleration : The rate of change of velocity with respect to time is known as **acceleration**. When the particle moves from P to P_1, if v is the velocity of particle at P and v_1 is the velocity of particle at P_1, then the average acceleration during the time Δt is given by

$$a_{avg} = \frac{\Delta v}{\Delta t}$$

Δv represents the difference in the velocity during the time interval Δt i.e. $v_1 - v$.

The instantaneous acceleration at time t is

$$a = \frac{dv}{dt} \qquad \ldots (5.2)$$

The sign or direction of acceleration depends on Δv.

When Δv is positive, it indicates increase in speed and the acceleration is positive.

When Δv is negative, it indicates decrease in speed and the acceleration is negative which is known as deceleration or retardation.

Acceleration and deceleration is shown in Fig. 5.1 (e) and Fig. 5.1 (f).

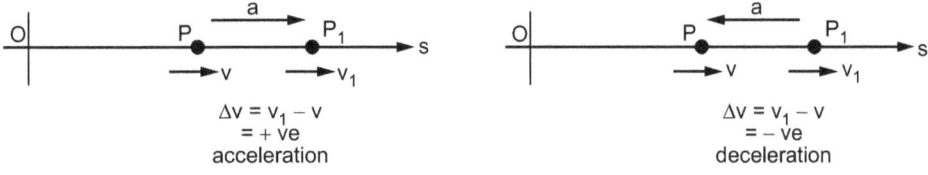

Fig. 5.1 (e)   **Fig. 5.1 (f)**

A differential relation involving displacement, velocity and acceleration can be written as,

$$a = \frac{dv}{dt}$$

$$a = \frac{dv}{ds} \cdot \frac{ds}{dt} \qquad \left(\text{where } \frac{ds}{dt} = v\right)$$

$$\therefore \quad a = v\frac{dv}{ds}$$

$$\therefore \quad \mathbf{a\ ds = v\ dv} \qquad \ldots (5.3)$$

5.2 EQUATION OF RECTILINEAR MOTION WITH UNIFORM ACCELERATION

When the acceleration is uniform, each of the three kinematic equations $a = \frac{dv}{dt}$, $v = \frac{ds}{dt}$ and $a\ ds = v\ dv$ may be integrated to obtain the equation of rectilinear motion with uniform acceleration.

(1) By definition, $\quad a = \frac{dv}{dt}$

$$a\ dt = dv$$

Integrating, $\quad a\int_0^t dt = \int_u^v dv \quad\quad \begin{bmatrix} t \to 0 \text{ to } t \\ v \to u \text{ to } v \end{bmatrix}$

$\therefore \quad a \cdot t = v - u$

$\therefore \quad \mathbf{v = u + at}$ ... (5.4)

In equation (5.4), velocity is a function of time.

(2) By definition, $\quad v = \dfrac{ds}{dt}$

$\therefore \quad ds = v\, dt \quad\quad \begin{bmatrix} s \to 0 \text{ to } s \\ t \to 0 \text{ to } t \end{bmatrix}$

Integrating, $\quad \int_0^s ds = \int_0^t v\, dt$

Substituting, $\quad v = u + a \cdot t$

$\therefore \quad \int_0^s ds = \int_0^t (u + a \cdot t)\, dt$

$\therefore \quad \mathbf{s = ut + \dfrac{1}{2} at^2}$ ... (5.5)

In equation (5.5), position is a function of time.

(3) $\quad\quad a\, ds = v\, dv \quad\quad \begin{bmatrix} s \to 0 \text{ to } s \\ v \to u \text{ to } v \end{bmatrix}$

Integrating, $\quad a\int_0^s ds = \int_u^v v\, dv$

$\therefore \quad as = \dfrac{v^2}{2} - \dfrac{u^2}{2}$

$\dfrac{v^2 - u^2}{2} = 2as$

$v^2 - u^2 = 2as$

$\mathbf{v^2 = u^2 + 2as}$ ... (5.6)

In equation (5.6), velocity is a function of position.

5.3 MOTION UNDER GRAVITY

When the particle is projected vertically in the air, then its motion is under the action of gravitational force. The motion of particle under the action of gravitational force is known as **motion under gravity**.

Characteristics of Motion Under Gravity :

1. Throughout the motion of particle, the gravitational acceleration is always in the downward direction. (g = – 9.81 m/s²)
2. At the maximum height, velocity must be zero (v = 0).

3. The velocity of particle at any height must be same in magnitude in upward or downward direction.
4. The time of motion for upward or downward journey must be same with reference to datum.
5. The equation of motion with constant gravitational acceleration (g) becomes

(a) $\quad v = u - gt \quad$ ... (5.7)

(b) $\quad s = ut - \dfrac{1}{2} gt^2 \quad$ ... (5.8)

(c) $\quad v^2 = u^2 - 2gs \quad$ ... (5.9)

5.4 VARIABLE ACCELERATION

Many times the acceleration of particle may not be constant, but varies from time to time. The four parameters - displacement, velocity, acceleration and time are related as follows.

(1) $\quad v = \dfrac{ds}{dt} \quad$ (Velocity as a function of time)

$$v\,dt = ds$$

Integrating, $\quad \int ds = \int v\,dt$

$$s = \int v\,dt$$

(2) $\quad a = \dfrac{dv}{dt} \quad$ (Acceleration as a function of time)

$$a\,dt = dv$$

Integrating, $\quad \int a\,dt = \int dv$

(3) $\quad a = \dfrac{dv}{dt} \quad$ (Acceleration as a function of position)

$$a = \dfrac{dv}{ds} \cdot \dfrac{ds}{dt} \quad \left(\text{where } \dfrac{ds}{dt} = v\right)$$

$$a = v\dfrac{dv}{ds}$$

Integrating, $\quad \int a\,ds = \int v\,dv$

(4) $\quad a = \dfrac{dv}{dt} \quad$ (Acceleration as a function of time)

$$a = \dfrac{d}{dt}\dfrac{ds}{dt}$$

$\therefore \quad a = \dfrac{d^2s}{dt^2}$

$$a\,dt^2 = d^2s$$

Double integrating, $\quad \int\int a\,dt^2 = \int\int d^2s$

When one or more of the above quantities are specified, the other can be obtained by differentiation or integration. In the process of integration, the constant of integration can be find by giving specified condition such as at t = 0, s = 0 and v = 0.

5.5 KINEMATICS OF CIRCULAR MOTION OF A PARTICLE

5.5.1 Introduction

In Kinematics of particle, we have been considering the motion of a mass center in a straight line i.e. motion of translation or translatory motion also termed as rectilinear motion, which results due to unbalanced force acting on mass centre, and there is no unbalanced moment. But when unbalanced force is zero and only an unbalanced moment or couple acts on body, it results in rotation of the body about some fixed point on the body is said to have the motion of rotation or the rotary motion. A body may also be subjected by an unbalanced force and couple thus have both type of motion i.e. translation as well as rotation, simultaneously. In this chapter, we shall study the kinematics of pure motion of rotation and combined motion of translation and rotation.

5.5.2 Angular Displacement

A body which moves in a circular path is said to have the angular displacement. Let us consider Ox be the axis of reference and body is moving along circular path from A to B in time 't'. Then the angular distance covered by the body is equal to AB and is measured by the angle θ. It is expressed in Radian.

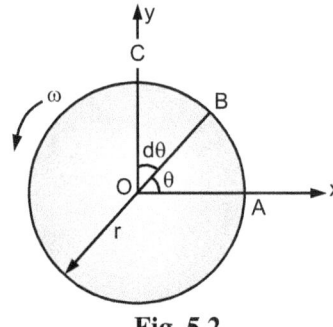

Fig. 5.2

5.5.3 Angular Velocity

Let the body further move to the position represented by the point C in time dt. If it is travelling angular distance dθ in time dt, the rate of change of angular displacement is called the **angular velocity**. It is represented by ω [Omega].

$$\omega = \frac{d\theta}{dt}$$

It is expressed in rad/sec because θ is measured in radians and t in seconds. The angular velocity of rotating body is also expressed by the number of revolutions, that the body makes in a unit time, which is normally a minute or sometimes in seconds and has units R.P.M. or R.P.S. [revolution per minute or seconds.] The R.P.M. of a body is written as N.

The angular velocity of rotating body may be uniform or variable. In uniform angular velocity, the body travels through equal angular displacement in equal time intervals but in variable velocity it travels through unequal distance [angular displacement in rotatory motion] in equal interval of time.

We know, by definition, $\omega = \dfrac{\text{angular displacement}}{\text{time taken}}$

If the speed of rotation is in revolutions per minute, then the angular displacement θ in one motion = $2\pi N$ rad

∴ $\omega = 2\pi N$ rad/minute {∵ 1 revolution = 2π rad.}

∴ $\omega = \dfrac{2\pi N}{60}$ rad/sec.

5.5.4 Angular Acceleration

It is defined as rate of change in angular velocity'. It is represented by α [alpha].

$$\alpha = \dfrac{d\omega}{dt} \text{ and is expressed in rad/sec}^2.$$

5.5.5 Equation of Angular Motion

Consider a body started with initial angular velocity ω_0, accelerated with angular acceleration α for time t, moving along the circular path. During time 't', it gains final angular velocity ω and has traversed 'θ' angular displacement.

From definition, α = Rate of change of angular velocity

$$\alpha = \dfrac{\text{Final velocity} - \text{Initial velocity}}{\text{Time}} = \dfrac{\omega - \omega_0}{t}$$

∴ $\omega = \omega_0 + \alpha \cdot t$ ...(5.10)

Angular displacement, θ = Av. Velocity × Time.

$$\theta = \dfrac{\{\omega + \omega_0\}}{2} \times t \qquad ...(5.11)$$

But, $\omega = [\omega_0 + \alpha t]$

$$\theta = \dfrac{[\omega_0 + \alpha t + \omega_0] \cdot t}{2}$$

$$\theta = \dfrac{1}{2}[2\omega_0 t + \alpha t^2]$$

$$\theta = \omega_0 t + \dfrac{1}{2}\alpha t^2 \qquad ...(5.12)$$

We know from equation (5.10) $\omega - \omega_0 = \alpha t$ ...(5.13)

and from equation (5.11) $2\theta = [\omega + \omega_0] t$

or $[\omega + \omega_0] = \dfrac{2\theta}{t}$ ...(5.14)

multiplying equation (5.13) and (5.14)

$$[\omega - \omega_0] \times [\omega + \omega_0] = \alpha t \times \dfrac{2\theta}{t}$$

$$\omega^2 - \omega_0^2 = 2\alpha\theta \text{ or } \omega^2 = \omega_0^2 + 2\alpha\theta \qquad ...(5.15)$$

Thus, for circular motion (rotational) we get three basic equations,

$$\omega = \omega_0 + \alpha t$$

$$\theta = \omega_0 t + \dfrac{1}{2}\alpha t^2$$

$$\omega^2 = \omega_0^2 + 2\theta\alpha$$

These equations are analogous to the equation for translatory motion.

5.6 RELATIONSHIP BETWEEN LINEAR AND ANGULAR MOTION

(a) Scalar Relation : Consider a body which rotates in a circular path of radius r with an angular velocity ω. Let v be its linear velocity at B when it has moved through an angle θ from OA and further moves through an angle $d\theta$ and occupies the position shown by the point C, where it has the velocity, $(v + dv)$.

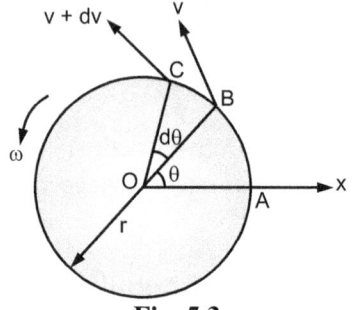

Fig. 5.3

$$\therefore \quad v = \text{tangential velocity at A}$$
$$= \lim_{\delta t \to 0} \frac{\text{Arc BC}}{\delta t}$$
$$\therefore \quad BC = r \cdot d\theta$$
$$v = \lim_{\delta t \to 0} \frac{r \cdot d\theta}{dt}$$
$$= \frac{r \cdot d\theta}{dt} = r\omega \qquad (\because \omega = d\theta/dt)$$

we also know that,

$$a = \frac{dv}{dt} = \frac{d \cdot r\omega}{dt} = \frac{r \cdot d\omega}{dt} \qquad (\because \alpha = d\omega/dt)$$

$$\therefore \quad a = r\alpha$$

Thus, the relationship between the linear and angular quantities.

$$s = r \cdot \theta, \quad v = r \cdot \theta \quad \text{and} \quad a = r \cdot \alpha$$

In general, linear quantity = r × angular quantity
where,   r = radius of the circular path.

(b) Vector's Relation : When we express the motion parameter as vector,

Thus,
$$v = \omega \times r \qquad \text{[A cross product]}$$
$$a = \frac{dv}{dt} = \frac{d}{dt}[\omega \times r]$$
$$a = \frac{d\omega}{dt} r + \omega \frac{dr}{dt}$$
$$a = \alpha \times r + \omega \times v$$
$$a = \alpha \times r + \omega \times [\omega \times r]$$

$\alpha \times r$ is the tangential acceleration,
$\omega \times [\omega \times r]$ is the normal acceleration.

$$a = a_t + a_n$$
$$\text{Total acceleration} = \sqrt{a_t^2 + a_n^2}$$
$$a_t = r\alpha \qquad \text{(acting tangentially)}$$
$$a_n = r\omega^2 \qquad \text{(acting towards center of rotation)}$$

5.7 KINETICS OF LINEAR MOTION

5.7.1 Introduction

As per the Newton's second law, a particle will accelerate when it is subjected to unbalanced force.

Kinetics is the study of the relationships between unbalanced force and the resulting changes in motion.

In succeeding articles, we will study kinetics of particle of rectilinear motion. Here we require combined knowledge of properties of forces, which we have developed in statics and the kinematics of particle of rectilinear motion covered in previous articles.

With the help of Newton's second law, we can combine these two topics and solve engineering problems involving force, mass and motion. In this chapter, we will study direct application of Newton's second law which is known as force-mass-acceleration method.

FORCE - MASS - ACCELERATION

5.8 NEWTON'S LAWS OF MOTION

Isaac Newton first presented three basic laws of governing the motion of a particle. Newton's three laws of motion can be stated as follows :

First law : A particle remains in its state of rest or of uniform motion in a straight line with a constant velocity, will remain in its state unless it is not subjected to an unbalanced force.

Second law : When an unbalanced force $\overline{F}$ acted upon a particle, the unbalanced force experiences an acceleration $\overline{a}$ that has the same direction as the force and the magnitude is directly proportional to the unbalanced force.

Third law : The mutual forces of action and reaction between the particles are equal, opposite and collinear.

The first and third laws were used extensively in developing the concept of statics. These laws are also considered in dynamics.

Newton's second law of motion forms the basis for the study of kinetics because this law relates the accelerated motion of a particle to the unbalanced force acting on it.

Statics is the special case of dynamics, since Newton's second law yields the result of his first law when the unbalanced force is equal to zero.

According to Newton's second law, an unbalanced force is directly proportional to the acceleration or rate of change of momentum.

Consider a particle with mass 'm' moving with velocity v, under the action of unbalanced force 'F'.

$$F \propto \text{Rate of change of momentum}$$

$$F \propto \frac{d}{dt}(mv)$$

$$F = K \frac{d}{dt}(mv)$$

$$F = Km\frac{dv}{dt} \quad \left(\because \frac{dv}{dt} = a\right)$$

$$\therefore \quad F = Kma$$

where K is a dimensionless constant to be determined in order to preserve the equality. The unit force is defined as 'a force which should be applied on a unit mass to produce unit acceleration'.

Hence, the Newton's law of motion may be written in mathematical form as

$$F = ma$$

This equation, which is known as equation of motion, is one of the most important formulations in mechanics. The S.I. unit of force is newton, which is represented by N.

5.8.1 Newton's Law of Gravitational Attraction

Newton postulated a law governing the mutual attraction between any two particles. In mathematical form, this law can be expressed as,

$$F = \frac{Gm_1m_2}{r^2} \quad \ldots (5.16)$$

where,
F = Force of attraction between the two particles
G = Universal constant of gravitation, according to experimental result, $G = 66.73 \times 10^{-12}$ m³/kg-s²
m_1, m_2 = Mass of each of the two particles
r = Distance between the centres of two particles

Any two particles or bodies have a mutual attractive gravitational force acting between them. This force is termed as the weight. Weight will be the only gravitational force considered in mechanics.

5.9 MASS AND WEIGHT

Mass is the property of matter by which we can compare the action of one body with respect to another.

This property indicates itself as a gravitational attraction between two bodies and provide a quantitative measure of the resistance of matter to a change in velocity. It is an absolute quantity.

Therefore the measurement of mass can be made at any location; while as weight of the body is not a absolute, since it is measured in a gravitational field and hence its magnitude depends on the location of measurement.

From equation (5.16), we can write a general expression to find the weight W of a particle having mass $m_1 = m$.

If m_2 is the mass of the earth and r is the distance between the earth centre and the particle, then, $g = \frac{Gm_2}{r^2}$. We have,

$$W = mg \quad \ldots (5.17)$$

In comparison with $F = ma$, g is termed as acceleration due to gravity.

5.10 THE EQUATION OF RECTILINEAR MOTION

If more than one force acts on a particle, the resultant force may be determined by a vector summation of all the forces. i.e. $\bar{F}_R = \Sigma \bar{F}$. In general, the equation of motion may be written as,

$$\Sigma F = ma \qquad \ldots (5.18)$$

Consider a particle P of mass m subjected to action of more than one forces i.e. F_1 and F_2, having an acceleration 'a' as shown in Fig. 5.4 (a).

We can represent forces F_1 and F_2 graphically as shown in Fig. 5.4 (b). If F_R is the resultant of two forces F_1 and F_2, as per Newton's second law, resultant force $F_R = \Sigma F$ produces the vector ma, its magnitude and direction can be represented graphically on the kinetic diagram as shown in Fig. 5.4 (c).

The equal sign between the free body and the kinetic diagram represents graphical equivalency i.e. $\Sigma F = ma$.

In a particular case, when $F_R = \Sigma F = 0$, then the acceleration is zero, so that the particle will either remain at rest or move along a straight line with constant velocity. This is the condition of static equilibrium or Newton's first law of motion.

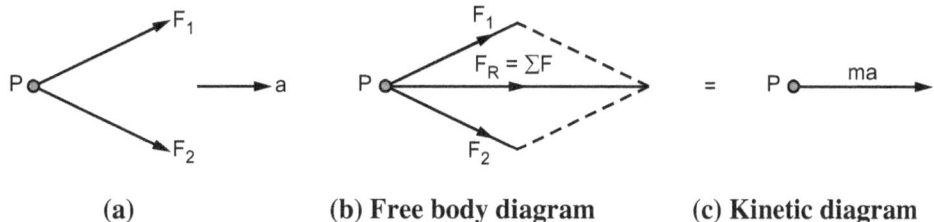

(a)   (b) **Free body diagram**   (c) **Kinetic diagram**

Fig. 5.4

Rectangular co-ordinates : When a particle is moving in the x-y plane, the forces acting on the particle as well as its acceleration, may be expressed in terms of i and j components as shown in Fig. 5.5.

Applying the equation of motion, we have,

$$\Sigma F = ma$$

$$\Sigma F_x i + \Sigma F_y j = m(a_x i + a_y j)$$

To satisfy the above equation, the i and j components of the left side must be equal to the corresponding components on the right side. Hence, we can write the following two equations of motion along x and y directions.

$$\left. \begin{array}{l} \Sigma F_x = ma_x \\ \Sigma F_y = ma_y \end{array} \right\} \qquad \ldots (5.19)$$

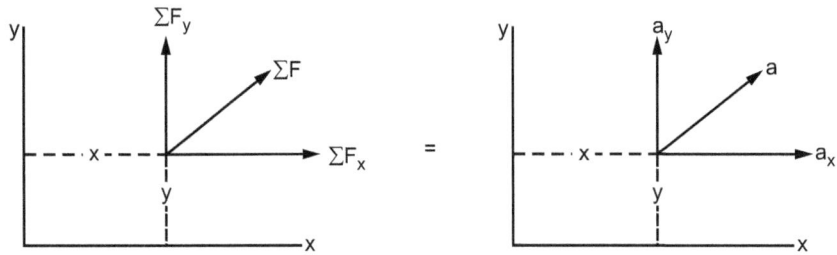

Fig. 5.5

5.11 D'ALEMBERT'S PRINCIPLE

The equation of motion, $\Sigma F = ma$, can also be written as $\Sigma F - ma = 0$. The term $(-ma)$ is called as inertia force or the D'Alembert force and is defined as 'the resistance to the change in condition of rest or of uniform motion of a body'. After applying D'Alembert force to a particle in motion, it comes under dynamic equilibrium and we can write equations of dynamic equilibrium as follows :

$$\Sigma F_x - ma_x = 0$$
$$\Sigma F_y - ma_y = 0 \qquad \ldots (5.20)$$

D'Alembert was the first to point out that the equation of motion can be written as equilibrium equation by introducing inertia or D'Alembert force in addition to the force acting on the system.

It should be clearly understood that the equation of motion of a particle and the equation of dynamic equilibrium of a particle are the two concepts of expression which differ only in the manner of writing the equation. However, the final result will be the same. D'Alembert's principle can be explained in the following example.

Consider a block of mass m resting on horizontal surface subjected to force F. Let μ_k be the coefficient of kinetic friction between the block and the horizontal surface. The F.B.D. of the block is shown in Fig. 5.6.

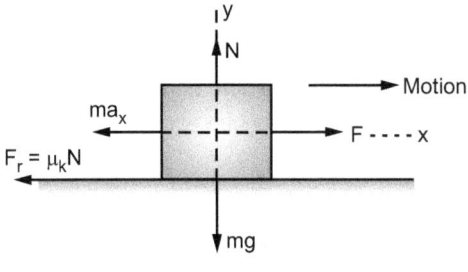

Fig. 5.6

According to D'Alembert's principle, equation of dynamic equilibrium is

$$\Sigma F_y - ma_y = 0 \qquad \ldots (\because a_y = 0)$$
$$N - mg = 0$$
$$N = mg$$
$$\Sigma F_x - ma_x = 0$$

$$F - \mu_k N - ma_x = 0$$
$$F - \mu_k mg - ma_x = 0$$
$$F = m(\mu_k g + a_x)$$

NUMERICAL EXAMPLES ON EQUATIONS OF MOTION

Example 5.1 :

The 50 kg crate is travelled along the floor with an initial velocity 7 m/s at x = 0. The coefficient of kinetic friction is μ_k = 0.40. Calculate the time required for the crate to come to rest and the corresponding distance x travelled. [Refer Fig. 5.7]

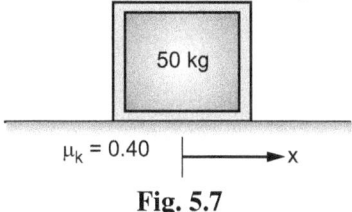

Fig. 5.7

Solution :

Given data : Initial velocity, u = 7 m/s
Final velocity, v = 0
Mass of the crate, m = 50 kg
Coefficient of kinetic friction, μ_k = 0.40.

As the crate travelled with initial velocity, u = 7 m/s (at x = 0) along the floor and come to rest, it decelerates and covered a distance x in time t.

F.B.D. of crate is as shown in Fig. 5.7 (a).

Using equations of motion normal to the plane and along the floor,

$$\Sigma F_y = ma_y \quad \ldots (\because a_y = 0)$$
$$-50 \times 9.81 + N = 50 \times 0$$
$$N = 490.5 \text{ N}$$
$$\Sigma F_x = ma_x$$
$$\mu_k \cdot N = ma_x$$
$$-0.4 \times 490.5 = 50 \times a_x$$
$$a_x = -3.924 \text{ m/s}^2$$
$$= 3.924 \text{ m/s}^2 \text{ (deceleration)}$$

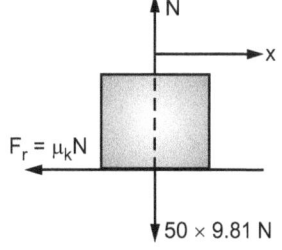

Fig. 5.7 (a) : F.B.D. of crate

Using equation of kinematics,
$$v^2 = u^2 + 2a_x \cdot x$$
$$0 = 49 + 2 \times (-3.924) x$$
$$x = \mathbf{6.24 \text{ m}} \quad \ldots \text{Ans.}$$
$$v = u + a_x t$$
$$0 = 7 + (-3.924) \times t$$
$$\therefore \quad t = \mathbf{1.784 \text{ s}} \quad \ldots \text{Ans.}$$

Example 5.2 :

100 N block is carefully placed with zero velocity on the inclined plane as shown in Fig. 5.8. If $\mu_s = 0.30$ and $\mu_k = 0.25$, determine the acceleration of the block if (a) $\theta = 15°$, (b) $\theta = 20°$.

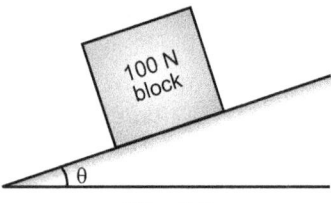

Fig. 5.8

Solution :

Given data : Initial velocity, u = 0

Weight of block, W = 100 N

As the initial velocity of the block is zero, possible motion of block is downward along the inclined plane and it is only possible when θ is more than $\phi = \tan^{-1} \mu_s$.

F.B.D. of block is as shown in Fig. 5.8 (a).

(a) When $\theta = 15°$

$\mu_k = 0.25$

$\phi = \tan^{-1} (0.30)$

$= 16.69°$

$\theta < \phi$, hence no motion

$\therefore$ a = 0   ... Ans.

Fig. 5.8 (a) : F.B.D. of block

(b) When $\theta = 20°$

$\phi = \tan^{-1} (0.30)$

$= 16.69°$

$\theta > \phi$, hence the block is moving downward along the plane.

Using equation of motion normal to the plane and along the plane,

$\Sigma F_y = ma_y,$ (normal to the inclined plane, $a_y = 0$)

$-100 \cos 20 + N = 0$

$N = 93.97 \text{ N}$

$\Sigma F_x = ma_x,$ (along the inclined plane)

$100 \sin 20 - 0.25 \times 93.97 = \dfrac{100}{9.81} \cdot a_x$

$34.20 - 23.493 = 10.194 \, a_x$

$a_x = 1.05 \text{ m/s}^2$ ... Ans.

Example 5.3 :

A man moves a crate by pushing horizontally against until it slides on the floor. If $\mu_s = 0.5$ and $\mu_k = 0.4$, with what acceleration does the crate begin to move ? Assume that the force exerted by the man at impending motion is maintained when sliding begins.

Solution :

Given data : Coefficient of static friction, $\mu_s = 0.5$.

Coefficient of kinetic friction, $\mu_k = 0.4$

Mass of crate is m.

Let P be the force required to push the crate on the floor.

Initially the crate is at rest condition.

Using equation of statics,

$$\Sigma F_y = 0$$
$$-mg + N = 0$$
$$N = mg$$
$$\Sigma F_x = 0$$
$$P - F_r = 0$$
$$P - 0.5\,N = 0$$
$$P = 0.5\,mg$$

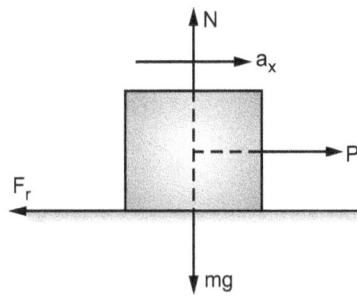

Fig. 5.9 : F.B.D. of crate

At the limiting condition, crate will impend the motion.

Using equation of motion,

$$\Sigma F_x = ma_x$$
$$0.5\,mg - 0.4\,mg = ma_x$$
$$a_x = 0.1\,g$$
$$= 0.981 \text{ m/s}^2 \qquad \text{... Ans.}$$

Example 5.4 :

Determine the minimum stopping distance s and the corresponding time t required by the truck, if the crate is not to slip forward. Take $\mu_s = 0.3$ and $\mu_K = 0.25$ between the crate and the flat bed of the truck which has a speed of 70 kmph.

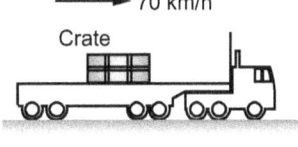

Fig. 5.10

Solution :

Given data : Initial velocity of truck, u = 70 km/h = 19.44 m/s

Final velocity of truck, v = 0.
Coefficient of static friction, $\mu_S = 0.3$
Coefficient of kinetic friction, $\mu_K = 0.25$
F.B.D. of crate is as shown in Fig. 5.10 (a).
Using equation of kinetics,

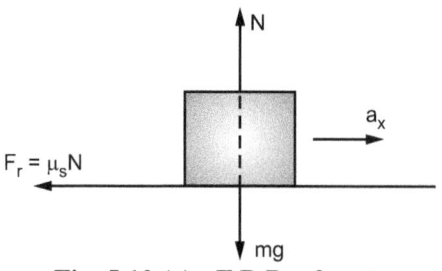

Fig. 5.10 (a) : F.B.D. of crate

$$\Sigma F_y = ma_y, \quad \ldots (\because a_y = 0)$$
$$-mg + N = 0$$
$$N = mg$$

$$\Sigma F_x = ma_x$$
$$-F = ma_x$$
$$-\mu_S N = ma_x$$
$$-\mu_S mg = ma_x$$
$$a_x = -0.3\,g$$

Using equation of kinematics,
$$a = \frac{dv}{dt}$$
$$dv = a\,dt$$
$$dv = (-0.3\,g)\,dt$$

Integrating on both sides,

$$\int_{19.44}^{0} dv = -0.3\,g \int_{0}^{t} dt \qquad \ldots (i)$$

$$19.44 = 0.3 \times g \times t$$

$$\therefore \quad t = \frac{19.44}{0.3 \times 9.81}$$

$$\therefore \quad t = \mathbf{6.606\ s} \qquad \ldots \text{Ans.}$$

From equation (i), $\quad v = 0.3 \times gt$

$$\frac{ds}{dt} = 0.3 \times gt$$

$$ds = 0.3 \times gt\,dt$$

Integrating on both sides,

$$\int_{0}^{s} ds = 0.3 \times 9.81 \int_{0}^{t} t\,dt$$

$$s = 0.3 \times 9.81 \times \frac{t^2}{2}$$

Substituting t = 6.606 s, we get,

$$s = 0.3 \times 9.81 \times \frac{(6.606)^2}{2}$$

$$\therefore \quad s = \mathbf{64.2\ m} \qquad \ldots \text{Ans.}$$

Example 5.5 :

A man weighs 700 N and supports a barbells which have a weight of 500 N. If he lift them 0.6 m in the air in 1.5 s, with uniform acceleration and starting from rest, determine the force exerted on his feet by the ground during the lift.

Solution :

Given data :
Weight of man, W_m = 700 N
Weight of barbells, W_b = 500 N
Lift of barbells, h = 0.6 m
Initial velocity of barbells, u = 0 and time, t = 1.5 s.

Fig. 5.11

Using equation of kinematics along y-direction,

$$s = ut + \frac{1}{2} at^2$$

$$0.6 = 0 + \frac{1}{2} a \times (1.5)^2$$

$$a = 0.533 \text{ m/s}^2$$

Consider F.B.D. of man and barbells at the floor and use equation of motion at floor. R be the force exerted by the ground on the feet of man.

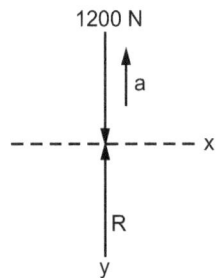

Fig. 5.11 (a) : F.B.D.

$$\Sigma F_y = ma_y$$

$$R - 1200 = \frac{500}{9.81} \times 0.533$$

$$R - 1200 = 27.18$$

$$R = 27.18 + 1200 = \mathbf{1227.18 \text{ N}} \qquad \text{... Ans.}$$

Example 5.6 :

Masses A and B, 30 kg each are connected by light inextensible rope passing over a smooth light pulley as shown in Fig. 5.12. Mass A slides over the smooth inclined plane making an angle of 30° with the horizontal. If the system is released from rest, find the distance moved by mass B in 2 s.

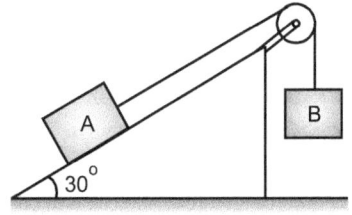

Fig. 5.12

Solution :

Given data : Mass of blocks A and B, $m_A = m_B$ = 30 kg

Let s be the distance travelled by block B in t = 2 s and a be the acceleration of the system. F.B.D.s of blocks A and B are shown in Fig. 5.12 (a) and (b).

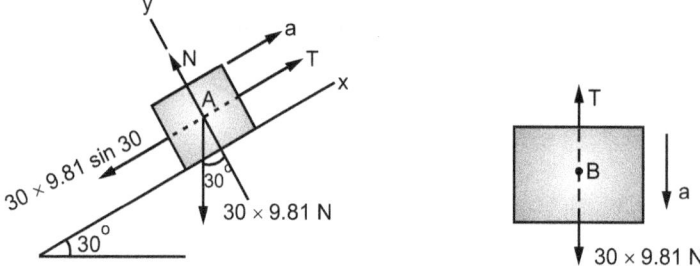

Fig. 5.12 (a) : F.B.D. of block A   Fig. 5.12 (b) : F.B.D. of block B

Consider F.B.D. of block A and using equation of kinetics along the inclined plane,
$$\Sigma F = m_A \cdot a$$
$$T - 30 \times 9.81 \sin 30 = 30 \, a$$
$$T - 147.15 = 30 \, a \qquad \ldots \text{(i)}$$

Consider F.B.D. of block B and using equation of motion,
$$\Sigma F_y = m_B \cdot a$$
$$30 \times 9.81 - T = 30 \, a$$
$$294.3 - T = 30 \, a \qquad \ldots \text{(ii)}$$

Solving equations (i) and (ii),
$$147.15 = 60 \, a$$
$$a = 2.4525 \text{ m/s}^2$$

Using equation of kinematics, distance travelled by block B in 2 s is given by,
$$s = ut + \frac{1}{2} at^2 \qquad \ldots (\because u = 0)$$
$$s = 0 + \frac{1}{2} \times 2.4525 \times (2)^2$$
$$s = \mathbf{4.905 \text{ m}} \qquad \ldots \textbf{Ans.}$$

Example 5.7 :

A crate having mass of 60 kg falls horizontally of the back of truck which is travelling at 80 km/h. Determine the coefficient of kinetic friction between the road and the crate, if the crate slides 45 m on the ground with no tumbling along the road before coming to rest. Assume the initial velocity of the crate along the road be 80 km/h. Refer Fig. 5.13.

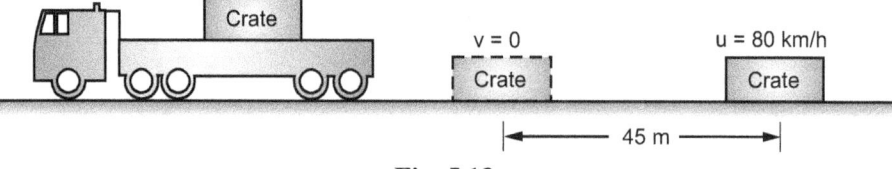

Fig. 5.13

Solution :

Given data : Mass of crate, m = 60 kg
Initial velocity of crate, u = 80 km/h = 22.222 m/s
Final velocity of crate, v = 0.
Distance travelled by the crate, s = 45 m

Let μ_K be the coefficient of kinetic friction and a be the acceleration of the crate. Using equation of kinematics, acceleration of the car is given by,

$$v^2 = u^2 + 2as$$
$$0 = (22.222)^2 + 2 \times a \times 45$$
∴ $$a = -5.487 \text{ m/s}^2$$
$$a = 5.487 \text{ m/s}^2 \text{ (deceleration)}$$

Consider F.B.D. of crate and using equation of kinetics along the road,

$$\Sigma F_y = ma_y \quad ... (\because a_y = 0)$$
$$N_C - 60 \times 9.81 = 0$$
$$N_C = 60 \times 9.81 \text{ N}$$
$$\Sigma F_x = ma_x$$
$$\mu_K N_C = 60 \, a$$
$$\mu_K \times 60 \times 9.81 = 60 \times 5.487$$
$$\mu_K = 0.559 \quad ... \text{ Ans.}$$

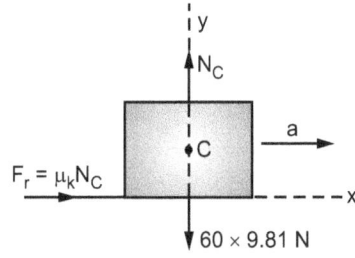

Fig. 5.13 (a) : F.B.D. of crate

Example 5.8 :

For what value(s) of the angle θ will the acceleration of the 2.5 kg block be 8 m/s² to the right when subjected to a force of 30 N. $\mu_S = 0.6$ and $\mu_K = 0.5$ between the block and the floor.

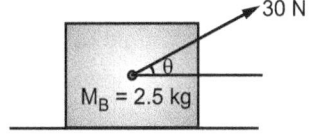

Fig. 5.14

Solution :

Given data :
Mass of block, $m_B = 2.5$ kg
Acceleration of the block, $a_B = 8$ m/s²
Applied force at an angle θ, P = 30 N
$\mu_S = 0.6$ and $\mu_K = 0.5$
Let θ be the angle made by force P = 30 N.

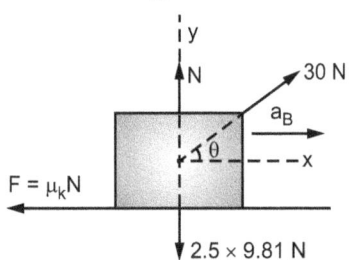

Fig. 5.14 (a) : F.B.D. of block

Consider F.B.D. of block and using equation of kinetics,

$$\Sigma F_y = m_B \cdot a_{By} \quad ... (\because a_{By} = 0)$$
$$N - 2.5 \times 9.81 + 30 \sin \theta = 0$$
$$N = 24.53 - 30 \sin \theta \quad ... \text{(i)}$$

$$\Sigma F_x = m_B a_{Bx}$$
$$30 \cos \theta - \mu_K N = 2.5 \times a_{Bx}$$
$$30 \cos \theta - 0.5 (24.53 - 30 \sin \theta) = 2.5 \times 8$$
$$30 \cos \theta + 15 \sin \theta = 32.265 \qquad \ldots \text{(ii)}$$

Dividing both sides of equation (ii) by $\cos \theta$,
$$30 + 15 \tan \theta = 32.263 \sec \theta$$

Squaring on both sides,
$$900 + 900 \tan \theta + 225 \tan^2 \theta = 32.263 (1 + \tan^2 \theta)$$
$$900 + 900 \tan \theta + 225 \tan^2 \theta = 1041 + 1041 \tan^2 \theta$$
$$\tan^2 \theta - 1.1029 \tan \theta + 0.1728 = 0$$
$$\tan \theta = \frac{1.1029 \pm 0.7247}{2}$$
$$\tan \theta = 0.9138 \text{ or } 0.1891$$
$$\theta = 10.7° \text{ or } 42.43° \qquad \ldots \text{Ans.}$$

Example 5.9 :

The 25 N block B rests on a smooth surface. Determine its acceleration when the 15 N block A is released from rest. What would be the acceleration of block B if the block at A was replaced by a 15 N force acting on the attached cord ?

Solution :

Given data : Weight of block B, $W_B = 25$ N

Weight of block A, $W_A = 15$ N

From equation of kinematics,
$$a_B = 2a_A \qquad \ldots \text{(i)}$$

Let T be the tension in the string. Considering F.B.D. of block B and using equation of motion,
$$\Sigma F = ma_B$$
$$\therefore \quad T = \frac{25}{9.81} a_B$$
$$\therefore \quad 9.81 T = 25 a_B$$
$$\therefore \quad 9.81 T = 50 a_A \qquad \ldots \text{(ii)}$$

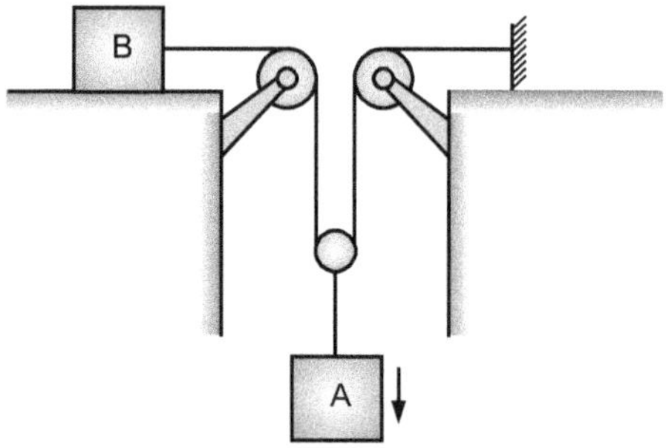

Considering F.B.D. of block A,
$$\Sigma F = ma_A$$
$$15 - 2T = \frac{15}{9.81} a_A$$
$$147.15 - 19.62 T = 15 a_A \qquad \ldots \text{(iii)}$$

Solving equations (ii) and (iii),
$$a_A = 1.2796 \text{ m/s}^2$$

From equation (i), $\quad \mathbf{a_B = 2.56 \text{ m/s}^2}$

Fig. 5.15 (a)

When 15 N block is replaced with 15 N force, acceleration a_A becomes zero and T = 7.5 N.

From F.B.D. of block B,
$$9.81 \times 7.5 = 25 a_B$$
$$a_B = 2.943 \text{ m/s}^2$$

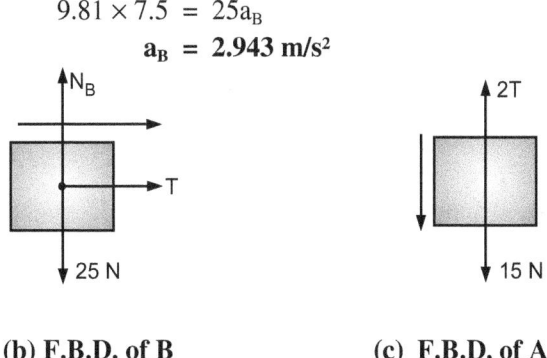

(b) F.B.D. of B   (c) F.B.D. of A

Fig. 5.15

Example 5.10 :

The conveyor belt is designed to transport packages of various weights. Each 10 kg package has a coefficient of kinetic friction μ_k = 0.15. If the speed of the conveyor is 5 m/s, and then it suddenly stops, determine the distance the package will slide on the belt before coming to rest.

Solution :

Given data :

Initial velocity of block, u = 5 m/s.

Final velocity of block, v = 0.

Mass of the block, m = 10 kg.

Coefficient of kinetic friction, μ_k = 0.15.

Considering F.B.D. of block and using equation of motion,
$$\sum F = ma$$
$$0.15 \times 10 \times 9.81 = 10a$$
$$\therefore \quad a = 1.4715 \text{ m/s}^2 \text{ (deceleration)}$$

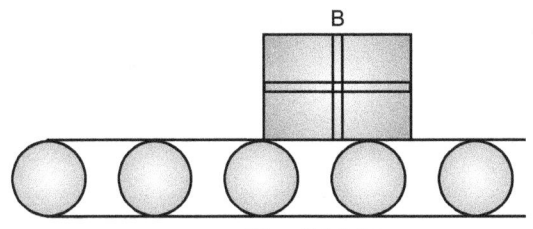

Fig. 5.16 (a)   Fig. 5.16 (b) : F.B.D. of block

Using equation of kinematics,
$$v^2 = u^2 + 2as$$
$$0 = 5^2 - 2 \times 1.4715 \times s$$
$$\therefore \quad s = 8.495 \text{ m} \qquad \qquad \text{... Ans.}$$

Example 5.11 :

Each of the three plates has a mass of 10 kg. If the coefficient of friction (static and kinetic) at each surface of contact are $\mu_s = 0.3$ and $\mu_k = 0.2$ respectively, determine the acceleration of each plate when the three horizontal forces are applied.

Solution :

Given data :
Mass of each plate, m = 10 kg
Coefficient of static friction, $\mu_s = 0.3$
Coefficient of kinetic friction, $\mu_k = 0.2$

Considering F.B.D. of block B : At the limiting condition, frictional force is more than the external force. Hence block B must be in static condition.
i.e. $\qquad a_B = 0 \qquad$ ... Ans.

Considering F.B.D. of block C and using equation of motion,
$$\sum F = ma$$
$$100 - 0.2 \times 10 \times 9.81 - 0.2 \times 20 \times 9.81 = 10 a_C$$
$$\therefore \qquad a_C = 4.114 \text{ m/s}^2 \qquad \text{... Ans.}$$

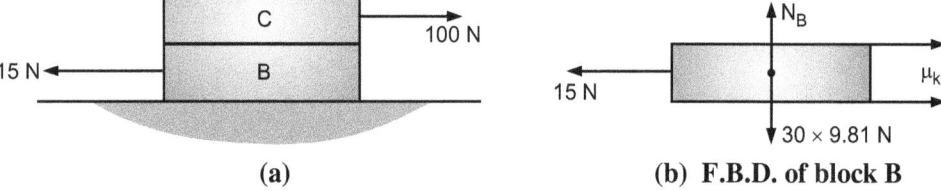

Considering F.B.D. of block D and using equation of motion,
$$\sum F = ma$$
$$0.2 \times 10 \times 9.81 - 18 = 10 a_D$$
$$a_D = 0.162 \text{ m/s}^2 \qquad \text{... Ans.}$$

(c) F.B.D. of block C   (d) F.B.D. of block D

Fig. 5.17

Example 5.12 :

Block A has a weight of 40 N and block B has a weight of 30 N. They rest on a surface for which the coefficient of kinetic friction is $\mu_k = 0.2$. If the spring has a stiffness of k = 300 N/m and it is compressed to 0.05 m, determine the acceleration of each block just after they are replaced.

Solution :

Given data :

Weight of block A, $W_A = 40$ N

Weight of block B, $W_B = 30$ N

Coefficient of kinetic friction, $\mu_k = 0.2$

Spring constant, $k = 300$ N/m

Compression of spring, $x = 0.05$

Considering F.B.D. of block A and using equation of kinetics,

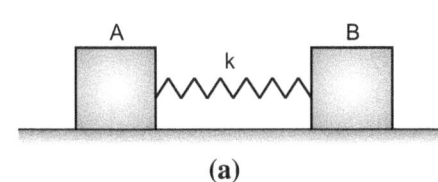
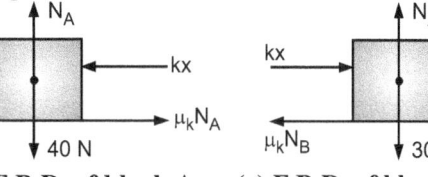

(a) (b) F.B.D. of block A (c) F.B.D. of block B

Fig. 5.18

$$\Sigma F = ma$$

$$300 \times 0.05 - 0.2 \times 40 = \frac{40}{9.81} a_A$$

∴ $\mathbf{a_A = 1.716 \text{ m/s}^2}$ ... Ans.

Considering F.B.D. of block B and using equation of motion,

$$\Sigma F = ma$$

$$300 \times 0.05 - 0.2 \times 30 = \frac{30}{9.81} a_B$$

∴ $\mathbf{a_B = 2.94 \text{ m/s}^2}$ ... Ans.

Example 5.13 :

The acceleration of a package sliding down section AB of incline ABC is 5.49 m/s². Assuming that the coefficient of kinetic friction is the same for each section, determine the acceleration of the package on section BC of the incline.

Solution :

Given data :

Mass of block be m.

a_{AB} be acceleration of package on incline AB.

Let μ_k be the coefficient of friction and a_{BC} be the acceleration of package on incline BC.

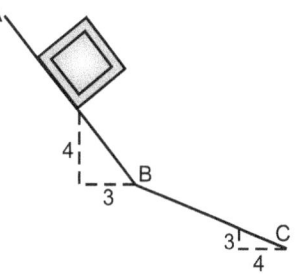

Fig. 5.19 (a)

Considering F.B.D. of package on incline AB and using equation of motion along the plane,

$$mg \sin 53.13 - \mu_k \, mg \cos 53.13 = m \times 5.49$$

∴ $-\mu_k \times 5.866 = -2.3549$

∴ $\mathbf{\mu_k = 0.4}$ ... Ans.

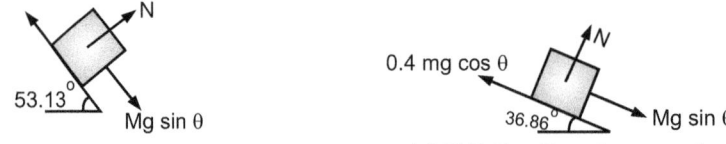

(b) F.B.D. of package on incline AB **(c) F.B.D. of package on incline BC**

Fig. 5.19

Considering F.B.D. of package on incline BC and using equation of motion along the incline,

$$mg \sin 38.86 - 0.4\, mg \cos 36.86 = ma_{BC}$$

$$a_{BC} = 2.745 \text{ m/s}^2 \qquad \text{... Ans.}$$

Example 5.14 :

A hockey player hits a puck so that it comes to rest in 9s after sliding 30 m on the ice. Determine (a) the initial velocity of puck, (b) the coefficient of friction between the puck and the ice.

Solution :

Given data :

Mass of hockey puck, m

Distance travelled, $x = 30$ m

Required time, $t = 9$s

Let v_o be the initial velocity of puck and μ_k be the coefficient of kinetic friction between hockey puck and ice.

Considering F.B.D. of hockey puck and using equation of motion along horizontal direction,

$$\Sigma F = ma$$

$$-\mu_k\, mg = ma$$

$$\therefore \qquad a = -\mu_k g$$

$$\therefore \qquad a = \mu_k g \text{ (deceleration)}$$

Using equation of kinematics,

$$v = u + at$$

$$\therefore \qquad 0 = v_o - \mu_k gt \qquad (\because v = 0)$$

$$\therefore \qquad v_o = \mu_k gt \qquad \text{... (i)}$$

$$s = ut + \frac{1}{2} at^2$$

$$\therefore \qquad 30 = \mu_k \times 9.81 \times 9 \times 9 - \frac{1}{2} \times \mu_k \times 9.81 \times 9^2$$

$$30 = 79.46\, \mu_k - 397.305\, \mu_k$$

$$30 = 397.305 \, \mu_k$$
$$\therefore \quad \mu_k = 0.0755$$

From equation (i),
$$v_0 = 0.0755 \times 9.81 \times 9$$
$$\mathbf{v_0 = 6.67 \text{ m/s}} \qquad \ldots \text{Ans.}$$

Example 5.15 :

The driver of a car, travelling along a straight level highway, suddenly applies a break so that the car slides 2s, covering a distance of 9.81 m before coming to rest. Assuming that during this time the car moved with constant deceleration, find the coefficient of friction between the tires and the highway.

Solution :

Given data :

Distance travelled, s = 9.81 m

Time required, t = 2s

Let a be the constant deceleration and μ be the coefficient of kinetic friction.

Using equation of kinematics, $\quad v = u + at \qquad (\because v = 0)$

$$a = -\frac{u}{t} \qquad \ldots \text{(i)}$$

Using
$$v^2 = u^2 + 2as$$
$$0 = u^2 - 2as$$

Substituting $\quad a = -\dfrac{u}{t}$

$$0 = u^2 - 2\frac{u}{2} \times 9.81$$

$\therefore \quad u^2 = 9.81 \, u$

$\therefore \quad u = 9.81 \text{ m/s}$

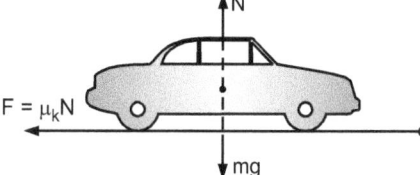

Fig. 5.20 : F.B.D. of car

Substituting u = 9.81 m/s in equation (1),

$$a = 4.905 \text{ m/s}^2$$

Considering F.B.D. of car and using equation of motion along the highway,

$$\mu_k mg = ma \quad \therefore \quad \mu = \frac{4.905}{9.81}$$

$$\boldsymbol{\mu_k = 0.5} \qquad \ldots \text{Ans.}$$

Example 5.16 :

Assuming that a car has sufficient power and that there is sufficient friction, find the maximum acceleration that it would be able to develop without tipping over backward.

Solution :

Considering F.B.D. of car and taking moment about B,

$$W \times b = \frac{W}{g} a \times h$$

$$\therefore \quad a = \frac{bg}{h}$$

Substituting the values of b = 0.8 m, h = 0.4 m,

$$a = \frac{0.8 \times 9.81}{0.4}$$

$$a = \mathbf{19.82 \text{ m/s}^2}$$

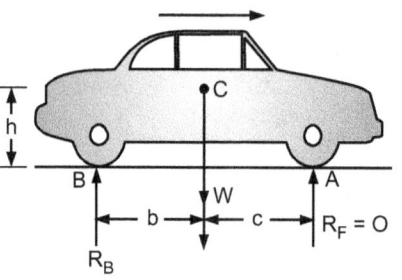

Fig. 5.21

Example 5.17 :

A smooth 10 N collar C fits loosely on the horizontal shaft. If the spring is unextended when s = 0, determine the velocity of the collar when s = 1 m if the collar is given an initial horizontal velocity of 4.5 m/s when s = 0.

Solution :

Considering F.B.D. of collar at s = 1 m. The acceleration is not constant, it varies with deformation of spring. The deformation of spring is zero at s = 0 and 0.414 m at s = 1 m.

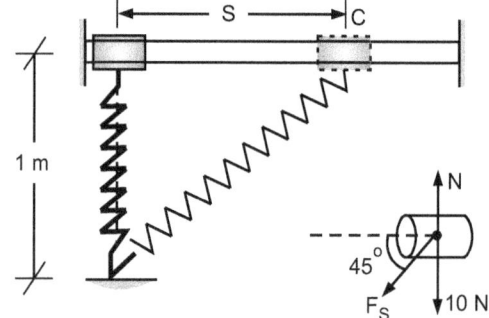

Fig. 5.22

Using equation of motion along the shaft,

$$\sum F_x = ma_x$$

$$-F_s = ma_t$$

$$-F_s = mv\frac{dv}{dx}$$

$$-65 \cdot x \cdot dx = m\, v\, dv$$

$$-65 \left[\frac{x^2}{2}\right]_0^{0.414} = \frac{10}{9.81} \left[\frac{v^2}{2}\right]_{4.5}^{v}$$

$$-5.5704 = \frac{10}{9.81 \times 2} [v^2 - 20.25]$$

$$-10.93 = v^2 - 20.25$$

$$v = \mathbf{3.05 \text{ m/s}} \quad \text{... Ans.}$$

5.12 WORK-ENERGY PRINCIPLE

5.12.1 Introduction

Now, we will integrate the equation of motion with respect to displacement to obtain work-energy principle. The equation of work-energy principle is useful for solving problems which involve force, velocity and displacement. The theorem of conservation of energy is introduced to solve the problem of kinetics of a particle.

5.13 WORK

When the particle or rigid body undergoes a displacement along the line of action of force, then the work done by the force is given by product of magnitude of force and displacement along the line of action of force.

The work done is positive when the displacement takes place in the direction of force and negative when the displacement takes place in opposite direction of force.

Let F be the force and s be the displacement.

$$\text{Work done} = F \times s \text{ Nm}$$
$$= F \times s \text{ joule} \qquad \ldots (1 \text{ Nm} = 1 \text{ joule})$$

5.13.1 Work by a Variable Force

If the particle undergoes a finite displacement along its path from s_1 to s_2 shown in Fig. 5.23 (a), the work is given by integration. If the force F is expressed as a function of position, $F = F(s)$; we can write,

$$\boxed{\text{Work done} = \int_{s_1}^{s_2} F \cos \theta \, ds} \qquad \ldots (5.21)$$

If the component of force $F \cos \theta$ is plotted against position s, [Fig. 5.23 (b)], the integral of equation (5.21) represents area under the curve from the position s_1 to s_2.

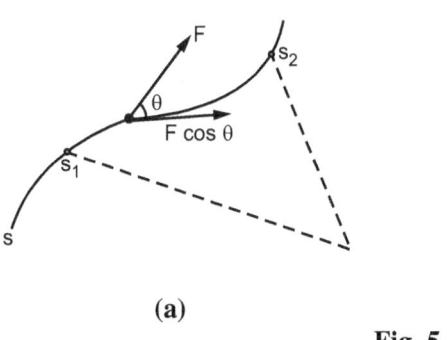

Fig. 5.23

5.13.2 Work by a Constant Force Along a Straight Line

If the force of constant magnitude F acts on a particle along the straight line path shown in Fig. 5.24 (a), the work done by the force F, when the particle is displaced from s_1 to s_2, is given by,

$$\text{Work done} = F \cos \theta \int_{s_1}^{s_2} ds$$

$$\boxed{\text{Work done} = F \cos \theta \, (s_2 - s_1)} \qquad \ldots (5.22)$$

The work done by a constant force F is the area of rectangle shown in Fig. 5.24 (b).

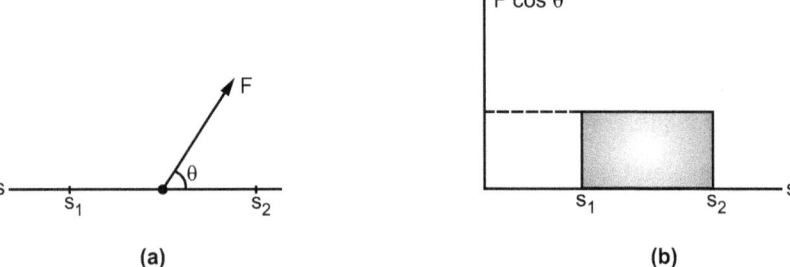

Fig. 5.24

5.13.3 Work By a Weight or Gravity Force

Consider a particle which moves up along the paths from position s_1 to s_2 as shown in Fig. 5.25. At an intermediate position, the displacement $ds = y_2 - y_1$. The work done by the gravity force is given by,

$$\text{Work done} = \int_{y_1}^{y_2} W \, dy$$

$$\text{Work done} = -W \, (y_2 - y_1) \qquad \ldots (5.23)$$

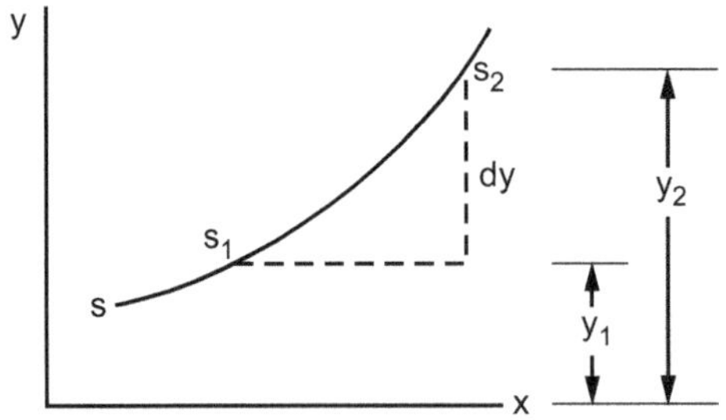

Fig. 5.25

The work done is equal to the product of particle's weight and vertical displacement. The work done is negative when $(y_2 - y_1)$ is positive and it is positive when $(y_2 - y_1)$ is negative.

5.13.4 Work by a Spring Force

When the spring is displaced by a distance x from its unstretched position, the magnitude of force induced in an elastic spring is $F_S = K \cdot x$, where K is the spring constant or spring stiffness or modulus of spring which is defined as 'force required for unit displacement' and its SI unit is N/m. If the spring is deformed from a position x_1 to x_2, the work done on the spring by F_S is positive, since in both the cases force and displacement are in the same direction, as shown in Fig. 5.26 (a).

$$\text{Work done} = \int_{x_1}^{x_2} F_S \, dx = \int_{x_1}^{x_2} Kx \, dx$$

$$\boxed{\text{Work done} = \frac{1}{2} K \left(x_2^2 - x_1^2\right)} \qquad \ldots (5.24)$$

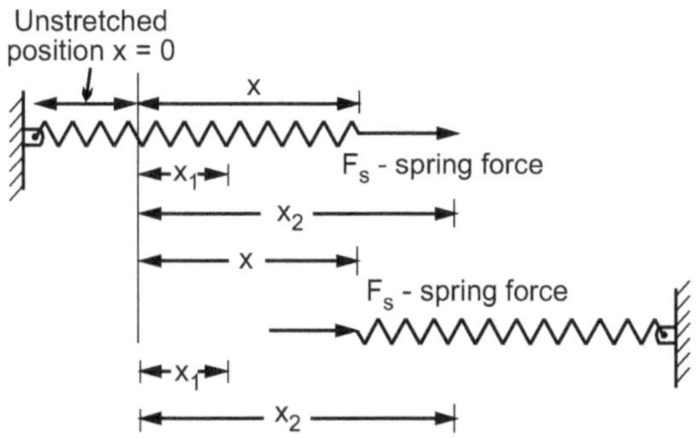

Fig. 5.26 (a)

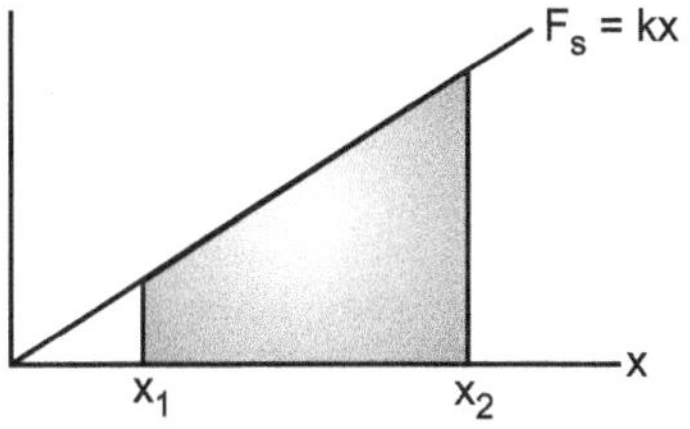

Fig. 5.26 (b)

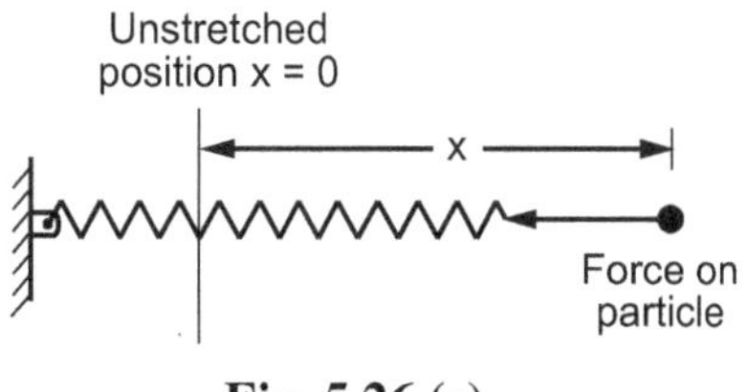

Fig. 5.26 (c)

The equation (5.24) represents the trapezoidal area shown in Fig. 5.26 (b). If the particle or body is attached to a spring, then the force F_S exerted on the particle is opposite to that of the spring, shown in Fig. 5.26 (c), hence the spring force will do the negative work on the particle when the particle is further moving so as to elongate or compress the spring. The equation (5.24) becomes,

$$\boxed{\text{Work done} = -\frac{1}{2} K \left(x_2^2 - x_1^2\right)} \qquad \ldots (5.25)$$

If the spring force acting on a particle and displacement are in the same direction, then the work done is positive, otherwise it is negative.

5.14 PRINCIPLE OF WORK-ENERGY

Consider a particle of mass m travelled from position s_1 to s_2 under the action of force ΣF, which changes the particle velocity u to v. According to Newton's second law,

$$\Sigma F = ma$$

$$\Sigma F = m \cdot \frac{dv}{ds} \cdot \frac{ds}{dt} \qquad \ldots \left(\because \frac{ds}{dt} = v \right)$$

$$\Sigma F = m \cdot \frac{dv}{ds} \cdot v$$

Integrating,
$$\Sigma F \int_{s_1}^{s_2} ds = m \int_u^v v \, dv$$

$$\boxed{\Sigma F (s_2 - s_1) = mv^2 - \frac{1}{2} mu^2} \qquad \ldots (5.26)$$

$$\Sigma \text{ Work done } = \text{Final K.E.} - \text{Initial K.E.}$$

When a particle of mass m is travelled from position s_1 to s_2 with velocity u to v, the work done by all the forces is equal to the change in kinetic energy is known as work-energy principle.

Equation (5.26) represents work-energy principle for a particle. The term on the left hand side is the sum of the work done by all the forces acting on the particle from the position s_1 to s_2. The term on the right hand side, defines the particle's final and initial kinetic energy respectively. These terms are positive scalar quantities since they do not depend on the direction of the particle velocity. Equation (5.26) is dimensionally homogeneous, hence unit of kinetic energy is N-m or joule. The convenient form of work-energy principle is as follows :

$$\boxed{\text{Initial K.E.} + \Sigma \text{ Work done } = \text{Final K.E.}} \qquad \ldots (5.27)$$

which states that the particle's initial kinetic energy plus the work done by all the forces acting on the particle, as it moves from initial position (s_1) to final position (s_2), is equal to the particle's final kinetic energy.

NUMERICAL EXAMPLES ON WORK-ENERGY PRINCIPLE

Example 5.18 :

A woman having mass of 70 kg stands in elevator which has a downward acceleration of 4 m/s² starting from rest. Determine the work done by her weight and the work of the normal force which the floor exerts on her when the elevator descends 6 m. Explain why work of these forces is different.

Solution :

Given data : Mass of woman, $m_w = 70$ kg

Acceleration of elevator, $a = 4$ m/s² ($\downarrow$)

Distance moved by elevator, $h = 6$ m ($\downarrow$)

Work done by woman's weight = $m_w \cdot g \cdot h = 70 \times 9.81 \times 6$

$$= 4120.2 \text{ Nm} = \mathbf{4.12 \text{ kJ}} \qquad \text{... Ans.}$$

Work done by normal force : Normal force is determined by considering F.B.D. of floor of elevator and using equation of kinetics,

$$\Sigma F_y = ma_y$$
$$70 \times 9.81 - N = 70 \times 4$$
$$N = 506.7 \text{ N}$$

Work done by normal force = $-N \times h$
$$= -506.7 \times 6$$
$$= -2440.2 \text{ Nm}$$
$$= \mathbf{-2.44 \text{ kNm or kJ}} \qquad \text{... Ans.}$$

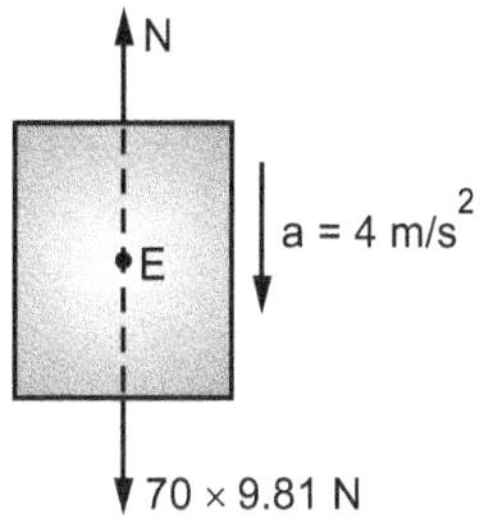

Fig. 5.27 : F.B.D. of elevator

Work done by the normal force is negative as the normal force and displacement are in opposite direction.

Example 5.19 :

The car having mass of 2 Mg is originally travelling at 2 m/s. Determine the distance it must be travelled by a force F = 4 kN in order to attain a speed of 5 m/s. Neglect the friction.

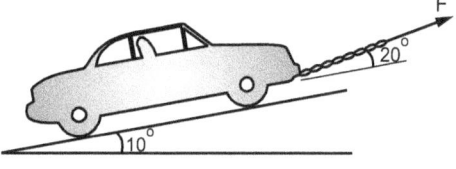

Fig. 5.28

Solution :

Given data :

Mass of car, m = 2 Mg = 2000 kg

Initial velocity of car, u = 2 m/s

Final velocity of car, v = 5 m/s

Let d be the distance travelled by the car along the inclined plane. Considering F.B.D. of car and using work-energy principle,

Initial K.E. + Σ Work done = Final K.E.

$$\frac{1}{2} \times 2000 \times 2^2 + 4000 \cos 20 \times d - 2000 \times 9.81 \sin 10 \times d = \frac{1}{2} \times 2000 \times 5^2$$

$$4000 + 3758.77\, d - 3406.97\, d = 25000$$

$$351.8\, d = 21000$$

$$\therefore \qquad d = \mathbf{59.69 \text{ m}} \qquad \text{... Ans.}$$

Example 5.20 :

Boxes are transported by a conveyor belt with a velocity v_0 on a fixed inclined at A where they slide and eventually fall at B. If $\mu_K = 0.4$, determine the velocity of the conveyor belt if the boxes are to have zero velocity at B.

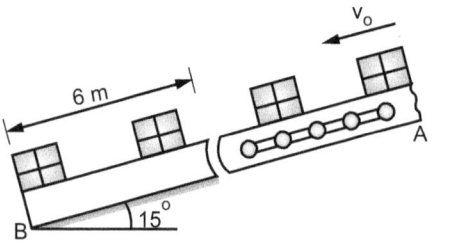

Fig. 5.29

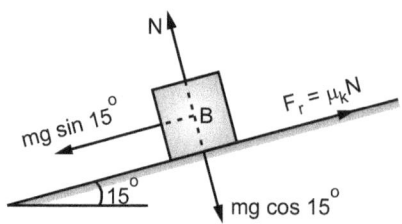

Fig. 5.29 (a) : F.B.D. of block

Solution :

Given data : Initial velocity of block at A, $v_A = v_0$

Final velocity of block at B, $v_B = 0$

Mass of block = m and $\mu_K = 0.4$

Distance travelled by block, x = 6 m

Let v_0 be the velocity of belt. Considering F.B.D. of block and using work-energy principle,

Initial K.E. + Σ Work done = Final K.E.

$$\frac{1}{2} m v_A^2 + mg \sin 15 \times x - \mu_K mg \cos 15 \times x = \frac{1}{2} m v_B^2$$

$$\frac{1}{2} m v_0^2 + mg \sin 15 \times 6 - 0.4 \, mg \cos 15 \times 6 = 0$$

$$\frac{1}{2} v_0^2 + 15.234 - 22.742 = 0$$

$$v_0^2 = 2 \times 7.508$$

∴ $v_0 = 3.875$ m/s   ... Ans.

Example 5.21 :

A package is projected 10 m up an inclined plane so that it just reaches the top of the inclined plane with zero velocity. If $\mu_K = 0.12$ between the package and the inclined plane, determine : (a) the initial velocity of the package at A and (b) the velocity of the package as it returns to its original position.

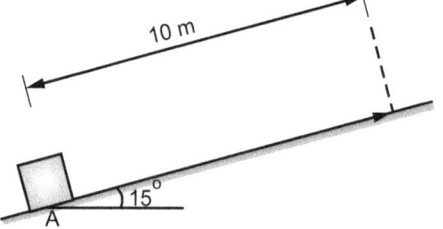

Fig. 5.30

Solution :

Given data : Distance travelled by the package, $x = 10$ m

Velocity of package at the top of inclined plane, $v = 0$

Coefficient of kinetic friction, $\mu_K = 0.12$

Let u_1 be the initial velocity of package at A and u_2 be the velocity of the package as it returns to its original position.

Consider F.B.D. of package for upward motion along the inclined plane and using work-energy principle,

Initial K.E. + Σ Work done = Final K.E.

$$\frac{1}{2} mu_1^2 + \mu_K\, mg \cos 15 \times x - mg \sin 15 \times x = \frac{1}{2} mv^2$$

$$\frac{1}{2} mu_1^2 - 0.12\, mg \cos 15 \times 10 - mg \sin 15 \times 10 = 0$$

$$\frac{1}{2} u_1^2 - 11.371 - 25.390 = 0$$

$$u_1^2 = 73.52$$

∴ $u_1 = $ **8.57 m/s**   ... Ans.

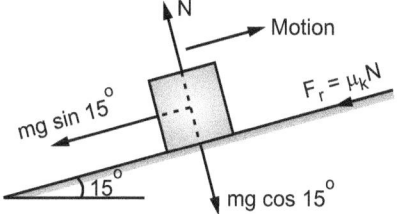 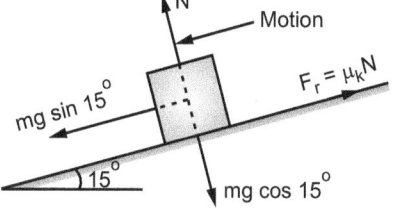

Fig. 5.31 (a) : F.B.D. of package   **Fig. 5.31 (b) : F.B.D. of package**

Consider F.B.D. of package for downward motion along the inclined plane and using work-energy principle,

Initial K.E. + Σ Work done = Final K.E.

$$\frac{1}{2} mv^2 + mg \sin 15 \times x - \mu_K\, mg \cos 15 \times x = \frac{1}{2} mu_2^2$$

$$0 + mg \sin 15 \times 10 - 0.12 \times mg \cos 15 \times 10 = \frac{1}{2} mu_2^2$$

$$25.39 - 11.37 = \frac{1}{2} mu_2^2$$

$$u_2^2 = 28.04$$

∴ $u_2 = $ **5.3 m/s**   ... Ans.

Example 5.22 :

A force, which varies with x as shown, pulls a 10 N body that is originally at rest, along a horizontal floor. If $\mu_K = 0.2$ between the body and the floor, determine (a) the work done by the force in moving the body from x = 0 to x = 8 m, (b) the speed of the body when it has travelled 3 m, (c) the speed of the body when it has travelled 8 m.

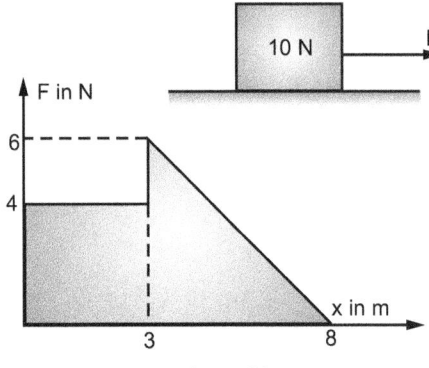

Fig. 5.32

Solution :

Given data : Initial velocity of body, u = 0

Weight of body, W = 10 N

Coefficient of kinetic friction, $\mu_K = 0.2$

(a) Work done by the body from x = 0 to x = 8 m is given by,

$$\text{Work} = \Sigma F \cdot x = 4 \times 3 + \frac{1}{2} \times 6 \times 5$$

$$= \mathbf{27 \ Nm} \qquad \text{... Ans.}$$

(b) Using work-energy principle from x = 0 to x = 3 m,

$$-\mu_K N \cdot x + F \cdot x + \frac{mu^2}{2} = \frac{mv^2}{2}$$

$$-0.2 \times 10 \times 3 + 4 \times 3 + 0 = \frac{10 \times v^2}{9.81 \times 2}$$

$$v^2 = 11.772$$

∴   v = **3.43 m/s - velocity of body at x = 3 m**   ... Ans.

(c) By the work-energy principle, from x = 0 to x = 8 m,

$$-0.2 \times 10 \times 8 + 4 \times 3 + \frac{1}{2} \times 6 \times 5 + 0 = \frac{10 \times v^2}{9.81 \times 2}$$

$$v^2 = 21.585$$

∴   v = **4.65 m/s - velocity of body at x = 8 m**   ... Ans.

Example 5.23 :

Two blocks A and B of mass 4 kg and 5 kg respectively, are connected by a chord, which passes over the pulleys as shown. A 3 kg collar C is placed on block A and the system is released from rest. After the blocks have moved 0.9 m, collar C is removed and blocks A and B continue to move. Determine the speed of block A just before it strikes the ground.

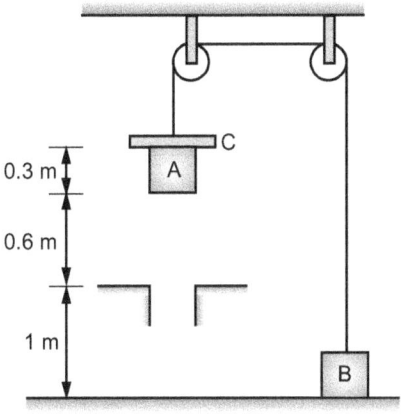

Fig. 5.33

Solution :

Given data :
Mass of block A, $m_A = 4$ kg
Mass of block B, $m_B = 5$ kg
Mass of block C, $m_C = 3$ kg
At h = 0.9, collar is removed.
Initial velocity of system, u = 0

Let v be the velocity of block A at h = 0.9 m ($\downarrow$), at which collar C is detached from block A and v_A be the velocity of the block A just before it strikes the ground.

Velocity of blocks A and B is same, since it is connected by single cord.

Using work-energy principle, from h = 0 to h = 0.9, displacement ($\downarrow$) of block A :

Initial K.E. + Σ Work done = Final K.E.

$$0 + 0 + (4 + 3) \times 9.81 \times 0.9 - 5 \times 9.81 \times 0.9 = \frac{1}{2} \times 7 \times v^2 + \frac{1}{2} \times 5 \times v^2$$

$$v^2 = 2.943$$

$$\therefore \quad v = 1.7155 \text{ m/s}$$

Using work-energy principle, after detaching the collar of 3 kg, downward displacement of block to strike the ground is (1 − 0.3) = 0.7 m.

Initial K.E. + Σ Work done = Final K.E.

$$\frac{1}{2} \times 4 \times (1.7155)^2 + \frac{1}{2} \times 5 \times (1.7155)^2 + 4 \times 9.81 \times 0.7 - 5 \times 9.81 \times 0.7 = \frac{4v_A^2}{2} + \frac{5v_A^2}{2}$$

$$v_A^2 = 1.4169$$

$$\therefore \quad v_A = \mathbf{1.19 \text{ m/s}} \qquad \text{... Ans.}$$

Example 5.24 :

Four identical packages are held in place by friction on a conveyor belt when its power supply is shut off. When the system is released from rest, package 1 leaves the belt at A just as package 4 comes into the inclined portion of the belt at B. Determine (a) the velocity of package 2 as it leaves the belt at A, (b) the velocity of package 3 as it leaves the belt at A. Neglect the mass of belt and rollers.

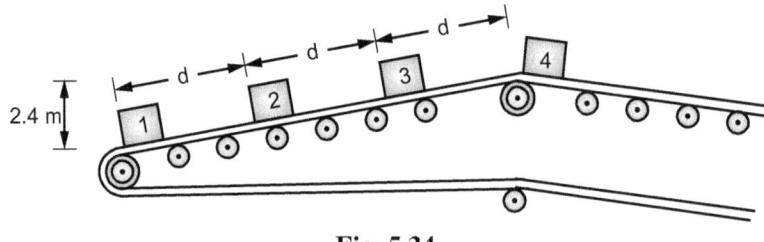

Fig. 5.34

Solution :

Given data : Mass of packages = m

Initial velocity of the packages, u = 0

Let v_2 be the velocity of package 2 as it leaves the belt at A and v_3 be the velocity of package 3 as it leaves the belt at A.

Vertical distance moved by package 2, $h_2 = \dfrac{2.4}{3} = 0.8$ m

Using work-energy principle,

$$\text{Initial K.E.} + \Sigma \text{ Work done} = \text{Final K.E.}$$

$$\frac{1}{2} mu^2 + mgh_2 = \frac{1}{2} mv_2^2$$

$$0 + m \times 9.81 \times 0.8 = \frac{1}{2} \times m \times v_2^2$$

$$v_2^2 = 15.696$$

∴ $v_2 = $ **3.96 m/s** ... **Ans.**

Vertical distance moved by package 3,

$$h_3 = \dfrac{2 \times 2.4}{3} = 1.6 \text{ m}$$

Using work-energy principle,

$$\frac{1}{2} mu^2 + mgh_3 = \frac{1}{2} mv_3^2$$

$$0 + m \times 9.81 \times 1.6 = \frac{1}{2} \times m \times v_3^2$$

$$v_3^2 = 31.392$$

∴ $v_3 = $ **5.6 m/s** ... **Ans.**

Example 5.25 :

A trailer truck has a 2000 kg cab and 8000 trailer. If it enters a 2% uphill grade at 65 km/h and reaches a speed of 100 km/h in 300 m, determine (a) the average force of traction at the cab wheels, (b) the average force in the coupling between the cab and the trailer.

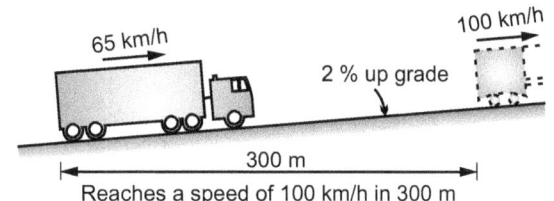

Fig. 5.35

Solution :

Given data : Mass of cab, $m_C = 2000$ kg

Mass of trailer, $m_t = 8000$ kg

Initial velocity of truck, $u = 65$ km/h $= 18.06$ m/s

Final velocity of truck, $v = 100$ km/h $= 27.78$ m/s

Distance travelled by truck, $s = 300$ m

Let P be the force of traction at the cab wheels and F be the average force in the coupling between the cab and trailer. Using work-energy principle,

Initial K.E. $+ \Sigma$ Work done $=$ Final K.E.

$$\frac{1}{2} \times mu^2 - mgx + P \times s = \frac{1}{2} mv^2$$

$$\frac{1}{2} \times 10000 \times (18.06)^2 - 10000 \times 9.81 \times 0.02 \times 300 + P \times 300 = \frac{1}{2} \times 10000 \times (27.78)^2$$

$$300 \, P = 2816424$$

$\therefore \qquad P = 9388$ N ... Ans.

Consider F.B.D. of the cab and using equation of kinetics, acceleration of cab is given by using equation of kinematics.

$$v^2 = u^2 + 2as$$
$$(27.78)^2 = (18.06)^2 + 2 \times a \times 300$$

$\therefore \qquad a = 0.743$ m/s^2

$$\Sigma F = ma$$
$$P - F = ma$$
$$9388 - F = 2000 \times 0.743$$

Fig. 5.35 (a)

$\therefore \qquad F = 7903$ N (Tension) ... Ans.

Example 5.26 :

The ball is released from the position A with a velocity of 3 m/s and swings in a vertical plane. At the bottom position, the cord strikes the fixed bar at B, and the ball continues to swing in the dashed arc. Determine the velocity of the ball as it passes position at C as shown in Fig. 5.36.

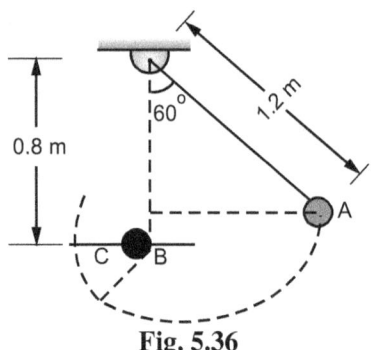

Fig. 5.36

Solution :

Given data : Initial velocity at A, u = 3 m/s
Mass of ball = m
Let v be the velocity of ball at C. Distance moved by ball in downward direction,
$$h = 0.8 - 1.2 \cos 60, \quad h = 0.2 \text{ m}$$

Using work-energy principle,
Initial K.E. + Σ Work done = Final K.E.
$$\frac{1}{2} mu^2 + mgh = \frac{1}{2} mv^2$$
$$\frac{1}{2} m \times 3^2 + m \times 9.81 \times 0.2 = \frac{1}{2} \times m \times v^2$$
$$4.5 + 1.962 = 0.5 v^2$$
$$v^2 = 12.924$$
$$v = \textbf{3.59 m/s} \qquad \text{... Ans.}$$

Example 5.27 :

Each of the two rubber bands, having a stiffness of K = 50 N/m, of the slingshot has an unstretched length of 200 mm. If it is pulled back to the position shown and released from rest, determine the speed of the 25 g pellet just after the rubber bands become unstretched. Neglect the mass of rubber bands and the change in elevation of the pellet while it is constrained by the rubber bands.

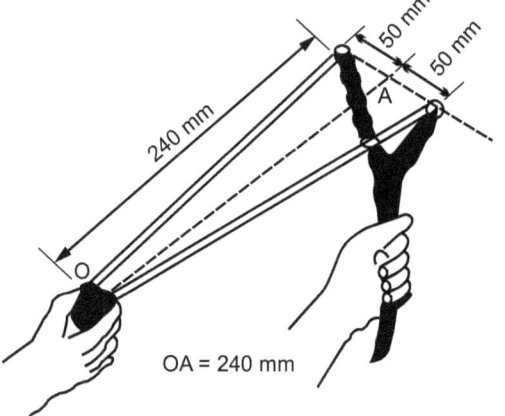

Fig. 5.37

Solution :

Given data : Stiffness of rubber band, k = 50 N/m
Mass of pellet, m = 25 g
Unstretched length, x_0 = 200 mm

Length after stretching, $x_1 = \sqrt{(240)^2 + (50)^2} = 245.15$ mm

Stretch, $x = x_1 - x_0 = 45.15$ mm

Initial velocity of pellet, $u = 0$

Let v be the velocity of the pellet just after the rubber bands become unstretched. Using work-energy principle,

$$\text{Initial K.E.} + \Sigma \text{ Work done} = \text{Final K.E.}$$

$$\frac{1}{2} mu^2 + kx^2 = \frac{1}{2} mv^2$$

$$0 + 50 \times \left(\frac{45.15}{1000}\right)^2 = \frac{1}{2} \times \frac{25}{1000} v^2$$

$$v^2 = 8.15409$$

$$v = 2.86 \text{ m/s} \qquad \text{... Ans.}$$

Example 5.28 :

A 10 kg collar slides smoothly along a vertical rod as shown in Fig. 5.38. The spring attached to the collar has an undeformed length of 100 mm and a spring constant of k = 600 N/m. If the collar is released from rest in position A, determine its velocity after it has moved 150 mm down to position B.

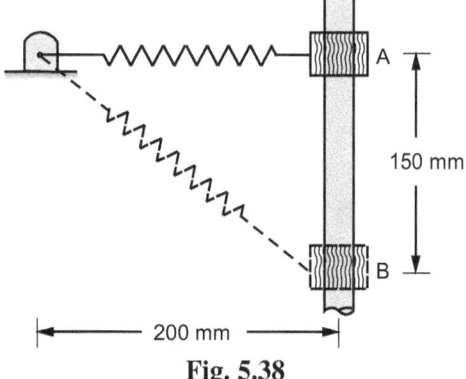

Fig. 5.38

Solution :

Given data :

Mass of collar, m = 10 kg

Undeformed length of spring, $L_o = 100$ mm

Length of spring at position A, $L_A = 200$ mm

Length of spring at position B, $L_B = \sqrt{(200)^2 + (150)^2} = 250$ mm

Initial velocity of collar, $u = 0$

Initial deformation of spring at A, $x_A = 100$ mm

Final deformation of spring at B, $x_B = 150$ mm

Let v be the velocity of collar when it has moved 150 mm down to position B. Using work-energy principle,

$$\text{Initial K.E.} + \Sigma \text{ Work done} = \text{Final K.E.}$$

$$\frac{1}{2} mu^2 + mgh - \frac{1}{2} k \left(x_B^2 - x_A^2\right) = \frac{1}{2} mv^2$$

$$0 + 10 \times 9.81 \times 0.15 - \frac{1}{2} \times 600 \times [(0.15)^2 - (0.10)^2] = \frac{1}{2} \times 10 \times v^2$$

$$14.715 - 3.75 = 5v^2$$

$$\therefore \qquad v^2 = 2.193$$

$$\therefore \qquad v = \mathbf{1.48 \ m/s} \qquad \text{... Ans.}$$

Example 5.29 :

A block of 5.25 kg slides 150 mm from rest down the 20° inclined plane as shown in Fig. 5.39. It hits a spring whose modulus is 1750 N/m. If $\mu_K = 0.20$, determine the maximum compression of the spring.

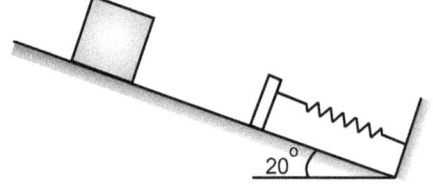

Fig. 5.39

Solution :

Given data :

Mass of block, m = 7.25 kg

Distance moved along the plane, d = 150 mm

Spring modulus, k = 1750 N/m

Coefficient of kinetic friction, $\mu_K = 0.20$

Initial velocity of block, u = 0 and Final velocity of block, v = 0

Let x be the maximum compression of spring.

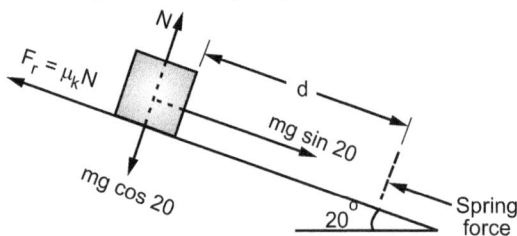

Fig. 5.39 (a) : F.B.D. of block

Considering F.B.D. of block and using work-energy principle,

$$\frac{1}{2} mu^2 + mg \sin 20 \times d - \mu_K \, mg \cos 20 \times d - \frac{1}{2} kx^2 = \frac{1}{2} mv^2$$

$$0 + 7.25 \times 9.81 \times \sin 20 \times 0.15 - 0.2 \times 7.25 \times 9.81 \times \cos 20 \times 0.15 - \frac{1}{2} \times 1750 \times x^2 = 0$$

$$3.649 - 2.005 - 875 x^2 = 0$$

$$\therefore \qquad x^2 = 1.8788 \times 10^{-3}$$

$$\therefore \qquad x = 0.04335 \text{ m}$$

$$\therefore \qquad x = \mathbf{43.35 \ mm} \qquad \text{... Ans.}$$

Example 5.30 :

Block A has a weight of 300 N and block B has a weight of 50 N. Determine the speed of block A after it moves 1.5 m down the plane, starting from rest. Neglect friction and mass of the cord and pulleys.

Solution :

Given data : Weight of block A, $w_A = 300$ N.
Weight of block B, $w_B = 50$ N.
Displacement of block A, $s_A = 1.5$.
Initial velocity of blocks A and B is $v_A = v_B = 0$.
From the concept of length of string,
$$2x_A = x_B, \quad 2v_A = v_B$$
At $\quad x_A = 1.5$ m, $x_B = 3$ m

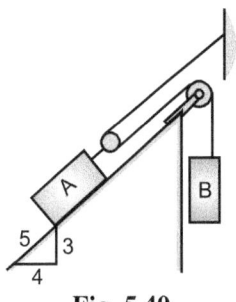

Fig. 5.40

Let v be the velocity of block A.
Using work-energy principle,
$$K.E._1 + \sum W.D. = K.E._2$$
$$0 + 0 + 300 \sin 36.87 \times 1.5 - 50 \times 3 = \frac{1}{2} \times \frac{300}{9.81} v^2 + \frac{1}{2} \times \frac{50}{9.81} (2v)^2$$
$$2354.413 = 500 v^2$$
$$v^2 = 4.709$$
$$\therefore \quad v = 2.17 \text{ m/s} \quad \text{... Ans.}$$

Example 5.31 :

The 2 kg smooth collar is attached to a spring that has an unstretched length of 3 m. If it is drawn to point B and released from rest, determine its speed when it arrives at point A.

Solution :

Given data : Mass of collar, $m_C = 2$ kg.
Unstretched length, $s_0 = 3$ m.
Initial velocity at B, $v_B = 0$.
Stretched length of spring is,
$$s_1 = \sqrt{3^2 + 4^2}, \quad s_1 = 5 \text{ m},$$
Deformation of spring = $(5 - 3)$, $s = 2$ m.

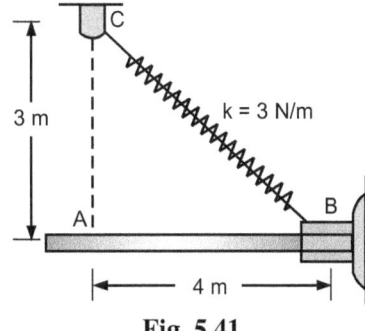

Fig. 5.41

Using work-energy principle,
$$K.E._1 + \sum W.D. = K.E._2$$
$$0 + \frac{1}{2} \cdot 3 \times 2^2 = \frac{1}{2} \times 2 \cdot v^2$$
$$v^2 = 6 \quad \therefore \quad v = 2.45 \text{ m/s} \quad \text{... Ans.}$$

Example 5.32 :

Marble having a mass of 5 g falls from rest at A through the glass tube and accumulate in the can at C. Determine the placement R of the can from the end of the tube and the speed at which the marble falls into the can. Neglect the size of the can.

Solution :

Given data : Mass of marble, m = 5 g.

Let v be the velocity of marble at C.
Using work-energy principle,

$$0 + \frac{5 \times 9.81 \times 3}{1000} = \frac{1}{2} \times \frac{5}{1000} \times v^2$$

$$58.86 = v^2$$

$$v = 7.672 \text{ m/s}$$

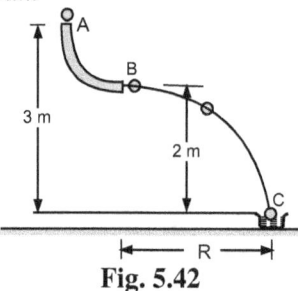

Fig. 5.42

Using equation of kinematics, time required to travel 2 m.

$$-2 = 0 - \frac{1}{2} \times 9.81 \times t^2$$

$$t = 0.6386 \text{ s}$$

Velocity of marble at B along horizontal direction is given by using work-energy principle,

$$0 + \frac{5 \times 9.81 \times 1}{1000} = \frac{1}{2} \times \frac{5}{1000} v_B^2 \quad \therefore \quad v_B = 4.429 \text{ m/s}$$

Using equation of kinematics along x-direction ($a_x = 0$),

$$s_x = R = 4.429 \times 0.6386 \quad \therefore \quad R = 2.83 \text{ m} \quad \ldots \text{ Ans.}$$

Example 5.33 :

The 100 kg stone is being dragged across the smooth surface by means of the truck T. If the towing cable passes over a small pulley at A, determine the speed of the stone when $\theta = 60°$. The stone is at rest when $\theta = 30°$ and the truck exerts the constant force F = 500 N on the cable at B.

Solution :

Given data : Mass of stone, m = 100 kg.
Constant force, F = 500 N.
At $\theta = 30°$, u = 0. At $\theta = 60°$, v = ?
Let v be the velocity of truck at $\theta = 60°$.

At $\theta = 30°$, $l(AC) = \sqrt{8^2 + (8/\tan 30)^2}$
$l(AC) = 16$ m

At $\theta = 60°$, $l(AC) = \sqrt{8^2 + (8/\tan 60)^2}$

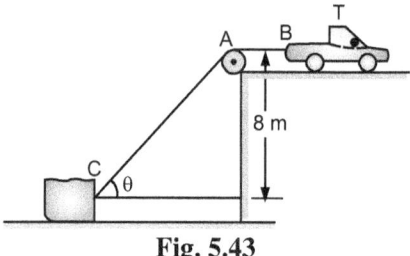

Fig. 5.43

$l(AC) = 9.24$ m

Deflection of cable, s = 16 – 9.24, s = 6.76 m.

Using work-energy principle, $KE_1 + \Sigma WD = KE_2$

$$\therefore \quad 500 \times 6.76 = \frac{1}{2} \times 100 \; v^2$$

$$\therefore \quad v = 8.22 \text{ m/s} \quad \ldots \text{ Ans.}$$

Example 5.34 :

The collar has a mass of 20 kg and slides along the smooth rod. Two springs are attached to it and ends of the rod as shown in Fig. 5.44. If each spring has an uncompressed length 1 m and the collar has a speed of 2 m/s when s = 0, determine the maximum compression of each spring due to the back and forth (oscillation) motion of the collar.

Solution :

Given data : Mass of collar, m = 20 kg.
Initial velocity of collar at s = 0 is, u = 2 m/s.

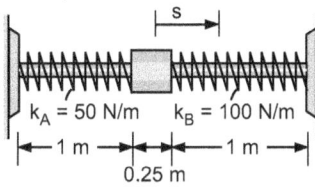

Fig. 5.44

When spring B is compressed by s, the spring A elongates by same amount of deformation. At the maximum compression and elongation of spring, its velocity becomes zero, v = 0.

Using work-energy principle,

$$\frac{1}{2} \times 20 \times 2^2 - \frac{1}{2} \times 50 \times s^2 - \frac{1}{2} \times 100 \, s^2 = 0$$

$80 = 150 \, s^2$, $\quad s^2 = 0.533$, $\quad$ **s = 0.73 m.** ... Ans.

Example 5.35 :

The small collar of mass m is released from rest at A and slides down the curved rod in the vertical plane. If m = 0.5 kg, b = 0.8 m and h = 1.5 m and if the velocity of the collar as it strikes the base B is 4.7 m/s after release of the collar from rest at A, calculate the work Q of friction. What happens to the energy which is lost ?

Solution :

Given data : Mass of collar, m = 0.5 kg.
Height of rod, h = 1.5 m.
Initial velocity, $v_A = 0$.
Final velocity, $v_B = 4.75$ m/s.
Using work-energy principle, $K.E._1 + \Sigma WD = K.E._2$

$$0 + 0.5 \times 9.81 \times 1.5 - Q = \frac{1}{2} \times 0.5 \times 4.7^2$$

Q is the work done due to frictional force.
$0 + 7.3575 - Q = 5.5225$
Q = 1.835 N.m

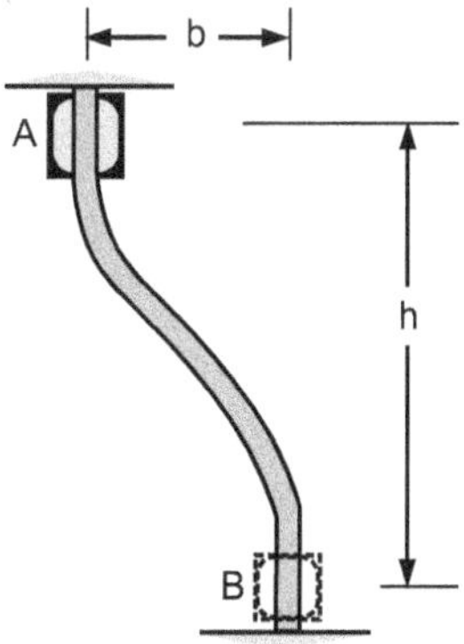

Fig. 5.45

Example 5.36 :

A car with a mass of 1500 kg starts from rest at the bottom of a 10% grade and acquires a speed of 50 km/h in a distance of 100 m with constant acceleration up the grade. What is the power P delivered to the drive wheels by the engine when the car reaches this speed ?

Solution :

Given data :

Mass of car, m = 1500 kg
Initial velocity of car, u = 0
Distance travelled, s = 100 m
Final velocity of car, v = 50 kmph, v = 13.89 m/s

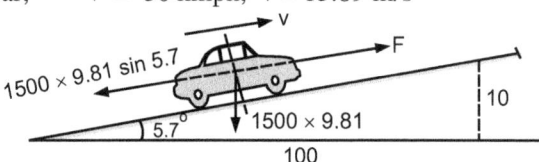

Fig. 5.46 : F.B.D. of car

Let a be the acceleration of the car considering equation of kinematics,

$$v^2 = u^2 + 2as$$
$$13.89^2 = 0 + 2 \times a \times 200$$
$$a = 0.965 \text{ m/s}^2$$

Considering F.B.D. of car and using equation of motion along the plane,

$$-1500 \times 9.81 \sin 5.71 - F = 1500 \times 0.965, \quad F = 2909 \text{ N}$$
$$\text{Power} = F \cdot v = 2909 \times 13.89$$
$$P = 40405 \text{ W}$$
$$\boxed{P = 40.4 \text{ kW}} \quad \text{... Ans.}$$

Example 5.37 :

A small block slides at a speed v on a horizontal surface. Knowing that h = 2.5 m, determine the required speed of the block if it is to leave the cylindrical surface BCD when θ = 40°.

Solution :

Given data : Mass of block, m.

Height, h = 2.5 m, θ = 45°.

Let v be the velocity of the block on horizontal plane and v_C be the velocity of block at C. Considering F.B.D. of block at C and using equation of motion along normal direction,

$$mg \cos 40 = \frac{mv_C^2}{2.5}$$
$$v_C = 4334 \text{ m/s}$$

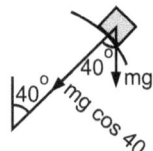

Fig. 5.47 (a)   **Fig. 5.47 (b) : F.B.D. of block at C**

Using work-energy principle (from B to C),

$$\frac{1}{2} m \cdot v^2 + mg(2.5 - 2.5\cos 40) = \frac{1}{2} \times m \times 4.334^2$$

$$v^2 = 2(9.39 - 5.74)$$

v = 2.7 m/s ... Ans.

Example 5.38 :

A package is projected 10 m up a 15° incline so that it just reaches the top of the incline with zero velocity. Knowing that the coefficient of kinetic friction between the package and incline is 0.12, determine (a) the initial velocity of the package at A, (b) the velocity of the package as it returns to its original position.

Solution :

Given data :

Mass of package, m; velocity of package at C, $v_C = 0$; distance travelled, s = 10 m.

Position of plane, $\theta = 15°$ with horizontal; coefficient of kinetic friction, $\mu_k = 0.12$

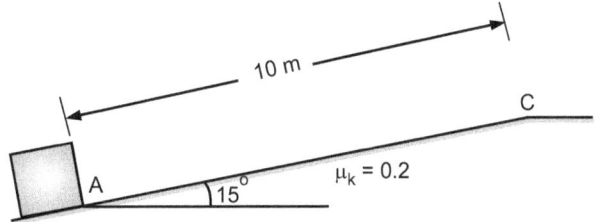

Fig. 5.48

Let v_A be the velocity of package at A and v be the velocity of package as it returns to its initial position.

Using work-energy principle along AC (up the plane),

$$\frac{1}{2} \times m \times v_A^2 - m \times 9.81 \times 10 \sin 15 - 0.12 \times m \times 9.81 \times \cos 15 \times 10 = 0$$

$v_A^2 = 73.52$ ∴ **v_A = 8.57 m/s** ... Ans.

Using work-energy principle along CA (down the plane),

$$0 + m \times 9.81 \times 10 \sin 15 - 0.12 \times m \times 9.81 \times \cos 15 \times 10 = \frac{1}{2} mv^2$$

$v^2 = 28.04$ ∴ **v = 5.3 m/s.** ... Ans.

Example 5.39 :

The system shown consisting of 20 kg collar A and 10 kg counter weight B, is at rest when a constant 500 N force is applied to collar A. (a) Determine the velocity of A just before it hits the support at C, (b) solve part (a) assuming that counter weight B is replaced by a 98 N downward force. Ignore friction and the mass of the pulleys.

Solution :

Given data : Mass of collar A, $m_A = 20$ kg.

Mass of counter weight B, $m_B = 10$ kg.

Constant force, $F = 500$ N.

Initial velocity of collar and weight B, $u = 0$.

Let v_A be the velocity of collar A just before it hits the support at C. From equation of kinematics, velocity of counter weight B is $v_B = 2v_A$.

Using work-energy principle,

(a) $0 + 0 + (500 + 20 \times 9.81) 0.6 - 10 \times 9.81 \times 1.2$

$= \dfrac{1}{2} \times 20\, v_A^2 + \dfrac{1}{2} \times 10\, (2v_A)^2$

$300 = 30 v_A^2 \quad \therefore \quad v_A = 3.16$ m/s ... **Ans.**

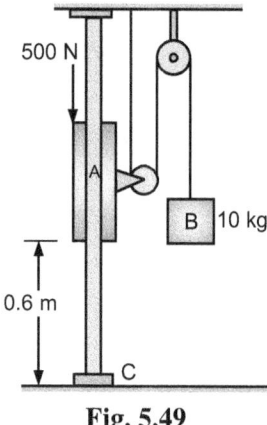

Fig. 5.49

(b) $0 + 0 + [(500 + 20 \times 9.81) - 2 \times 98.1] \times 0.6 = \dfrac{1}{2} \times 20 \times v_A^2$

$300.12 = 10 v_A^2 \quad \therefore \quad v_A = 5.48$ m/s ... **Ans.**

Example 5.40 :

The particle of mass m moves rectilinearly along x-axis under the action of force $F = kx$, where k is constant. Find the velocity v as a function of displacement x if the initial conditions of motion are $x_0 = 0$ and $\dot{x}_0 = v_0$.

Solution :

Given data : Mass of particle, m.

Initial displacement, $x = 0$; Initial velocity, $v = v_0$.

Force, $F = kx$.

Let, v be the velocity of particle at a displacement x.

Using work-energy principle, $K.E._1 + \sum W.D. = K.E._2$.

$$\dfrac{1}{2} \cdot m \cdot v_0^2 + \int_0^x kx\, dx = \dfrac{1}{2} m v^2$$

$$\dfrac{m v_0^2}{2} + \dfrac{k x^2}{2} = \dfrac{1}{2} m v^2$$

$\therefore \qquad v^2 = v_0^2 + \dfrac{k x^2}{m}$

$\therefore \qquad v = \sqrt{v_0^2 + \dfrac{k x^2}{m}}$ ... **Ans.**

5.15 CONSERVATIVE FORCES

A unique type of force acting on a particle depends on the net change in the particle's position and independent of the particle's velocity and acceleration. If the work done by this force in moving the particle from one position to another is independent of path followed by the particle, this force is known as **conservative force**. The weight of the particle and spring force are two examples of conservative forces.

Weight : The work done by the weight of the particle is independent of the path of the particle and it depends only on the particle's vertical displacement. If Δy is positive upward displacement, then the work done by the weight is

$$\text{Work done} = -W \Delta y$$

Elastic spring : The work done by the elastic spring on a particle is independent of the path of the particle and depends on the deformation of spring. If the spring is elongated or compressed from position x_1 to x_2, then the work done by the spring is

$$\text{Work done} = -\frac{1}{2} K (x_2^2 - x_1^2)$$

Friction : Work done by the friction on a particle depends on the path of the particle. Friction is non-conservative force. Longer the path, the work done is more.

Potential energy : The energy which comes from the position of particle is known as potential energy. The potential energy is the work done on a particle by the conservative force when it moves from a given position to datum. The gravitational potential energy of the particle is,

$$\text{P.E.} = mgy$$

where y is position of particle w.r.t. datum. If y is upward, P.E. is positive and if y is downward, P.E. is negative.

Elastic potential energy : If an elastic spring is deformed by a distance x from its undeformed position, the elastic potential energy is,

$$\text{P.E.} = \frac{1}{2} Kx^2$$

The potential energy is always positive, when the spring is returned to its undeformed position.

5.16 CONSERVATION OF ENERGY

When the particle is subjected to conservative and non-conservative forces, the work done by the conservative forces is written in the form of potential energy. According to work-energy principle,

$$\text{Initial (K.E. + P.E.)} + \Sigma \text{ Work done} = \text{Final (K.E. + P.E.)}$$

Σ Work done is the work done by non-conservative force. If only conservative force is acting on a particle, then we have,

$$\text{K.E. (1)} + \text{P.E. (1)} = \text{K.E. (2)} + \text{P.E. (2)} \qquad \ldots (5.28)$$

Equation (5.28) is known as **conservation of energy**.

NUMERICAL EXAMPLES ON CONSERVATION OF ENERGY

Example 5.41 :

The collar has a weight of 40 N. If it is released from rest at a height of h = 0.6 m from the top of the uncompressed spring, determine the speed of the collar after it falls and compresses the spring 0.09 m. (Refer Fig. 5.50)

Solution :

Given data :

Weight of collar, W = 40 N

Downward distance travelled by collar, h = 0.6 m

Compression of spring, x = 0.09 m

Spring constant, k = 500 N/m

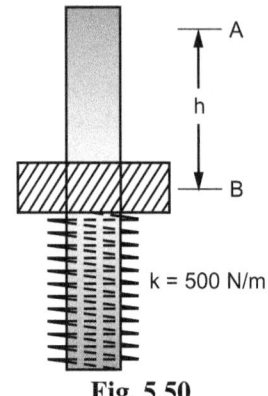

Fig. 5.50

Let v be the velocity of collar after it falls from h = 0.6 m and compress the spring 0.09 m.

Take the datum at h = 0 and use conservation of energy. The gravitational potential energy is – mgh, since the collar is below the datum line.

$$K.E._A + P.E._A = K.E._B + P.E._B$$

$$0 + 0 = \frac{1}{2} \times \frac{40}{9.81} v^2 + \left[\frac{1}{2} Kx^2 - Wh\right]$$

$$0 = \frac{1}{2} \times \frac{40}{9.81} v^2 + \frac{1}{2} \times 500 \times (0.09)^2 - 40(0.6 + 0.09)$$

$$0 = 2.038 v^2 + 2.205 - 27.6$$

∴ $v^2 = 12.461$

∴ $v^2 = \mathbf{3.53 \ m/s}$ ... Ans.

Example 5.42 :

The 2 kg smooth collar is attached to a spring that has an unstretched length of 3 m. If it is drawn to point B and released from rest, determine its speed when it arrives at point A.

Solution :

Given data : Mass of collar, m = 2 kg

Unstretched length, L_o = 3 m

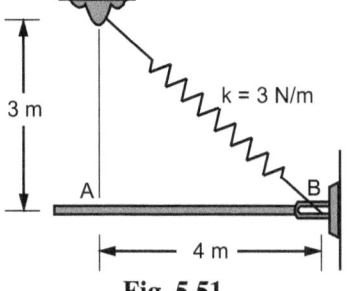

Fig. 5.51

Length after stretching, $L = \sqrt{3^2 + 4^2} = 5$ m, Spring constant, k = 3 N/m

Velocity of collar at B, u = 0, Elongation of the spring, $x = L - L_o = 5 - 3 = 2$ m

For convenience, take datum at AB. Let v be the velocity of collar when it arrives at A. Using conservation of energy,

$$K.E._B + P.E._B = K.E._A + P.E._A$$

Gravitational potential energy is zero, since the collar is moving along the datum line AB.

$$0 + \frac{1}{2} Kx^2 = \frac{1}{2} mv^2 + 0$$

$$\frac{1}{2} \times 3 \times (2)^2 = \frac{1}{2} \times 2 \times v^2$$

$$v^2 = 6$$

∴ v = **2.45 m/s** ... **Ans.**

Example 5.43 :

The collar has a weight of 40 N. If it is pushed down so as to compress the spring 0.6 m and then released from rest (h = 0), determine its speed when it is displaced h = 1.35 m. The spring is not attached to the collar. Neglect friction.

Solution :

Given data : Weight of collar, W = 40 N. (Refer Fig. 5.52)

Compression of spring, x = 0.6 m.

Displacement of spring, x = 1.35 m.

v be the velocity of collar when it is displaced by h = 1.35 m.

Considering compressed position of spring is datum and using conservation of energy,

$$\frac{1}{2} \times \frac{40}{9.81} v^2 = \frac{1}{2} \times 500 \times 0.6^2 - \frac{40}{9.81} \times 9.81 \times 1.35$$

$$2.0387 v^2 = 36$$

$$v^2 = 17.658$$

v = **4.2 m/s** ... **Ans.**

Example 5.44 :

The collar has a weight of 40 N. If it is released from rest at a height h = 0.6 from the top of the uncompressed spring, determine the speed of the collar after it falls and compresses the spring 0.09 m.

Solution :

Given data : Weight of collar, W = 40 N.

Height, h = 0.6.

Spring constant, k = 500 N/m.

Compression of spring, x = 0.09 m.

Initial velocity of collar, u = 0.

Considering datum as compressed position of spring and using conservation of energy.

$$KE_1 + PE_1 = KE_2 + PE_2$$

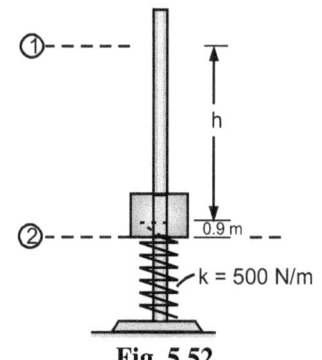

Fig. 5.52

$$\therefore \quad 0 + 40 \times (0.6 + 0.09) = \frac{1}{2} \times \frac{40}{9.81} v^2 + \frac{1}{2} \times 500 \times 0.09^2$$

$$v^2 = 12.545, \quad \mathbf{v = 3.54 \text{ m/s}} \qquad \text{... Ans.}$$

Example 5.45 :

Point P on the 2 kg cylinder has an initial velocity $v_o = 0.8$ m/s as it passes position A. Neglect the mass of the pulleys and cable and determine the distance y of point P below A when the 3 kg cylinder has acquired an upward velocity of 0.6 m/s.

Solution :

Given data : Mass of cylinder A, $m_A = 2$ kg.
Mass of cylinder B, $m_B = 3$ kg.
Initial velocity of cylinder A, $u_A = 0.8$ m/s
Final velocity of cylinder B, $v_B = 0.6$ m/s.
Let y be the distance below A when cylinder B acquired upward velocity of 0.6 m/s.
From concept of length of string,
$$x_A = 2x_B, \quad v_B = 2v_B$$
$$\therefore \quad u_B = 0.4 \text{ m/s}.$$
$$y = 2x_B \quad \therefore \quad x_B = y/2.$$

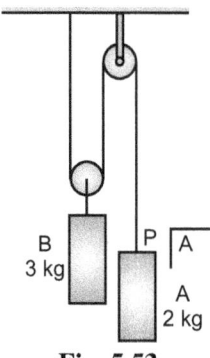

Fig. 5.53

Considering datum at A and using conservation of energy

$$\frac{1}{2} \times 2 \times 0.8^2 + \frac{1}{2} \times 3 \times 0.4^2 = \frac{1}{2} \times 2 \times 1.2^2 + \frac{1}{2} \times 3 \times 0.6^2 - 2 \times 9.81 y + 3 \times 9.81 \times y/2$$

$$0.8 = 1.98 - 4.905 y, \quad 4.905 y = 1.98 - 0.88 \quad \therefore \quad \mathbf{y = 0.224 \text{ m}}. \qquad \text{... Ans.}$$

Example 5.46 :

The simple pendulum shown in Fig. 5.54 is released from rest at A with the string horizontal and swing downward under the influence of gravity. Express the velocity v of the bob as a function of angle θ.

Solution :

Given data : Weight of pendulum - W.
Velocity of pendulum at A, $v_A = 0$.
Length of pendulum - L.
Let v be the velocity of pendulum at B.
Considering datum at B and using conservation of energy,

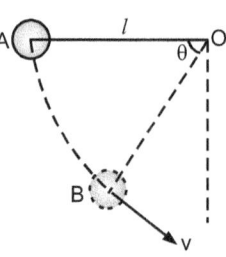

Fig. 5.54

$$0 + Wl \sin \theta = \frac{1}{2} \cdot \frac{W}{g} v^2$$
$$v^2 = 2gl \sin \theta$$
$$\therefore \quad \mathbf{v = \sqrt{2gl \sin \theta}} \qquad \text{... Ans.}$$

Example 5.47 :

If the pendulum shown in Fig. 5.55 is released from rest in its position of unstable equilibrium as shown, find the value of the angle φ defining the position in its downward fall at which the axial force in the rod changes from compression to tension.

Solution :

Given data : Weight of pendulum - W.
Initial velocity of pendulum at A, $v_A = 0$.
Length of pendulum - l.
Let v be the velocity of pendulum at B.
Considering datum at B and using conservation of energy,

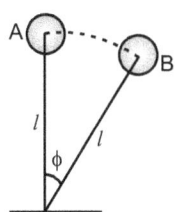

Fig. 5.55 (a)

$$0 + W(l - l\cos\theta) = \frac{1}{2} \cdot \frac{W}{g} \cdot v^2$$

$$v^2 = 2gl(1 - \cos\theta)$$

Considering F.B.D. of pendulum bob at B and using equation of motion along normal axis,

$$\sum F_x = ma_n$$

$$W\cos\theta = \frac{W}{g} \cdot \frac{2gl(1 - \cos\theta)}{l}$$

$$\cos\theta = 2 - 2\cos\theta$$

$$3\cos\theta = 2$$

$$\cos\theta = \frac{2}{3}$$

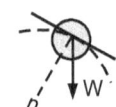

Fig. 5.55 (b) : F.B.D. of pendulum bob

∴ $\theta = 48.19°$

5.17 IMPULSE-MOMENTUM PRINCIPLE

5.17.1 Introduction

In the succeeding articles we will integrate the equation of motion with respect to time to obtain principle of impulse and momentum. The equation of impulse-momentum is useful for solving problems involving force, velocity and time. The conservation of momentum and coefficient of restitution are introduced to solve the problems of impact.

5.18 IMPULSE AND MOMENTUM

Impulse : The change in momentum produced by a force on the particle within an infinite short interval of time is known as **impulse**.

$$\boxed{\text{Impulse} = \text{Force} \times \text{Time}}$$

$$= F \cdot t$$

Its S.I. unit is N-s.

Momentum : The amount of motion possessed by a particle during the motion which depends upon the mass and the velocity of the particle is known as **momentum**. It is the product of mass and velocity of the particle.

$$\boxed{\text{Momentum} = \text{Mass} \times \text{Velocity}}$$

$$= m \times v$$

Its S.I. unit is kg-m/s or N-s.

Impulse-Momentum Principle : According to Newton's second law of motion,

$$\Sigma F = ma$$

$$\Sigma F = m \cdot \frac{dv}{dt}$$

Integrating between the limits $v = u$ at $t = t_1$ and $v = v$ at $t = t_2$,

$$\Sigma \int_{t_1}^{t_2} F \cdot dt = m \int_u^v dv$$

$$\Sigma \int_{t_1}^{t_2} F \cdot dt = mv - mu \qquad \ldots (5.29)$$

$$\boxed{\Sigma \text{ Impulse} = \text{Final momentum} - \text{Initial momentum}}$$

Equation (5.29) is known as impulse-momentum principle. If the magnitude or direction of a force varies, the impulse of the force is determined by integration. If the force is constant for the time interval $(t_2 - t_1)$, the impulse of the force is $F(t_2 - t_1)$.

The following equation represents the principle of linear impulse-momentum for the particle in the x and y directions respectively.

$$\left. \begin{array}{l} \Sigma F_x (t_2 - t_1) = m (v_x - u_x) \\ \Sigma F_y (t_2 - t_1) = m (v_y - u_y) \end{array} \right\} \qquad (5.30)$$

While solving numerical problems, impulse in the direction of motion is considered positive.

5.19 CONSERVATION OF MOMENTUM FOR SYSTEM OF PARTICLES

Rewriting impulse-momentum principle in the following form,

$$mu + \Sigma F (t_2 - t_1) = mv$$

When the sum of the external impulses acting on a system of particle is zero, the above equation reduces to a simplified form

$$\boxed{\Sigma mu = \Sigma mv} \qquad \ldots (5.31)$$

This equation is known as the conservation of momentum for a system of particle. It states that sum of linear momentum for a system of particles remains constant throughout the period t_1 to t_2.

NUMERICAL EXAMPLES ON IMPULSE-MOMENTUM PRINCIPLE

Example 5.48 :

The winch delivers a horizontal force F, which varies as shown, to the cable at A. The pulley carries a 70 kg block B. If B is originally moving upwards at 3 m/s, determine the speed of the block at t = 18 s.

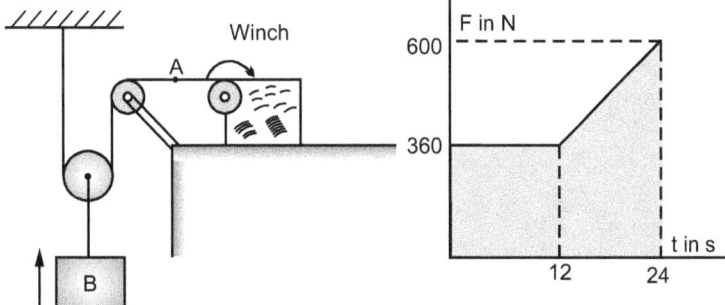

Fig. 5.56

Solution :

Given data : Mass of pulley, m = 70 kg

Initial velocity of block, u = 3 m/s

Let v be the velocity of the block at t = 18 s

From Fig. 5.56, at t = 18 s, impulsive force is given by

$$\text{Impulsive force} = \frac{600 - 360}{2} + 360 = 480 \text{ N}$$

Considering F.B.D. of block and using impulse-momentum principle,

$$\Sigma Ft = m(v - u)$$

$$2\left[360 \times 12 + \left(\frac{360 + 480}{2}\right) \times 6\right] - 70 \times 9.81 \times 18 = 70(v - 3)$$

$$13680 - 12360.6 = 70v - 210$$

$$\therefore \quad v = \frac{1529.4}{70}$$

$$\therefore \quad v_B = \mathbf{21.85 \text{ m/s}} \quad ...\text{ Ans.}$$

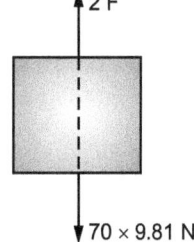

Fig. 5.56 (a) :
F.B.D. of block

Example 5.49 :

An 8 kg cylinder C rests on a 4 kg platform A supported by a cord which passes over the pulleys D and E and is attached to a 4 kg block B. Knowing that the system is released from rest, determine : (a) the velocity of block B after 0.8 s, (b) the force exerted by the cylinder on the platform.

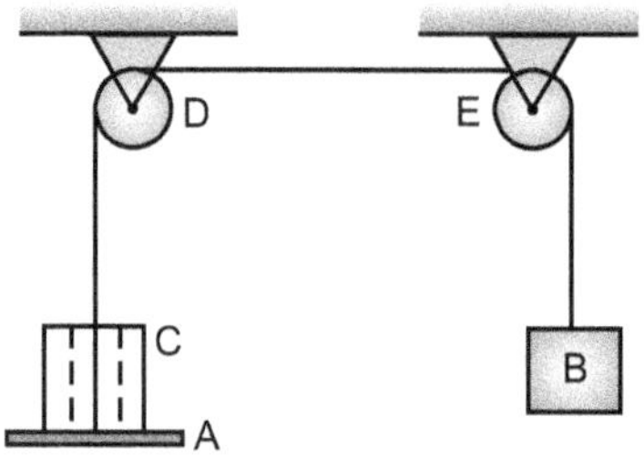

Solution :

Given data :

Mass of cylinder, $m_C = 8$ kg

Mass of platform A, $m_A = 4$ kg

Mass of block B, $m_B = 4$ kg

Fig. 5.57

Let v be the velocity of block B at t = 0.8 s.

From the equation of kinematics, $v_C (\uparrow) = v_B (\downarrow)$

Using impulse-momentum principle for the system,

$$\Sigma Ft = m(v - u)$$
$$12 \times 9.81 \times 0.8 - 4 \times 9.81 \times 0.8 = 12(v_C - 0) + 4(v_B - 0)$$
$$62.784 = 16 v$$

∴ $\qquad v = \mathbf{3.924 \text{ m/s}}$ ... **Ans.**

Let R be the force exerted by the cylinder on the platform and using impulse-momentum principle to cylinder,

$$8 \times 9.81 \times 0.8 - R \times 0.8 = 8(3.924 - 0)$$
$$-0.8 R = -31.392$$

∴ $\qquad R = \mathbf{39.24 \text{ N}}$ ... **Ans.**

Example 5.50 :

The system is released from rest. Determine the time it takes for the velocity of A to reach 0.6 m/s. Neglect friction and mass of pulleys.

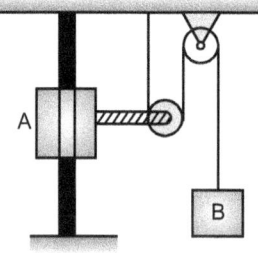

Fig. 5.58

Solution :

Given data :

Mass of block A, $m_A = 15$ kg

Mass of block B, $m_B = 10$ kg

Initial velocity of system, $u_A = u_B = 0$

Let t be the time at which block A will attain the velocity of 0.6 m/s. Considering F.B.D. of block A and using impulse-momentum principle,

$$\Sigma F \cdot t = m(v - u)$$
$$15 \times 9.81 \times t - 2T \cdot t = 15(0.6 - 0)$$
$$147.15\, t - 2T \cdot t = 9 \qquad \ldots (i)$$

Fig. 5.58 (a) : F.B.D. of block A   **Fig. 5.58 (b) : F.B.D. of block B**

Considering F.B.D. of block B and using impulse-momentum principle,

$$\Sigma Ft = m(v_B - u_B)$$

From equation of kinematics,

$$2x_A + x_B = \text{Constant}$$
$$2v_A + v_B = 0$$
$$v_B = 1.2 \text{ m/s } (\uparrow)$$
$$10 \times 9.81 \times t - T \cdot t = 10(-1.2 - 0)$$
$$98.1\, t - T \cdot t = -12 \qquad \ldots (ii)$$

Solving equations (i) and (ii), **t = 0.673 s** ... Ans.

Example 5.51 :

The slider block B is at rest in a smooth track shown in Fig. 5.59. The block B moves after it is hitted by another block A travelling at a speed of 8 m/s. Take e = 0.4 and the mass of the block to be 1.5 kg. Find the average force exerted by the block A during the impact, which lasts for 5 milliseconds.

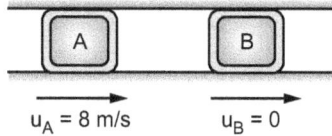

Fig. 5.59

Solution :

Given data : Mass of each block, $m_A = m_B = 1.5$ kg
Initial velocity of block A, $u_A = 8$ m/s
Initial velocity of block B, $u_B = 0$
Coefficient of restitution, e = 0.4

Let v_1 be the velocity of block A and v_2 be the velocity of block B after impact. Considering impact of blocks A and B and using conservation of momentum,

$$m_A u_A + m_B u_B = m_A v_1 + m_B v_2$$
$$1.5 \times 8 + 1.5 \times 0 = 1.5 \times v_1 + 1.5 \times v_2$$
$$v_1 + v_2 = 8 \qquad \ldots \text{(i)}$$

Using coefficient of restitution, $\quad e = \dfrac{v_2 - v_1}{u_1 - u_2}$

$$0.4 = \dfrac{v_2 - v_1}{8 - 0}$$
$$v_2 - v_1 = 3.2 \qquad \ldots \text{(ii)}$$

Solving equations (i) and (ii), $\quad v_1 = 2.4$ m/s

$$v_2 = 5.6 \text{ m/s}$$

Now using impulse-momentum principle for block A,

$$\Sigma Ft = m(v_1 - u_1)$$
$$F \times 0.005 = 1.5(8 - 2.4)$$
$$F = \mathbf{1.68 \text{ kN}} \qquad \ldots \text{Ans.}$$

Example 5.52 :

Two 70 kg men stand on 100 kg cart, which is at rest. Determine the final speed of the cart, if one of the men runs at a speed of 1.5 m/s and jumps on the cart at one end and then the other runs at the same speed and jumps on the same end.

1.5 m/s relative to the cart

Fig. 5.60

Solution :

Given data : Mass of each man, $m_m = 70$ kg

Mass of cart, $m_c = 100$ kg

Initial velocity of men, $u = 1.5$ m/s

Let v be the common velocity of second man and cart. Considering jumps of first man with velocity $u_1 = 1.5$ m/s from the cart and using conservation of momentum,

$$m_m u_1 = (m_m + m_c) v$$
$$70 \times 1.5 = (70 + 100) v$$
$$\therefore \qquad v = 0.62 \text{ m/s}$$

Let v_C be the velocity of the cart at which the second man jumps. Considering jumps of second man with velocity $v = 0.62$ m/s from the cart and using conservation of momentum,

$$m_m \, v + m_C \times v = m_C \, v_C$$
$$70 \times 0.62 + 100 \times 0.62 = 100 \, v_C$$
$$\therefore \quad v_C = \mathbf{1.054 \text{ m/s}} \qquad \text{... Ans.}$$

Example 5.53 :

Two swimmers A and B, having a mass of 75 kg and 55 kg respectively, are at the diagonally opposite ends of 140 kg raft. A starts walking towards B at a speed of 2 m/s relative to raft. Determine (a) the speed of the raft if B does not move, (b) the speed relative to raft, with which B must walk towards A if the raft not to move.

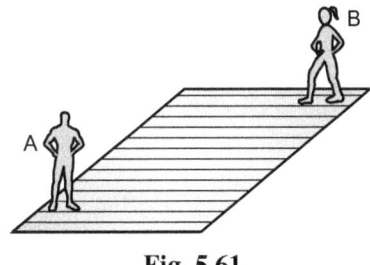

Fig. 5.61

Solution :

Given data : Mass of swimmer A, $m_A = 75$ kg

Mass of swimmer B, $m_B = 55$ kg

Mass of raft, $m_R = 140$ kg

Velocity of swimmer A relative to raft, $u_A = 2$ m/s

(a) A starts walking towards B, if B does not move ($u_B = 0$). Let v_R be the common velocity of raft and swimmer B. Using conservation of momentum,

$$m_A \, u_A = (m_B + m_R) \, v_R$$
$$85 \times (2 - v_R) = (55 + 140) \, v_R$$
$$\therefore \quad v_R = \mathbf{0.607 \text{ m/s}} \qquad \text{... Ans.}$$

(b) Let v_B be the velocity of swimmer B relative to raft if raft is not to move. Using conservation of momentum,

$$m_A \, u_A = m_B \, v_B + m_R \, v_R \qquad \text{... (where } v_R = 0\text{)}$$
$$\therefore \quad m_A \, (2 - v_R) = 55 \times (v_B - v_R) + 140 \times v_R$$
$$\therefore \quad 85 \times 2 = 55 \times v_B$$
$$\therefore \quad v_B = \mathbf{3.09 \text{ m/s}} \qquad \text{... Ans.}$$

Example 5.54 :

A 2 kg collar, which can slide on a frictionless vertical rod, is acted upon by a force P that varies in magnitude as shown in Fig. 5.62. If the collar is initially at rest, determine the maximum velocity of the collar.

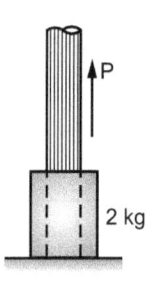

Fig. 5.62

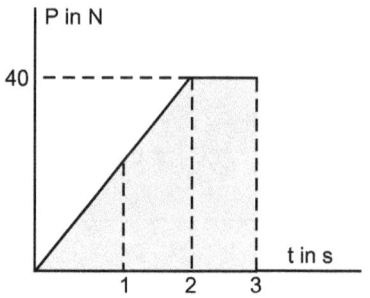

Fig. 5.62 (a)

Solution :

Given data : Mass of collar, $m_C = 2$ kg

Initial velocity of collar, $u = 0$

Let v be the maximum velocity of the collar. A 2 kg collar can slide on a vertical rod when $P \geq 2 \times 9.81$ i.e. weight of collar acting downward at time t. For limiting condition,

$$P = 2 \times 9.81$$

From P-t diagram, [Refer Fig. 5.62 (b)]

$$\frac{2 \times 9.81}{t} = \frac{40}{2}$$

$$t = 0.981 \text{ s}$$

Force at $t = 0.981$ s is 2×9.81

$$P = 19.62 \text{ N}$$

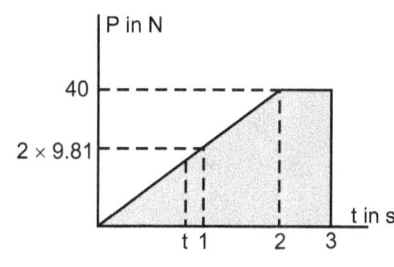

Fig. 5.62 (b)

Using impulse-momentum principle,

$$\Sigma F \cdot t = m(v - u)$$

$$-2 \times 9.81 \times (3 - 0.981) + \frac{19.62 + 40}{2} \times (2 - 0.981) + 40 \times 1 = 2(v - 0)$$

$$-39.613 + 30.376 + 40 = 2v$$

∴ $\quad 2v = 30.763$

∴ $\quad v = \mathbf{15.38 \text{ m/s}}$ ... **Ans.**

PROBLEMS FOR PRACTICE

Problem No. 1 : A child having a mass of 22 kg sits on a swing and is held in the position shown by second child. Neglecting the mass of the swing, determine the tension in rope AB (a) while the second child holds the swing with his arms outstretched horizontally, (b) immediately after the swing is released. (Refer Fig. 5.63).

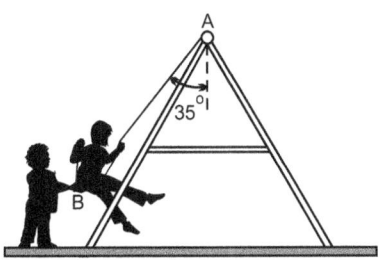

Fig. 5.63

Answer : T = 131.46 N, T = 84.39 N

Problem No. 2 : A 200 N suitcase slides from rest 6 m down the smooth ramp. Determine the point where it strikes the ground at C. How long does it take to go from A to C ? (Refer Fig. 5.64)

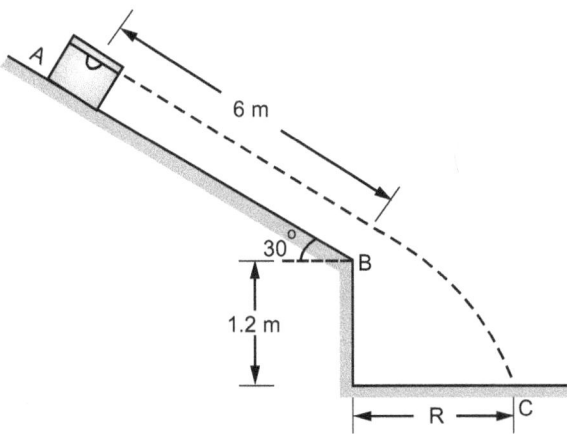

Fig. 5.64

Answer : t = 1.8 s, R = 1.59 m

Problem No. 3 : Block A has a mass of 40 kg and block B has a mass of 8 kg. The coefficients of friction between all surfaces of contact are $\mu_S = 0.20$ and $\mu_K = 0.15$. If P = 4 N (→), determine (a) the acceleration of block B, (b) the tension in the cord. (Refer Fig. 5.65)

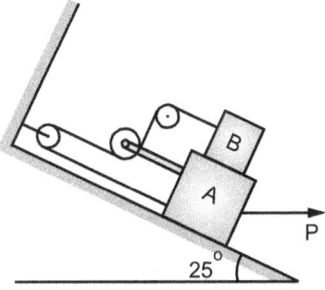

Fig. 5.65

Answer : $a_B = 1.794$ m/s^2, T = 58.2 N

Problem No. 4 : Boxes A and B are at rest on a conveyor belt that is initially at rest. The belt is suddenly started in an upward direction so that slipping occurs between the belt and the boxes. If $\mu_K = 0.30$ between the box A and the belt and 0.32 between the box B and the belt, determine the initial acceleration of each block. (Refer Fig. 5.66)

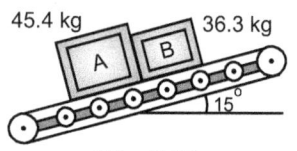

Fig. 5.66

Answer : $a_B = 0.493$ m/s^2, $a_A = 0.304$ m/s^2

Problem No. 5 : A package is at rest on a conveyor belt, which is initially at rest. The belt is started and moves to the right for 1.3 s with a constant acceleration of 2 m/s². The belt then moves with a constant deceleration a_2 and comes to rest after a total displacement at 2.2 m. If $\mu_S = 0.35$ and $\mu_K = 0.25$ between the package and the belt, determine (a) the largest allowable a_2 of the belt, (b) the displacement of the package relative to the belt as the belt comes to stop. (Refer Fig. 5.67)

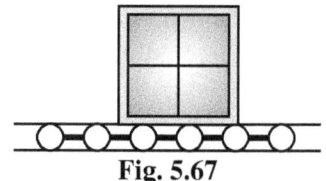

Fig. 5.67

Answer : $a_2 = 6.63$ m/s^2 (deceleration), s = 0.32 m

Problem No. 6 : A shunting engine with two bogies is moving on a straight level track. The mass of the engine is 15000 kg and that of the each bogie is 10000 kg. The frictional resistance to motion is 1 kN for the engine and 0.75 kN for each bogie. If the acceleration is 2 m/s², compute the tractive force exerted by the engine and the tension in the two connecting couplings. If the speed is 18 km/h, find the h.p. developed by the engine. (Refer Fig. 5.68)

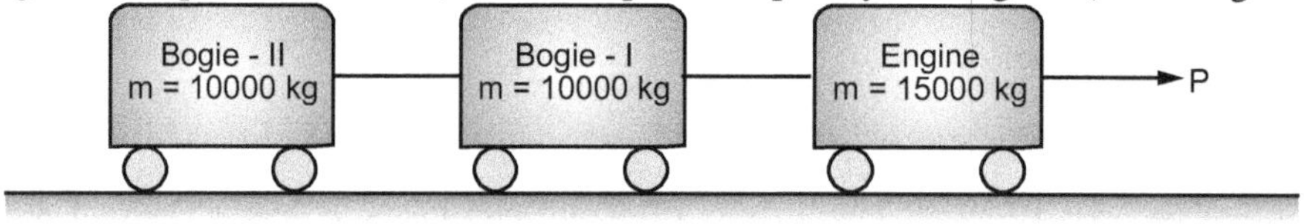

Fig. 5.68

Answer : T = 20.75 kN, T$_1$ = 41.5 kN, P = 72.5 kN, Power = 485.93 hp.

Problem No. 7 : The speed of 17.5 kN car is plotted over the 30 s time period. Determine the tractive force F acting on the car needed to cause the motion at t = 5s and at t = 20s. (Refer Fig. 5.69)

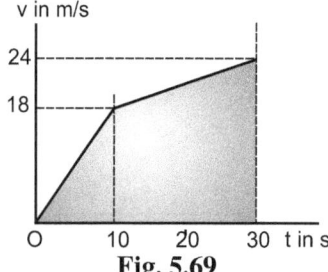

Fig. 5.69

Answer : F$_{20}$ = 0.535 kN

Problem No. 8 : Block B rests on a smooth surface. If the coefficient of static friction, $\mu_s = 0.4$ and kinetic friction $\mu_k = 0.3$, determine the acceleration of each block if block A is pushed by horizontal force of (a) P = 30 N, (b) 250 N. (Refer Fig. 5.70)

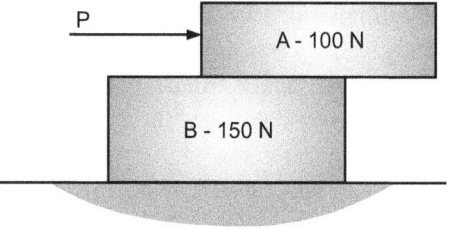

Fig. 5.70

Answer : $a = 1.177$ m/s², $a_A = 21.58$ m/s²

Problem No. 9 : The block shown is observed to have a velocity $v_1 = 20$ ft/sec as it passes point A and a velocity $v_2 = 10$ ft/sec as it passes point B on the incline. Calculate the coefficient of kinetic friction μ_k between the block and the incline if x = 30 ft and $\theta = 15°$. (Refer Fig. 5.71)

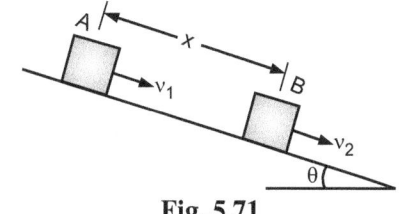

Fig. 5.71

Answer : $\mu_k = 0.429$

Problem No. 10 : In anticipation of long 7° upgrade, a bus driver accelerates at a constant rate of 1 m/s² while still on level section of the highway. Knowing that the speed of the bus is 100 kmph as it begins to climb the grade and that the driver does not change the setting of his throttle or shift gears, determine the distance travelled by the bus up the grade when his speed has decreased to 80 kmph.

Answer : s = 711 m

Problem No. 11 : If an automobile's breaking distance from 90 kmph is 50 m on level pavement, determine the automobile's breaking distance from 90 kmph when it is (a) going up 5° incline, (b) going down 3 percent incline.

Answer : $a = 6.25$ m/s² (deceleration), F = – 6.25 mN, s = 44 m, s = 52.5 m

Problem No. 12 : A 20 kg package is at rest on an incline when a force P is applied to it. Determine the magnitude of P if 10 s is required for the package to travel 5 m up the incline. The static and kinetic coefficient of friction between the package and the incline are 0.4 and 0.3 respectively. (Refer Fig. 5.72)

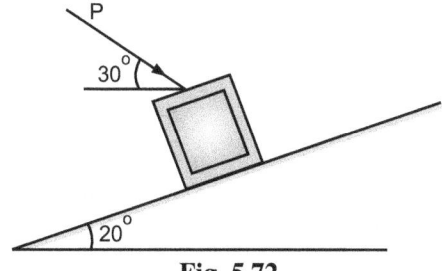

Fig. 5.72

Answer : 301.1 N

Problem No. 13 : The collar has a mass of 20 kg and is supported on the smooth rod. The attached springs are both compressed 0.4 m when d = 0.5 m. Determine the speed of the collar after the applied force F = 100 N causes it to be displaced so that d = 0.3 m. When d = 0.5 m, the collar is at rest.

Answer : v = 2.344 m/s

Problem No. 14 : The 2 kg collar is released from rest at A and slides down the inclined fixed rod in the vertical plane. The coefficient of kinetic friction is 0.4. Calculate (a) the velocity v of the collar as it strikes the spring and (b) the maximum deflection x of the spring.

Answer : v = 2.56 m/s, x = 99.09 mm

Problem No. 15 : The 0.5 kg collar slides with negligible friction along the fixed spiral rod, which lies in the vertical plane. The rod has the shape of spiral r = 0.3 θ, where r is in meters and θ is in radians. The collar is released from rest at A and slides to B under the action of a constant radial force T = 10 N. Calculate the velocity v of the slider as it reaches B.

Answer : v_B = 5.3 m/s

Problem No. 16 : The 7 kg collar A slides with negligible friction on the fixed vertical shaft. When the collar is released from rest at the bottom position shown, it moves up the shaft under the action of the constant force F = 200 N applied to the cable. Calculate the shiffness k which the spring must have if its maximum compression is to be limited to 75 mm. The position of the smaller pulley at B is fixed.

Answer : k = 8790 N/m

Problem No. 17 : A small block slides at a speed v = 3 m/s on a horizontal surface at a height h = 1 m above the ground. Determine the angle θ at which it will leave the cylindrical surface BCD.

Problem No. 18 : A package block weighing 90 N is projected up a 25° incline with an initial velocity of 7.4 m/s. Determine :

(1) the maximum distance 'x' the block will move up the incline.

(2) velocity of the block as it returns to its original position.

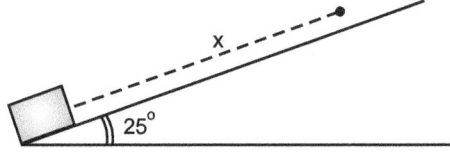

Fig. 5.73

Answer : (1)   x =4.63 m

(2)   v =4.67 m/s.

Problem No. 19 : A body of mass 400 kg starts from rest and moves along a straight line under the action of a force which varies as square of the time from the start. The magnitude of the force was found out to be 400 N at 15 seconds from the start. Calculate the velocity of the body after 10 seconds from start.

Answer : (1)   v =1.48 m/s

Problem No. 20 : A boy of mass 50 kg stands on an elevator. Determine the force exerted by the boy on the floor of the elevator when the elevator moves
(1) upwards with constant acceleration of 2 m/s²
(2) downwards with constant acceleration of 2 m/s².
(3) downwards with constant acceleration of 9.81 m/s².

Answer : (1) R = 590 N
(2) R = 390 N
(3) R = 0

Problem No. 21 : A man weighing 637 N dives vertically down into a swimming pool from a diving board of height 6 m above the water level. He is found to go down by 3 m into the water and then starts rising upwards. Assuming total water resistance to be constant during the downward motion in water, find the resisting force.

Answer : (1) v = 10.85 m/s (↓) (This is the velocity with which the man strikes the water)
(2) R = 1911 N

Problem No. 22 : A block of wood A of mass 5 kg is resting on a table. A string attached to A runs over a pulley and carries a mass of 5 kg at the other end. A wooden block B of mass 3 kg is placed on top of the block A. If the coefficient of friction between block A and the table is 0.25 and between block B and block A is 0.4, determine the acceleration of block A when
(a) block B is held fixed by means of a string.
(b) A and B are connected by string passing over smooth pulleys.

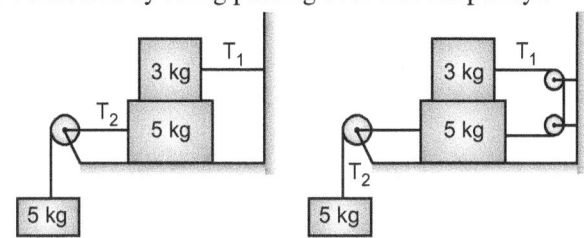
Fig. 5.74

Answer : (a) a = 1.766 m/s²
T_1 = 11.77 N
T_2 = 40.22 N
(b) a = 0.453 m/s²
T_1 = 13.13 N
T_2 = 46.78 N

Problem No. 23 : The world records for the shotput and discuss throw are 30 m and 80 m respectively. Assuming that their respective masses are 7 kg and 2 kg respectively, compare the work done by the champions in making their record throw if each trajectory starts at an elevation of 3 m and has an angle of projection of 45° w.r.t. horizontal.

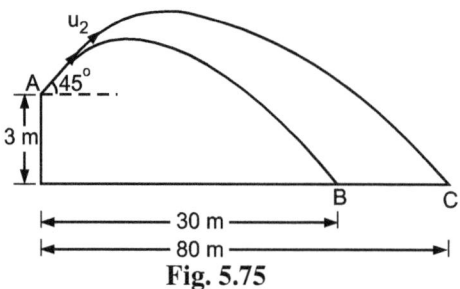

Fig. 5.75

Answer : (1) For AB, $u_1 = 16.36$ m/s
For AC, $u_2 = 27.51$ m/s
(2) K.E. = 936.77 J (shotput)
K.E. = 756.8 J (discuss)
(3) **Note :** As the work done is equal to the K.E. imparted to the object at the instant of projection, the champion throwing shotput does more work than the champion throwing discuss.

Problem No. 24 : Three blocks of masses m_1, m_2 and m_3 are connected by two cords as shown.
(a) Determine the acceleration of the system and the tensions in the cords.
(b) If $m_1 = m_2 = m$
$\mu_1 = \mu_2 = 0.3$
$m_3 = 2m$
Find a, T_1 and T_2

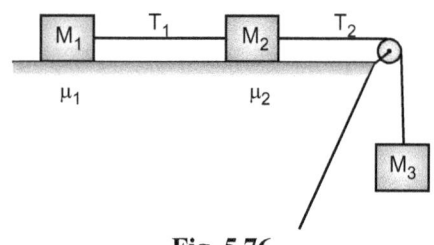

Fig. 5.76

Answer : (a) $a = \dfrac{(m_3 - \mu_1 m_1 - \mu_2 m_2) g}{(m_1 + m_2 + m_3)}$

$T_1 = m_1 (\mu_1 g + a)$

$T_2 = m_3 (g - a)$

(b) $a = 4.578$ m/s^2
$T_1 = 7.52$ N
$T_2 = 10.464$ N

Problem No. 25 : A horizontal force of 100 N is exerted on block A of mass 20 kg which is tied by an inclined string to block B of mass 5 kg as shown. If μ between the plane and the blocks A and B are 0.25 and 0.5 respectively, calculate the acceleration of the system and tension in the string.

Fig. 5.77

Answer : (1) T = 28.05 N
(2) a = 1.1 m/s^2

Problem No. 26 : Two blocks A and B weighing 100 kg and 75 kg respectively are connected to each other as shown.
(a) Determine the acceleration of block B.
(b) Now, if instead of block A, a vertical downward force of (100 × 9.81) is applied, would the acceleration remain same ?

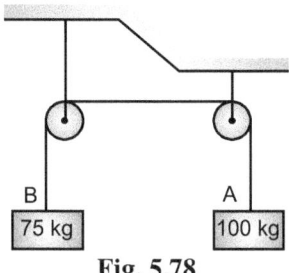

Fig. 5.78

Answer : (a) a = 1.4 m/s², T = 840.75 N
(b) a = 3.27 m/s², T = 981 N

Problem No. 27 : An aeroplane having a mass of 320 mg has four engines each of which produces a constant thrust of 165 kN during the take off roll. Determine the length of the runway and the take-off time if the take-off speed is 200 kmph. μ between the tyres and the runway is 0.1.

Answer : (a) a = 1.0815 m/s²
(b) s = 1426.63 m
(c) t = 51.36 s.

Problem No. 28 : Two equal masses m each are connected at the two ends of a smooth rope passing over a smooth pulley as shown. An additional mass 'm_1' is placed on one of the two masses. If the system moves with a constant acceleration, find the magnitude of mass "m_1".

Answer : $m_1 = \dfrac{2 \cdot m \cdot a}{(g - a)}$

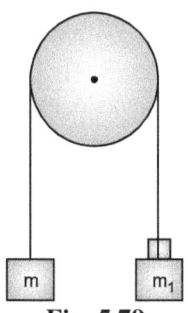

Fig. 5.79

Problem No. 29 : Masses m_1 and m_2 are placed on smooth inclined planes which make angles α_1 and α_2 respectively with the horizontal. The masses are connected with each other by an inextensible string which passes over a smooth pulley. Determine acceleration of the system released from rest.

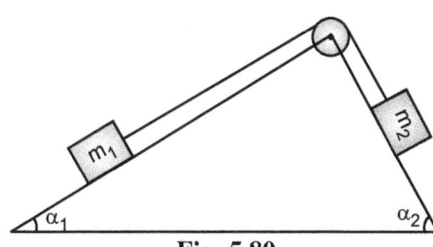

Fig. 5.80

Answer : $a = \left[\dfrac{m_1 \sin \alpha_1 - m_2 \sin \alpha_2}{(m_1 + m_2)} \right] g$

Problem No. 30 : A mass m resting on a smooth table is connected to two masses m_1 and m_2 by strings as shown. Find the acceleration of the system.

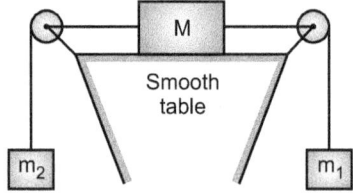

Fig. 5.81

Answer : $\quad a = \dfrac{g(m_1 - m_2)}{(m + m_1 + m_2)}$

Problem No. 31 : A horizontal force F is applied to a 75 kg body on smooth horizontal surface. There is a variation of F with time. If the body starts from rest, compute the velocity after 6 seconds and after 13 seconds.

Answer :
Area of F-t diagram = Impulse
$$v_6 = 1.2 \text{ m/s}$$
$$v_{13} = 4 \text{ m/s}$$

Problem No. 32 : A 2 kg mass attached to a spring slides along a horizontal circular guide without friction. The undeformed length of the spring is 150 mm and stiffness is 200 N/m. Determine the velocity of the mass as it passes point D
(1) directly from A to D,
(2) passing through B and C.

Answer : In both cases, the work done is same and hence, the velocity will be same.
$$v = 1.732 \text{ m/s}.$$

Problem No. 33 : At the instant shown in Fig. 5.82, the 2 kg block B is moving downward with a speed of 1 m/s. Determine the velocity of 4 kg block A when t = 1 s. Assume that $\mu_K = 0.15$ between the horizontal plane and the block A.

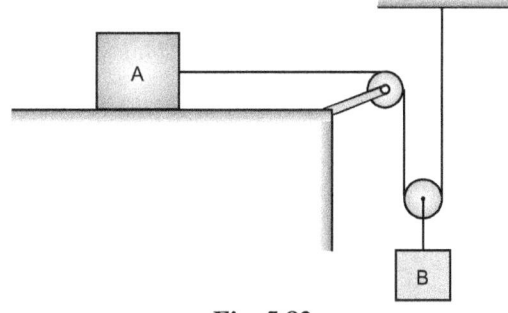

Fig. 5.82

Answer : v = 2.87 m/s

CHAPTER SIX
IMPACT AND COLLISION

6.1 IMPACT

Impact : When two bodies collide with each other during a very short interval of time, causing impulsive force to be exerted between the bodies is known as *impact*.

Line of impact : Line joining the centroids of two colliding particles is known as line of impact.

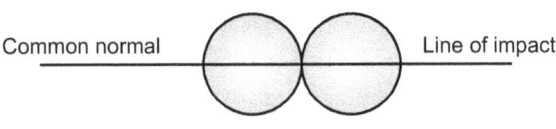

Fig. 6.1

Central impact : When the velocities of two colliding particles are along the line of impact, then it is known as central impact.

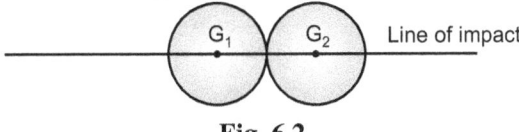

Fig. 6.2

Eccentric impact : If the mass centres of the colliding bodies are not located on line of impact, the impact is called the 'eccentric impact'. Eccentric impact is shown in Fig. 6.3.

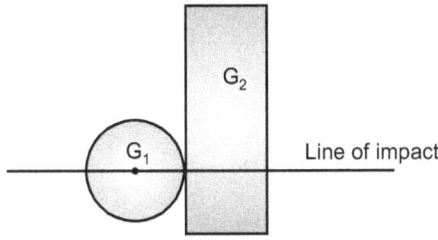

Fig. 6.3

Direct impact : If the velocities of the two bodies before collision are colinear with the line of impact, it is called 'direct impact'. The direct impact is shown in Fig. 6.4.

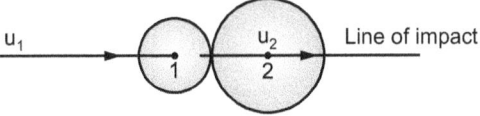

Fig. 6.4

Oblique impact : The impact which is not direct is called oblique or 'indirect impact'. The oblique impact is shown in Fig. 6.5.

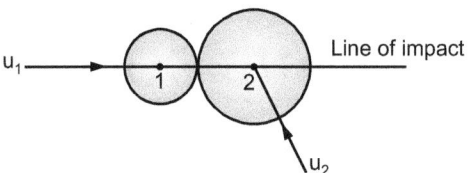

Fig. 6.5

Deformation : During impact, the two bodies undergo change in shape and size during a very short interval of time. This is known as deformation.

Restitution : After deformation, the two bodies try to regain their original shape and size during a short interval of time. This is known as restitution.

Coefficient of restitution : Consider two particles having mass m_1 and m_2. Let u_1 and u_2 be the initial velocities of particles before impact and v_1 and v_2 be the final velocities of particles after impact ($u_1 > u_2$).

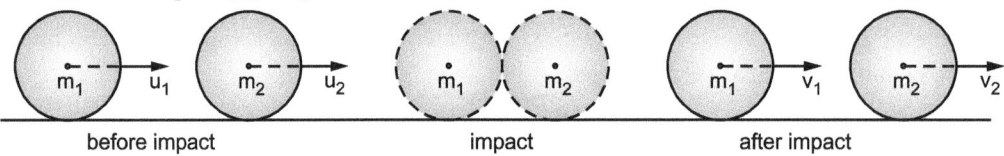

Fig. 6.6

Relative velocity of approach = $u_1 - u_2$

Relative velocity of separation = $v_2 - v_1$

The ratio of relative velocity of separation to relative velocity of approach is known as coefficient of restitution and it is denoted by e.

$$e = \frac{v_2 - v_1}{u_1 - u_2} \qquad \ldots (6.1)$$

During the impact, momentum is conserved.

$$m_1 u_1 + m_2 u_2 = m_1 v_1 + m_2 v_2 \qquad \ldots (6.2)$$

During the impact, energy is not conserved

and Loss in kinetic energy = Initial K.E. – Final K.E.

6.1.1 Types of Impact

(i) Perfectly elastic impact : During the perfectly elastic impact, velocities are interchanged after impact.

(a) Coefficient of restitution, $e = 1$.

(b) Momentum is conserved.

$$m_1 u_1 + m_2 u_2 = m_1 v_1 + m_2 v_2$$

(c) Kinetic energy is conserved.

$$\frac{1}{2} m_1 u_1^2 + \frac{1}{2} m_2 u_2^2 = \frac{1}{2} m_1 v_1^2 + \frac{1}{2} m_2 v_2^2$$

(ii) Partially elastic impact :

(a) Coefficient of restitution varies inbetween 0 to 1.

(b) Momentum is conserved.
$$m_1u_1 + m_2u_2 = m_1v_1 + m_2v_2$$

(c) Kinetic energy is not conserved.
$$\text{Loss of K.E.} = \text{Initial K.E.} - \text{Final K.E.}$$

(iii) Plastic impact :
In the plastic impact, after impact, both the particles are moving with same velocity.

(a) Coefficient of restitution, $e = 0$

(b) Momentum is conserved.
$$m_1u_1 + m_2u_2 = m_1v_1 + m_2v_2$$

(c) Kinetic energy is not conserved.
$$\text{Loss of K.E.} = \text{Initial K.E.} - \text{Final K.E.}$$

NUMERICAL EXAMPLES ON IMPACT

Example 6.1 :

Two identical balls A and B move towards each other and make direct central impact. Ball B moves with an initial velocity u_B. After the impact, ball A is stopped. Derive a formula for the ratio of the initial velocity of ball A, u_A before the collision in terms of u_B and the coefficient of restitution e. Explain the motion of the balls after the impact when $e = 0$ and when $e = 1$.

Solution :

Given data : Velocity of ball A before impact = u_A

Mass of each ball, $m_A = m_B = m$

Velocity of ball B before impact = u_B

Coefficient of restitution = e

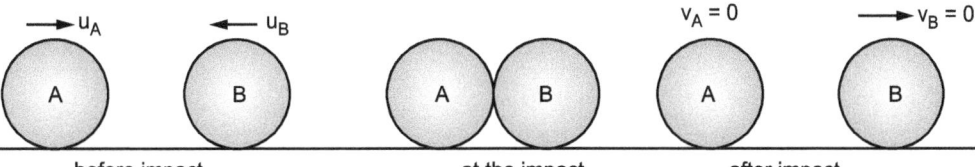

Fig. 6.7

Using coefficient of restitution, $\quad e = \dfrac{v_2 - v_1}{u_1 - u_2}$

$$e = \dfrac{v_B}{u_A + u_B}$$

$$e(u_A + u_B) = v_B \qquad \ldots \text{(i)}$$

Using conservation of momentum,

$$m_A u_A + m_B u_B = m_A v_A + m_B v_B$$

$$m u_A - m u_B = 0 + m v_B$$

$$u_A - u_B = v_B$$

$$u_A = v_B + u_B \qquad \ldots \text{(ii)}$$

Substituting $v_B = e(u_A + u_B)$ in equation (ii),

$$u_A = e(u_A + u_B) + u_B$$

$$u_A - e u_A = e u_B + u_B$$

$$u_A(1 - e) = u_B(1 + e)$$

$$u_A = \frac{(1 + e)}{(1 - e)} u_B \qquad \ldots \text{Ans.}$$

When $e = 0$, then $\quad u_A = u_B \qquad \ldots$ Ans.

When $e = 1$, then $\quad u_A = \infty \qquad \ldots$ Ans.

Example 6.2 :

Two spheres A and B of radius 25 mm are travelling along the same straight path in the opposite direction. Sphere A of mass 1.2 kg is moving with 5 m/s towards right and the sphere B of mass 2.4 kg is moving with 2.5 m/s towards left. If the coefficient of restitution is 0.80, find the final velocities of the sphere.

Solution :

$$m_1 = 1.2 \text{ kg}, \quad u_1 = 5 \text{ m/s}$$

$$m_2 = 2.4 \text{ kg}, \quad u_2 = -2.5 \text{ m/s}$$

$\therefore \qquad m_1 u_1 + m_2 u_2 = m_1 v_1 + m_2 v_2$

$\therefore \qquad 1.2 \times 5 - 2.4 \times 2.5 = 0 = 1.2 v_1 + 2.4 v_2$

$\therefore \qquad v_1 = -2 v_2$

Also $\qquad \dfrac{v_2 - v_1}{u_1 - u_2} = 0.80$

$\therefore \qquad \dfrac{v_2 - v_1}{7.5} = 0.80$

$\therefore \qquad v_2 - v_1 = 6.00$

$\therefore \qquad 3 v_2 = 6$

$\therefore \qquad v_2 = \mathbf{2 \text{ m/s}} (\rightarrow) \qquad \ldots$ **Ans.**

and $\qquad v_1 = -2 \times 2 = \mathbf{-4 \text{ m/s}}$ i.e. $(\leftarrow) \qquad \ldots$ **Ans.**

Example 6.3 :

A 20 Mg rail wagon moving at 0.5 m/s to the right collides with a 35 Mg wagon at rest. If after the collision, the 35 Mg wagon is observed to move to the right at 0.3 m/s, determine the coefficient of restitution between the wagons.

Solution :

$m_1 = 20$ Mg, $u_1 = 0.5$ m/s, $v_1 = ?$
$m_2 = 35$ Mg, $u_2 = 0,$ $v_2 = 0.3$ m/s

$$m_1 u_1 + m_2 u_2 = m_1 v_1 + m_2 v_2$$

∴ $10 + 0 = 20 v_1 + 10.5$

∴ $20 v_1 = -0.5$

∴ $v_1 = -\dfrac{0.5}{20} = -0.025$ m/s

$$\dfrac{v_2 - v_1}{u_1 - u_2} = e$$

∴ $e = \dfrac{0.3 + 0.025}{0.50} = \mathbf{0.65}$ ... **Ans.**

Example 6.4 :

A bullet of mass 20 grams and moving horizontally with 800 m/s strikes a block of wood of mass 5 kg through its centre, the block being suspended by a vertical wire from a point 2 m above the centre. To what angle with the vertical will the block and the embedded shot swing ?

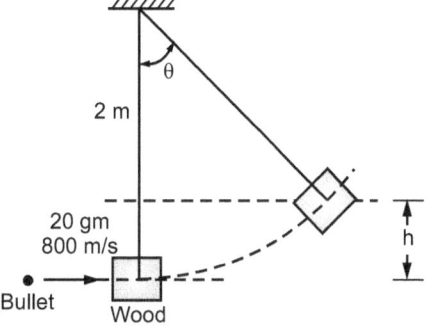

Fig. 6.8

Solution :

Refer to Fig. 6.8. Using the principle of conservation of momentum,

$$20 \times 10^{-3} \times 800 = (20 \times 10^{-3} + 5) v_c$$

∴ $v_c = $ Common velocity $= \dfrac{20 \times 10^{-3} \times 800}{5.02}$

∴ $v_c = 3.187$ m/s

$$\text{K.E.} = \dfrac{1}{2} \times 5.02 \times 3.187^2 = 25.49 \text{ J}$$

Taking datum as a horizontal line through lowest position of the block and applying the principle of conservation of energy.

$$5.02 \times 9.81 \times h = 25.49$$

∴ $$h = 0.518 \text{ m}$$

∴ $$\cos \theta = \frac{2 - 0.518}{2} = 0.741$$

$$\theta = 41.18°$$ ... **Ans.**

Example 6.5 :

Fig. 6.9 shows spheres A and B suspended by cards 2.5 m and 2.0 m and 2.0 m long respectively. Masses of the spheres A and B are 1.5 kg and 2 kg respectively. Sphere A is pulled to a position 'A', 500 mm above A and released from rest. Sphere B is at rest when struck by A with direct impact. After impact, the sphere B rises to a height of 300 mm above its lowest point. Determine the coefficient of restitution.

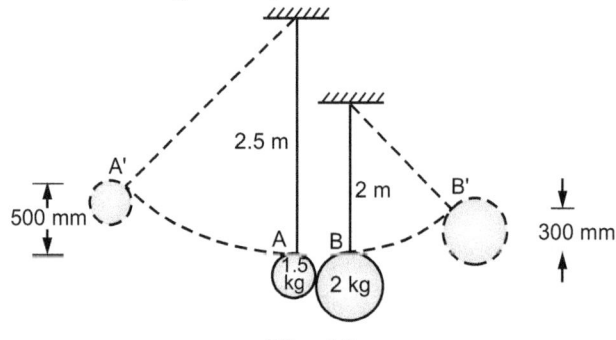

Fig. 6.9

Solution :

For sphere A, u_A = Striking velocity of sphere A
$$= \sqrt{2gh_A} = [2 \times 9.81 \times 0.5]^{1/2} = 3.13 \text{ m/s}$$

For sphere B, v_B = Velocity after impact
$$= \sqrt{2 \times 9.81 \times 0.3} = 2.426 \text{ m/s}$$

Using the principle of conservation of momentum duringh the impact,

Moment of before impact = Momentum after impact

∴ $$m_A \times u_A + m_B \times u_B = m_A \times v_A + m_B \times v_B$$

Here
$$m_A = 1.5 \text{ kg}; \quad u_A = 3.13 \text{ m/sec}$$
$$m_B = 2 \text{ kg}; \quad u_B = 0$$
$$v_B = 2.426 \text{ m/sec}$$

∴ $$1.5 \times 3.13 + 0 = 1.5 \times v_A + 2 \times 2.426$$

∴ v_A = Velocity of sphere A, after the impact

$$\therefore \quad v_A = -0.105 \text{ m/s} = 0.105 \text{ m/s} (\leftarrow)$$

$$e = \frac{v_B - v_A}{u_A - u_B} = \frac{2.426 - (-0.105)}{3.13 - 0} = 0.809 \quad \text{... Ans.}$$

Example 6.6 :

A small rubber ball is released from a height of 800 mm on a horizontal floor. After the first bounce it rises to a height of 480 mm. Compute the coefficient of restitution. Upto what height it will rise after the second bounce ?

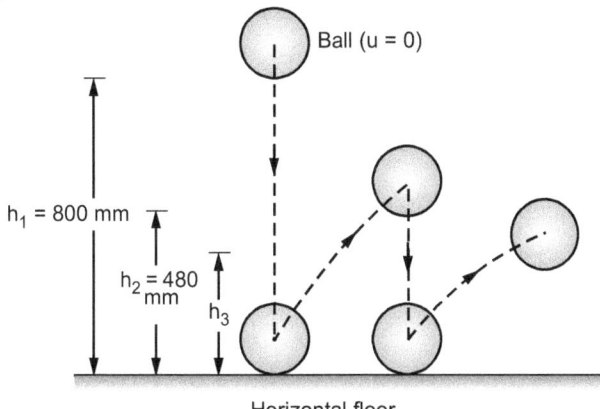

Fig. 6.10

Solution :

Given data : Height of drop of ball, $h_1 = 800$ mm

Height of first bounce, $h_2 = 480$ mm

Let e be the coefficient of restitution and h_3 be the height of ball after second bounce. Consider first impact of ball with horizontal floor. Velocity of ball before impact is determined by considering motion of ball under gravity.

$$v^2 = u^2 - 2gh \quad \text{... (}\because u = 0\text{)}$$
$$v^2 = 0 - 2 \times g \,(-h_1)$$
$$v = \sqrt{2gh_1} = u_1$$

Velocity of ball after impact,

$$v^2 = u^2 - 2gh \quad \text{... (}\because v = 0\text{)}$$
$$0 = u^2 - 2gh_2$$
$$u = \sqrt{2gh_2} = v_1$$

The velocity of horizontal floor before and after impact is zero i.e. $u_2 = v_2 = 0$

$$e = \frac{\text{Relative velocity of separation}}{\text{Relative velocity of approach}}$$

$$e = \frac{\sqrt{2gh_2}}{\sqrt{2gh_1}} = \sqrt{\frac{h_2}{h_1}} \quad \text{... (i)}$$

$$e = \sqrt{\frac{480}{800}} = 0.77 \qquad \text{... Ans.}$$

From equation (i), $\quad 0.77 = \sqrt{\frac{h_3}{480}}$

∴ $\qquad h_3 = 288$ mm $\qquad$ ... Ans.

Example 6.7 :

A ball of mass 0.5 kg is dropped on the floor from a height of 5 m. After striking the floor, it rebounds to a height of 3 m. Find the impulse of the force acting on the ball during its contact with the floor. Assuming the contact to last for 1/50 second, find the average force exerted by the floor on the ball.

Solution :

Given data : Mass of ball, $m_B = 0.5$ kg

Height of drop, $h_1 = 5$ m

Height of rebounce, $h_2 = 3$ m

Time of contact, $t = \frac{1}{50}$ s

Let F be the impulse and R be the force exerted by the floor on the ball.

Considering impact between ball and horizontal floor, velocity of ball before impact is,

$$u_1 = \sqrt{2gh_1}$$
$$u_1 = \sqrt{2 \times 9.81 \times 5}$$
$$u_1 = 9.9045 \text{ m/s } (\downarrow)$$

Velocity of ball after impact,

$$v = \sqrt{2gh_2}$$
$$v = \sqrt{2 \times 9.81 \times 3}$$
$$v = 7.672 \text{ m/s } (\uparrow)$$

Using impulse-momentum principle,

$$\Sigma Ft = m(v - u)$$
$$(R - 0.5 \times 9.81) \times \frac{1}{50} = 0.5 [7.672 - (-9.9045)]$$
$$R = 50 \times 0.5 \times (7.672 + 9.9045) + 0.5 \times 9.81$$
$$R = \mathbf{444.32 \text{ N}} \qquad \text{... Ans.}$$

$$\text{Impulse} = m(v - u)$$
$$\text{Impulse} = 0.5 \times (7.672 + 9.9045)$$
$$\text{Impulse} = \mathbf{8.788 \text{ N-s}} \qquad \text{... Ans.}$$

Example 6.8 :

A simple pendulum, as shown in Fig. 6.11, is released from rest when it was in horizontal position OA and falls in a vertical plane under the influence of gravity. If it strikes a vertical wall at B and coefficient of restitution $e = 0.5$, find angle ϕ defining its total rebound.

Solution :

Given data :

Velocity of pendulum before impact = u_1

Velocity of pendulum after impact = v_1

As the wall is fixed, its velocity before and after the impact is zero i.e. $u_2 = v_2 = 0$

Coefficient of restitution, $e = 0.5$

Velocity of pendulum before impact,

$$v^2 = u^2 - 2gh \qquad \ldots (\because u = 0)$$
$$v^2 = 0 - 2g \times (-l)$$
$$v = u_1 = \sqrt{2gl}$$

Consider impact between pendulum and vertical wall.

The coefficient of restitution, $\quad e = \dfrac{v_2 - v_1}{u_1 - u_2}$

$$0.5 = \dfrac{0 - v_1}{\sqrt{2gl} - 0}$$
$$v_1 = -0.5\sqrt{2gl}$$
$$v_1 = 0.5\sqrt{2gl} \ (\uparrow)$$

Using conservation of energy after impact,

$$\text{K.E.} = \text{P.E.}$$
$$\tfrac{1}{2} mv_1^2 = mgh$$
$$\tfrac{1}{2} \times (0.5\sqrt{2gh})^2 = gh$$
$$h = 0.25\, l$$

From geometry of Fig. 6.11 (a),

$$\cos \phi = \dfrac{(l - h)}{l}$$

$$\cos \phi = 0.75$$
$$\phi = \mathbf{41.4°} \qquad \ldots \textbf{Ans.}$$

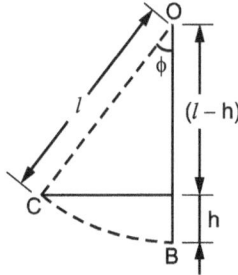

Fig. 6.11 (a)

Example 6.9 :

The 400 kg ram R of a pile driver is designed to fall 1.5 m from rest and strikes the top of a 300 kg pile partially driven in the ground. The deeper the penetration, the greater is the tendency for the ram to rebound as a result of the impact. Calculate the velocity of the pile immediately after the impact if the resistance is high and a ram is found to rebound to a height of 100 mm above the point of impact.

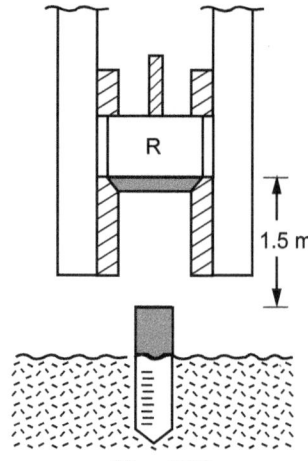

Fig. 6.12

Solution :

Given data :

Mass of ram, $m_1 = 400$ kg

Mass of pile, $m_2 = 300$ kg

Height of fall, $h = 1.5$ m

Height of rebound, $h_1 = 0.1$ m

Let u_1 and u_2 be the velocities of ram and pile before impact. v_1 and v_2 be the velocities of ram and pile after impact.

Velocity of ram before impact is determined by considering fall of ram.

Motion under gravity, $\quad v^2 = u^2 - 2gh \quad\quad\quad$ ... ($\because u = 0$)

$\quad\quad\quad\quad\quad\quad\quad\quad\quad\quad v^2 = -2 \times 9.81 \times (-1.5)$

$\quad\quad\quad\quad\quad\quad\quad\quad\quad\quad v = 5.425 \text{ m/s} = u_1 \ (\downarrow)$

Velocity of pile before impact, $\quad u_2 = 0$

Velocity of ram after impact, $\quad v^2 = u^2 - 2gh$

$\quad\quad\quad\quad\quad\quad\quad\quad\quad\quad u^2 = 2 \times 9.81 \times 0.1$

$\quad\quad\quad\quad\quad\quad\quad\quad\quad\quad u = 1.4 \text{ m/s}$

$\quad\quad\quad\quad\quad\quad\quad\quad\quad\quad v_1 = 1.4 \text{ m/s} \ (\uparrow)$

Velocity of pile after impact is determined by conservation of momentum.

$\quad\quad\quad\quad\quad\quad\quad m_1 u_1 + m_2 u_2 = m_1 v_1 + m_2 v_2$

$\quad\quad\quad\quad\quad -400 \times 5.425 + 0 = 400 \times 1.4 + 300 \times v_2$

$\quad\quad\quad\quad\quad\quad\quad\quad\quad\quad v_2 = -9.1 \text{ m/s}$

$\quad\quad\quad\quad\quad\quad\quad\quad\quad\quad v_2 = \mathbf{9.1 \text{ m/s}} \ (\downarrow) \quad\quad\quad\quad\quad\quad\quad\quad\quad$ ... Ans.

Example 6.10 :

Block A of mass m is released from rest and falls a distance h to strike the plate B of mass 2 m which is attached to a spring. The coefficient of restitution between A and B is e. Determine the velocity of the plate, in terms of h and e, just after the collision.

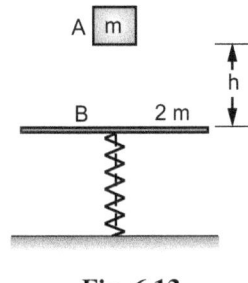

Fig. 6.13

Solution :

Given data : Mass of block A, $m_1 = m$

Mass of plate B, $m_2 = 2m$

Velocity of block A before impact, $v^2 = u^2 - 2gh$ ... ($\because u = 0$)

$u_1 = \sqrt{2gh}$

Velocity of plate B before impact, $u_2 = 0$.

Consider impact between block A and plate B. v_1 and v_2 be the velocities of block A and plate B after impact.

From coefficient of restitution, $\quad e = \dfrac{v_2 - v_1}{u_1 - u_2}$

$$e = \dfrac{v_2 - v_1}{\sqrt{2gh} - 0}$$

$$v_2 - v_1 = e\sqrt{2gh} \qquad \ldots \text{(i)}$$

Using conservation of momentum,

$$m_1 u_1 + m_2 u_2 = m_1 v_1 + m_2 v_2$$

$$m \times \sqrt{2gh} + 0 = mv_1 + 2mv_2$$

$$v_1 + 2v_2 = \sqrt{2gh} \qquad \ldots \text{(ii)}$$

Solving equations (i) and (ii),

$$3v_2 = e\sqrt{2gh} + \sqrt{2gh}$$

$$3v_2 = (1 + e)\sqrt{2gh}$$

$$v_2 = \dfrac{1}{3}(1 + e)\sqrt{2gh} \qquad \ldots \text{Ans.}$$

Example 6.11 :

A 1 kg block B is moving with a velocity of 2 m/s as it hits the 0.5 kg sphere A, which is at rest and hanging from a chord attached at O. If $\mu_K = 0.6$ between the block and horizontal surface and e = 0.8 between the block and sphere, determine after impact, (a) the maximum height h reached by the sphere, (b) the distance x travelled by the block.

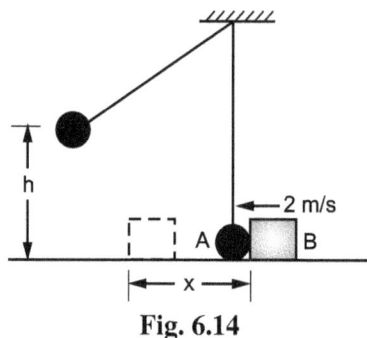

Fig. 6.14

Solution :

Given data : Mass of block B, $m_1 = 1$ kg

Mass of sphere A, $m_2 = 0.5$ kg

Velocity of block before impact, $u_1 = 2$ m/s

Velocity of sphere before impact, $u_2 = 0$

Coefficient of kinetic friction, $\mu_K = 0.6$

Coefficient of restitution, e = 0.8

Velocity of block and sphere after impact is v_1 and v_2.

Let h be the maximum height reached by the sphere and x be the distance travelled by block.

Considering the impact between the block and sphere and using conservation of momentum,

$$m_1 u_1 + m_2 u_2 = m_1 v_1 + m_2 v_2$$
$$1 \times 2 + 0.5 \times 0 = 1 \times v_1 + 0.5 \times v_2$$
$$v_1 + 0.5 v_2 = 2 \quad \ldots \text{(i)}$$

From coefficient of restitution,

$$e = \frac{v_2 - v_1}{u_1 - u_2}$$

$$0.8 = \frac{v_2 - v_1}{2 - 0}$$

$$v_2 - v_1 = 1.6 \quad \ldots \text{(ii)}$$

Solving equations (i) and (ii),

$$v_1 = 0.8 \text{ m/s}$$
$$v_2 = 2.4 \text{ m/s}$$

Now using equation of kinematics for sphere,

$$v^2 = u^2 - 2gh \quad \ldots (\because v = 0)$$
$$u^2 = 2gh$$

(Here u is the velocity of sphere after impact i.e. $v_2 = 2.4$ m/s)

$$h = \frac{(2.4)^2}{2 \times 9.81}$$

∴ $h = 294$ mm ... Ans.

Using work-energy principle for the block,

$$\frac{m_1 v_1^2}{2} - \mu mgx = 0$$

$$\frac{1 \times (0.8)^2}{2} - 0.6 \times 1 \times 9.81 \, x = 0$$

∴ $x = 54.4$ mm ... Ans.

Example 6.12 :

Two identical steel balls are connected by a rigid bar of negligible mass and are dropped in the horizontal position from a height of 150 mm above the heavy steel and brass base plates. e = 0.6 between the ball and the steel base and e = 0.4 between the other ball and the brass base. Assuming that both the balls make the impact simultaneously, determine the angular velocity of the bar immediately after the impact.

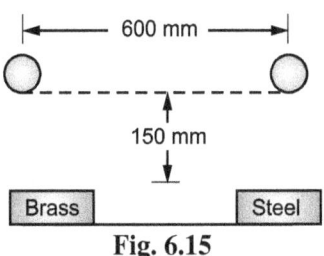

Fig. 6.15

Solution :

Given data :

Coefficient of kinetic friction between steel ball and steel base = 0.6

Coefficient of kinetic friction between the steel ball and brass plate = 0.4

Velocity of steel ball before impact is determined by considering motion of steel balls with rigid bar under gravity.

$$v^2 = u^2 - 2gh \quad \quad ... (\because u = 0)$$

$$v^2 = -2 \times 9.81 \times (-0.15)$$

$$u_1 = 1.72 \text{ m/s} (\downarrow)$$

Brass and steel plate rest on horizontal surface, hence its velocities before and after impact must be zero i.e. $u_2 = v_2 = 0$. Consider impact of left steel ball and brass plate. Let v_{1L} be the velocity of steel ball (left) after impact.

$$e = \frac{v_2 - v_1}{u_1 - u_2}$$

$$0.4 = \frac{0 - v_{1L}}{-1.72 - 0}$$

$$v_{1L} = 0.688 \text{ m/s} (\uparrow)$$

Consider impact of right steel ball and steel plate. Let v_{1R} be the velocity of steel ball after impact.

$$e = \frac{v_2 - v_1}{u_1 - u_2}$$

$$0.6 = \frac{0 - v_{1R}}{-1.72 - 0}$$

$$v_{1R} = 1.032 \text{ m/s} (\uparrow)$$

Now consider rotation of rigid bar.

$$v_{1L} + r\omega_{rod} = v_{1R}$$

$$0.688 + 0.6\, \omega_{rod} = 1.032$$

∴ $\quad \omega_{rod} = $ **0.573 rad/s (angular velocity of rigid bar)** ... Ans.

PROBLEMS FOR PRACTICE

Problem No. 1 : The 300 kg and 400 kg mine cars are rolling in opposite directions along track with the respective speeds of 0.6 m/s and 0.3 m/s. Upon impact, the cars become coupled together. Just before the impact, a 100 kg stone leaves the delivery chute with a velocity of 1.2 m/s in the direction shown in Fig. 6.16 and lands in the 300 kg car. Calculate the velocity v of the system after the stone has come to rest relative to the car.

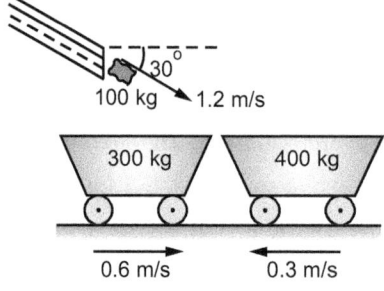

Fig. 6.16

Answer : $v = 0.205$ m/s

Problem No. 2 : Two cars of same mass collide head on at C. After the collision, the cars skid on the road with their brakes locked and come to stop in the position shown in the lower part of Fig. 6.17. If the speed of car A just before the impact was 5 km/h and $\mu_K = 0.3$ between the tyre and road, determine (a) the speed of the car B just before impact, (b) the effective coefficient of restitution.

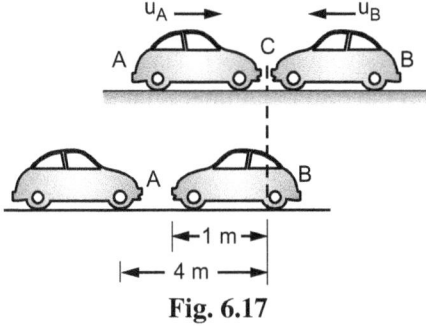

Fig. 6.17

Answer : $u_B = 8.67$ m/s ($\leftarrow$), $e = 0.241$

Problem No. 3 : A 70 g ball B dropped from a height $h_o = 1.5$ m reaches a height $h_2 = 0.25$ m after bouncing twice from identical 210 g plates. Plate A rests directly on hard ground, while plate C rests on foam-rubber mat. Determine (a) 'e' between the plates and the ball, (b) the height h_1 of the ball's first bounce.

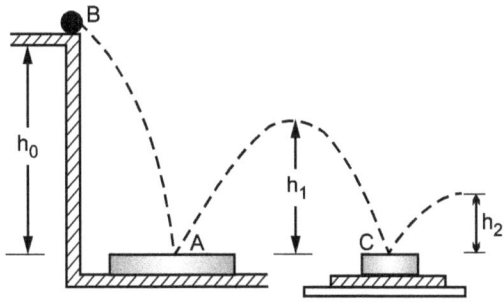

Fig. 6.18

Answer : $h = 1.234$ m, $e = 0.93$

Problem No. 4 : The three blocks shown in Fig. 6.19 are identical. Block B and block C are at rest when block B is hitted by block A, which is moving with a velocity of 3 m/s. After the impact, which is assumed to be perfectly plastic, the velocity of blocks A and B decreases due to friction; while block C picks up speed, until all the three blocks are moving with the same velocity v. If $\mu_K = 0.2$ between all the surfaces, determine (a) the time required for the three blocks to reach the same velocity v, (b) the total distance travelled by each block during that time.

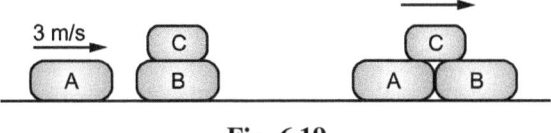

Fig. 6.19

Answer : $t = 0.255$ s, $x_C = 63.79$ mm, x_A or $x_B = 255$ mm

Problem No. 5 : A 1.5 kg block B is attached to an undeformed spring of constant 80 N/m and is resting on a horizontal surface when it is struck by an identical block A moving at a speed of 5 m/s. If e = 1 for the impact and $\mu_S = 0.5$, $\mu_K = 0.3$ between the blocks and the surface, determine the final position of (a) block A and (b) block B.

Answer : (a) $x_A = 2.98$ m ($\rightarrow$ from point of impact)

(b) x = 0.632 m (maximum compression of spring)

SHIVAJI UNIVERSITY
UNIVERSITY QUESTION PAPERS
Applied Mechanics
Dec. 2014

Time : 3 Hours   Total Marks : 100

Section - I

1. (a) The resultant of force 100 N and 200 N is also equal to 200 N in magnitude. Find the resultant of the 100 N force with a 400 N force which is in the same direction as the 200 N force. Also find its direction. **[08]**

    (b) A regular pentagon ABCDE has forces 100 N, 200 N, 300 N and 400 N along the directions AB, AC, AD and AE respectively. Find the resultant force in magnitude and direction. **[08]**

2. (a) Explain the term 'Limiting Frictional Forces' and state the factors on which it depends. **[08]**

    (b) An extensible string ABCD is connected to a ridid ceiling at A and D. It supports two loads of 100 N and 400 N as shown in the Fig. 1. Find the reactions at A and D and the tension in the BC region of the cable. **[10]**

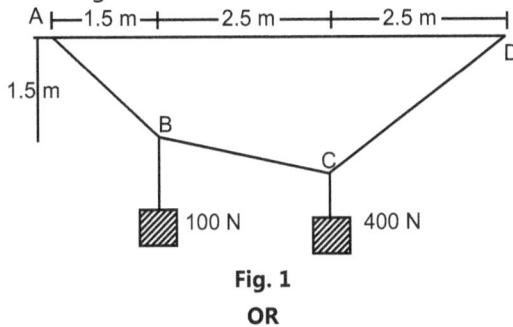

Fig. 1

OR

(b) A simply supported beam ABC has hinge support at A at roller support at B. The overhanging portion BC is of length 1.5 m and the base of the roller support makes an angle of 40° with the horizontal. Find the reactions for the loading as shown in the Fig. 2. **[10]**

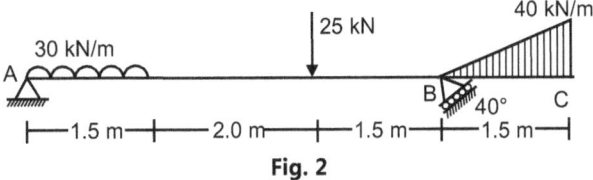

Fig. 2

3. (a) Explain the terms : Perfect Truss, Stable Truss and Unstable Truss. **[06]**

    (b) Analyze the truss and tabulate all the member forces in the truss loaded and configured as shown in the Fig. 3 below **[10]**

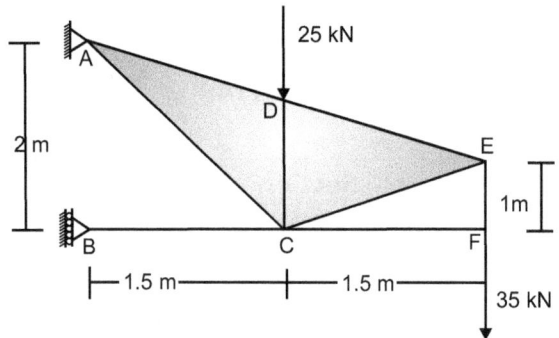

Fig. 3

Section – II

4. (a) Define and explain : Centre of gravity, Centroid, Radius of gyration. **[06]**
(b) Find the radius of gyration for the plane lamina shown besides about the centroidal Horizontal axis. **[10]**

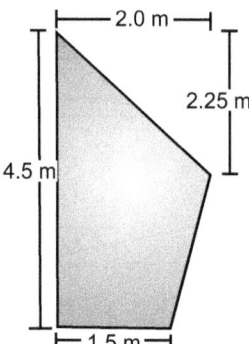

Fig. 4

5. (a) An in-extensible string, passing over a fixed pulley, carries two loads of 100 N and 400 N as shown in the Fig. 5. Find the tension in the string and the acceleration of the moving. **[08]**

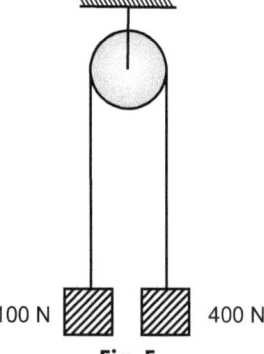

Fig. 5

OR

(a) A mass of 150 Kg slides down a rough plane, starting with a velocity of 36 Kmph. The plane is inclined and makes an angle of 15° with the horizontal and the co-efficient for dynamic friction between the plane and sliding body is 0.365 uniform. Find the distance travelled by the mass before it comes to rest. **[08]**

(b) A flywheel of mass 10 Kg has radius of gyration about its rotational axis as 0.24 meters. It is subjected to a torque of 1.152 N.m about the axis of rotation. Find the time taken by the fly-wheel to complete 1225 revolutions, starting from rest. **[04]**

(c) Define Inertia Force and Centrifugal Force and discuss their importance in study of applied mechanics. **[06]**

6. (a) Discuss the characteristics referred in study of impact. **[06]**

(b) Two identical marbles of same mass hit each other while approaching each other at a uniform speed of 10 m/sec. If the coefficient of restitution for the colliding bodies is 0.8, find the velocities with which they move after the impact. **[05]**

(c) What would be the velocities if one marble has double the mass of other marble in above example. **[05]**

Applied Mechanics (S.U.) University Question Papers

May 2015

Time : 3 Hours Total Marks : 100

Section - I

1. (a) Explain the following terms : [04]
   (i) Resultant and Equilibrant
   (ii) Moment and Couple.

   (b) A square ABCD of 60 mm side is subjected to force 10 N, 20 N, 30 N and 40 N along the side AB, AC, BD and AD respectively. Find the magnitude, direction and position of the resultant force with respect to A. Refer Fig. 1. [12]

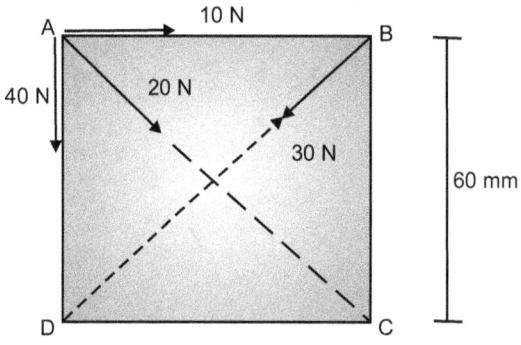

Fig. 1

2. (a) Explain in detail the types of loadings of the beam with neat sketches. [04]

   (b) Determine the force 'P' required to begin rolling a uniform cylinder of mass 'm' over the obstruction of height 'h' as shown in Fig. 2. [14]

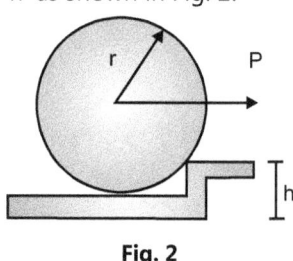

Fig. 2

OR

   (b) A beam has been loaded and supported as shown in Fig. 3 given below. Determine the reactions at the support points 'A' and 'B'.

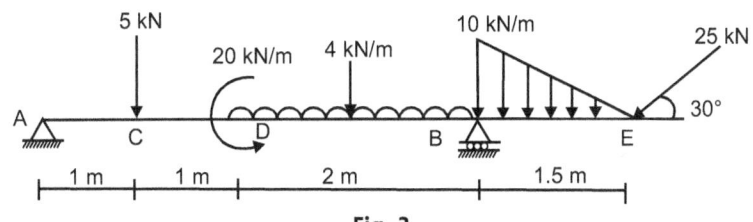

Fig. 3

3. (a) Name the different methods of finding out the forces in the members of a perfect frame. Which one is used where and why? [04]
   (b) Determine the forces in the all the members of the cantilever truss loaded and supported as shown in Fig. 4. [12]

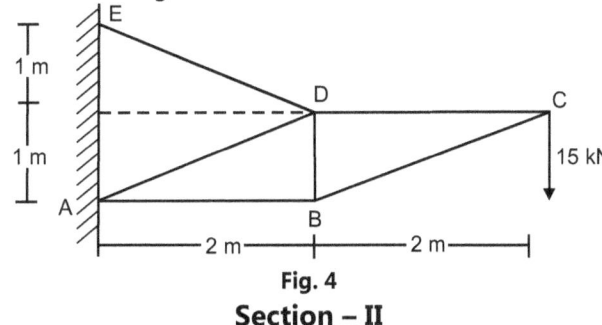

Fig. 4

Section – II

4. (a) State and explain: [06]
   (i) Parallel axis theorem (ii) Perpendicular axis theorem
   (b) Determine the moment of inertia of the L-section shown in the Fig. 5. (All dimensions are in mm). [10]

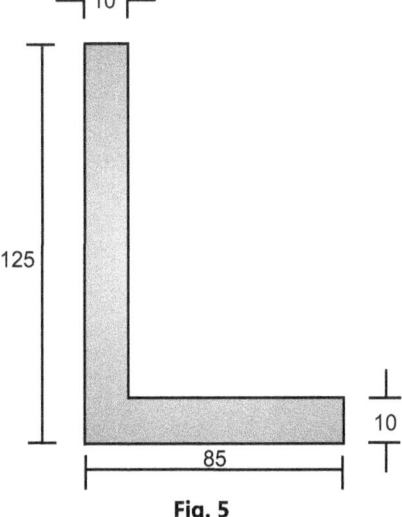

Fig. 5

5. (a) Write D'Alembert's equation of motion and compare it with Newton's second law of motion. [03]

(b) Determine the tension in the string and acceleration of block C and D weighing 1400 N and 400 N connected by and intensible string as shown in Fig. 6. Assume pully is frictionless and weightless. [12]

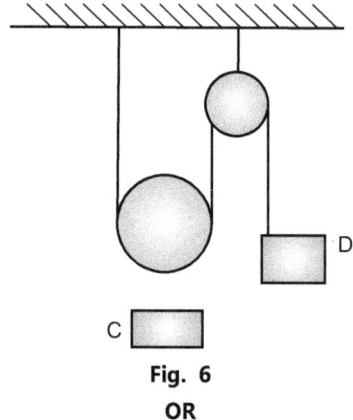

Fig. 6

OR

(b) A steam engine weighing 500 kN starts from rest and moves up an incline 1 : 150 with a uniform acceleration. It attains a maximum velocity of 64.8 kmph in an interval of 1 km. after which the steam is suddenly shut off. Assuming the tractive restiance of 15 N/kN. Determine :
 (i) Maximum power developed
 (ii) Energy spent by locomotive
 (iii) Average power developed [12]

(c) State and explain principle of conservation of energy. [03]

6. (a) What are the different types of impact. [02]

(b) Direct central impact occurs between a 300 N body moving to the right with velocity of 6m/sec and 150 N body moving to the left with a velocity of 10m/sec. Find the velocity of each body after impact if the coefficient of restitution is 0.8. [10]

(c) State and explain impulse momentum principle. [04]

www.ingramcontent.com/pod-product-compliance
Lightning Source LLC
Chambersburg PA
CBHW082036230426
43670CB00016B/2678